Journal of Biblical Literature

Volume 127
2008

GENERAL EDITOR
JAMES C. VANDERKAM
University of Notre Dame
Notre Dame, IN 46556

A Quarterly Published by
THE SOCIETY OF BIBLICAL LITERATURE

JOURNAL OF BIBLICAL LITERATURE
PUBLISHED QUARTERLY BY THE
SOCIETY OF BIBLICAL LITERATURE
(Constituent Member of the American Council of Learned Societies)

EDITOR OF THE JOURNAL

General Editor: JAMES C. VANDERKAM, University of Notre Dame, Notre Dame, IN 46556

EDITORIAL BOARD

Term Expiring
2008: ELLEN B. AITKEN, McGill University, Montreal, Quebec H3A 2T5 Canada
MICHAEL JOSEPH BROWN, Emory University, Atlanta, GA 30322
TERENCE L. DONALDSON, Wycliffe College, Toronto, ON M5S 1H7 Canada
STEVEN FRIESEN, University of Texas at Austin, Austin, TX 78712
JENNIFER GLANCY, Le Moyne College, Syracuse, New York 13214
A. KATHERINE GRIEB, Virginia Theological Seminary, Alexandria, VA 22304
ARCHIE C. C. LEE, The Chinese University of Hong Kong, Shatin New Territories, Hong Kong SAR
DANIEL MARGUERAT, Université de Lausanne, CH-1015 Lausanne, Switzerland
RICHARD D. NELSON, Perkins School of Theology, So. Methodist Univ., Dallas, TX 75275
DAVID L. PETERSEN, Candler School of Theology, Emory University, Atlanta, GA 30322
YVONNE SHERWOOD, University of Glasgow, Glasgow, Scotland, G12 8QQ, United Kingdom
LOREN T. STUCKENBRUCK, University of Durham, Durham, England, DH1 3RS, United Kingdom
PATRICIA K. TULL, Louisville Presbyterian Theological Seminary, Louisville, KY 40205
2009: DAVID L. BARR, Wright State University, Dayton, OH 45435
THOMAS B. DOZEMAN, United Theological Seminary, Dayton, OH 45406
ELIZABETH STRUTHERS MALBON, Virginia Polytechnic Institute and State University, Blacksburg, VA 24061-0135
MARTTI NISSINEN, University of Helsinki, FIN-00014 Finland
EUNG CHUN PARK, San Francisco Theological Seminary, San Anselmo, CA 94960
TURID KARLSEN SEIM, University of Oslo, N-0315 Oslo, Norway
BENJAMIN D. SOMMER, Northwestern University, Evanston, IL 60645
LOUIS STULMAN, University of Findlay, Findlay, OH 45840
2010: BRIAN BRITT, Virginia Polytechnic Institute and State University, Blacksburg, VA 24061-0135
JOHN ENDRES, Jesuit School of Theology at Berkeley, Berkeley, CA 94709
MICHAEL FOX, University of Wisconsin, Madison, WI 53706
STEVEN FRAADE, Yale University, New Haven, CT 06520-8287
MATTHIAS HENZE, Rice University, Houston, TX 77251
STEPHEN MOORE, Drew University, Madison, NJ 07940
CATHERINE MURPHY, Santa Clara University, Santa Clara, CA 95053
EMERSON POWERY, Lee University, Cleveland, TN 37312
ADELE REINHARTZ, University of Ottawa, Ottawa, ON K1N 6N5 Canada
RICHARD STEINER, Yeshiva University, New York, NY 10033-3201
SIDNIE WHITE CRAWFORD, University of Nebraska-Lincoln, Lincoln, NE 68588-0337

Editorial Assistant: Monica Brady, University of Notre Dame, Notre Dame, IN 46556

President of the Society: Jonathan Z. Smith, University of Chicago, Chicago, IL 60637; *Vice President:* David Clines, University of Sheffield, Sheffield S10 2TN England; *Chair, Research and Publications Committee:* Benjamin G. Wright III, Lehigh University, Bethlehem, PA 18015; *Executive Director:* Kent H. Richards, Society of Biblical Literature, 825 Houston Mill Road, Suite 350, Atlanta, GA 30329.

The *Journal of Biblical Literature* (ISSN 0021–9231) is published quarterly. The annual subscription price is US$35.00 for members and US$150.00 for nonmembers. Institutional rates are also available. For information regarding subscriptions and membership, contact: Society of Biblical Literature, Customer Service Department, P.O. Box 133158, Atlanta, GA 30333. Phone: 866-727-9955 (toll free) or 404-727-9498. FAX: 404-727-2419. E-mail: sblservices@sbl-site.org. For information concerning permission to quote, editorial and business matters, please see the Spring issue, p. 2.

The Hebrew font used in *JBL* is SBL Hebrew and is available from www.sbl-site.org/Resources/default.aspx.

The JOURNAL OF BIBLICAL LITERATURE (ISSN 0021–9231) is published quarterly by the Society of Biblical Literature, 825 Houston Mill Road, Suite 350, Atlanta, GA 30329. Periodical postage paid at Atlanta, Georgia, and at additional mailing offices. POSTMASTER: Send address changes to Society of Biblical Literature, P.O. Box 133158, Atlanta, GA 30333.

PRINTED IN THE UNITED STATES OF AMERICA

Articles are indexed in *Religion Index One: Periodicals;* book reviews in *Index to Book Reviews in Religion,* American Theological Library Association, Evanston, Illinois. Both indexes are also found in the ATLA Religion Database on CD-ROM.

EDITORIAL MATTERS OF THE *JBL*

1. Contributors should consult the Journal's Instructions for Contributors (http://www.sbl-site.org/Publications/PublishingWithSBL/JBL_Instructions.pdf).
2. If a MS of an article, critical note, or book review is submitted in a form that departs in major ways from these instructions, it may be returned to the author for retyping, even before it is considered for publication.
3. Submit *two* hard copies of the MS of an article or critical note. Manuscripts will not be returned.
4. Manuscripts and communications regarding the content of the *Journal* should be addressed to James C. VanderKam at the address given on the preceding page (or correspondence only at the following e-mail address: jvanderk@nd.edu).
5. Permission to quote more than 500 words may be requested from the Rights and Permissions Department, Society of Biblical Literature, 825 Houston Mill Road, Suite 530, Atlanta, GA 30329, USA (E-mail: sblexec@sbl-site.org). Please specify volume, year, and inclusive page numbers.

BUSINESS MATTERS OF THE SBL
(not handled by the editors of the *Journal*)

1. All correspondence regarding membership in the Society, subscriptions to the *Journal*, change of address, renewals, missing or defective issues of the *Journal*, and inquiries about other publications of the Society should be addressed to Society of Biblical Literature, Customer Service Department, P.O. Box 133158, Atlanta, GA 30333. Phone: 866-727-9955 (toll-free) or 404-727-9498. FAX 404-727-2419. E-mail: sbl@sbl-site.org.
2. All correspondence concerning the research and publications programs, the annual meeting of the Society, and other business should be addressed to the Executive Director, Society of Biblical Literature, The Luce Center, 825 Houston Mill Road, Atlanta, GA 30329. (E-mail: sblexec@sbl-site.org).
3. Second Class postage paid at Atlanta, Georgia, and at additional mailing offices.

Presidential Address
by
KATHARINE DOOB SAKENFELD

President of the Society of Biblical Literature 2007
Annual Meeting of the Society of Biblical Literature
November 18, 2007
San Diego, California

Introduction given by Jonathan Z. Smith
Vice President, Society of Biblical Literature

Good evening, and welcome to this much-anticipated occasion. It is my privilege and pleasure to introduce to you our president, Katharine Doob Sakenfeld, otherwise known as the William Albright Eisenberger Professor of Old Testament Literature and Exegesis at Princeton Theological Seminary, where she has remained an active influence for the span of her distinguished teaching and scholarly career, an influence amplified by her role as the seminary's longtime director of Ph.D. studies.

Many of you will also know her in her more recent capacity as the general editor of *The New Interpreter's Dictionary of the Bible*—an undertaking that, if my experience as the editor of a dictionary of religion is any guide, is a task more demanding than that which our guild is wont to attribute to the fabled "Redactor."

I shall not attempt to predict how Professor Sakenfeld will answer, tonight, her own question, "Whose Text Is It?," except to wager that it will defy the standard association-dialogue: "If I say 'flower,' you say 'fragrance'; if I say 'Bible,' you say 'mine,' or 'ours.'" Her repeated travels and experiences in Asia; her attention to the role of women in both biblical and contemporary situations, as represented by her Interpretation Commentary volume on Ruth (1999); her co-edited issue of *Semeia, Reading the Bible as Women: Perspectives from Africa, Asia and Latin America* (1997); as well as the conjoining of these dual interests in her striking and moving *Just Wives? Stories of Power and Survival in the Old Testament and Today* (2003) guarantee a more complex and provocative answer to her question than that traditionally proffered—one that actively seeks to take account of the voices of those often classified as powerless alongside those of the publicly powerful.

I previously knew Katharine's work only through the impersonal medium of the printed page, most especially several treatments of the book of Numbers. There one gains a sense of an individual who engages in meticulously detailed exegeses in the service of larger questions. Serving with her, this year, on the SBL council has introduced me to a person of uncommon practical wisdom, one who is relentlessly on point, and an individual—thank God—full of fun and good humor.

Her students testify at length to her role as their mentor, to her capacity for working endlessly and effectively to gain them support—*if,* they stress, they have earned it. Others speak of Kathy the music lover, the photographer, the avid reader of histories, as well as of her delight in bird-watching. As an aside, I would note that the presence of this avian avocation among SBL members is, on the basis of an informal survey, perhaps the most noteworthy distinction of interests between them and the members of the AAR.

More than one of her students and colleagues have spoken of her "pack-rat" practices (perhaps a vernacular translation of the term "historian"). One wrote: "Tell Kathy that you plan to visit some place that she has been [to] in earlier years, and she will bring forth her maps, tour guide [books], her notes. . . ." Just think, if the Israelites in their wanderings, or Paul in his, had done and produced the same—some number of us might no longer have a subject matter!

I am delighted and honored to present to you, this evening, Katharine Doob Sakenfeld, who will deliver the 2007 Presidential Address, "Whose Text Is It?"

Whose Text Is It?

KATHARINE DOOB SAKENFELD
katharine.sakenfeld@ptsem.edu
Princeton Theological Seminary, Princeton, NJ 08542

It was exactly twenty years ago that Professor Elisabeth Schüssler Fiorenza gave her landmark presidential address entitled "The Ethics of Biblical Interpretation: Decentering Biblical Scholarship."[1] There she argued for the need for biblical scholarship to "continue its descriptive-analytic work . . . for understanding of ancient texts and their historical location" while also "exploring the power/knowledge relations inscribed in contemporary biblical discourse and in the biblical texts themselves." In such an approach, the work of those "traditionally absent from the exegetical enterprise would not remain peripheral or non-existent for biblical scholarship," but "could become central to the scholarly discourse of the discipline."[2] My address to you this evening is intended to further this call for a shift in our self-understanding of our scholarly work. We have made progress in the past twenty years, but work remains to be done.

My particular focus was provoked in a session I attended at the SBL annual meeting two years ago. In introducing a session on feminism and postcolonialism, a moderator reported that she had been asked why the session had been organized around a book on African women's voices published a few years earlier (i.e., not hot off the press), to which her response had been "because nobody seems to be listening." The authors experienced their claim to ownership of the text, at least within the guild, as being discounted or overridden. Attempting to listen to global feminist voices within biblical studies has been a key theme of my own work, but devel-

---

[1] Elisabeth Schüssler Fiorenza, "The Ethics of Biblical Interpretation: Decentering Biblical Scholarship," *JBL* 107 (1988): 3–17; reprinted in *Presidential Voices: The Society of Biblical Literature in the Twentieth Century* (ed. Harold W. Attridge and James C. VanderKam; Atlanta: Society of Biblical Literature, 2006), 217–31; subsequent references are to the reprint edition. For a more extensive and updated treatment of her perspective, see her volume *The Power of the Word: Scripture and the Rhetoric of Empire* (Minneapolis: Fortress, 2007).

[2] Schüssler Fiorenza, "Ethics of Biblical Interpretation," 230–31.

oping viable modes of engagement between white Euro-Atlantic feminists and global feminism remains a challenge. That challenge, however, is but one component of the much larger question of how we all as scholars engage one another over a wide range of dividing lines, since we all claim texts as our own through our acts of interpretation.

I will first approach the question of "Whose text?" and competing claims to ownership in a wide-sweeping overview and then turn more specifically to feminist postcolonial interpretation as a particular example. Before launching into the overview, let me note that I will use more "I" language and anecdotal material than is usual for the presidential address. I want the style of my speaking to reflect my perspective that being more self-consciously contextual, more public rather than less so about the personal in our work, is critically important to a way forward in any mutual engagement across dividing lines.

I. "Whose Text?" In Our Descriptive Analytical Work

The question "Whose text?" as I am posing it has two principal dimensions: first, who claims a particular text as important; and, second, how are competing interpretive claims to be negotiated when more than one group has a stake in the same text. I find it helpful to remember that the question, thus conceived, has actually been with us for a long time in our traditional descriptive and analytical research. In the field of text criticism, for example, the degree of differences among manuscript families, as well as evidence of intentional scribal emendations, has led to theories of different schools or centers with different manuscript choices. Here interpretive claims are expressed through variations in the text itself, and scholars ask what kind of contextual hermeneutical and identity claims may lie behind the different manuscript traditions.

Studies of canon formation whether of the TNK or the NT are a second, well-established locus of exploration of "Whose text?" The emphasis on Judaisms (plural) of the Second Temple period and beyond, and our knowledge of the many extant Christian writings as well as those that were lost to us and not canonized, provide rich fodder for exploring ancient ownership claims to different texts and competing interpretive claims for texts held in common.

A third example of our scholarly historical inquiry into "Whose text?" is found in the recent heightened interest in the history of interpretation. Biblical scholars are increasingly collaborating across disciplines of history, music, and art to discover more about the religious-social-political-cultural contexts that have affected interpreters' selection of and perspective on texts over the centuries. The good questions that we have tried to ask and answer over many decades about the ancient biblical texts in their own compositional contexts are now being asked about subsequent readers and readings.

In short, the question "Whose text is it?" with its attendant issues of contested identities and hermeneutics is scarcely new to our discipline. But the question has seemed safe so long as it applied to the past and so long as the question of why we ourselves as scholars choose to study particular texts or ask certain questions or reach certain conclusions was not part of the discussion. However heated the debates about the ancient world of the texts and their meanings within that world of the past (and we know those debates can be fiery), the conversations about our own places in relation to our work turn out to be more difficult.

II. "Whose Text?" The Current Landscape

Recent discussion of our own places in relation to our work is multidimensional; I have organized it under five headings, each of which represents a major fault line across which issues of ownership ("Whose text?") are in tension. These five are academic methods; religious/secular interpretation; Jewish and Christian/other readers; sociocultural traditions, including cultural, ethnic, gender, economic, and political dimensions; and "ordinary"/"expert" readers. This schema is obviously porous, and after commenting on each of the five I will hasten to reiterate the inevitability of their interaction.

The first set of divisions concerns academic methods. None of us would even pretend to be able to control all of the subspecialties of method in biblical scholarship, even if we restricted ourselves to a particular smaller corpus of the material such as pentateuchal narrative or Johannine literature. I include this category not because we are unwilling to recognize the expertise of others, but to raise the question of how we value that expertise. To the extent that hermeneutics says to textual criticism, "I have no need of you," or vice versa, a fault line is made visible. To the extent that those engaged in comparative study of ancient texts speak of literary critics as too lazy to learn cognate languages, or literary critics disparage or ignore possible illumination from extrabiblical sources, a fault line is present. Perhaps the widest fissure in method lies between those who are committed to focusing on identity hermeneutics and those who are disinterested in this broad approach or continue to question its academic value.

My second category, the division between religious and secular interpretation, is sometimes also described as between confessional and nonconfessional or between devotional and academic interpretation.[3] Whatever the nomenclature, the

---

[3] For confessional/nonconfessional language, see, e.g., Philip Davies, *Whose Bible Is It Anyway?* (2nd ed.; London: T&T Clark, 2004), esp. 13–15, 33–35. For devotional/academic language, see, e.g., "The Bible and Public Schools," in *Finding Common Ground: A First Amendment Guide to Religion and Public Schools* (ed. C. C. Haynes and O. Thomas; rev. ed.; Nashville: First Amendment Center, 2007), 121–33. Online: http://www.firstamendmentcenter.org/PDF/FCGchapter

central issue is how (and, for many people, whether) the text can be introduced, discussed, and interpreted in a manner that does not privilege the perspective of a particular religious or faith tradition. Our Society for many decades has sought to provide a forum for such a nonconfessional approach, and much of our work as a Society has been predicated upon the assumption that we can engage in such work. Here in the United States, we associate this fault line also with the controversies around teaching the Bible in our public (government-owned and funded) schools. The SBL is currently cooperating in efforts to help local communities discern what the academic study of the Bible apart from contemporary religious claims might look like in local high school classrooms. Yet we are aware that many of us are adherents of Judaism or Christianity, and that a great many of the college undergraduate teaching posts in our field in the United States exist because students (mostly Christian in this case) want or are required by their church-related institutions to learn something "academic" about the basic document of the Judeo-Christian tradition.[4] How this divide between religious and secular interpretation should be maintained and whether that is even possible are matters of continuing and sometimes heated debate.

My third broad category takes note of the fault line between those who acknowledge biblical texts as a part of their own faith heritage and those who study biblical texts out of curiosity about a religious tradition other than their own and often from a culture other than their own. Here I have in mind particularly the divide between Jewish and Christian (but predominantly Christian in terms both of numbers and of cultural influence) interpreters, on the one hand, and readers from other cultural and religious traditions, on the other; I include the question of how biblical interpretation may be informed by comparative work growing out of other living religious traditions and their texts. What place do readers from other cultural and religious traditions have at the table of biblical interpretation? And what responsibility do Christian and Jewish biblical scholars have to become more engaged with other religious texts and traditions? The matter is of theoretical scholarly significance and also of practical import, here in North America, but especially in a global perspective. Scholars as diverse as Wayne Meeks and R. S. Sugirtharajah have identified this as a key frontier, urging its importance upon Western biblical scholars.[5] Those of us who teach in North America and Europe are challenged

---

11.pdf (accessed Nov. 11, 2007). The SBL is one of many signatories to the position statement on this topic printed in this chapter.

[4] See American Academy of Religion, "AAR Survey of Undergraduate Religion and Theology Programs in the U.S. and Canada: Further Data Analysis: Summary of Results" (paper presented at the annual meeting of the AAR, Atlanta, Nov. 24, 2003). Online: http://aarweb.org/Programs/Department_Services/Survey_Data/Undergraduate/dataanalysis-20040309.pdf (accessed Oct. 25, 2007).

[5] See Wayne A. Meeks, "Why Study the New Testament?" *NTS* 51 (2005): 168–69. In numerous publications, R. S. Sugirtharajah has urged the importance of comparing selected biblical

to prepare our students to engage rather than to ignore this divide. This fault line points us in two directions: it points back to my previous consideration of the debate about a secular or nonconfessional academic discourse; it also points ahead to my fourth category of sociocultural divides. Religious differences could be theoretically erased under the former category or incorporated into the latter; I have lifted out religious pluralism for separate notice to underscore the need for more sustained attention to other sacred texts and to perspectives from other religious traditions.

My fourth fault line, then, is sociocultural, which may include diverse religious traditions but in which I am focusing, as I indicated earlier, on the broad range of racial-ethnic, political, economic, gender, and cultural differences among interpreters and the resulting multifaceted tensions in claims to "ownership" of texts. If the dividing lines internal to my first four broad categories were complex, here they become even more so, since each interpreter, whether using one academic method or another, whether working in a religious or a secular context, whether working with his or her own faith documents or other texts, participates in this whole range of dimensions of sociocultural experience. The issue is not whether any one of us participates, but how that reality impacts our work. Among those who speak and write from a perspective of identity hermeneutics, fragmentation of perspectives is on the increase. No longer, for example, are categories such as Asian voices or even Southeast Asian voices adequate, but groups and individuals from different subcultures of many regions are distinguishing themselves. It is my own judgment that such fragmentation is a positive sign, even as it was a positive first step when black or liberation or white feminist interpretations (categories that we now recognize as quite broad) initially arose some decades ago. Ever smaller and more focused groups are considering their identity in relation to and/or in resistance to the text, seeking to make their own meaning and challenging what could become hegemonic interpretations even by their nearer neighbors. In the face of such fragmentation, however, constructive mutual engagement becomes even more difficult to achieve.

The fifth and last fault line that I would identify is that between so-called ordinary and so-called expert readers. The more usual discussion of this fault line has identified "expert" readers as those such as ourselves (members of the SBL) who have special academic training in the guild's methods of approaching biblical texts. Depending on our particular training we may rightly be viewed as more expert than ordinary interpreters in our various technical specializations. Gerald West, Musimbi Kanyoro, Hans de Wit, and others remind us, however, that all readers bring some sort of expertise to the text.[6] Thus, this divide may be better identified

---

themes and motifs to materials from Asian religious texts (see, e.g., *Postcolonial Reconfigurations: An Alternative Way of Reading the Bible and Doing Theology* [St. Louis: Chalice, 2003], 107–8).

[6] See, most recently, Gerald West, ed., *Reading Other-Wise: Socially Engaged Biblical Schol-*

as between academic and nonacademic readers, recognizing that even with such a label there will be a continuum. Nonacademic or ordinary readers bring their own life experiences to the text, offering expertise often very different from ours, and the experiences of these nonacademic, sometimes nonliterate, readers may open up remarkably fresh avenues of analysis. Vincent Wimbush's important Institute for Signifying Scriptures project is drawing our attention to the significance of this approach to expertise in all cultural settings, including North America.[7]

As I indicated at the outset, these five categories of fault lines are heuristic and reflective of major threads of discussion in recent literature about the character of biblical scholarship for the twenty-first century. I expect that most of you have found your own resonance with the question of "Whose text?" primarily in one or two of the categories, although the interpenetration of the categories should be apparent.

In the face of this complexity it is a natural temptation for each of us to proceed with doing whatever interests us without worrying much about these fault lines. I say "for each of us," but I think that temptation, such as it is, is mostly for those of us who find ourselves by reason of birth and circumstance in relatively more privileged positions as part of the white Eurocentric academy. For many others in our midst, however, the struggle to find a venue for their work, and the struggle to have it taken seriously, is part and parcel of their academic life. It is their experience that, again in the words of the moderator of that panel two years ago, "Nobody seems to be listening." The effort to gain recognition for their claim to ownership of the text remains an uphill battle.

III. A Possible Way Ahead

In acknowledgment of that uphill battle, I want to focus now on possibilities for recognizing the claim to ownership of those who are not part of the privileged majority, for having their interpretive voices taken seriously, with special attention to the global context of our work.

Our Society has taken structural steps in the right direction. Subsidies for bringing international scholars and specifically international women scholars to the North American annual meeting are to be applauded, although six to eight

---

ars Reading with Their Local Communities (SemeiaSt 62; Atlanta: Society of Biblical Literature, 2007), esp. 1–3; Musimbi R. Kanyoro, *Introducing Feminist Cultural Hermeneutics: An African Perspective* (London: Sheffield Academic Press, 2002); Hans de Wit et al., eds., *Through the Eyes of Another: Intercultural Reading of the Bible* (Elkhart, IN: Institute of Mennonite Studies, 2004). West emphasizes that among "ordinary readers" his particular interest is in "the poor, the working class, and the marginalized" (p. 2), and de Wit offers an extended discussion of the category of "ordinary reader" (pp. 5–19).

[7] See the Institute's Web site at http://iss.cgu.edu/about/index.htm (accessed Nov. 12, 2007).

guests among several thousand attendees hardly form a critical mass. Our international meetings are potentially another step, insofar as they do not simply export Eurocentric presentations to holiday locations, but rather enable scholars from outside the West to participate in more significant numbers. We have begun a project of making scholarly papers in native languages from across the world available electronically on our Web site, with the selection process conducted by local or regional associations of biblical scholars in Asia, Africa, and Latin America. Beyond such structural steps, what strategies may be helpful?

In approaching this question I recall one of my most difficult evenings in Asia. The women who joined me for conversation had agreed to be present as a courtesy to my host, but they were nonetheless quite frank. "We are tired of Westerners coming to tell us what to think," they said, and then added, "we are equally tired of being asked what we think. We need dialogue, a two-way conversation." On that we were agreed, but how to proceed eluded us. What might enable us to meet, as Kwok Pui-lan eloquently puts it, as equal subjects for sharing of our treasures?[8] In my subsequent experience, focusing conversation around a particular text has proved to be one helpful way of addressing such an impasse. With that in mind, let me sharpen my question of "Whose text?" Thus far in asking "Whose text is it?" I have spoken about "text/texts" rather generically. It is my conviction, however, that we can often proceed further toward mutual engagement if we focus the question of "Whose text?" not on the Bible as a whole (whatever its boundaries in various religious traditions) but rather on individual texts, or on much smaller bodies of texts that introduce particular characters or political or sociocultural topics.

IV. A Test Probe

Given this perspective on the value of a focal text, I turn now to offering a brief postcolonial reflection on a particular biblical story and character. As postcolonial feminists from among the colonized are calling for women like myself (and men as well) to engage their work and their approach,[9] I as a first-world, white feminist can perhaps best make clear my sense of my place by describing myself as a "pro-postcolonial feminist" (on the analogy of a "pro-woman man" entering into white feminist biblical interpretation). I emphasize that I am making no claim to "having it right" in what follows. My goal is to model publicly the risk that I invite

---

[8] For the image of shared treasures, see Kwok Pui-lan, "Discovering the Bible in the Non-Biblical World," in *Voices from the Margin: Interpreting the Bible in the Third World* (ed. R. S. Sugirtharajah; new ed.; Maryknoll, NY: Orbis Books, 1995), 303; reprinted from *Semeia* 47 (1989).

[9] See, e.g., Kwok Pui-lan, *Postcolonial Imagination and Feminist Theology* (Louisville: Westminster John Knox, 2005), 127, 167; Musa W. Dube, "Toward a Post-Colonial Feminist Interpretation," in *Reading the Bible as Women: Perspectives from Asia, Africa, and Latin America* (ed. P. A. Bird et al.; *Semeia* 78; Atlanta: Scholars Press, 1997), 20, 22.

other first-world interpreters to take: recognizing global ownership of biblical texts by attempting to engage biblical interpretation across difficult dividing lines.

I have chosen for my test probe Judges 4–5, the story of Deborah and Barak, Sisera and Jael, chapters that have received extensive treatment by numerous white first-world feminists. Although postcolonial feminist writers have produced already an impressive body of work on selected biblical texts, most notably within the OT on the story of Rahab and on the story of Ruth, Naomi, and Orpah, I have not yet uncovered publications from a specifically postcolonial perspective on Judges 4–5.[10] It is possible that this apparent lacuna is not a reality, since the sources included in database searches are still limited largely to North Atlantic languages and publications (yet another sign, of course, of the hegemonic interpretive context I am highlighting here).[11] There may well be publications in Asia, Africa, or Latin America that do deal with Judges 4–5 from a postcolonial perspective, and there may be various forms of oral communication to which access is even more difficult.

My choice of this text and of the figure of Jael in particular may be an awkward selection. For me as a white, first-world feminist to offer any postcolonial reflection before others have spoken may seem out of place. Yet I choose this text because of a prior experience that does place it for me squarely in this domain, with the hope that postcolonial feminist writers will choose to explore it further in response and correction. That experience, as I have recounted elsewhere, took place some years ago in discussing this story with Korean women church leaders.[12] I expressed the discomfort that I and many women peers in North America experience with Jael's murder of Sisera, to which the response came swiftly: "your place as a U.S. woman

---

[10] On Ruth, see, e.g., Musa W. Dube, "The Unpublished Letters of Orpah to Ruth," in *The Feminist Companion to the Bible,* vol. 3, *A Feminist Companion to Ruth* (ed. Athalya Brenner; FCB; Sheffield: Sheffield Academic Press, 1999), 145–50; eadem, "Divining Ruth for International Relations," in *Other Ways of Reading: African Women and the Bible* (ed. Musa W. Dube; Global Perspectives on Biblical Scholarship 2; Atlanta: Society of Biblical Literature, 2001), 179–95; Laura E. Donaldson, "The Sign of Orpah: Reading Ruth through Native Eyes," in *A Feminist Companion to Ruth,* 130–44; on Rahab, see Musa W. Dube, *Postcolonial Feminist Interpretation of the Bible* (St. Louis: Chalice, 2000), esp. 76–80, 121–24.

Uriah Y. Kim considers the significance of postcolonial interpretation for Judges generally but without focused attention on chs. 4–5 ("Who Is the Other in the Book of Judges," in *Judges and Method: New Approaches in Biblical Studies* [ed. Gale A. Yee; 2nd ed.; Minneapolis: Fortress, 2007], 161–82).

[11] Hans de Wit observes the tendency to overlook Spanish-language scholarship in his comparison of Latin American and non–Latin American treatments of Judges 4 ("Leyendo con Yael," in *Los caminos inexhauribles de la Palabra: Las relecturas creativas en la Biblia y de la Biblia: Homenaje de colegas y discipulos a J. Severino Croatto* [ed. Guillermo Hansen; Buenos Aires: Lumen-ISEDET, 2000], 11–66).

[12] See my "Deborah, Jael, and Sisera's Mother: Reading the Scriptures in Cross-Cultural Context," in *Women, Gender, and Christian Community* (ed. Jane Dempsey Douglass and James F. Kay; Louisville: Westminster John Knox, 1997), 13–22.

is with Sisera's mother, waiting to count the spoils." In retrospect this was surely a postcolonial (or neocolonial economic) reading and challenge, although none of us marked it as such at the time. I note also, and not insignificantly, that this observation was offered by a so-called ordinary (i.e., nonacademic) reader. She was not a biblical scholar; she had never to my knowledge studied Hebrew. But she was certainly an expert in relating the text to her life and the political context of our two nations.

With her response in mind, let me explore further how I imagine the story might be viewed through a postcolonial lens. My hermeneutical strategy, following a range of postcolonial writers, will be to explore possible points of contact between biblical actors and contemporary readers, even as did my Korean conversation partner in pointing me to Sisera's mother. This approach resonates, for instance, with the concept of "story field" as a locus for negotiating readings as proposed by postcolonial interpreter Laura Donaldson.[13] I choose it also because it fits closely with the way in which many "ordinary" (i.e., nonacademic) readers typically engage the Bible, thus providing an important bridge of contact across that divide.

I begin by stepping back from the character of Jael in order to problematize the place of Israel relative to the Canaanites. To be sure, these chapters, like the OT generally, view the situation through Israelite eyes. But the situation in Judges is not exactly the same as the picture in the book of Joshua, where the invading Israelites are taking control of Canaanite land. In Joshua, the experience of the Canaanites provides a connecting point of identity for contemporary peoples whose land has been or is being taken over by outside forces. As Robert Alan Warrior, among others, has emphasized, this is the Joshua narrative's portrayal of Israel and Canaan, regardless of what happened historically, and this has been the portrayal used as warrant by land-grabbing colonizing powers.[14] The scenario in Judges, however, is potentially more complicated. From the narrowest viewpoint on our narrative, it is now the Israelites who are under the oppressive hand of the Canaanites, without regard for how the Israelites came to be present. At this narrative level, a contemporary subject people might read this story in a liberationist mode alongside the exodus story and identify with the Israelites in their effort to throw off an oppressive yoke, even if those same readers have identified themselves with the Canaanites in the context of Joshua.[15]

---

[13] Laura E. Donaldson, *Decolonizing Feminisms: Race, Gender, and Empire-Building* (Chapel Hill: University of North Carolina Press, 1992), 139.

[14] Robert Alan Warrior, "A Native American Perspective: Canaanites, Cowboys, and Indians," in *Voices from the Margin: Interpreting the Bible in the Third World* (ed. R. S. Sugirtharajah; 3rd ed.; Maryknoll, NY: Orbis Books, 2006), 235–41; reprinted from *Christianity and Crisis* 49 (1989).

[15] De Wit finds examples of such liberationist readings of Judges in Latin American sources ("Leyendo con Yael").

Such an initial view of Judges 4–5 is immediately complicated, however, by the theological framing of the text, since it is Israel's deity who has allowed Israel's oppression, and it is Israel's deity who will accomplish Israel's deliverance. Does this theological stance inevitably make Israel actually the dominant cultural and political power in the story? I would propose that this is not necessarily the case; the story can still be read as a story of a weak Israel rejecting the temptation to participate in the Canaanites' religious-cultural hegemony, to which they have thus far succumbed, and trying to stake out their own sociocultural as well as physical space. On the other hand, we know enough of modern colonial history to see how readily the story of Judges 4–5 can be read from the perspective of Israel's dominance, all the more so as the theological framing ties the themes of Judges back to Joshua. The image in Judges is still one of recent arrivals, now pictured as a weaker/small group, trying to establish themselves in the midst of powerful but despised native inhabitants, inhabitants who have temporarily, but only temporarily, overrun the intruding outsiders. In such a reading, the colonized are again the Canaanites. Parallels are legion to modern stories of "settlers" who described themselves as "beleaguered," and to original inhabitants who have resented and resisted their presence.

Thus far I have suggested that it might be possible for contemporary postcolonial subjects to identify with either of the two sides in the conflict, depending on what level of the narrative and what points of contact are selected. The corollary is that those like myself who live on the side of Empire, of the colonizers, historically and/or at the present moment, must consider our own place.[16] On my first, narrower level of reading, we may find ourselves as Canaanites, as my Korean respondent had powerfully pointed out. At the second level, however, we will find ourselves instead as Israelites, participating in a sociopolitical and even religious community that imagines itself as rightly called to the role of colonizer even while experiencing a temporary setback. I suspect that for those of us who are a part of Empire yet seek to resist its impulse this latter identification with Israel is more difficult. To be a Canaanite in this story, for me to be Sisera's mother, means to be in the wrong: reading with the grain of the text, the Canaanites are in the wrong, and the connection is straightforward. However, to identify myself as an Israelite in this story while maintaining a postcolonial lens requires first that as a colonizer I view Israel's weak and overrun position nonetheless as one of Empire, already a difficult mental step for a relatively privileged first-world reader to hold on to, and second

---

[16] Postcolonial scholars have varying ways of distinguishing between imperialism and colonialism, as well as neocolonialism; see, e.g., Dube, "Toward a Post-Colonial Feminist Interpretation," 15; R. S. Sugirtharajah, *The Postcolonial Biblical Reader* (Oxford: Blackwell, 2006), 16–17. None of these concepts, of course, is precisely parallel either culturally or geopolitically to the situation of the Israelites and Canaanites as portrayed in Joshua-Judges. The issues of control of land and resources, emphasis on cultural distinctiveness, and regarding the other as inferior are features shared by the biblical narrative and imperial/colonial impulses.

that I must choose whether and how to resist that identity for the sake of the Canaanites. As one who is immersed in the Western Judeo-Christian faith tradition, the mental gymnastics of standing within yet against ancient Israel as it seeks to defeat Jabin and Sisera are complex, to say the least.

These potential connecting points are subject to even further complication if we ask after ancient Israel's own possible perspectives on the story and how Canaan may have been a cipher for imperial powers for some ancient hearers. If we undertake an experiment in historical imagination, overhearing the story late in the monarchy in the era of Judah's King Josiah, we find Judah as a small blip on the world scene dominated first by the Assyrian Empire but soon by the rising Babylonians.[17] Perhaps, as Judah dreams of some degree of independence from Mesopotamian might and Egyptian pressure, we can imagine the story of Deborah and Barak as a warrant for Josiah's mysterious decision to go to battle against Pharaoh Neco at Megiddo. A people and leader who have recently turned afresh toward devotion to Yhwh, at least as the narrator of 2 Kings portrays them, seek to throw off a foreign yoke. This time, however, the battle ends in quite the opposite way with the death of Judah's leader rather than defeat of the enemy, and Judah's status as puppet or pawn of imperial powers remains unchanged.

If we move ahead in our imagination into the Persian era, when Judah is officially part of another empire, a standing army is no more, and prophecy has taken a quite different shape, perhaps the story becomes colonized Judah's nostalgia for bygone days, or perhaps a call to repentance in hopes of restoring former glory, or perhaps even part of the Persian colonizer's strategy for maintaining order[18]—if Judah's deity has not sent another Deborah in these latter days, then submission to Persia/Canaan must be the intent of Judah's god. Each of these readings equates ancient empires with Canaan, but now there is no deliverance for the subjugated. Even if the story wants to portray Israel as the powerful center, even if it is resistance literature rather than a tool of Empire, it is preserved in a community that experiences its life as colonized and without serious prospect of change. Attention to historical context seems to make a pipe dream of the hope implicit in an anticolonial reading. In the absence of prospects for change, Empire becomes more

---

[17] For an important treatment of Josiah and 2 Kings from a postcolonial perspective, see Uriah Y. Kim, *Decolonizing Josiah: Toward a Postcolonial Reading of the Deuteronomistic History* (Bible in the Modern World 5; Sheffield: Sheffield Phoenix, 2005). For a more abbreviated interpretation of Jael, along with Rahab and Ruth, from the perspective of colonized Judah, see my "Postcolonial Perspectives on Premonarchic Women," in *To Break Every Yoke: Essays in Honor of Marvin L. Chaney* (ed. Robert B. Coote and Norman K. Gottwald; Sheffield: Sheffield Phoenix, 2007), 192–203.

[18] For an approach suggesting that some biblical texts functioned to support the interest of the Persians, see Jon Berquist, "Postcolonialism and Imperial Motives for Canonization," *Semeia* 75 (1996): 15–36; idem, *Judaism in Persia's Shadow: A Social and Historical Approach* (Minneapolis: Fortress, 1995), esp. 131–36.

secure, and the effort to resist complicity with Empire, whether from within or from without, becomes correspondingly more difficult.

Thus far my proposed patterns of reading have bypassed Jael and the Kenites; I turn now to the question of Jael's social location. Jael is presented to us in the usual rendering as the wife of Heber the Kenite, who is not Israelite yet by tradition would be affiliated with Israel as a descendant of Moses' father-in-law. Yet Heber had separated himself from his kinfolk, moved his tent into Canaanite territory, and "made peace" (4:17) with the king of the Canaanite forces. Heber (who never personally appears in the story) is thus a borderland figure, both geographically and ethnically, one who cannot belong fully to either side, who has eschewed his ties even to his own liminal Kenite group, and who apparently has chosen to align himself with the seemingly dominant side (Canaan) rather than with the kinship side (Israel).[19] On this reading of the text, we are told nothing explicitly about the ethnicity of Jael or of her personal loyalties, despite the assumption of many commentators that she is a loyal Kenite. It is conceivable that Heber had married outside his clan, either an Israelite woman or a Canaanite woman.[20]

Some scholars have argued that the word *Heber* is not a proper name but a common noun.[21] In this case Jael would be presented to us clearly as a Kenite, but with no reference to her marital status. For my purpose here, however, the central point is that none of these readings suggests that Jael as a woman had any part in the decision to encamp away from other Kenites or from Israel or to join in alliance with Canaan. The text does not tell us anything about her loyalties. No matter which ethnicity we presume for Jael, Israel's victory in battle and Sisera's appearance at her tent force her to make a choice.

Although white feminist interpretations of Jael are enormously diverse, a number tend to interpret her killing of Sisera as an act of self-defense. Themes include Jael's defense of herself against a male intruder into women's private space (especially in the poem) and thus against a threat of rape, and Jael's defense of herself against being discovered harboring the enemy (especially in the prose account), and thus against a threat of death.[22] This "defense" or implicit justification of Jael's

---

[19] Baruch Halpern has suggested that the Kenites may have been working for Israel, despite appearances ("Sisera and Old Lace: The Case of Deborah and Yael," in *The First Historians: The Hebrew Bible and History* [San Francisco: Harper & Row, 1988], 85–87).

[20] If we imagine Jael as a Canaanite, we might align her intertextually with Rahab; if we imagine her as Israelite, connections with Judith of much later tradition might be more apt. For comparison of these other characters, see Musa W. Dube, "Rahab Says Hello to Judith: A Decolonizing Feminist Reading," in *Toward a New Heaven and a New Earth: Essays in Honor of Elisabeth Schüssler Fiorenza* (ed. Fernando Segovia; Maryknoll, NY: Orbis Books, 2003), 54–72.

[21] See Susan Ackerman, "What If Judges Had Been Written by a Philistine?" *BibInt* 8 (2000): 37–38, and bibliography there.

[22] For the former, see Ann Wansbrough, "Blessed Be Jael among Women: For She Challenged Rape," in *Women of Courage: Asian Women Reading the Bible* (ed. Lee Oo Chung et al.;

need to kill Sisera for her own survival serves to defuse some readers' discomfort (even revulsion) with the tent-peg scene, but it also can lead to downplaying the poem's explicit celebration of Jael's action—"most blessed of women be Jael" (5:24). The "defense" theme also stands in contrast to oral reports of women from other cultures who compare Jael to women in their own traditions who are celebrated for assassination of enemy leaders in times of military crisis.[23]

As my Korean conversation partner suggested, women who champion the overthrow of oppressors can identify with Jael. Given Jael's complex liminal status and its possible permutations, however, I would covet more conversation about Jael with women reflecting on their varied positions as postcolonial subjects. Imagining us gathered around a table, I hope we could consider questions such as these: Stepping back from the specific circumstance of war and murder/assassination, how might Jael's liminality illuminate ways in which you find yourself caught between colonizer and colonized because of gender structures in either or both cultures? Where does Jael's lack of agency in finding herself placed between Israel and Canaan resonate with you as an individual or with the circumstances of your community as colonized? When may your circumstances have meant that you have found no home on either side? In the moment of crisis, does Jael's action represent genuine agency or only forced choice? Does Jael's predicament mirror choices you have been forced to make, and what have been the possibilities and costs of refusing to choose? Is there reason to resist identifying with Jael simply because she takes sides so quickly? Does her action simply reinforce and reinscribe the construction of "absolute, incompatible contrasts"[24] that postcolonial analysis seeks to dismantle?

And what of myself, or of other first-world white feminists? Is our only place with Sisera's mother? I hesitate to consider any additional option without postcolonial conversation partners at the ready to correct my blind spots. I have asked myself whether I dare to claim any place with Jael as a woman whose tent inevitably lies between the camps. I can interpret my catalogue of questions about Jael in a way that allows me to speak of my own liminal place in a kyriarchal world.[25] But the risk of taking over (colonizing) yet again a space that may better belong rightly to my colonized sisters seems great. So for now I ask instead whether there is another place of liminality that could arise from committing oneself to hearing and advo-

---

Seoul: Asian Women's Resource Centre for Culture and Theology, 1992), 101–22; for the latter, see Danna Nolan Fewell and David M. Gunn, "Controlling Perspectives: Women, Men, and the Authority of Violence in Judges 4 & 5," *JAAR* 58 (1990): 396.

[23] I heard such comparisons from several groups of Asian women; Gale A. Yee also reports such a comparison ("By the Hand of a Woman: The Metaphor of the Woman Warrior in Judges 4," *Semeia* 61 [1993]: 106).

[24] See John J. Collins, "The Zeal of Phinehas: The Bible and the Legitimation of Violence," *JBL* 122 (2003): 18.

[25] The term "kyriarchy," coined by Elisabeth Schüssler Fiorenza, gathers up the multiple and intertwined hierarchies of a world of Empire.

cating for the Jaels of the postcolonial world. Might there be an unnamed woman of Israel, or of Canaan, depending on where a first-world white woman places herself in the story, an unnamed woman who supports Jael in some small way by resisting the power and the strategies of her own people? Such a midrash I would like to explore with the guidance of my postcolonial sisters.

Whose story is it? Whose text is it? I have claimed this particular text for myself in the hope of giving it away, and in the hope of receiving eventually a gift from other interpreters in a mutual sharing of treasures.

V. Conclusion

In conclusion, let me quickly pull the zoom lens back from postcolonial feminism and this one text to the wide angle on the question of "Whose text?" with which I began. Each year as I greet new students entering my institution's Ph.D. program, I begin with that phrase more traditionally used only at the conferral of the doctoral degree, "Welcome to the company of scholars." In those remarks, my primary emphasis is on the word "company." The challenge I put to them, and now to you is this: Acknowledging our need for the gifts and contributions of sister and brother scholars, let us not decide so easily that the contribution of the "other" does not count as worthy scholarship, whether because we perceive its method and data as too politically motivated (read "postcolonial") or alternatively too old fashioned and even hegemonic (read "Eurocentric or patriarchal") or whether because we perceive the work as nonacademic (read "too much reporting on 'ordinary' readers"), or whether because we reject the method as too vague or too psychological or too whatever else causes any of us to "other" that approach and its practitioners.

Each text really does belong at least potentially to all of us, and to people across the world who may never know anything of the work we do in these halls. But text by text, each text will belong to different ones of us in vastly different and sometimes painfully different ways. Given this reality, let us not be content with a state of static tolerance in which we simply ignore one another. Rather, let us be on the move toward that ethical calling to become a company of scholars who rejoice in working with and learning from those least like ourselves and who show special generosity of spirit to those whose struggle to be heard is more difficult than our own.

Building Houses and Planting Vineyards: The Early Inner-Biblical Discourse on an Ancient Israelite Wartime Curse

JEREMY D. SMOAK
jeremysmoak@hotmail.com
University of California, Los Angeles, Los Angeles, CA 90095

Notions of building and planting have profound significance in the discourse of biblical literature. One important indication of this is the inner-biblical discourse of a wartime curse, which threatens Israel in the following words, "You will build a house, but you will not live in it. You will plant a vineyard, but you will not harvest its fruit" (Deut 28:30). A survey of biblical literature reveals that this particular curse held an especially prominent place in the discourse of ancient Israel and early Judaism.[1] Over a dozen biblical texts contain formulations of, or allusions to, this particular curse and its imagery (Amos 5:11; 9:14; Isa 5:1–17; Zeph 1:13; Jer

Much of the research for this article was supported by a fellowship from the University of California, Los Angeles. I thank the University of California, Los Angeles, and the Department of Near Eastern Languages and Cultures for their support of this project. I also thank William M. Schniedewind, Aaron Burke, Jacob Wright, Elizabeth Carter, and Daniel Smith-Christopher for their comments on the article or the ideas expressed therein.

[1] For previous discussions of this curse or the imagery found therein, see Robert Bach, "Bauen und Planzen," in *Studien zur Theologie der alttestamentlichen Überlieferungen* (ed. Rolf Rendtorff and Klaus Koch; Neukirchen-Vluyn: Neukirchener Verlag, 1961), 22; Daniel L. Smith-Christopher, *The Religion of the Landless: The Social Context of the Babylonian Exile* (Bloomington, IN: Meyer-Stone Books, 1989), 133–36; Shalom M. Paul, "Literary and Ideological Echoes of Jeremiah in Deutero-Isaiah," in *Proceedings of the 4th World Congress of Jewish Studies* (Jerusalem: Magnes, 1970), 102–20; Adele Berlin, "Jeremiah 29:5–7: A Deuteronomic Allusion [Deut 20:5–10]," *HAR* 8 (1984): 3–11; Carey Ellen Walsh, *The Fruit of the Vine: Viticulture in Ancient Israel* (HSM 60; Winona Lake, IN: Eisenbrauns, 2000).

6:9–15; 29:5, 28; 31:4; Deut 20:5–6; 28:30; Isa 62:6–9; 65:21; Ezek 28:26; 36:36). The following study traces the origins and early inner-biblical discourse of the curse in the eighth and seventh centuries B.C.E.[2] Placement of the early biblical occurrences of the curse against certain historical moments allows one to see the ways in which various historical processes influenced its different biblical formulations. A study of the historical motivations behind the curse's literary history also points to its attractiveness as a persistent motif in biblical literature.

I. Neo-Assyrian Military Tactics, Siege Warfare, and the Background of the Curse in Biblical Discourse

Scholars have long noted that the threat of war forms the background of the present curse. It is during wartime that the fulfillment of one's labors, such as the harvesting of a vineyard, is thwarted. Assyrian textual and iconographic sources, however, suggest that a more specific, and interrelated, aspect of Assyrian siege warfare stands behind the curse's imagery. One of the major developments that accompanied the increasing Assyrian presence in the southern Levant during the eighth century was the rise of siege warfare as the dominant mode of battle.[3] Assyrian sources indicate that siege warfare increasingly displaced open-field battles beginning in the eighth century. Assyrian iconography of this period increasingly

---

[2] In the present study, I adopt the terminology of inner-biblical discourse as opposed to inner-biblical exegesis for two main reasons. First, the term "inner-biblical discourse" emphasizes that there is a close connection between historical phenomena and the contours of exegetical traditions in biblical literature. That is, students of this method envision an intimate relationship between social and historical contexts and the evolution of interpretation in society. This emphasis is partly a reaction to the other approaches to inner-biblical interpretation, which also give peripheral attention to the broader aspects of cultural discourse. Second, the term "inner-biblical discourse," in contrast to "inner-biblical exegesis," stresses that ancient Israelite interpretive systems were not primarily textual in nature. For more on the terminology of inner-biblical discourse, see William M. Schniedewind, *Society and the Promise to David: The Reception History of 2 Samuel 7:1–17* (New York/Oxford: Oxford University Press, 1999), 7–9. For other critiques of the approaches of inner-biblical exegesis, see Lyle M. Eslinger, "Inner-biblical Exegesis and Allusion: The Question of Category," *VT* 42 (1992): 48–49; James L. Kugel, "The Bible's Earliest Interpreters," *Prooftexts* 7 (1987): 275–76.

[3] See Israel Eph'al, *Siege and Its Ancient Near Eastern Manifestations* (in Hebrew; Jerusalem: Magnes, 1996); idem, "Ways and Means to Conquer a City, Based on Assyrian Queries to the Sungod," in *Assyria 1995: Proceedings of the 10th Anniversary Symposium of the New-Assyrian Text Corpus Project, Helsinki, September 7–11, 1995* (ed. Simo Parpola and Robert M. Whiting; Helsinki: Neo-Assyrian Text Corpus Project, 1997), 49–54; idem, "On Warfare and Military Control in the Ancient Near Eastern Empires: A Research Outline," in *History, Historiography and Interpretation: Studies in Biblical and Cuneiform Literatures* (ed. Hayim Tadmor and Moshe Weinfeld; Jerusalem: Magnes, 1983), 88–106; Alfred C. Mierzejewski, "La technique de siège assyrienne aux IX–VII siècles avant notre ère," *Etudes et Travaux* [Warsaw] 7 (1970): 11–20; see also A. Leo Oppenheim, "Siege-documents from Nippur," *Iraq* 17 (1955): 69–89.

depicts the Assyrians laying siege to a well-fortified city, as opposed to meeting an enemy in an open field.

The advent of siege warfare brought with it new military tactics and battle techniques, many of which are alluded to in Assyrian and biblical sources. One of the most devastating military tactics that the Assyrians employed during a siege was the destruction of the agricultural support systems.[4] Several Assyrian iconographic sources depict Assyrian soldiers chopping down trees, orchards, and other vegetation surrounding an enemy city. Such imagery is paralleled in the Assyrian textual sources, which often describe the king or the military destroying the vegetation of their enemies. For instance, in the Suhu annals of Shalmaneser III, the king boasts, "We will go and attack the houses of the land of Suhu; we will seize his cities of the steppe; and we will cut down their fruit trees."[5] In the Nimrud Monolith, Shalmaneser also boasts, "Ahuni, son of Adini . . . I shut up in his city, carried off the crops of his (fields), cut down his orchards."[6] Such descriptions of the destruction of orchards and other types of vegetation are found in many other Assyrian inscriptions.

Scholars have long sought to understand the exact purpose behind the Assyrian destruction of agricultural support systems. Several studies have claimed that the destruction of trees and other vegetation enabled the Assyrians to build additional equipment during a prolonged siege.[7] Other scholars have argued that the destruction of vegetation was a "face saving device employed in a report about an uncompleted siege."[8] More recent studies, however, argue that a close examination of the order of events in the iconographic sources suggests an alternative explanation. These studies emphasize that the destruction of agricultural support systems in the iconographic sources always occurs during or directly after the successful destruction and looting of a city.[9] The iconography at Sennacherib's Southwest

---

[4] On this military tactic, see Erika Bleibtreu, "Zerstörung der Umwelt durch Bäumefällen und Dezimierung des Löwenbestandes in Mesopotamien," in *Der orientalische Mensch und seine Beziehungen zur Umwelt: Beiträge zum 2. Grazer Morgenländischen Symposion (2.–5. März 1989)* (ed. Bernhard Scholz; Graz, 1989), 219–33; Steven W. Cole, "The Destruction of Orchards in Assyrian Warfare," in *Assyria 1995*, ed. Parpola and Whiting, 29–40; Oded Bustani, "Cutting Down the Gardens in the Descriptions of the Assyrian Kings—A Chapter in Assyrian Historiography," in *Michael: Historical, Epigraphical and Biblical Studies in Honor of Prof. Michael Heltzer* (ed. Yitzhak Avishur and Robert Deutsch; Tel Aviv: Archaeological Center Publications, 1999), 27*–36*.

[5] Grant Frame, *Rulers of Babylonia: From the Second Dynasty of Isin to the End of Assyrian Domination (1157–612 BC)* (RIMB 2; Toronto: University of Toronto Press, 1995), 295.

[6] *ARAB*, 1:229, text 620.

[7] See Cole, "Destruction of Orchards," 34.

[8] Hayim Tadmor, *The Inscriptions of Tiglathpileser III, King of Assyria* (Jerusalem: Israel Academy of Sciences and Humanities, 1994), 79.

[9] See Michael G. Hasel, *Military Practice and Polemic: Israel's Laws of Warfare in Near Eastern Perspective* (Berrien Springs, MI: Andrews University Press, 2005).

Palace is particularly instructive in this regard. In a scene depicting the siege of the city of Dilbat, Assyrian soldiers cut down date palms while other soldiers remove spoil from the conquered city.[10] The scene places the destruction of vegetation alongside the burning of city buildings and the removal of the city's population. It is also during this stage of the siege in many Assyrian sources that the local inhabitants are removed from their homes and deported from the city.

A similar picture emerges from the iconography of Sennacherib's palace at Nineveh. In a scene depicting Sennacherib's capture of Illubru, Assyrian soldiers are depicted carrying away the spoils of the city and leading the inhabitants out of the city into captivity.[11] In the same scene, an Assyrian soldier is pictured hacking down a tree while all of these events transpire. A bronze relief of Shalmaneser III also depicts Assyrian soldiers chopping down trees during the final stages of the destruction of a city in Urartu.[12] Again, the order of events clearly connects the decimation of the city's vegetation with the final stages of destruction after the Assyrians had taken the city.

The order of events described in several Assyrian textual sources largely parallels that of the iconographic sources. That is, a review of the Assyrian inscriptions shows that descriptions of the destruction of vegetation often follow or occur in close connection with the description of the destruction of a city. For example, the annals of Sargon II also closely connect the decimation of vegetation with the destruction of a city:

> Into Ulhu, the store-city of Ursa I entered triumphantly; to the palace, his royal abode, I marched victoriously. The mighty wall, which was made of stone from the lofty mountain, with iron axes and iron hoes I smashed like a pot and leveled it to the ground.... Into his pleasant gardens, the adornments of his city which were overflowing with fruit and wine ... came tumbling down.... His great trees, the adornment of his palace, I cut down like millet (?), and destroyed the city of his glory, and his province I brought to shame. The trunks of all those trees which I had cut down I gathered together, heaped them in a pile and burned them with fire. Their abundant crops, which (in) garden and marsh were immeasurable, I tore up by the root and did not leave an ear to remember the destruction.[13]

Again, the sequence of events described in the annals is important. The description of the destruction of vegetation follows the description of the breach of the city walls and the final capture of the city. The narration of the conquest of other cities

---

[10] John Malcom Russell, *Sennacherib's Palace without Rival at Nineveh* (Chicago: University of Chicago Press, 1991), 154, fig. 78.

[11] Ibid., 70–71, fig. 39.

[12] Leonard W. King, *Bronze Reliefs from the Gates of Shalmaneser, King of Assyria, B.C. 860-825* (London: British Museum, 1915), pl. VIII, band II/2, upper register.

[13] *ARAB*, 2:87, text 161.

follows the same order of events. The description of Sargon II's conquest of the land of Aiadi states,

> I sent up large numbers of troops against their cities and they carried off large quantities of their property, their goods. Their strong walls, together with 87 cities of their neighborhood, I destroyed, I leveled to the ground. I set fire to the houses with them, and made the beams of their roofs like flame. Their heaped-up granaries I opened and let my army devour unmeasured quantities of barley. Their orchards I cut down, their forests I felled; all their tree trunks I gathered together and set them on fire.[14]

A number of Assyrian textual sources specify vineyards or wine as an object that was singled out by the Assyrians following a successful siege. For instance, in his description of the looting of Ulhu, Sargon boasts, "Its guarded wine cellars I entered, and the widespreading hosts of Assur drew the good wine from the bottles like river water."[15] Later in the inscription's description of Sargon's conquest of the lands of the Manneans and Nairi, the king brags, "I cut down great quantities of its vines, I made an end to its drinking." The iconographic and textual sources described above may indicate that the Assyrians destroyed vegetation only as punishment of a rebellious or incompliant enemy.[16] The destruction of viticulture quoted above likely followed the breach of city walls or the capture of the city in the inscriptions.

A number of Assyrian campaign narratives also contain descriptions of the destruction of houses and other physical structures following descriptions of a successful siege. Several textual sources situate descriptions of the destruction of houses close to descriptions of the destruction of agriculture. For example, in the description of Sargon's conquest of the land of Aiadi quoted above, the king boasts that he "set fire to the houses" and then "cut down their orchards."[17] Several other textual sources also associate houses and agriculture as objects of destruction. The order of events is similar in Sargon's description of his conquest of the lands of the Manneans and Nairi. After his successful scaling of the wall of their cities, Sargon brags, "I set fire on their beautiful dwellings, and made the smoke thereof rise and cover the face of heaven like a storm. . . . I cut down its splendid orchards, I cut down great quantities of its vines, making an end of its drinking."[18] A similar description of a successful siege occurs in Sargon's Letter to Assur recounting the events of his eighth campaign. In the description of his conquest of the city of Ushkaia in Urartu, Sargon claims that he set fire to the dwellings and then left its

---

[14] Ibid., 92, text 167.
[15] Ibid., 87, text 161.
[16] Hasel, *Military Practice and Polemic*, 62.
[17] *ARAB*, 2:91, text 166.
[18] Ibid., 90, text 164.

fields as if destroyed by a flood.¹⁹ Sennacherib's annals also often pair descriptions of the destruction of homes, or the deportation of people from homes, with descriptions of the devastation of vegetation.²⁰

The Assyrian iconographic and textual sources described above provide a compelling setting in which to place the curse's early history in biblical discourse. That is, the Assyrian iconographic and textual sources point to a specific moment during an Assyrian siege as the background of the curse. The pairing of the destruction of vineyards, or other vegetation, with the destruction of houses in the curse reflects the pairing of these activities during the final stages of a successful Assyrian siege. The curse threatened the successful capture and destruction of a city, which culminated in the removal of people from their homes and the destruction of their life-support systems. As a result, the curse came to symbolize the threats that a successful Assyrian siege posed, namely, the deportation of the population and the destruction of its agriculture.

II. Building and Planting in the Eighth Century b.c.e.: From Curse to Promise of National Restoration

The earliest biblical formulation of the curse appears in Amos 5:11, which directs the curse at the administrative elite of the northern kingdom:

> Therefore, because you levy a straw tax on the poor and exact a grain tax from him, you have built houses of hewn stone, but you will not live in them. You have planted lush vineyards, but you will not drink their wine.

Several aspects of this formulation of the curse stand out as significant in relation to the other biblical formulations of the curse. First, the language of the curse in this passage has been modified in order to connect it explicitly with the activities of the elite of the northern kingdom. In this way, the formulation of the curse in this verse has been adapted for its immediate literary context. The targets of the curse in this verse are not merely "houses" and "vineyards," as in the other formulations of the curse, but rather "houses of hewn stone" (בתי גזית) and "lush vineyards" (כרמי חמד).²¹ These linguistic transformations serve to specify further the audience to

---

[19] Ibid., 85, text 158.

[20] David D. Luckenbill, *The Annals of Sennacherib* (Chicago: University of Chicago Press, 1924), 58–59.

[21] For another use of the expression כרם חמד in biblical literature, see Isa 27:2. This is the only occurrence of בתי גזית in the Hebrew Bible. Scholars connect the latter expression with the presence of ashlar masonry at many urban sites in the north during this period. For examples of ashlar masonry at sites in the north, see Ronny Reich, "Palaces and Residences in the Iron Age," in *The Architecture of Ancient Israel: From the Prehistoric to the Persian Periods* (ed. Aaron Kempinski and Ronny Reich; Jerusalem: Israel Exploration Society, 1992), 202–22; Yigal Shiloh, *The Proto-Aeolic Capital and Israelite Ashlar Masonry* (Jerusalem: Israel Exploration Society, 1979).

which the curse is directed by threatening materials connected to the administrative elite of Israel, such as quality building material and prime agricultural land.

Past commentators regarded this verse as an insertion by a later redactor based on the presence of the unique expression לכן יען at the beginning of v. 14 and the fact that the verse uses the second person plural in contrast to the previous verse, which uses the third person.[22] Recent archaeological work suggests that this particular formulation of the curse should be read in the context of the northern kingdom during the eighth century B.C.E. Excavations at several sites in the northern kingdom demonstrate that this period witnessed an emerging socioeconomic stratification of society, marked by growing administrative upper classes.[23] This phenomenon is particularly evident in the residential quarters at several sites where one sees a growing disparity in the size and construction of domestic dwellings during this period.[24] For instance, Hazor Stratum VI contains several houses that may be identified as luxurious buildings belonging to wealthy or administrative elite based on their size, location, and type of construction.[25] This picture of an increased social stratification in the northern kingdom is also consistent with the depiction of the northern society in certain parts of Amos and other eighth-century prophets.[26]

An emphasis on "lush vineyards" also coincides with the agricultural picture of the northern kingdom during this period. Recent studies emphasize that this period was marked by a transformation in the structure of viticulture industries in

---

[22] K. W. Neubauer, "Erwägungen zu Amos 5:4–15," *ZAW* 78 (1966): 313; Hans Walter Wolff, *Joel and Amos: A Commentary on the Books of the Prophets Joel and Amos* (Hermeneia; Philadelphia: Fortress, 1977), 233; Artur Weiser, *Die Profetie des Amos* (BZAW 53; Giessen: Töpelmann, 1929), 197. More recent studies, however, stress the literary unity of ch. 5; see esp. Shalom M. Paul, *Amos: A Commentary on the Book of Amos* (Hermeneia; Philadelphia: Fortress, 1991), 171–72; Francis I. Andersen and David Noel Freedman, *Amos: A New Translation with Introduction and Commentary* (AB 24A; New York: Doubleday, 1989), 496–97; Jan de Waard, "The Chiastic Structure of Amos 5:1–17," *VT* 27 (1977): 170–77.

[23] Avraham Faust, "Socioeconomic Stratification in an Israelite City: Hazor VI as a Test Case," *Levant* 31 (1999): 179–90; Shulamit Geva, *Hazor, Israel: An Urban Community of the 8th Century B.C.E* (BAR International Series 543; Oxford: BAR, 1989). On the issue of the emergence of social stratification during the Iron II period, see also Shmuel Vargon, "The Social Background of Reproach Prophecies from the Latter Half of the 8th Century" (in Hebrew), in *Proceedings of the Ninth World Congress of Jewish Studies, 1985: Division A* (Jerusalem: Magnes, 1986), 81–86 [Hebrew]; Alexander H. Joffee, "The Rise of Secondary States in the Iron Age Levant," *JESHO* 45 (2003): 425–67; William G. Dever, "Social Structure in Palestine in the Iron II Period on the Eve of Destruction," in *The Archaeology of Society in the Holy Land* (ed. Thomas E. Levy; London: Leicester, 1995), 416–31.

[24] For an overview of this phenomenon at several cities, see Ze'ev Herzog, *Archaeology of the City: Urban Planning in Ancient Israel and Its Social Implications* (Monograph Series 13; Tel Aviv: Emery and Claire Yass Archaeology Press, 1997), 211–57.

[25] Faust, "Socioeconomic Stratification," 185–86.

[26] See Izabela Jaruzelska, "Social Structure in the Kingdom of Israel in the Eighth Century B.C. as Reflected in the Book of Amos," *FO* 29 (1992–93): 91–117.

the north.[27] These studies argue that during the eighth century small local vineyards were increasingly usurped by elites in urban centers in order to form larger and more economically profitable agricultural estates. This process was undoubtedly part of a larger strategy by the royal court and other elites to benefit from burgeoning trade networks on the Phoenician coast during this period.[28] Consequently, rural villagers were placed in an increasingly disenfranchised position compared to that of the ruling classes, who benefited the most from the new trading markets. Recent excavations and surveys of various regions of the north support this general economic picture.[29]

The socioeconomic picture described above suggests that the formulation of the curse in Amos 5:11 would have resonated well in the context of eighth-century Israel. Moreover, the fact that the increased stratification of urban sites contrasts sharply with the situation at rural sites in the northern kingdom may suggest that the urbanization of the north might have been the motivating social force behind this passage.[30] That is, the formulation of the curse here in Amos 5 may reflect the growing animosity between urban and rural sectors of the northern kingdom.

The fall of the north in the late eighth century followed by the ambitious political reforms of Hezekiah triggered a radical reformulation of the curse in biblical discourse. Amos 9:14-15, which should be read in this context, reformulates the curse into a blessing that forecasts the restoration of the north:

---

[27] See Marvin L. Chaney, "Systemic Study of the Israelite Monarchy," *Semeia* 37 (1986): 72–73; idem, "Bitter Bounty: The Dynamics of Political Economy Critiqued by the Eighth-Century Prophets," in *The Bible and Liberation: Politics and Social Hermeneutics* (rev. ed.; ed. Norman K. Gottwald and Richard A. Horsley; Maryknoll, NY: Orbis Books, 1993), 250–63; see also Morris Silver, *Prophets and Markets: The Political Economy of Ancient Israel* (Boston: Kluwer-Nijhoff, 1983), 49–52; John A. Dearman, "Prophecy, Property, and Politics," *SBLSP* 1984 (ed. Kent H. Richards; Chico, CA: Scholars Press, 1984), 389–91. On the Samaria ostraca and their relation to this process, see Anson F. Rainey, "Wine from Royal Vineyards," *BASOR* 245 (1982): 57–62.

[28] On the trade networks of this period in the north, see esp. Moshe Elat, "Trade and Commerce," in *The World History of the Jewish People*, vol. 4/2, *The Age of the Monarchies: Culture and Society* (ed. Abraham Malamat; Jerusalem: Massada, 1979), 185–86; idem, "Phoenician Overland Trade within the Mesopotamian Empires," in *Ah, Assyria . . . : Studies in Assyrian History and Ancient Near Eastern Historiography Presented to Hayim Tadmor* (ed. Mordechai Cogan and Israel Eph'al; Jerusalem: Magnes, 1991), 21–35; Shulamit Geva, "Archaeological Evidence for the Trade Between Israel and Tyre," *BASOR* 248 (1982): 69–72; David C. Hopkins, "The Dynamics of Agriculture in Monarchical Israel," in *SBLSP* 1983 (ed. Kent H. Richards; Chico, CA: Scholars Press, 1983), 195–96.

[29] See Shimon Dar, *Landscape and Pattern: An Archaeological Survey of Samaria 800 B.C.E.–636 C.E* (BAR International Series 308; Oxford: BAR, 1986), 147–60; Edward F. Campbell, *Shechem II: Portrait of a Hill Country Vale; The Shechem Regional Survey* (Archaeological Reports 2; Atlanta: Scholars Press, 1991), 109–12.

[30] On differences between rural and urban sites in the Iron II period, see esp. Avraham Faust, "The Rural Community in Ancient Israel during Iron Age II," *BASOR* 317 (2000): 17–39; idem, "Differences in Family Structure between Cities and Villages in Iron Age II," *TA* 26 (1999): 233–52.

> I will restore the fortunes of my people Israel; they shall rebuild ruined cities and live in them, they shall plant vineyards and drink their wine. They shall cultivate gardens and eat their fruit. I will plant them upon their land. And they shall never again be plucked up out of the land that I have given them, says the Lord your God.

These verses are part of a larger literary unit encompassing 9:11–15, which centers on the restoration of the north. The close repetition of the vocabulary of the curse in these verses indicates that the passage draws on Amos 5. Several studies have noted that the presence of shared vocabulary between vv. 11–15 and the woe oracle in ch. 5 indicates that these verses were composed as a response to, or a commentary on, that chapter.[31] For instance, several of the promises found in vv. 11–15 represent reversals of disasters forecast in Amos 5, such as the promise that the people of Israel would be "replanted" on "their ground" (אדמתם), which echoes the threaten of 5:2 that maiden Israel will be abandoned upon "her land" (אדמתה).[32] Verses 11–15 also repeat other significant verbs used in ch. 5, such as קום and נפל.[33]

Some past studies have preferred to assign these verses to the exilic or postexilic periods because of their optimistic flavor, which many regard as too dissimilar to the tone of the rest of the book.[34] More recent studies, however, point out that the exilic and postexilic periods are not the only plausible contexts for these verses.[35] William M. Schniedewind suggests that these verses "were added when the book of Amos received its final form in the Hezekian period."[36] This interpretation would read the reformulation of the curse in these verses as part of the political ambitions of Hezekiah, who hoped to restore the former "golden age" of David and Solomon. A setting in the late eighth century during the reforms of Hezekiah provides a compelling context in which to read this particular reformulation of the curse. The key to this interpretation rests in an understanding of the meaning of the expression "restoring the fortunes" (שבתי את־שבות) at the opening of v. 14. Extrabiblical inscriptions demonstrate that one of the central connotations of this expression involves the restoration of a dynasty's formerly held territory.[37] Understood in

---

[31] Paul, *Amos*, 288–89; Schniedewind, *Society and the Promise to David*, 64.

[32] Paul, *Amos*, 288–89.

[33] For instance, the promise in 9:11 that God will raise (אקים) the "fallen booth of David" echoes 5:2, which uses similar verbs: "Fallen, no more to rise (לא־תוסיף קום), is maiden Israel."

[34] See, most recently, Kenneth E. Pomykala, *The Davidic Dynasty Tradition in Early Judaism: Its History and Significance for Messianism* (Atlanta: Scholars, 1995); James Luther Mays, *Amos: A Commentary* (OTL; London: SCM, 1969), 164–65; W. A. G. Nel, "Amos 9:11–15: An Unconditional Prophecy of Salvation during the Period of the Exile," *OTE* 2 (1984): 81–97; Julius Wellhausen, *Die Kleinen Propheten übersetzt und erklärt* (Berlin: Reimer, 1898), 96. Other scholars argue for the lateness of these verses on linguistic grounds; see Wolff, *Joel and Amos*, 352–53.

[35] Paul, *Amos*, 288–89; Andersen and Freedman, *Amos*, 893.

[36] Schniedewind, *Society and the Promise to David*, 63–65.

[37] See, e.g., Joseph A. Fitzmyer, *The Aramaic Inscriptions of Sefire* (rev. ed.; BibOr 19A; Rome: Pontifical Biblical Institute, 1995), 140–41, Stele III, 24, which states, "When (the) gods

this light, the promise of "restoring the fortunes," accompanied by a reversed form of the curse, functioned as propaganda that envisioned the restoration of northern territory to the Davidic dynasty.[38]

The reference to the repossession of "the remnant of Edom" in v. 12 should also be read along these lines. Subjugation of Edomite territory was one of the major accomplishments attributed to David (2 Sam 8:13–14), and it appears that most Judean kings were able to hold this territory.[39] The events surrounding the Syro-Ephraimite war, however, forced Ahaz to turn his attention northward, which allowed Edom to rebel and recapture this territory.[40] The promise of a restoration of this territory to Judah makes sense against this background and should be seen as part of the propaganda associated with the rise of Hezekiah.

The slight modifications in the language of the promise in these verses compared to that of Amos 5 also support a late-eighth-century date. The substitution of "ruined cities" (ערים נשמות) in the place of "houses" as the objects that will be rebuilt should be read in the context of the fall of the northern kingdom in 721 B.C.E. That is, the envisioning of a rebuilding of "ruined cities" fits a context immediately after the Assyrian devastation of the north, which culminated in the fall of Samaria in 721 B.C.E. However, placed in the context of these verses and, more specifically, in the context of the promise of "raising the ruins" of the "fallen booth of David" (v. 11), the expression "ruined cities" must also be read as connoting the rebuilding of the Davidic dynasty.[41]

---

struck [my father's] house, [it came to belong] to another. Now, however, (the) gods have *brought about the return* of the house of my father." For a similar use of the verb שוב, see the expression in the Mesha inscription "but Kemosh restored it." For a discussion of this expression in the Mesha inscription, see Patrick D. Miller, "A Note on the Meshaʿ Inscription," *Or* 38 (1969): 161–64. Several biblical texts also associate this idiom with the restoration of formerly held territory. See, e.g., Zeph 2:7, "The seacoast shall become the possession / of the remnant of the house of Judah, / on which they shall pasture, / and in the houses of Ashkelon / they shall lie down at evening. / For the LORD their God will be mindful of them / *and restore their fortunes* [שב שבותם]." See also Ps 126:1, 4. For discussions of the use of the expression in biblical literature, see E. L. Dietrich, שוב שבות: *Die endzeitlich Wiederherstellung bei den Propheten* (BZAW 49; Giessen: Töpelmann, 1925); William L. Holladay, *The Root* שוב *in the Old Testament with Particular Reference to Its Usage in Covenantal Contexts* (Leiden: Brill, 1958), 113; E. Preuschen, "Die Bedeutung von שוב שבות im alten Testament," *ZAW* 15 (1985): 1–74; E. Baumann, "שוב שבות: Eine exegetische Untersuchung," *ZAW* 47 (1929): 17–44.

[38] On the subject of Hezekiah's reforms, see Andrew G. Vaughn, *Theology, History, and Archaeology in the Chronicler's Account of Hezekiah* (Atlanta: Scholars Press, 1999).

[39] On Judah's control of Edomite territory during the monarchic period, see John R. Bartlett, *Edom and the Edomites* (JSOTSup 77; Sheffield: JSOT Press, 1989), 103–61. Recent excavations in Edom, however, suggest that much of the chronology of ancient Edom is now in need of revision.

[40] Cf. 2 Kgs 16:5–6; 2 Chr 28:16–17. On the background of these events, see Bustani Oded, "The Historical Background of the Syro-Ephraimite War Reconsidered," *CBQ* 34 (1972): 153–65; Roger Tomes, "The Reason for the Syro-Ephraimite War," *JSOT* 59 (1993): 55–71.

[41] See William M. Schniedewind, *How the Bible Became a Book: The Textualization of*

Perhaps the most significant literary aspect of these verses concerns the way in which the language of the reconfigured curse plays on the language of other phrases in vv. 11–15. For instance, the statement in v. 11 that God will "build it" (בניתיה), referring to the "booth of David" (סכת דויד), echoes the promise of the reformulated curse that Israel will rebuild (בנו) the "ruined cities" (ערים נשמות). In addition, the promise that Israel will plant (נטע) is echoed by v. 15, which states, "I will plant (נטע) them on their ground." These wordplays endow the reformulated curse with connotations related to an anticipated restoration of the north under the leadership of the Davidic dynasty.

III. Reformulating the Curse for the Political and Demographic Contexts of Seventh-Century Judah

The events of the seventh century B.C.E. provoked new and diverse applications and formulations of the curse in late Judean society. Continued Assyrian involvement in the southern Levant, the rise of the Babylonian Empire, and the persistent threats of dislocation and exile provided contexts in which the imagery of building and planting held increased significance. Moreover, the increase in viticulture industries in the environs of Jerusalem and adjacent regions offered new contexts for continuing discourse about the curse in Judean society.[42] Several texts from this period illustrate the curse's continued prominence in the discourse in ancient Israel (Zeph 1:13; Deut 20:5–6; 28:30, Jer 31:4). One notable example occurs in Zeph 1:13 as part of another woe oracle directed against the inhabitants of Judah and Jerusalem:

> And their wealth will be for plunder and their houses for desolation. Though they build houses, they will not live in them; though they plant vineyards, they will not drink their wine.

In contrast to the formulation of the curse in Amos 5:11, this verse formulates the curse in the third person plural, referring back to the plural subjects of v. 12, namely,

---

Ancient Israel (Cambridge/New York: Cambridge University Press, 2004), 87–88, who suggests that the reference to "ruins" in v. 11 refers "to the division of the 'house of David,' not to the destruction of Judah" (p. 88).

[42] Avraham Faust and Ehud Weiss, "Judah, Philistia, and the Mediterranean World: Reconstructing the Economic System of the Seventh Century B.C.E.," *BASOR* 338 (2005): 79–80; Gershon Edelstein, Ianir Milevski, and Sara Aurant, *The Rephaim Valley Project: Villages, Terraces, and Stone Mounds; Excavations in Manahat, Jerusalem 1987–1989* (Jerusalem: Israel Exploration Society, 1998); David Amit, "Farmsteads in Northern Judaea (Betar Area), Survey," *Explorations and Surveys in Israel* 10 (1991): 147–48; Gershon Edelstein and Ianir Milevski, "The Rural Settlement of Jerusalem Re-evaluated: Surveys and Excavations in the Repha'im Valley and Mevesseret Yerushalayim," *PEQ* 126 (1994): 2–23; James B. Pritchard, *The Winery, Defenses, and Soundings at Gibeon* (Museum Monographs; Philadelphia: University Museum, 1964).

"those who linger over their wine dregs" and "those who say in their hearts." Beyond this modification, the passage formulates the curse in less precise language than that of Amos 5:11. As a result, the objects that this formulation of the curse targets do not carry the specific linguistic connotations pointing to a particular stratum of society. The author of these verses configures the curse in more generic fashion in order to accommodate the broader audience targeted by the oracle.

Although many commentators assign Zeph 1:13b to a late editor,[43] recent studies emphasize that there is no reason to separate it from vv. 7–13a, because futility curses are rather prominent in preexilic prophetic texts.[44] Nevertheless, there is considerable debate concerning the precise historical setting behind these verses. Several recent studies read these verses in the context of the early years of Josiah's rebellion against Assyrian hegemony.[45] These studies argue that vv. 7–13 should be understood as propaganda warning Judeans who do not support Josiah's rebellion that the "day of YHWH" is near.

Several aspects of the curse's literary relationship to Zeph 1:7–13 suggest reading the reapplication of the curse here in the context of seventh-century Judah. First, the verb בנה in the curse plays on the phrase "those living in the Maktesh" (ישבי המכתש) in v. 11. That is, the threat that those who have built houses will not live in them likely refers back to this phrase in v. 11. It is also possible that the threat against houses in the curse is meant to echo, or play on, the expression of the previous verse (v. 13), which states that "their wealth will be plundered and *their houses laid waste*" (והיה חילם למשסה ובתיהם לשממה). If one accepts these linguistic connections, then a setting in the early years of Josiah's reforms becomes a more interesting context in which to read the curse in this passage. The curse against houses and vineyards, reapplied here as part of Josiah's reforms, threatens items associated with the urbanization and industrialization of Jerusalem and its environs during the late eighth and seventh centuries B.C.E.[46] These developments are compelling con-

---

[43] See Karl Elliger, *Die Propheten Nahum, Habakuk, Zephanja, Haggai, Sacharja, Maleachi* (Göttingen: Vandenhoeck & Ruprecht, 1982), 65; Hubert Irsigler, *Gottesgericht und Jahwetag: Die Komposition Zef 1,1-2,3, untersucht auf der Grundlage der Literarkritik des Zefanjabuches* (St. Ottilien: EOS, 1977), 105–6; Klaus Seybold, *Nahum, Habakkuk, Zephanja* (Zurich: Theologischer Verlag, 1991), 99; John M. Powis Smith, William H. Ward, and Julius A. Bewer, *A Critical and Exegetical Commentary on Micah, Zephaniah, Nahum, Habakkuk, Obadiah, and Joel* (ICC; Edinburgh: T&T Clark, 1911), 203.

[44] Marvin A. Sweeney, *Zephaniah: A Commentary* (Hermeneia; Philadelphia: Fortress, 2003), 95; J. J. M. Roberts, *Nahum, Habakkuk, and Zephaniah* (OTL; Louisville: Westminster John Knox, 1991), 181; Adele Berlin, *Zephaniah: A New Translation with Introduction and Commentary* (AB 25A; New York: Doubleday, 1994), 88–89.

[45] Sweeney, *Zephaniah*, 95; idem, "A Form-Critical Reassessment of the Book of Zephaniah," *CBQ* 53 (1991): 388–408. On the subject of Josiah's revolt against Assyria, see Frank Moore Cross Jr. and David Noel Freedman, "Josiah's Revolt against Assyria," *JNES* 12 (1953): 56–58; Nadav Na'aman, "The Kingdom of Judah under Josiah," *TA* 18 (1991): 3–71.

[46] On the demographic and economic developments of Judah during the reign of Manasseh,

texts in which to read the curse here in Zephaniah, since such developments occurred during the reign of Manasseh. Thus, the curse becomes a threat aimed at the inhabitants of Jerusalem and Judah who became wealthy by cooperation with the pro-Assyrian policies of Manasseh.

Three other references to the curse that should be read in relation to the demographic, economic, and political developments of the seventh century B.C.E. are Deut 20:5–6; 28:30; and Jer 31:4–5. Deuteronomy 20:5–6 stipulates that a person who has built a house but not yet dedicated it or planted a vineyard but not yet harvested its wine is exempt from participation in military service:[47]

> Then the officials shall address the troops, saying: "Has anyone built a new house but not dedicated it? He should go back to his house, so that he does not die in battle and another dedicate it. Has anyone planted a vineyard but not yet harvested its fruit? He should go to his house, so that he does not die in battle and another be first to harvest its fruit. Has anyone become engaged to a woman but not yet married her? He should go back to his house, so that he does not die in battle and another marry her."

The second reference to the curse in the book of Deuteronomy appears in the list of curses that warn against disobedience to the laws of chs. 12–26: "If you pay the bride-price for a wife, another man shall enjoy her. If you build a house, you shall not live in it. If you plant a vineyard, you shall not harvest it" (28:30).

Two aspects of these variations stand out as particularly significant in relation to the other usages of the curse in biblical literature. First, the language of these formulations deviates from earlier examples. In contrast to previous variations, which use שתה ("to drink"), these passages use the verb חלל ("to pollute, or harvest"). The use of this verb in relation to vineyards occurs only in these passages and two additional contexts (Lev 19:23–25; Jer 31:5).[48] This terminological variation serves to highlight the agricultural dimensions of the motif, as opposed to the enjoyment of its produce. In this way, the variation brings the curse in line with the broader concerns of the book of Deuteronomy, such as the affairs of the countryside as opposed to those of the urban elite.

Two developments associated with the late Judean monarchy may stand behind the emphasis on agricultural and rural concerns in this formulation of the curse. First, the seventh century witnessed a revitalization of occupation in several

---

see Israel Finkelstein, "The Archaeology of the Days of Manasseh," in *Scripture and Other Artifacts: Essays on Bible and Archaeology in Honor of Philip J. King* (ed. Michael D. Coogan, J. Cheryl Exum, and Lawrence E. Stager; Louisville: Westminster John Knox, 1994), 169–87; Magen Broshi, "The Expansion of Jerusalem in the Reigns of Hezekiah and Manasseh," *IEJ* 24 (1974): 21–26.

[47] On the military exemptions of Deuteronomy 20, see Alexander Rofé, "The Laws of Warfare in the Book of Deuteronomy," in idem, *Deuteronomy: Issues and Interpretation* (OTS; London: T&T Clark, 2002), 160–61; Adele Berlin, "Jeremiah 29:5–7," 3–11.

[48] See also the discussion of חלל in Carey Ellen Walsh, *The Fruit of the Vine*, 71–78.

rural sectors of Judah. A birth of settlement occurred in the eastern and southern portions of Judah during the reign of Manasseh.[49] In addition, excavations and surveys in the western foothills and northern hills also indicate increasing settlement activity during this time.[50] Other work demonstrates that the western foothills witnessed a revival as part of Assyria's attempt to capitalize on the olive oil potential of the southern Levant.[51] Recent work in the environs of Jerusalem also points to a flourishing of villages and farmsteads around the capital.[52] These demographic shifts are reflected in the overall tone of the laws of Deuteronomy, which emphasize rural, rather than urban, matters. Accordingly, an emphasis on the agricultural dimensions of the curse follows this general trend.

Second, the late eighth and seventh centuries saw a shift in the military and administrative policies of Assyria in the southern Levant, which primarily affected the rural countryside. Beginning in the reign of Tiglath-pileser III, the Assyrians began pillaging and burning large portions of rural territory and deporting the

---

[49] See Amihai Mazar, "Iron Age Fortresses in the Judaean Hills," *PEQ* 114 (1982): 87–109; Frank Moore Cross and József T. Milik, "Explorations in the Judaean Buqêʿah," *BASOR* 142 (1956): 5–17; Nadav Naʾaman, "The Negev in the Last Days of the Kingdom of Judah," *Cathedra* 42 (1987): 5–6; Baruch Halpern, "Sibyl, or the Two Nations? Archaism, Kinship, Alienation, and the Elite Redefinition of Traditional Culture in Judah in the 8th–7th Centuries B.C.E.," in *The Study of the Ancient Near East in the Twenty-first Century: The William Foxwell Albright Centennial Conference* (ed. Jerrold S. Cooper and Glenn M. Schwartz; Winona Lake, IN: Eisenbrauns, 1996), 291–338; idem, "Jerusalem and the Lineages in the Seventh Century BCE: Kinship and the Rise of Individual Moral Liability," in *Law and Ideology in Monarchic Israel* (ed. Baruch Halpern and Deborah W. Hobson; JSOTSup 124; Sheffield: JSOT Press, 1991), 11–107; Avi Ofer, "The Monarchic Period in the Judean Highland: A Spatial Overview," in *Studies in the Archaeology of the Iron Age in Israel and Jordan* (ed. Amihai Mazar; JSOTSup 331; Sheffield: Sheffield Academic Press, 2001), 14–37.

[50] J. B. Pritchard, "Industry and Trade at Biblical Gibeon," *BA* 23 (1960): 23–29.

[51] On the southern Levant during the seventh century B.C.E., see, most recently, Faust and Weiss, "Judah, Philistia and the Mediterranean World," 71–92; see also Seymour Gitin, "Tel Miqne-Ekron in the 7th Century B.C.E.: The Impact of Economic Innovation and Foreign Cultural Influences on a Neo-Assyrian Vassal City-State," in *Recent Excavations in Israel: A View to the West; Reports on Kabri, Nami, Miqne-Ekron, Dor, and Ashkelon* (ed. Seymour Gitin; Colloquia and Conference Papers 1; Dubuque, IA: Archaeological Institute of the West, 1995), 61–79; idem, "The Neo-Assyrian Empire and Its Western Periphery: The Levant, with a Focus on Philistine Ekron," in *Assyria 1995*, ed. Parpola and Whiting, 77–103; David Eitam, "The Olive Oil Industry at Tel Miqne-Ekron in the Late Iron Age," in *Olive Oil in Antiquity: Israel and Neighboring Countries from the Neolithic to the Early Arab Period* (ed. David Eitam and Michael Heltzer; History of the Ancient Near East/Studies 7; Padua: Sargon, 1996), 167–96; Lynn Tatum, "King Manasseh and the Royal Fortress at Horvat ʿUza," *BA* 54 (1991): 135–45.

[52] On the subject of rural sites in the Iron II period, see esp. Avraham Faust, "The Farmstead in the Highlands of Iron Age II Israel," in *The Rural Landscape of Ancient Israel* (ed. Aren M. Maeir, Shimon Dar, and Zeʾev Safrai; BAR International Series; Oxford: BAR, 2003), 91–104; Edelstein and Milevski, "Rural Settlement of Jerusalem Re-evaluated," 23; Shimon Gibson, "Investigating Jerusalem's Rural Landscape," *Levant* 23 (1985): 139–55.

inhabitants of several areas of this region. This shift in dealing more directly with large rural populations, as opposed to just the urban ruling elite, is reflected in the extant Assyrian treaties of this period, which address entire populations, rather than kings or ruling elites.[53] This shift in Assyrian diplomacy is also reflected in the outlook of the book of Deuteronomy, which addresses its stipulations in general terms to the entire population of Israel. The curses of Deuteronomy 28 threaten activities associated with the general populace instead of the ruling dynasty. The formulation of the curse in this list of curses reflects these Assyrian diplomatic shifts in the eighth and seventh centuries B.C.E.

Another allusion to the curse motif that should be read in the context of the politics of the seventh century B.C.E. is Jer 31:4–5:

> Again I shall build you so that you may be built, maiden Israel; again you shall adorn your timbrels and go forth in the dance of the merrymakers; again you shall plant vineyards in the mountains of Samaria; the planters shall plant and enjoy. For there shall be a day when sentinels will call in the hill country of Ephraim: "Come, let us go up to Zion, to the LORD our God."

The similarities between the phrases "you shall plant vineyards" (תטעי כרמים) and "the planters shall plant and enjoy" (נטעו נטעים וחללו) in v. 5 indicate that the verse draws on the variation of the curse from Deuteronomy. Like Amos 9:14, however, the motif is formulated here as a promise that envisions a repopulating of the north, accompanied by the planting of vineyards. This oracle in Jeremiah, as well as several of the surrounding oracles in chs. 30–31, appears to draw on imagery from Amos 9:11–15. For instance, the statement in Jer 30:18 concerning the "restoring of fortunes" (שב שבות) echoes Amos 9:14, which states that God will restore the fortunes (שבתי את־שבות) of Israel. In addition, the expression at the beginning of Jer 31:4, "Again I will build you so that you may be built," may draw on similar building imagery found in Amos 9:11. Although one should not push the issue too far, these similarities make one wonder if the author of these oracles in Jeremiah knew the text from Amos.

The other language of Jer 31:4–5 suggests that the reformulation of the curse in the passage is intimately tied to notions of victory in war. The phrases of the preceding verse involving the adorning of tambourines and the dancing of "merrymakers" are usually associated with celebrations following success in battle (Exod 15:20; Judg 11:34; 1 Sam 18:6).[54]

The background and date of the various oracles found in Jeremiah 30–31 have

---

[53] On this aspect of Neo-Assyrian treaties, see John S. Holladay Jr., "Assyrian Statecraft and the Prophets of Israel," *HTR* 63 (1970): 29–51; Moshe Weinfeld, *Deuteronomy and the Deuteronomic School* (Oxford: Clarendon, 1972), 101.

[54] William L. Holladay, *Jeremiah 2: A Commentary on the Book of the Prophet Jeremiah, Chapters 26–52* (Hermeneia; Philadelphia: Fortress, 1989), 183.

received considerable discussion during the past century. Consensus scholarship views these chapters as a conglomeration of different oracles from different social and historical periods.[55] Scholars are divided, however, concerning to which periods to assign the various oracles. Several recent studies suggest that a core of material in these chapters (30:5–7, 12–15, 18–21; 31:1a, 2–6, 9b, 15–17, 18–22) dates from the early years of the prophet and reflects early support for the political and religious reforms of Josiah.[56] Such a context provides a compelling setting in which to read the utilization of the motif of building and planting. The fact that vv. 4–6 envision the return of northerners to "the mountains of Samaria" (v. 5) and "the hill country of Ephraim" (v. 6b) in order to rejoin the Zion cult (v. 6b) is consistent with the political and religious aspirations of Josiah's reforms.[57]

V. Conclusion

A study of the early inner-biblical discourse of the present curse reveals that several factors stand behind its prominence and persistence in the discourse of biblical literature. First, although scholars have long noted that the threat of war forms the background of the curse, an examination of certain Assyrian sources suggests that the curse's imagery should be linked to the rise of siege warfare, which began to affect ancient Israel in the eighth century B.C.E. In the context of siege warfare, the imagery of the curse came to symbolize the horrors associated with a successful siege, namely, the exile of the inhabitants and the destruction of their subsistence

---

[55] Siegmund Böhmer, *Heimkehr und neuer Bund: Studien zu Jeremia 30–31* (GTA 5; Göttingen: Vandenhoeck & Ruprecht, 1976); Norbert Lohfink, "Der junge Jeremia als Propagandist und Poet: Zum Grundstock von Jer 30–31," in P.-M. Bogaert et al., *Le Livre de Jérémie: Le prophète et son milieu, les oracles et leur transmission* (BETL 54; Leuven: Leuven University Press, 1981), 351–68; Konrad Schmid, *Buchgestalten des Jeremiabuches: Untersuchungen zur Redaktions- und Rezeptionsgeschichte von Jer 30–33 im Kontext des Buches* (WMANT 72; Neukirchen-Vluyn: Neukirchener Verlag, 1996); William McKane, "The Composition of Jeremiah 30–31," in *Texts, Temples, and Traditions: A Tribute to Menahem Haran* (ed. Michael V. Fox; Winona Lake, IN: Eisenbrauns, 1996), 187–94.

[56] See Marvin A. Sweeney, "Jeremiah 30–31 and King Josiah's Program of National Restoration and Religious Reform," *ZAW* 108 (1996): 569–83; W. L. Holladay, *Jeremiah 2*, 156–57.

[57] Sweeney, "Jeremiah 30–31," 580–81; idem, *King Josiah of Judah: The Lost Messiah of Israel* (Oxford/New York: Oxford University Press, 2001), 208–33; on the political and religious reforms of Josiah, see Na'aman, "Kingdom of Judah under Josiah," 3–71; Naomi Steinberg, "The Deuteronomic Law Code and the Politics of State Centralization," in *The Bible and the Politics of Exegesis: Essays in Honor of Norman K. Gottwald on His Sixty-fifth Birthday* (ed. David Jobling, Peggy L. Day, and Gerald T. Sheppard; Cleveland: Pilgrim, 1991), 161–70; Norbert Lohfink, "The Cult Reform of Josiah of Judah," in *Ancient Israelite Religion: Essays in Honor of Frank Moore Cross* (ed. Patrick D. Miller Jr., Paul D. Hanson, and S. Dean McBride; Philadelphia: Fortress, 1987), 459–75.

systems. Since the realities of siege warfare and exile repeatedly struck at ancient Israel and Judah from the eighth to sixth centuries B.C.E., the curse's imagery resonated over a broad historical horizon.[58] The persistence of such phenomena in the southern Levant provided a climate in which discourse surrounding the curse held continued significance.

Second, the relatively imprecise and vague nature of the curse's imagery allowed it to be customized and reformulated for various historical and social circumstances. This characteristic of the curse's language also allowed it to signify both concrete realities, such as exile, and more theologically abstract ideas, such as God's planting of Israel. This aspect of the curse is a hallmark of many biblical motifs.[59] In fact, many texts suggest a convergence of both the tangible and the abstract dimensions of the curse's language, which are difficult to separate. For instance, Amos 9:11–15 links the more tangible dimensions of a physical repopulating of the north with the more theologically imaginative notions of God's replanting of his people.

The melding of the tangible and abstract aspects of the curse's language receives further definition in the exilic and postexilic discourse over the curse. A number of exilic and postexilic texts transform the curse into a promise of return, which will be characterized by security and stability (Jer 29:5, 28; Ezek 28:26; 36:36; Isa 62:6–9; 65:21). These texts further highlight the significance of the curse and its imagery in biblical literature and point to the persistence of such imagery in the cultural discourse of ancient Israel.

---

[58] On the recurring nature of exile and deportation from the eighth to sixth centuries B.C.E., see Thomas L. Thompson, "The Exile in History and Myth: A Response to Hans Barstad," in *Leading Captivity Captive: "The Exile" as History and Ideology* (ed. Lester L. Grabbe; JSOTSup 278; Sheffield: Sheffield Academic Press, 1998), 101–8; Bustenay Oded, "The Settlements of the Israelite and Judean Exiles in Mesopotamia in the 8th–6th Centuries B.C.E.," in *Studies in Historical Geography and Biblical Historiography: Presented to Zechariah Kallai* (ed. Gershon Galil and Moshe Weinfeld; VTSup 81; Leiden: Brill, 2000), 91–103; idem, "Observations on the Israelite/Judean Exiles in Mesopotamia during the Eighth-Sixth Centuries BCE," in *Immigration and Emigration within the Ancient Near East: Festschrift E. Lipiński* (ed. Karel van Lerberghe and Antoon Schoors; OLA 65; Leuven: Peeters, 1995), 205–12; Israel Eph'al, "Assyrian Domination in Palestine," in *The World History of the Jewish People*, vol. 4/1, *The Age of the Monarchies: Political History* (ed. Abraham Malamat; Jerusalem: Massada, 1979), 276–89, 364–68.

[59] On this aspect of biblical motifs, see esp. Shemaryahu Talmon, "Literary Motifs and Speculative Thought in the Hebrew Bible," *Hebrew University Studies in Literature and the Arts* 16 (1988): 150–68; idem, "The Desert Motif in the Bible and Qumran Literature," in *Biblical Motifs: Origins and Transformations* (ed. Alexander Altmann; Brandeis University, Philip W. Lown Institute of Advanced Judaic Studies, Studies and Texts 3; Cambridge, MA: Harvard University Press, 1966); Michael A. Fishbane, *Biblical Interpretation in Ancient Israel* (Oxford: Clarendon, 1985); idem, "The Well of Living Water—A Biblical Motif and Its Ancient Transformation," in *Sha'arei Talmon: Studies in the Bible, Qumran, and the Ancient Near East Presented to Shemaryahu Talmon* (ed. Michael A. Fishbane and Emanuel Tov; Winona Lake, IN: Eisenbrauns, 1992), 3–16.

The Zohar

The Zohar
Pritzker Edition, Volume Four

Translation and Commentary by DANIEL C. MATT

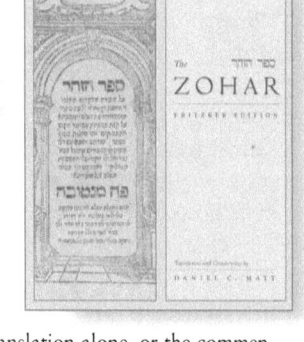

Sefer ha-Zohar (The Book of Radiance) has amazed and overwhelmed readers ever since it emerged mysteriously in medieval Spain toward the end of the thirteenth century. Written in a unique, lyrical Aramaic, this masterpiece of Kabbalah exceeds the dimensions of a normal book; it is virtually a body of literature, comprising over twenty discrete sections. The bulk of the *Zohar* consists of a running commentary on the Torah, from Genesis through Deuteronomy. This fourth volume of *The Zohar: Pritzker Edition* covers the first half of Exodus.

"A powerfully poetic rendition of this spiritual masterpiece... Matt's new *Zohar* is a classic already. The edition alone, or the translation alone, or the commentary alone would be a major contribution. The whole is a work of art."
—*Journal of the American Academy of Religion*

"Daniel C. Matt is giving us what I hardly thought possible: a superbly fashioned translation and commentary that opens up the *Zohar* to the English-speaking world."

—Harold Bloom,
Yale University

"Daniel Matt's work is superior to any other available translation of the *Zohar* because of its superb poetic language, the exegetical contribution of its copious notes, and its superior underlying Aramaic text, which was specially prepared by Dr. Matt from numerous original *Zohar* manuscripts and serves as the basis for his translation. Both the general English reader and scholars in the field of religious studies will benefit tremendously from this new series of volumes."

—Moshe Idel,
Hebrew University of Jerusalem

Zohar: The Pritzker Edition
$49.95 cloth

800.621.2736   www.sup.org

שמעו והעידו בבית יעקב:
Invoking the Council as Witnesses in Amos 3:13

DAVID E. BOKOVOY
bokovoy@brandeis.edu
Brandeis University, Waltham, MA 02453

One of the chief perils in the exegesis of ancient writings is that we should take figuratively that which in origin was meant quite realistically.
—H. Wheeler Robinson, "The Council of Yahweh," *JTS* 45 (1944): 151.

Throughout the diverse and oftentimes opposing perspectives featured in the Bible, at least one concept appears consistently: the God of ancient Israel was not alone. True, unlike many of *his* ancient Near Eastern contemporaries, the biblical God never appears explicitly fraternizing with a legitimate female consort, nor do biblical authors typically provide a detailed description of their deity interacting with other divine beings—male or female—yet nonetheless, according to the religious texts preserved in the Hebrew Bible, Israel's celestial monarch shared his universe with a variety of gods.[1] As is typical of other ancient Near Eastern traditions, biblical texts regularly depict these deities serving in council with the high God of the universe.[2] Indeed, the idea of a Near Eastern-like heavenly assembly is now so

---

[1] In the Hebrew Bible, "God" is always treated as grammatically masculine; therefore, I have intentionally elected to use the third person masculine pronoun to describe the main biblical deity. As Marc Zvi Brettler has explained concerning the issue, "historical-critical methodology is indebted to the norms of the past which it is trying to recapture, rather than the preferences of contemporary religious practice" (*How to Read the Bible* [Philadelphia: Jewish Publication Society, 2005], 294 n. 9).

[2] Even the so-called radical monotheism witnessed in later biblical texts such as Deutero-Isaiah and Deut 32:29 may in fact preserve a henotheistic theology. See Nathan MacDonald, *Deuteronomy and the Meaning of "Monotheism"* (FAT 2/1; Tübingen: Mohr Siebeck, 2003); Hans Rechenmacher, *"Ausser mir gibt es keinen Gott!": Eine sprach- und literaturwissenschaftliche Studie zur Ausschliesslichkeitsformel* (Arbeiten zu Text und Sprache im Alten Testament 49: St. Ottilien:

well entrenched in our contemporary approach to the Bible that it would seem that the topic has been all but exhausted.[3] Although critical scholarship has provided an important foundation for understanding the attestation and role of the divine council in the Hebrew Bible, none of these studies has carried the implications of this knowledge to its logical conclusion for Amos 3:13:

שמעו והעידו בבית יעקב נאם־אדני יהוה אלהי הצבאות:

Hear and witness against the House of Jacob, says my Lord Yahweh, the God of Hosts.

Unlike Amos 6:14, which features the book's only other attestation of the phrase אלהי הצבאות, "God of Hosts," Amos 3:13 appears without an explicitly marked addressee summoned via imperatives. In Amos 6:14, אלהי הצבאות clearly speaks directly to the House of Israel. The addressee for אלהי הצבאות in Amos 3:13, however, is not so apparent. In Amos 3:13 the subject of the masculine plural imperatives seems to represent the same nonspecified group that is commanded to *proclaim* (השמיעו) and *speak* (ואמרו) in Amos 3:9:

EOS, 1997); Michael S. Heiser, "The Divine Council in Late Canonical and Non-Canonical Second Temple Jewish Literature" (Ph.D. diss., University of Wisconsin-Madison, 2004). The term "radical monotheism" was popularized by Tikva Frymer-Kensky, *In the Wake of the Goddesses: Women, Culture, and the Biblical Transformation of Pagan Myth* (New York: Free Press, 1992). However, a detailed critique of the radical monotheistic reading of these late biblical texts extends beyond the scope of my current analysis.

[3] The groundbreaking study for the imagery of the divine council in the Hebrew Bible was H. Wheeler Robinson, "The Council of Yahweh," *JTS* 45 (1944): 151–57. After Robinson, see Frank Moore Cross, "The Council of Yahweh in Second Isaiah," *JNES* 12 (1953): 274–77; G. Cooke, "The Sons of (the) God(s)," *ZAW* 76 (1974): 22–47; E. C. Kingsbury, "The Prophets and the Council of Yahweh," *JBL* 83 (1964): 279–86; M. E. Polley, "Hebrew Prophecy within the Council of Yahweh, Examined in its Ancient Near Eastern Setting," in *Essays on the Comparative Method* (ed. Carl D. Evans et al.; Scripture in Context 1; PTMS 34; Pittsburgh: Pickwick, 1983), 141–56; Werner H. Schmidt, *Königtum Gottes in Ugarit und Israel: Zur Herkunft der Königsprädikation Jahwes* (BZAW 80; Berlin: Töpelmann, 1961), 69–72; Patrick D. Miller, "The Divine Council and the Prophetic Call to War," *VT* 18 (1968): 100–107. Although dated, the primary study for the divine council imagery in the Hebrew Bible remains E. Theodore Mullen, *The Assembly of the Gods: The Divine Council in Canaanite and Early Literature* (HSM 24; Cambridge, MA: Harvard University Press, 1973). More recently, see Patrick D. Miller, "Cosmology and World Order in the Old Testament," *HBT* 9 (1987): 53–78, repr. in idem, *Israelite Religion and Biblical Theology: Collected Essays* (JSOTSup 267; Sheffield: Sheffield Academic Press, 2000), 422–44; Lowell K. Handy, *Among the Host of Heaven: The Syro-Palestinian Pantheon as Bureaucracy* (Winona Lake, IN: Eisenbrauns, 1994); Martti Nissinen, "Prophets and the Divine Council," in *Kein Land für sich Allein: Studien zum Kulturkontakt in Kanaan, Israel/Palästina und Ebirnari für Manfred Weippert zum 65. Geburtstag* (ed. Ulrich Hübner and Ernst Axel Knaur; OBO 186; Göttingen: Vandenhoeck & Ruprecht, 2002), 4–19.

השמיעו על־ארמנות באשדוד ועל־ארמנות בארץ מצרים
ואמרו האספו על־הרי שמרון וראו מהומת רבות בתוכה
ועשוקים בקרבה

> Proclaim in the fortresses of Ashdod
> and in the fortresses of the land of Egypt!
> Say: "Gather on the hills of Samaria,"
> and witness the great outrages within her
> and the oppression in her midst.

When interpreted with a textual sensitivity directed toward the fundamental administrative role fulfilled by the council in ancient Near Eastern tradition—including the Hebrew Bible—the masculine plural imperatives in Amos 3 seem to present an invocation spoken by אלהי הצבאות to the deities of the divine council, directing the heavenly host to serve as witnesses against the house of Jacob.[4]

Amos 3:13 commences with two masculine plural imperatives, the first a *qal* and the second a *hiphil*. Traditionally, the reason these imperatives issue a dual command to an unspecified audience to "hear" and "testify" has befuddled most interpreters. Explanations for the audience have ranged from "foreign prophets" to an indefinite group representing "any who might hear."[5] In their assessment of the imperative, for example, Bruce Waltke and M. O'Connor suggest that "apostrophe with the imperative is usually directed to unspecified or indefinite persons; the personifying jussive is comparable."[6] In other words, interpreters following Waltke and O'Connor would view texts such as Amos 3:9, 13, which feature a series of undefined masculine plural imperatives, as "apostrophe," meaning an address to an absent or simply imaginary audience. However, given the fundamental role fulfilled by the divine council as witnesses and messengers, the use of apostrophe in cases such as Amos 3:9, 13, where God calls on an audience in the plural seems questionable. After all, why would אלהי הצבאות simply resort to invoking an *imaginary* audience when—according to most biblical texts—God had a very *real* צבא ("host") he could summon?[7]

---

[4] Concerning references to the designation צבא as a title for "the heavenly entourage of Yahweh," *HALOT* (study ed., 2001, 2:995) lists 1 Kgs 22:19; 2 Chr 18:18; Pss 103:21; 148:2, with an individual from that group in Josh 5:14, and Dan 8:11.

[5] For a general survey of previous analyses, see William Rainey Harper, *A Critical and Exegetical Commentary on Amos and Hosea* (ICC; 1905; repr., Edinburgh: T&T Clark, 1973), 82; James Luther Mays, *Amos: A Commentary* (OTL; Philadelphia: Westminster, 1976), 68–69; Francis I. Andersen and David Noel Freedman, *Amos: A New Translation with Introduction and Commentary* (AB 24A; New York: Doubleday, 1989), 410; Karl Möller, *A Prophet in Debate: The Rhetoric of Persuasion in the Book of Amos* (JSOTSup 372; Sheffield: Sheffield Academic Press, 2003), 93.

[6] *IBHS*, 572–73.

[7] Marjorie O'Rourke Boyle attempts to apply form criticism to Amos 3 ("The Covenant

Recognizing the inherent problem associated with previous attempts to interpret this passage, the most immediate candidate for an audience for the plural imperatives in 3:9, 13 appears in 3:7.

כי לא יעשה אדני יהוה דבר כי אם־גלה סודו אל־עבדיו הנביאים:

Indeed, my Lord God does nothing unless he revealed his council to his servants the prophets.

In its present form, Amos 3:7 serves as a segue to the summons given by אלהי הצבאות in vv. 9 and 13, instructing the סוד ("council") to *proclaim* (השמיעו), *speak* (ואמרו), *hear* (שמעו), and *witness* (והעידו)—all in the plural.[8]

Most assuredly, the oracles presented in Amos 3 do not derive from a single authorial hand. Critical studies suggest that in fact Amos 3:7, which presents the concept of God's council or סוד, may be a later textual insertion, so that with its undefined masculine plural imperatives, Amos 3:13 is most likely earlier than the statement concerning God's סוד.[9] If correct, this theory of textual development may suggest that an ancient editor who recognized the traditional role fulfilled by the council as witnesses may have been inspired to include the assessment offered in v. 7 by the invocation expressed by אלהי הצבאות. As witnessed in Dan 8:10, late

---

Lawsuit of the Prophet Amos: III 1–IV 13," *VT* 21 [1971]: 338–62). Concerning the invocation of witnesses for the trial Yahweh brings against Israel, Boyle states, "The litigation opens with a summons issued to Israel to hear the announcement of Yahweh's complaint and to acknowledge its justice. The witnesses for the prosecution are the defendant itself, Israel (iii 1); and neighbors, Egypt and Ashdod (iii 9), the Samaritans (iii 12) and probably the Samaritan women of Bashan (iv 1)" (p. 343). Boyle specifically states, however, that "Amos does not call the heavenly pantheon," a tradition which she acknowledges was a "common procedure of later OT prophetic tradition" (ibid.). For a general survey of the genre and scholarly observations, see Kirsten Nielsen, *Yahweh as Prosecutor and Judge: An Investigation of the Prophetic Lawsuit (Rîb-Pattern)* (JSOTSup 9; Sheffield: University of Sheffield, 1978). For critiques that question the actual attestation of a distinct *Gattung* within biblical texts, see Dwight R. Daniels, "Is There a 'Prophetic Lawsuit' Genre?" *ZAW* 99 (1987): 339–60; and Michael DeRoche, "Yahweh's *rîb* against Israel: A Reassessment of the So-Called 'Prophetic Lawsuit' in the Preexilic Prophets," *JBL* 102 (1983): 563–74. For a consideration of the *rîb* in the book of Amos, see José Luis Barriocanal Gómez, "'¡Buscad a Yhwh y viviréis¡' Am 5,1–27: una relectura de la tradición del éxodo," *Burgense* 40 (1999): 423–60.

[8] Concerning references to the designation סוד as a title for the "council of the holy ones," *HALOT* (study ed., 2001, 1:745) lists Ps 89:8; for the "confidential discussion in the assembly of Yahweh," *HALOT* lists Jer 23:18–22; Job 15:8. As Dexter E. Callender, Jr., explains, "Generally speaking, the word *sôd*, translated both 'council' and 'counsel', is used in the Hebrew Bible to refer to a group or to that which transpires within a given group. When used to signify a group, it is used with reference both to humankind (e.g., Ezek 13:9) and to the divine realm (e.g., Ps 89:8)" (*Adam in Myth and History: Ancient Israelite Perspectives on the Primal Human* [HSS 48; Winona Lake, IN: Eisenbrauns, 2000], 144).

[9] For a consideration of Amos 3:7 as a late textual insertion, see A. Graeme Auld, "Amos and Apocalyptic Vision, Prophecy, Revelation," in *Storia e tradizioni di Israele: Scritti in onore di J. Alberto Soggin* (ed. Daniele Garrone and Felice Israel; Brescia: Paideia, 1991), 1–13.

biblical authors recognized the term הצבא, or "the host," as a reference to the heavenly assembly:

ותגדל עד־צבא השמים ותפל ארצה מן־הצבא ומן־הכוכבים ותרמסם:

It grew as high as the host of heaven and it hurled some of the heavenly host and some of the stars to the ground and trampled them.

Granted, interpreting the intended addressee of Amos 3:13 as the council presents a hypothesis that cannot be proved. I simply suggest that readers remain open to the possibility that the summons spoken by אלהי הצבאות may specifically invoke the constituents of the heavenly צבא. Prophetic oracles such as Jer 2:12, which do provide a specific addressee, offer evidence that the types of literary constructions featured in Amos 3 may specifically invoke the heavenly realm:

שמו שמים על־זאת ושערו חרבו מאד נאם־יהוה:

Be appalled, O heavens, at this; Be horrified, utterly dazed! — says Yahweh.

This pattern is not unique to the Bible. The first incantation from the Babylonian anti-witchcraft compilation known as *Maqlû* provides evidence that these literary forms were an important part of at least some ancient Near Eastern traditions (tablet 1, lines 13–14):

> *ilū rābûtu šimā dabābī*
> *dīnī dīnā*
>
> Oh great gods hear my litigation
> Judge my case![10]

Hence, with a set of plural imperatives (*šimā* and *dīnā*) addressed specifically to the "great gods" of the council who could serve in the ritual lawsuit as a judicial force, this text provides a theoretical model that interpreters can (with some caution) apply to related biblical constructs, including Amos 3:13.

The fact that biblical passages such as Amos 3: 9 and 13 preserve the same literary construct as that attested in ancient Near Eastern texts such as *Maqlû* tablet 1 (which directly invokes the great gods of the council) but avoid any explicit reference to those deities may suggest that some authors wished to preserve the literary judgment form and perhaps even the very theological construct of the council while simultaneously avoiding an explicit reference to the other "great gods" in the assembly of אלהי הצבאות. This convention may ultimately reflect a similar ideology to the

---

[10] For the text of Maqlû, see G. Meier, *Die assyrische Beschwörungssammlung Maqlû* (AfO Beiheft 2; Berlin: Biblio-Verlag, 1937). Lines 4–12 of Maqlû I present an incantation depicting a legal conflict between two adversaries that explains the plaintiff's request to the court that it convene, hear the case, and examine the evidence of witchcraft; for a translation and detailed discussion of Maqlû I 1–36, see Tzvi Abusch, *Babylonian Witchcraft Literature: Case Studies* (BJS 132; Atlanta: Scholars Press, 1987), x–xii, 85–147.

view witnessed in the Covenant Collection of Exodus in the following charge (Exod 23:13):

ושם אלהים אחרים לא תזכירו לא ישמע על־פיך

Do not mention the name of other gods; it shall not be heard upon your mouth.[11]

This theory of the nonspecified audience in Amos 3:13 parallels the somewhat ambiguous references to the divine council in the opening chapters of Genesis (see 1:26; 3:22).[12] In the same way that the Priestly source presents God directing the other nonspecified deities to create a human in their image, and the J source depicts the deity speaking to an unspecified group of gods concerning the human, the author(s) of Amos 3 may have presented God commanding the nonspecified members of the council to act as witnesses in his ריב against Israel. Rather than a case of apostrophe, this literary technique may have been designed to reinforce intentionally the importance of focusing one's attention on Israel's deity, who, from the author's perspective, served as the אלהי הצבאות. In view of the trend, evidenced in Exod 23:13 and the opening chapters of Genesis, of avoiding explicit reference to other deities, one can appropriately theorize that the plural imperatives in Amos 3 represent an example of Israel's deity summoning the council as his witnesses and messengers.

If correct, this hypothesis would explain the final title, אלהי הצבאות, in the series of seemingly redundant epithets given Israel's God: אדני יהוה אלהי הצבאות, "Lord," "Yahweh," "God of Hosts."[13] Ultimately, this interpretation of the unit works well with biblical cosmology, which, in the words of Patrick D. Miller, tends to view the divine council as "a fundamental symbol for the Old Testament understanding of how the government of human society by the divine world is carried out."[14] This reading of Amos 3:13 as a summoning of God's assembly coheres with the general judicial role fulfilled by the council throughout ancient Near Eastern traditions.[15]

---

[11] Since the council of deities does appear explicitly in other biblical texts, clearly not all biblical authors felt compelled to follow this literary trend.

[12] A number of exegetes have suggested that the plural references in the Bible's first two creation stories are an allusion to the divine council; see, e.g., Simon B. Parker, "Council," *DDD*, 395. As Mark S. Smith has observed, a Ugaritic parallel in *KTU* 1.16 V presents El in a more explicit depiction informing the divine council that he will create a being; see Smith, *The Early History of God: Yahweh and Other Deities in Ancient Israel* (Grand Rapids: Eerdmans, 2002), 145 n. 143. Objections to this reading such as the one raised by Claus Westermann that "it is impossible that P should have understood the plural in this way, not only because he was not familiar with the idea of a heavenly court, but also because of his insistence on the uniqueness of Yahweh, besides whom there could be no other heavenly being" (*Genesis 1–11: A Continental Commentary* [Minneapolis: Fortress, 1994], 144–45) are clearly problematic. However, a detailed evaluation extends beyond the scope of the present focus.

[13] Cf., however, Hos 12:6: ויהוה אלהי הצבאות יהוה זכרו.

[14] Miller, "Cosmology and World Order," 432.

[15] In reality, the biblical view of the council seems congruent with the general perspective

Reflecting secular institutions, the heavenly council of the gods in ancient Near Eastern thought formed an important judicial body, governing the affairs of the cosmos. As Richard J. Clifford has explained concerning the Phoenician depiction of the assembly, "as elsewhere in the ancient Near East, the assemblies are pictured as subordinate to individual gods, although the assembly's consent seems necessary for important decisions."[16] The view of the council as a cosmic judicial institution appears prominently in Mesopotamian thought. In one of the Akkadian literary texts from Ur, the invocation of the gods to serve as witnesses in a judicial decision assumes a prominent role in the appeal made by one Kuzulum against his adversary, Elani:

> He swore, "I am doing you no wrong";
> He said, "These gods are my witnesses."[17]

In Esarhaddon's memorial stele commemorating the restoration of the city of Babylon, the Assyrian king invoked a curse upon any ruler who in future days might destroy Esarhaddon's inscribed name, shatter the record, or eradicate Babylon's freedom:

> In Upshuginna, the court of the assembly of the gods, the abode of judgment, may he [i.e., Marduk] impugn [lit., make evil] his word. May he command that his life (last) not a single day.[18]

Similarly, the judicial responsibilities assumed by the council appear in the Sumerian myth of Enlil and Ninlil, in which the assembly holds the male deity legally accountable for raping the goddess Ninlil. As Enlil returns to the city of Nippur, the assembly arrests him and the council of the "fifty great gods, and the seven gods of (formulating) decisions" issue a verdict against "the sex offender Enlil," declaring that the deity must "leave town!"[19] Another important example that illustrates the judicial responsibilities of the divine council in Mesopotamian tradition is the Sumerian Lament over the City of Ur. Though historical analysis suggests that Ur fell during the reign of Ibi-Sin (ca. 2028–2004 B.C.E.), as a result of a joint attack by the Elamites from the east and the Amorites from the west, "in a deeper, truer sense," explains Thorkild Jacobsen, "the barbaric hordes were a storm, Enlil's storm, wherewith the god himself was executing a verdict passed on Ur and its people by

---

witnessed in ancient Near Eastern texts. For an introduction to the idea of the council in ancient Near Eastern thought that discusses its fundamental judicial role, see Thorkild Jacobsen, *The Treasures of Darkness: A History of Mesopotamian Religion* (New Haven: Yale University Press, 1976), 86–87.

[16] Richard J. Clifford, "Phoenician Religion," *BASOR* 279 (1990): 57.
[17] U.I6900 F, as cited in C. J. Gadd, "Two Sketches from the Life at Ur," *Iraq* 25 (1963): 179.
[18] "Esarhaddon; The Building Inscriptions," *ARAB* 2:249.
[19] See "Enlil and Ninlil" in Thorkild Jacobsen, *The Harps That Once—: Sumerian Poetry in Translation* (New Haven: Yale University Press, 1987), 174.

the assembly of the gods."[20] Conceptually, these Mesopotamian texts provide a possible background for understanding the biblical depictions of the council.[21] If this is so, then אלהי הצבאות seeking the assembly's assistance in Amos 3 to serve as messengers and witnesses reflects a common ancient Near Eastern ideology.

As illustrated through Isa 41:21–23, the notion of gods presenting a case before the members of the heavenly assembly is not foreign to biblical thought:

קרבו ריבכם יאמר יהוה הגישו עצמותיכם יאמר מלך יעקב:
יגישו ויגידו לנו את אשר תקרינה
הראשנות מה הנה הגידו ונשימה לבנו
ונדעה אחריתן או הבאות השמיענו:
הגידו האתיות לאחור ונדעה כי אלהים אתם
אף־תיטיבו ותרעו ונשתעה ונראה יחדו:

> Submit your case, says Yahweh;
>   Offer your pleas, says the King of Jacob.
> Let them approach and tell us
>   what will happen.
> Tell us what has occurred,
>   And we will take note of it;
> Or announce to us what will occur,
>   That we may know the outcome.
> Foretell what is yet to happen,
>   That we may know that you are gods!
> Do anything, good or bad,
>   That we may be awed and see.

Though presented as a religious taunt designed to support Yahweh's supremacy, ultimately the concept of gods presenting a legal case in Isaiah 41 supports the possibility that אלהי הצבאות may have performed a similar act in Amos 3.

In a judicial context, one of the clearest examples of a biblical text describing the responsibility of the divine council to judge the nations of the earth is Psalm 82:

---

[20] Thorkild Jacobsen, "Mesopotamia: The Cosmos as a State," in H. Frankfort et al., *Before Philosophy: The Intellectual Adventure of Ancient Man; An Essay on Speculative Thought in the Ancient Near East* (Baltimore: Penguin Books, 1949), 154. For a critical edition of "The First Ur Lament," see Samuel Noah Kramer, *Lamentation over the Destruction of Ur* (AS 12; Chicago: University of Chicago Press, 1940); for translations, see M. Witzel, "Die Klage über Ur," *Or* n.s. 14 (1945): 185–234; 15 (1946): 46–63; Samuel Noah Kramer, trans., "Lamentation over the Destruction of Ur," *ANET*, 455–63; Jacobsen, *Harps That Once—*, 447–74; Jacob Klein, trans., "Lamentation over the Destruction of Sumer and Ur," *COS* 1:535–39.

[21] James Ackerman discusses the implications for the Hebrew Bible of Mesopotamian depictions of the council as a judicial body ("An Exegetical Study of Psalm 82" [Th.D. diss., Harvard University, 1966], 186–210).

אלהים נצב בעדת־אל בקרב אלהים ישפט׃
עד־מתי תשפטו־עול ופני רשעים תשאו׃
שפטו־דל ויתום עני ורש הצדיקו׃
פלטו־דל ואביון מיד רשעים הצילו׃
לא ידעו ולא יבינו בחשכה יתהלכו ימוטו כל־מוסדי ארץ׃
אני־אמרתי אלהים אתם ובני עליון כלכם׃
אכן כאדם תמותון וכאחד השרים תפלו׃
קומה אלהים שפטה הארץ כי־אתה תנחל בכל־הגוים׃

> God has taken his place in the divine council;
>   in the midst of the gods he holds judgment:
> "How long will you judge unjustly
>   and show partiality to the wicked?
> Give justice to the weak and the orphan;
>   maintain the right of the lowly and the destitute.
> Rescue the weak and the needy;
>   deliver them from the hand of the wicked.
> They have neither knowledge nor understanding,
>   they walk around in darkness;
>   all the foundations of the earth are shaken.
> I say, 'You are gods,
>   children of the Most High, all of you;
> nevertheless, you shall die like mortals,
>   and fall like any prince.'"
> Rise up, O God, judge the earth;
>   for all the nations belong to you!

In its present form, this text depicts אלהים standing in the עדה accusing the other deities of rendering poor judgment.[22] This use of עדה as a technical term for God's heavenly council provides important evidence for the roles associated with the heavenly assembly in Israelite thought. As Jacob Milgrom illustrates, though עדה frequently carries the general nuance of "assembly" as a bureaucratic expression, the Priestly term describes:

> a political body invested with legislative and judicial functions, such as 1) to bring trial and punish violators of the covenant, be they individuals (Num. 35:12, 24–25; Josh. 20:5, 9), cities, or tribes (Josh. 22:16; Judg. 21:10); 2) arbitrate intertribal disputes (Judg. 21:22; cf. v. 16); 3) crown kings (I Kings 12:20) and 4) reprimand its own leaders (Josh. 9:18–19).[23]

---

[22] For a historical survey of Psalm 82 that is sensitive to these issues, see Simon Parker, "The Beginning of the Reign of God: *Psalm* 82 as Myth and Liturgy," *RB* 102 (1995): 532–59.

[23] Jacob Milgrom, *Studies in Cultic Theology and Terminology* (SJLA 36; Leiden: Brill, 1983), 5–6.

The use of עדה in Psalm 82 as a reference to God's administrative assembly parallels Ps 89:6–7, which refers to the council as the קהל קדשים, "assembly of the holy ones." Psalm 82, therefore, clearly assumes that the אלהים of the divine council held the responsibility to judge, like the members of an earthly עדה or קהל, and to do so righteously.

With its view of the heavenly עדה, Psalm 82 establishes a strong precedent for the deity's invoking the divine council in a judicial context through the use of masculine plural imperatives, the precise pattern featured in Amos 3:9, 13. Indeed, as Frank Moore Cross explains, "the proclamation of Yahweh to his council frequently appears in early poetic or epic sources couched in a series of plural imperatives."[24] Through parallelism, the council in Psalm 82 receives two sets of mandates, both of which the author creates through a dual set of masculine plural imperatives: הצדיקו/שפטו and הצילו/פלטו (vv. 3–4). Hence, Psalm 82 reflects the grammatical pattern evidenced in Amos 3:13 with the dual command שמעו and והעידו (as well as the directive in Amos 3:9).

Several texts in the Hebrew Bible parallel the view of the council deities operating as a judicial court as in Psalm 82. "Yahweh's מלאך witnessed ויעד unto Joshua," reports Zech 3:6, with a *hiphil* form of עוד and a prepositional ב that reflects the grammar of Amos 3:13. As a God from the heavenly assembly, Yahweh himself could appear to be invoked by the *hiphil* form of עוד to serve as a witness, for example, in Ps 50:7 and Mal 2:14:

שמעה עמי ואדברה ישראל ואעידה בך אלהים אלהיך אנכי:
(Ps 50:7)

> Hear, O my people, and I will speak;
> I will witness against you O Israel:
> I am God, even your God.

ואמרתם על־מה על כי־יהוה העיד בינך ובין אשת נעוריך אשר אתה בגדתה בה והיא חברתך ואשת בריתך:
(Mal 2:14)

> But you ask, "Because of what?" Because Yahweh witnesses between you and the wife of your youth with whom you have broken faith, though she is your partner and covenanted spouse.

These biblical texts illustrate that the concept of a divine being serving as a witness via the *hiphil* form of עוד (occurring in Amos 3:13 as an imperative) is not, therefore, an unusual motif.

The image of a divine witness serving in the heavenly assembly was especially comforting to Job, who declared: גם־עתה הנה־בשמים עדי ושהדי במרומים, "Surely now my witness is in heaven; / He who can testify for me is on high" (16:19). For

---

[24] Cross, "Council of Yahweh," 276–77 n. 8.

the author of Job 16:19, a divine עד in heaven may have served as a type of antithesis to the שטן figure of Job 1–2. Indeed, Job's שטן simply parallels the standard ancient Near Eastern view of council members functioning in a judicial capacity. For the author of the introductory prose section of the book of Job, the heavenly council serves as the sphere where decisions concerning punishments—whether earned or not—are decided upon and then carried out by representatives of the council such as השטן. Thus, אלהי הצבאות of Amos may have sought the assistance of these types of heavenly beings in his invocation presented in 3:13.

Though seldom viewed in this manner, the Aqedah may provide an additional example of a divine council member functioning in the role of witness. In Gen 22:12, God's heavenly מלאך appears suddenly, informing Abraham that he has successfully passed God's test:

ויאמר אל־תשלח ידך אל־הנער ואל־תעש לו מאומה כי עתה ידעתי כי־ירא
אלהים אתה ולא חשכת את־בנך את־יחידך ממני:

> And he said, "Do not raise your hand against the boy, or do anything to him. For now I know that you fear God, since you have not withheld your son, your favored one, from Me."

The immediate switch from the words expressed personally by the מלאך to the words spoken by God through his messenger need not present an interpretive challenge. As a messenger whom God had *sent*, the מלאך spoke the words of God as direct speech. However, the clause עתה ידעתי כי־ירא אלהים, "now I know that you fear God," may reflect the view of the מלאך as council witness. In addition to this occurrence in Gen 22:12, the expression עתה ידעתי כי appears only three times in the Hebrew Bible (see Exod 18:11; Judg 17:13; Ps 20:7).[25] None of the instances of the statement עתה ידעתי כי is spoken by Israel's deity. Apart from Genesis 22, the phrase is spoken by a human being who can serve as a witness to God's extraordinary power. It seems most likely, therefore, that the initial portion of the utterance spoken by the מלאך in Gen 22:12 represents the role of the מלאך as a witness to God's ability to fulfill the covenant described in vv. 15–18 followed by the message ולא חשכת את־בנך את־יחידך ממני, "since you have not withheld your son, your favored one, from me." Conceptually, this example of a divine council member serving as a messenger and a witness may therefore relate to the invocation of the צבא to שמעו and העידו in Amos 3:13.

These traces of the invocation of divine witnesses in the context of decision making provide important evidence for the possibility that Amos 3:13 invokes the heavenly council to *listen* and *testify* against Jacob. As a final consideration of the evidence for council witnesses in biblical thought, attention should be given to the invocation directed toward natural forces in the Hebrew Bible. This tradition has

---

[25] See also 1 Kgs 17:24, in which a human witness speaks the words עתה זה ידעתי כי, and 1 Sam 24:21, in which a human witness says, ועתה הנה ידעתי כי.

led to a series of distinct interpretations. Clearly, the summoning of "heaven and earth" to function as witnesses has important implications for understanding the biblical view of council deities. Statements such as העידתי בכם היום את־השמים ואת־ הארץ, "I call heaven and earth this day to witness against you" (Deut 4:26), in the context of Moses' literary sermon featured in Deuteronomy 4, seem, at first glance, to suggest that the natural forces may function as witnesses, summoned to provide testimony concerning the violation of important religious obligations.[26] However, in 1959 G. Ernest Wright offered an intriguing suggestion concerning these types of invocations. He argued that readers should "interpret such passages in the light of the Divine Assembly, the members of which constitute the host of heaven and of earth."[27] For Wright, the summoning of heaven and earth would provide a type of merism or "polar expression" whereby the speaker addresses *all* of the gods of the council through the antithetical word pair. Wright's thesis proves compelling, for as Cross argued, the biblical lawsuit oracle "undoubtedly has its origins in the conceptions of the role of Yahweh's heavenly assembly as a court."[28] Wright's insightful proposal, however, met with almost immediate opposition, principally from Herbert Huffmon, who offered a summary and critique, stating:

> One basic problem with interpreting heaven and earth, the mountains and the hills, and the foundations of the earth, as members of the divine assembly is that there is no direct evidence for it. In Mesopotamia, the divine assembly was a council of the gods, a pantheon. The natural elements, as such, were not members of the gods, a pantheon, as is shown by the fact that in the many catalogues of deities preserved from ancient Mesopotamian or Anatolian sources there is—apart from one particular type of list—no mention of these natural phenomena *per se*.[29]

In his criticisms, however, Huffmon misinterpreted Wright's argument, which does not state that heaven and earth appear in the biblical invocation of witnesses as distinct members of the assembly, but rather that the polar expression *refers* to the divine assembly, "the members of which constitute the host of heaven and of earth." In reality, the way in which the word pair "heaven and earth" often appears in ancient Near Eastern texts supports Wright's thesis.

The apparent biblical use of "heaven and earth" as a reference to *all* of the members of the assembly both "high and low" parallels the language of the Assyr-

---

[26] In 1950, commentator R. B. Y. Scott suggested that these invocations "derived from the manner of the adjudication of disputes and the hearing of complaints 'in the gates.' 'Hear ye, . . . Give ear . . . ,' introducing a complaint, calls for the attention of witnesses" ("The Literary Structure of Isaiah's Oracles," in *Studies in Old Testament Prophecy: Presented to Theodore H. Robinson on His Sixty-fifth Birthday, August 9th, 1946* [ed. H. H. Rowley; New York: Scribner, 1950], 79).

[27] George Ernest Wright, *The Old Testament against Its Environment* (SBT 2; London: SCM, 1950), 36.

[28] Cross, "Council of Yahweh," 274 n. 3.

[29] Herbert Huffmon, "The Covenant Lawsuit in the Prophets," *JBL* 78 (1959): 291.

ian vassal treaties of Esarhaddon, which typically commence with a lengthy list of the Mesopotamian deities invoked as witnesses to the treaty.[30] In the vassal treaties, the record of theophoric names appears with two subdivisions that create a sense of literary closure within the list:

> All the gods dwelling in heaven and earth, the gods of Assyria, the gods of Sumer and Akkad, the gods of every (foreign) country.
>
> You are adjured by all the gods of Sumer and Akkad, adjured by the gods of heaven and earth.[31]

In both divisions, the word pair "heaven and earth" parallels the terms "Sumer and Akkad," that is, "south and north" as a reference to "all the gods" of the assembly. The phrase "heaven and earth" denotes the gods of Assyria, the gods of Sumer and Akkad, the gods of *every* foreign country.

Perhaps of even greater import for understanding the expression "heaven and earth" as a reference to the gods who constitute the council are the biblical references to heaven and earth as the location where Israel's deity resides, for example, Josh 2:11:

> ונשמע וימס לבבנו ולא־קמה עוד רוח באיש מפניכם כי יהוה אלהיכם הוא
> אלהים בשמים ממעל ועל־הארץ מתחת:
>
> When we heard about it, we lost heart, and no man had any more spirit left because of you; for Yahweh your God, he is a God in heaven above and on earth below. (See also Deut 4:29; 1 Kgs 8:23; Eccl 5:1; 2 Chr 6:14; 20:6.)

From the perspective of these statements concerning Israel's deity, who is a God בשמים ממעל ועל־הארץ מתחת, "in heaven above and on earth below," the invoca-

---

[30] George E. Mendenhall noted that Deuteronomy shares the structure of second-millennium B.C.E. Hittite treaties, which include an invocation to heaven and earth ("Covenant Forms in Israelite Tradition," *BA* 23 [1954]: 2–22, repr. in *BARead* 3:25–53). Since Mendenhall's article appeared, however, a number of first-millennium Assyrian vassal treaties of the early seventh century (published in 1958) have been shown to have closer and more direct connections to Deuteronomy than the earlier Hittite treaties; see esp. Moshe Weinfeld, *Deuteronomy and the Deuteronomic School* (Oxford: Clarendon, 1972; repr., Winona Lake, IN: Eisenbrauns, 1992), 59–178; and the earlier article of R. Frankena, "The Vassal-Treaties of Esarhaddon and the Dating of Deuteronomy," *OtSt* 14 (1965): 122–54. See also the detailed study of Dennis J. McCarthy, *Treaty and Covenant: A Study in Form in the Ancient Oriental Documents and in the Old Testament* (new ed.; AnBib 21; Rome: Biblical Institute Press, 1978). For critiques of Mendenhall, Weinfeld, and McCarthy, see E. W. Nicholson, "Covenant in a Century of Study since Wellhausen," *OtSt* 24 (1986): 54–69; repr. in *A Song of Power and the Power of Song: Essays on the Book of Deuteronomy* (ed. Duane L. Christensen; Sources for Biblical and Theological Study 3; Winona Lake, IN: Eisenbrauns, 1993), 78–93; Nicholson, *God and His People: Covenant and Theology in the Old Testament* (Oxford: Clarendon, 1986), 56–82.

[31] D. J. Wiseman, trans., "The Vassal-Treaties of Esarhaddon," *ANET*, 534–35.

tion of the word pair "heaven and earth" as a witness would conceptually allude to the being(s) who constitute the two realms.

According to this proposal, the polar expression "heaven and earth" in the Bible may be an instance of metonymy, in which the place denotes the things located within it.[32] The Hebrew Bible contains a number of examples of this specific literary convention.

Psalm 33:8:

ייראו מיהוה כל־הארץ ממנו יגורו כל־ישבי תבל:

Let all the earth fear Yahweh;
　　let all the inhabitants of the world dread Him.

Genesis 11:1:

ויהי כל־הארץ שפה אחת ודברים אחדים:

And the whole earth was of one language, and of one speech.

2 Chronicles 32:20:

ויתפלל יחזקיהו המלך וישעיהו בן־אמוץ הנביא על־זאת ויזעקו השמים

And for this cause Hezekiah the king and the prophet Isaiah the son of Amoz, prayed and cried to heaven.

Psalm 89:6–7:

ויודו שמים פלאך יהוה אף־אמונתך בקהל קדשים:
כי מי בשחק יערך ליהוה ידמה ליהוה בבני אלים:

The heavens praise your wonders, O Yahweh,
　　Your faithfulness, too, in the assembly of holy beings.
For who in the skies can equal Yahweh,
　　can compare with Yahweh among the gods.

This final use of metonymy proves especially useful for the present analysis. Through synonymous parallelism, שמים corresponds to קהל קדשים, whereas the term שחק functions as a synonym for בני אלים. Both lines, therefore, move from a description of "heaven," that is, the place, toward a parallel term for the divine beings living within the celestial sphere. Therefore, in view of the general ancient Near Eastern and biblical evidence, even the invocation of natural forces in the Bible provides evidence for the council as the intended audience summoned in Amos 3.

---

[32] See E. W. Bullinger, *Figures of Speech Used in the Bible, Explained and Illustrated* (London: Eyre & Spottiswoode, 1898; repr., Grand Rapids: Baker, 1968), 573–81; G. Ammanuel Mikre-Sellassie, "Metonymy in the Book of Psalms," *BT* 44 (1993): 418–24.

Finally, a connection between Amos 3: 9, 13 and the summoning of heaven and earth for a divine trial appears in Ps 50:4–7:

יקרא אל־השמים מעל ואל־הארץ לדין עמו:
אספו־לי חסידי כרתי בריתי עלי־זבח:
ויגידו שמים צדקו כי־אלהים שפט הוא:
שמעה עמי ואדברה ישראל ואעידה בך אלהים אלהיך אנכי:

He summoned the heavens above,
    and the earth, for the trial of His people.
"Bring in My devotees,
    who made a covenant with Me over sacrifice!"
Then the heavens proclaimed His righteousness,
    for He is a God who judges.
"Listen, My people, and I will speak,
    O Israel, and I will bear witness against you;
I am God, your God."

In the course of the trial, the heavens offer a witness that Yahweh is a righteous god. As a deity in the case, Yahweh himself promises to bear witness against his people. Conceptually, the ריב presented in Psalm 50 relates to the council imagery in Amos 3. Just as the gods of the council appear in Amos 3:9 summoned by אלהי הצבאות to speak (יאמרו), God himself promises to speak (ואדברה) in Psalm 50. In the same way that the gods are apparently invoked in Amos 3:13 to bear witness (השמיעו), so Yahweh, as a god of the council, appears in Psalm 50 promising his people ואעידה בך, "I will bear witness against you."

"Listen and witness against the House of Jacob," declares אלהי הצבאות in Amos's judgment oracle in 3:13. Since in many biblical texts this type of invocation reflects traditional responsibilities allocated to the heavenly host, a synchronic reading of Amos 3, which includes an explicit reference to the סוד, may provide the intended addressee for the undefined masculine plural imperatives. Notwithstanding his supremacy, the God of ancient Israel was not alone, and perhaps, from the perspective of the author(s) of Amos 3, this deity could invoke his סוד to assist in the important process of rendering a divine judgment.

Religious Studies from Chicago

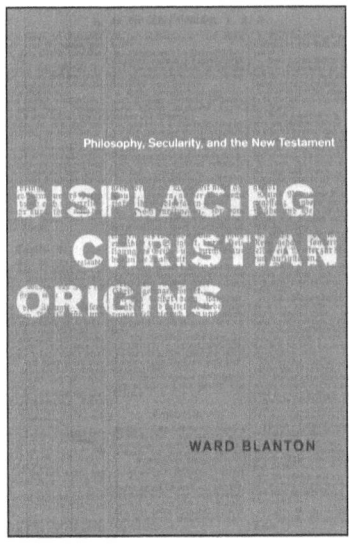

DISPLACING CHRISTIAN ORIGINS
Philosophy, Secularity, and the New Testament
Ward Blanton

"In this academic tour de force, Ward Blanton drags early scholarship on Jesus and Christian beginnings out of the closet of a history of an academic subdiscipline where it has been safely hidden. In a surprising but convincing move, he puts 19th and 20th New Testament scholarship in the context of the expansion of modern technology in the production and dissemination of literature. Thus, the construction of history becomes part of the production of modernity."
—Halvor Moxnes, University of Oslo
Paper $22.50

THE CHRISTIANITY READER
Edited by Mary Gerhart and Fabian Udoh

The Christianity Reader is a landmark sourcebook for the study of Christianity's historical diversity. With newly edited, annotated, and translated primary texts, along with supplemental analytical essays, the volume allows Christianity, at long last, to speak in its many voices.
Paper $40.00

THE UNIVERSITY OF CHICAGO PRESS   WWW.PRESS.UCHICAGO.EDU

Praxis of the Voice:
The Divine Name Traditions in the *Apocalypse of Abraham*

ANDREI A. ORLOV
andrei.orlov@mu.edu
Marquette University, Milwaukee, WI 53201

A large portion of the *Apocalypse of Abraham*, a Jewish work known only in its Slavonic translation, deals with the celestial tour of the eponymous hero of the text. In the work's elaborate account of the tour, which depicts Abraham's initiation into the heavenly mysteries, an important detail often found in other apocalyptic texts is missing. The authors of the Slavonic work seem deliberately to eschew anthropomorphic depictions of the deity that often mark climactic points in other early Jewish apocalyptic accounts. This reluctance to endorse traditions of the divine form appears to be quite unusual, given that other features of the pseudepigraphon exhibit explicit allusions to motifs and themes of the Merkabah tradition. Several distinguished scholars of early Jewish mysticism have previously noted that the *Apocalypse of Abraham* might represent one of the earliest specimens of Merkabah mysticism, the Jewish tradition in which the divine form ideology arguably receives its most advanced articulation.[1] Yet despite many suggestive allusions in

---

[1] On the Jewish mystical traditions in the *Apocalypse of Abraham*, see George H. Box and Joseph I. Landsman, *The Apocalypse of Abraham* (Translations of Early Documents; London: SPCK, 1918), xxix–xxx; Mary Dean-Otting, *Heavenly Journeys: A Study of the Motif in Hellenistic Jewish Literature* (Judentum und Umwelt 8; Frankfurt am Main: Lang, 1984), 251–53; Ithamar Gruenwald, *Apocalyptic and Merkavah Mysticism* (AGJU 14; Leiden: Brill, 1980), 55–56; David J. Halperin, *The Faces of the Chariot: Early Jewish Responses to Ezekiel's Vision* (TSAJ 16; Tübingen: Mohr Siebeck, 1988), 103–13; Alexander Kulik, *Retroverting the Slavonic Pseudepigrapha: Toward the Original of the Apocalypse of Abraham* (Text-critical Studies 3; Leiden/Boston: Brill, 2004), 83–88; Belkis Philonenko-Sayar and Marc Philonenko, *L'Apocalypse d'Abraham: Introduction, texte slave, traduction et notes* (Semitica 31; Paris: Adrien Maisonneuve, 1981), 28–33; Christopher Rowland, *The Open Heaven: A Study of Apocalyptic in Judaism and Early Christianity* (New York:

53

their depiction of the heavenly realities, the authors of the *Apocalypse of Abraham* appear very reluctant to endorse one of the most crucial tenets in the divine chariot lore: the anthropomorphic depiction of the Glory of God. The reluctance seems rather puzzling in view of some close similarities in angelological imagery that the *Apocalypse of Abraham* shares with the first chapter of the book of Ezekiel, the formative account of the Merkabah tradition, where the ideology of the divine form looms large.[2]

It has been previously noted that the seer's vision of the divine throne found in the *Apocalypse of Abraham* relies significantly on Ezekiel's account and stands in direct continuity with Merkabah tradition.[3] At the same time, however, scholars observe that the Slavonic pseudepigraphon shows attempts to depart from the overt anthropomorphism of this prophetic book. Christopher Rowland, for example, notes that the shift from anthropomorphism is apparent in the portrayal of the divine throne in ch. 18 of the *Apocalypse of Abraham*. Notwithstanding the many allusions to Ezekiel 1 in the depiction of the throne room in chs. 18 and 19 of the *Apocalypse*, Rowland highlights a radical paradigm shift in the text's description of the deity, noting "a deliberate attempt . . . to exclude all reference to the human figure mentioned in Ezek 1." For Rowland, this shift entails that "there was a definite trend within apocalyptic thought away from the direct description of God."[4]

Crossroad, 1982), 86–87; Ryszard Rubinkiewicz, *L'Apocalypse d'Abraham en vieux slave: Édition critique du texte, introduction, traduction et commentaire* (Towarzystwo Naukowe Katolickiego Uniwersytetu Lubelskiego: Źródła i monografie 129; Lublin: Société des lettres et des sciences de l'Université catholique de Lublin, 1987), 76–83; Michael E. Stone "Apocalyptic Literature," in *Jewish Writings of the Second Temple Period: Apocrypha, Pseudepigrapha, Qumran Sectarian Writings, Philo, Josephus* (ed. M. E. Stone; CRINT 2/2; Assen: Van Gorcum, 1984), 383–441; Gershom Scholem, *Major Trends in Jewish Mysticism* (New York: Schocken Books, 1961), 52, 57–61, 72; idem, *Jewish Gnosticism, Merkabah Mysticism, and Talmudic Tradition* (New York: Jewish Theological Seminary, 1965), 23–24; idem, *Kabbalah* (Library of Jewish Knowledge; New York: Quadrangle, 1974), 18.

[2] Ryszard Rubinkiewicz provides a helpful outline of usage of Ezekielian traditions in the *Apocalypse of Abraham* (*L'Apocalypse d'Abraham*, 87). He notes that "among the prophetic books, the book of Ezekiel plays for our author the same role as Genesis in the Pentateuch. The vision of the divine Throne (*Apoc. Ab.* 18) is inspired by Ezek 1 and 10. Abraham sees the four living creatures (*Apoc. Ab.* 18:5-11) depicted in Ezek 1 and 10. He also sees the wheels of fire decorated with eyes all around (*Apoc. Ab.* 18:3), the throne (*Apoc. Ab.* 18:3; Ezek 1:26), the chariot (*Apoc. Ab.* 18:12 and Ezek 10:6); he hears the voice of God (*Apoc. Ab.* 19:1 and Ezek 1:28). When the cloud of fire rises up, he can hear 'the voice like the roaring sea' (*Apoc. Ab.* 18:1; Ezek 1:24). There is no doubt that the author of the *Apocalypse of Abraham* takes the texts of Ezek 1 and 10 as sources of inspiration."

[3] John J. Collins, *The Apocalyptic Imagination: An Introduction to Jewish Apocalyptic Literature* (2nd ed.; Grand Rapids: Eerdmans, 1998), 228–29. Collins also notes that Abraham's vision "stands in the tradition of *1 En.* 14, conveying a sense of the visionary's experience of awe and terror" (p. 229).

[4] Rowland, *Open Heaven*, 86–87.

These observations about anti-anthropomorphic tendencies of the Slavonic apocalypse are intriguing and deserve further investigation. Even a cursory look at the text reveals that, despite an extensive appropriation of the visionary motifs and themes, the authors appear to be avoiding anthropomorphic depictions of the deity and some other celestial beings.[5] This tendency leads to the creation of a new apocalyptic imagery that combines traditional and novel elements. This article will investigate these new conceptual developments in the *Apocalypse of Abraham* and seek to understand their place in the larger anticorporeal ideology of the Slavonic pseudepigraphon.

I. The Biblical Background of the Shem Tradition

The *Apocalypse of Abraham* is a Jewish work probably composed in Palestine in the early centuries of the Common Era.[6] The text can be divided into two parts.[7]

---

[5] Anti-anthropomorphic reinterpretation of Ezekiel's vision can be detected also in the Targums. For extensive discussion of the avoidance of anthropomorphism in the Targum to Ezekiel 1, see Halperin, *Faces of the Chariot*, 120–23.

[6] On the date and provenance of the *Apocalypse of Abraham*, see Box and Landsman, *Apocalypse of Abraham*, xv–xix; Philonenko-Sayar and Philonenko, *L'Apocalypse d'Abraham*. 34–35; Ryszard Rubinkiewicz, "Apocalypse of Abraham," *OTP* 1:681–705, at 683; idem, *L'Apocalypse d'Abraham en vieux slave*, 70–73; Alexander Kulik, "К датировке 'Откровения Авраама'" [About the Date of the *Apocalypse of Abraham*], in *In Memoriam: Ja. S. Lurè* (ed. N. M. Botvinnik and Je. I. Vaneeva; St. Petersburg, 1997), 189–95; idem, *Retroverting the Slavonic Pseudepigrapha*, 2–3.

[7] For the published Slavonic manuscripts and fragments of the *Apoc. Ab.*, see Ioan Franko, "Книга о Аврааме праотци и патриарси" [The Book about the Forefather and the Patriarch Abraham], in *Апокріфи і легенди з українських рукописів* [The Apocrypha and the Legends from the Ukrainian Manuscripts](5 vols.; Monumenta Linguae Necnon Litterarum Ukraino-Russicarum [Ruthenicarum] 1–5; L'vov: Schevchenka, 1896–1910), 1:80–86; Alexander I. Jacimirskij, "Откровение Авраама" [The Apocalypse of Abraham], in *Библиографический обзор апокрифов в южнославянской и русской письменности (Списки памятников) Выпуск 1. Апокрифы ветхозаветные* [The Bibliographical Survey of Apocryphal Writings in South Slavonic and Old Russian Literature, vol. 1, The Old Testament Pseudepigrapha] (Petrograd: Russian Imperial Academy of Sciences, 1921), 99–100; P. P. Novickij, ed., "Откровение Авраама" [The Apocalypse of Abraham], in *Общество любителей древней письменности* [The Society of Lovers of Ancient Literature] 99.2 (St. Petersburg: Markov, 1891); Ivan Ja. Porfir'ev, "Откровение Авраама" [The Apocalypse of Abraham], in *Апокрифические сказания о ветхозаветных лицах и событиях по рукописям соловецкой библиотеки* [The Apocryphal Stories about Old Testament Characters and Events according to the Manuscripts of the Solovetzkoj Library] (Sbornik Otdelenija russkogo jazyka i slovesnosti Imperatorskoj akademii nauk 17.1; St. Petersburg: Russian Academy of Sciences, 1877), 111–30; Philonenko-Sayar and Philonenko, *L'Apocalypse d'Abraham*, 36–105; Alexander N. Pypin, *Ложные и отреченные книги славянской и русской старины, Памятники старинной русской литературы, издаваемые графом Григорием Кушелевым-Безбородко Том 3* [The False and Rejected Books of Slavonic and Russian

The first part (chs. 1–8) of the work represents a haggadic account of Abraham's rejection of the religious practices of his father, Terah. The second, apocalyptic part covers the rest of the work (chs. 9-32) and depicts the patriarch's ascension to heaven, where he is accompanied by his *angelus interpres,* Yahoel, during his initiation into the heavenly and eschatological mysteries.

The first eight chapters of the pseudepigraphon take the form of midrashic elaboration and recount the early years of Abraham, who is depicted as a reluctant helper to his idolatrous father, Terah. The conceptual developments found in this section of the work, especially in the depictions of the idolatrous figures, seem to play an important role in the work's overall retraction of the anthropomorphic understanding of the deity. Possibly mindful of the broader extrabiblical context of Abraham's biography and his role as the fighter against the idolatrous practices of his father, the work's authors seem to be appropriating the patriarch's story for their anticorporeal agenda.[8] In the depictions of the idol Bar-Eshath ("the Son of Fire")[9] and some other humanlike figures, whose features are vividly reminiscent of the familiar attributes of the anthropomorphic portrayals of the deity in Ezekiel and

---

Antiquity: Memorials of Ancient Russian Literature Edited by Count Gregory Kushelev-Bezborodko, vol. 3 (St. Petersburg: Kulesh, 1860–62), 24–36; Rubinkiewicz, *L'Apocalypse d'Abraham en vieux slave,* 98–256; Izmail I. Sreznevskij, "Книги Откровения Авраама" [The Apocalypse of Abraham], in *Известия Императорской академии наук по отделению русского языка и словесности. Том 10* [Proceedings of the Imperial Academy of Sciences, Division of Russian Language and Literature, vol. 10] (St. Petersburg: Russian Academy of Sciences, 1861–63), 648–65; Nikolaj S. Tihonravov, *Памятники отреченной русской литературы* [Memorials of Russian Apocryphal Literature] (2 vols.; St. Petersburg/Moscow: Obschestvennaja Pol'za, 1863), 1:32–77.

For the translations of the *Apoc. Ab.,* see Nathanael Bonwetsch, *Die Apokalypse Abrahams: Das Testament der vierzig Märtyrer* (Studien zur Geschichte der Theologie und der Kirche, Bd.1, Heft 1; Leipzig: Deichert, 1897); Box and Landsman, *Apocalypse of Abraham,* 35–87; Mario Enrietti and Paolo Sacchi, "Apocalisse di Abramo," in *Apocrifi dell'Antico Testamento* (ed. Paolo Sacchi et al.; 5 vols.; Turin/Brescia: Unione tipografico-editrice torinese, 1981–97), 3:61–110; Kulik, *Retroverting the Slavonic Pseudepigrapha,* 9–35; A. Pennington, "Apocalypse of Abraham," *AOT,* 363–491; Donka Petkanova, "Откровение на Авраам" [The Apocalypse of Abraham], in *Старобългарска Есхатология. Антология* [Old Bulgarian Eschatology: Anthology] (ed. D. Petkanova and A. Miltenova; Slavia Orthodoxa: Sofiya: Slavica, 1993), 17–30; Belkis Philonenko-Sayar and Marc Philonenko, "Die Apokalypse Abrahams," *JSHRZ* 5.5 (Gütersloh: Mohn, 1982), 413–60; Paul Rießler, "Apokalypse des Abraham," in *Altjüdisches Schrifttum außerhalb der Bibel* (Freiburg: F. H. Kerle, 1928), 13–39; 1267–69; Rubinkiewicz, "Apocalypse of Abraham," *OTP* 1:681–705; idem, "Apocalypsa Abrahama," in *Apokryfy Starego Testamentu* (ed. R. Rubinkiewicz; Warsaw: Oficyna Wydawnicza "Vocatio," 1999), 460–81.

[8] For the background of this story in the book of *Jubilees,* Josephus, Philo, and the later rabbinic materials (*Gen. Rab.* 38:13; *Tanna debe Eliahu* 2:25; *S. Eliahu R.* 33), see Box and Landsman, *Apocalypse of Abraham,* 88–94; Rubinkiewicz, *L'Apocalypse d'Abraham en vieux slave,* 43–49.

[9] On Bar-Eshath and the background of this name, see Kulik, *Retroverting the Slavonic Pseudepigrapha,* 63.

some other biblical and pseudepigraphical accounts, one can detect a subtle polemic against the divine body traditions. I have previously discussed the scope and nature of the anti-anthropomorphic developments in the first part of the *Apocalypse of Abraham*.[10] The current article can be seen as a continuation of the ongoing inquiry into the anti-anthropomorphic tendencies of the *Apocalypse*, as it will deal with the polemical developments in the second, apocalyptic section of the pseudepigraphon. The second portion of the Slavonic pseudepigraphon takes the form of a visionary account and deals with celestial and eschatological revelations to Abraham after his open renunciation of idolatrous practices.

One of the important features of this section of the text is the authors' apparent anti-anthropomorphic attitude, reflected in their peculiar portrayals of the deity and the heavenly hosts in chs. 8–19. Although the apocalyptic imagery found in this portion of the pseudepigraphon appears to stem from the theophanic paradigm of the early Merkabah speculations, similar to those found in Ezekiel 1, *1 Enoch* 14,[11] and the *Exagoge* of Ezekiel the Tragedian, the authors of the Slavonic text appear to exhibit consistent efforts to refashion this traditional theophanic imagery in accordance with a new anti-anthropomorphic template that insists on expressing the divine presence in the form of the deity's voice.[12] In his comparative analysis of the accounts from Ezekiel and the *Apocalypse of Abraham*, Rowland notes that, while preserving the angelology of Ezekiel's account, the author of the Slavonic apocalypse carefully avoids anthropomorphic descriptions of the *Kavod*, replacing them with references to the divine voice.

These anti-anthropomorphic tendencies can be observed already in the very beginning of the apocalyptic section of the work. The very first manifestation of the deity to the seer found in ch. 8 takes the form of a theophany of the divine voice, depicted as coming from heaven in a stream of fire.[13] This peculiar expression of

---

[10] Andrei A. Orlov, *"The Gods of My Father Terah": Abraham the Iconoclast and the Anti-Anthropomorphic Tendencies of the Apocalypse of Abraham* (forthcoming).

[11] George W. E. Nickelsburg notices that "Abraham's ascent and throne vision stand in a tradition that stretches from *1 En.* 12–16 to the medieval mystical texts" (*Jewish Literature between the Bible and the Mishnah: A Historical and Literary Introduction* [2nd ed.; Minneapolis: Fortress, 2005], 288).

[12] On the hypostatic voice of God, see James H. Charlesworth, "The Jewish Roots of Christology: The Discovery of the Hypostatic Voice," *SJT* 39 (1986): 19–41.

[13] Scholars have previously noted that the patriarch's vision reflected in the second part of the Slavonic apocalypse seems to be reminiscent not only of Ezekiel 1 but also of the visionary account in Genesis 15 ("with an allusion to Gen 22 insofar as the sacrifices are located on a high mountain" [Collins, *Apocalyptic Imagination*, 226]). Thus, Box notes that "the apocalyptic part of the book is based upon the story of Abraham's sacrifices and trance, as described in Gen. xv" (Box and Landsman, *Apocalypse of Abraham*, xxiv). In both Genesis and the *Apocalypse of Abraham*, the patriarch is asked to prepare sacrifices, and the content of the sacrifices is also very similar. Yet the theophanic tradition of the divine voice does not play a prominent role in Genesis 15. Although the latter text mentions the word of God given to Abraham, it does not say anything

the deity as the voice erupting in a fiery stream will subsequently become a customary theophanic expression, appearing multiple times in the apocalypse, including in the climactic account of the revelation given to Abraham in the seventh firmament. There, in his vision of the throne room, which evokes memories of Ezekelian angelology, the hero of the faith sees not the humanlike form of God but the deity's formless voice.

This tendency to replace the anthropomorphic depiction of the deity with expressions of the divine voice or name is, of course, not a novel development of the authors of the *Apocalypse of Abraham* but a specimen of the long-lasting tradition whose roots can be found already in the biblical materials.

The Hebrew Bible reveals complicated polemics for and against anthropomorphic understandings of God. Scholars argue that the anthropomorphic imagery found in biblical materials was "crystallized" in the Israelite priestly ideology known to us as the Priestly source. Moshe Weinfeld points out that the theology of worship delineated in the Priestly source depicts God in "the most tangible corporeal similitudes."[14] In the Priestly tradition God is understood to have created humanity in his own image (Gen 1:27) and is thus frequently described as possessing a humanlike form.[15] Scholars have shown that the anthropomorphism of the Priestly authors appears to be intimately connected with the place of divine habitation—the deity possesses a human form and needs to reside in a house or tabernacle.[16] Weinfeld argues that the anthropomorphic position was not entirely an invention of the Priestly tradition but derived from early preexilic sacral conceptions about divine corporeal manifestations found in Mesopotamian literature.[17] Scholars observe that the Priestly understanding of the corporeal representation of the deity finds its clearest expression in the conception of the "Glory of God" (כבוד יהוה).[18] This conception is always expressed in the Priestly tradition in the symbolism grounded in mythological corporeal imagery. One of the paradigmatic accounts of the portrayal of the divine *Kavod* can be found in the first chapter of the book of Ezekiel, which can be seen as the manifesto of the Priestly corporeal ideology. There the *Kavod* is portrayed as an enthroned human form enveloped by fire.

---

about the voice in the fire, a standard theophanic formula found in the *Apocalypse of Abraham*. It is also noteworthy that at the end of the Genesis account, the patriarch sees the vision of a fiery phenomenon—a smoking fire pot with a blazing torch.

[14] Moshe Weinfeld, *Deuteronomy and the Deuteronomic School* (Oxford: Clarendon, 1972), 191.

[15] Ludwig Köhler ("Die Grundstelle der Imago-Dei Lehre, Genesis i, 26," *TZ* 4 [1948]: 16–17) and Weinfeld (*Deuteronomy and the Deuteronomic School,* 199) argue that the phrase, "in our image, after our likeness" precludes the anthropomorphic interpretation that the human being was created in the divine image.

[16] Weinfeld, *Deuteronomy and the Deuteronomic School,* 191.

[17] Ibid., 199.

[18] Ibid., 200–201.

While containing forceful anthropomorphic ideologies, the Hebrew Bible also attests to polemical narratives contesting the corporeal depictions of the deity. Scholars have long noted a sharp opposition in the book of Deuteronomy and the Deuteronomic school to early anthropomorphic developments. In fact, the Deuteronomic school is widely thought to have initiated the polemic against the anthropomorphic and corporeal conceptions of the deity, which was subsequently adopted by the prophets Jeremiah and Deutero-Isaiah.[19] Seeking to dislodge ancient anthropomorphism, the book of Deuteronomy and the Deuteronomic school promulgated an anticorporeal theology of the divine name with its conception of sanctuary (tabernacle) as the exclusive dwelling of God's Name.[20] Gerhard von Rad argues that the Deuteronomic formula "to cause his name to dwell" (לשכן שמו) advocates a new understanding of the deity that challenges the popular ancient belief that God actually dwells within the sanctuary.[21] It is noteworthy that, although the Deuteronomic *Shem* ideology does not completely abandon the terminology pertaining to the concept of the divine glory (*Kavod*),[22] it markedly voids it of any corporeal motifs. Weinfeld observes that "the expression כבוד, when occurring in Deuteronomy, does not denote the being and substantiality of God as it does in the earlier sources but his splendor and greatness," signifying "abstract and not corporeal qualities."[23]

One of the early examples of the polemical interaction between the corporeal ideology of the divine form (*Kavod*), which is often labeled in the theophanic accounts as the divine face (*Panim*), and the incorporeal theology of the divine name possibly occurs in Exodus 33, where, upon Moses' plea to behold the divine *Kavod*, the deity offers an aural alternative by promising to reveal to the seer his name:

> Then Moses said, "Now show me your glory (כבדך)." And the Lord said, "I will cause all my goodness to pass in front of you, and I will proclaim my name (וקראתי בשם), the LORD, in your presence ... but," he said, "you cannot see my face (פני), for no one may see me and live." (Exod 33:18–20)

This account appears to highlight the opposition between visual and aural revelations, focusing on the possibility of encountering the deity not only through

---

[19] Ibid., 198.

[20] Tryggve N. D. Mettinger observes that the concept of God in the *Shem* theology is "strikingly abstract.... God himself is no longer present in the Temple, but only in heaven. However, he is represented in the Temple by his Name" (*The Dethronement of Sabaoth: Studies in the Shem and Kabod Theologies* [ConBOT 18; Lund: Wallin & Dalholm, 1982], 124). See also Weinfeld, *Deuteronomy and the Deuteronomic School*, 193.

[21] Weinfeld, *Deuteronomy and the Deuteronomic School*, 193.

[22] This tendency for polemical reinterpretation of the imagery of the rival paradigm is also observable in the *Kavod* tradition, which in its turn uses the symbolism of the divine voice and other aspects of the *Shem* symbolism.

[23] Weinfeld, *Deuteronomy and the Deuteronomic School*, 206.

the form but also through the sound. One mode of revelation often comes at the expense of the other—the idea hinted at in Exodus 33 and articulated more explicitly in Deut 4:12, "You heard the sound of words, but saw no form (תמונה)." Scholars point to a paradigm shift in Deuteronomy's switch of the revelatory axis from the visual to the aural plane.[24] In this new, theo-aural, as opposed to theo-phanic, understanding, even God's revelation to Moses on Mount Sinai in Exodus 19, an event marking a vital nexus of the visual anthropomorphic paradigm, becomes now reinterpreted in the terms of its aural counterpart. Deuteronomy 4:36 describes the Sinai theophany as the hearing of the divine voice: "Out of heaven he let you hear his voice, that he might discipline you; and on earth he let you see his great fire and you heard his words out of the midst of the fire." Here the revelation is received not in the form of tablets, the media that might implicitly underline the corporeality of the deity; rather "the commandments were heard from out of the midst of the fire . . . uttered by the Deity from heaven."[25] This transcendent nature of the deity's revelation that now chooses to manifest itself as the formless voice in the fire eliminates any need of its corporeal representation in the form of the anthropomorphic glory of God.

The depiction of the deity's activity and presence as the voice in the fire thus becomes one of the distinctive features of the *Shem* theology.[26] The classic example of this imagery can be found in the account of God's appearance to Elijah on Mount Horeb in 1 Kgs 19:11–13:

> He said, "Go out and stand on the mountain before the LORD, for the LORD is about to pass by." Now there was a great wind, so strong that it was splitting mountains and breaking rocks in pieces before the LORD, but the LORD was not in the wind; and after the wind an earthquake, but the LORD was not in the earthquake; and after the earthquake a fire, but the LORD was not in the fire; and after the fire a sound of sheer silence. When Elijah heard it, he wrapped his face in his mantle and went out and stood at the entrance of the cave. Then there came a voice to him that said, "What are you doing here, Elijah?"

This passage vividly recalls the description found in ch. 8 of the *Apocalypse of Abraham*, where the deity is described as "the voice of the Mighty One coming down from the heavens in a stream of fire." And although the fire is not mentioned directly in the account in 1 Kings 19, the fiery nature of the divine voice is implicitly reaffirmed through the portrayal of the seer wrapping his face in the mantle to shield himself from the dangerous nature of the encounter with the divine voice.

---

[24] Ibid., 207.

[25] Ibid.

[26] Mettinger notes that "it is not surprising that the Name of God occupies such central position in a theology in which God's words and voice receive so much emphasis" (*Dethronement of Sabaoth*, 124).

II. THE VOICE OF THE MIGHTY ONE:
THE AURAL MYSTICISM OF THE *APOCALYPSE OF ABRAHAM*

Keeping in mind the aforementioned biblical specimens relating to the *Kavod* and the *Shem* conceptual developments, we will next examine the imagery of the divine presence in the *Apocalypse of Abraham*.

The Revelation of the Divine Sound

Depictions of theophanies of the divine voice in the *Apocalypse of Abraham* reveal marked similarities to the traditions in Deuteronomic and Deuteronomistic materials.[27] Already in ch. 8, which marks a transition to the apocalyptic section of the work and narrates the patriarch's response to the divine call in the courtyard of Terah's house, the divine presence is depicted as "the voice of the Mighty One" coming down in a stream of fire.[28] This self-disclosure of God in the formless "voice" (Slav. *глас*) rather than some angelic or divine form becomes a standard description adopted by the author(s) of the apocalypse to convey manifestations of the deity.[29]

The divine voice appears continually in the narrative. More notably, in *Apoc. Ab.* 9:1 the voice of "the primordial and mighty God" commands Abraham to bring sacrifices, and in ch. 10 it appoints the angel Yahoel as a celestial guide of the exalted patriarch.

Similar to the developments in the *Kavod* tradition, the aural expression of the deity evokes veneration. The epiphany of the divine voice is repeatedly depicted as accompanied by the veneration of the seer, in a fashion that recalls the veneration of the *Kavod* in the apocalyptic visionary accounts. Thus, in the dramatic portrayal of the seer's encounter of the aural revelation of the deity in *Apoc. Ab.* 10:1-3,

---

[27] The affinities with the Deuteronomic materials can be seen also in the implicit and explicit connections between the vision of Abraham and the Deuteronomic version of Moses' Sinai encounter. In this respect David Halperin notes that the author of the *Apocalypse of Abraham* "gives us several clues that he is modeling Abraham's experience after Moses' at Sinai. The most obvious of these is his locating the experience at Mount Horeb, the name that Deuteronomy regularly uses for Sinai" (*Faces of the Chariot*, 109–10). Halperin also notices the allusion to the Deuteronomistic traditions, including the story of Elijah.

[28] *Apoc. Ab.* 8:1: "The voice (*глас*) of the Mighty One came down from heaven in a stream of fire, saying and calling, 'Abraham, Abraham!'" Kulik, *Retroverting the Slavonic Pseudepigrapha*, 16; Philonenko-Sayar and Philonenko, *L'Apocalypse d'Abraham*, 54.

[29] See, e.g., *Apoc. Ab.* 18:2 "And I heard a voice (*глас*) like the roaring of the sea, and it did not cease because of the fire." Kulik, *Retroverting the Slavonic Pseudepigrapha*, 24; Philonenko-Sayar and Philonenko, *L'Apocalypse d'Abraham*, 76.

the visionary's spirit is said to have been affrighted and his soul to have fled him—he "became like a stone (быхъ яко камыкъ), and fell down upon the earth (и падохъ [яко] ниць на земли)."³⁰

Transformational prostration of an adept during his dramatic encounter with the deity is not a novel feature and is customarily encountered in theophanic narratives as early as the book of Ezekiel, which depicts a visionary's prostration while approaching the glory of God.³¹ There is, however, a significant difference between these two mystical traditions, since in the *Apocalypse of Abraham* the visionary's prostration occurs not before the divine form but before the divine voice. Veneration of the divine sound can be found in other parts of the text where not only Abraham but also his celestial companion, Yahoel, is depicted as a worshiper of this peculiar divine manifestation:

> And while he was still speaking, behold, a fire was coming toward us round about, and a sound was in the fire like a sound of many waters, like a sound of the sea in its uproar. An angel bowed with me and worshiped (и покляче съ мною ангелъ и поклонися). (*Apoc. Ab.* 17:1–2)³²

The Singer of the Eternal One

It is important not to underestimate the figure of Abraham's celestial guide in the theological framework of the Slavonic apocalypse. Indeed, Yahoel can be seen as one of the decisive symbols for understanding the overarching theological thrust of the pseudepigraphon. The *Apocalypse of Abraham* defines him as the mediation of "my [God] ineffable name (неизрекомаго имени моего)."³³ Even apart from this explanation of the guide's spectacular office, the peculiar designation *Yahoel* (Slav. *Иаоиль*) in itself reveals unequivocally the angelic creature as the representation of the divine name. It is no coincidence that in the text, which exhibits similarities to the Deuteronomic *Shem* theology, the angelic guide of the protagonist is introduced as the Angel of the Name. Scholars have previously noted the formative role of the figure of the Angel of the Name (or the Angel of Yhwh) in the conceptual framework of the Deuteronomic and Deuteronomistic *Shem* ideologies. According to one of the hypotheses, the figure of the Angel of the Lord (or the Angel of the Divine Name) found in the book of Exodus constituted one of the conceptual roots

---

³⁰ Kulik, *Retroverting the Slavonic Pseudepigrapha*, 17; Rubinkiewicz, *L'Apocalypse d'Abraham en vieux slave*, 126; Philonenko-Sayar and Philonenko, *L'Apocalypse d'Abraham*, 58.

³¹ See also *1 Enoch* 71; *2 Enoch* 22.

³² Kulik, *Retroverting the Slavonic Pseudepigrapha*, 22; Philonenko-Sayar and Philonenko, *L'Apocalypse d'Abraham*, 72.

³³ Kulik, *Retroverting the Slavonic Pseudepigrapha*, 17; Rubinkiewicz, *L'Apocalypse d'Abraham en vieux slave*, 128; Philonenko-Sayar and Philonenko, *L'Apocalypse d'Abraham*, 58.

of the *Shem* theology. Tryggve N. D. Mettinger observes that "it appears that when the Deuteronomistic theologians chose *shem*, they seized on a term which was already connected with the idea of God's presence. Exod 23:21 tells us how God warned Israel during her wanderings in the desert to respect his angel and obey his voice, 'for my name is in him.'"[34]

Yahoel can be seen as both a manifestation and a nonmanifestation of the divine name. He is in many ways a paradoxical figure at once reaffirming the divine presence through the mediation of the Tetragrammaton and challenging its overt veneration.[35] This ambiguity in his role of mediating the divine presence is very similar to the later role, in the Merkabah tradition, of the angel Metatron, who represents not only the divine name but also the form of the deity, his *Shi^cur Qomah*.[36] In his role as a representation of the divine body, the great angel finds himself in a rather awkward position, as he becomes a stumbling block for the infamous visionary of the Talmud, Elisha b. Abuyah, who according to *b. Hag.* 15a took Metatron as the second deity in heaven, which led him to the heretical conclusion about two "powers" (ב' רשויות) in heaven. Still, in both accounts (talmudic and pseudepigraphical) the difference between the deity and his angelic manifestation is properly reaffirmed. In the *Apocalypse of Abraham*, Yahoel prevents Abraham from venerating him by putting the patriarch on his feet. In *b. Hag.* 15a the distance between the deity and his vice-regent, the angel Metatron, is reaffirmed even more radically—the supreme angel is publicly punished in front of the celestial hosts with sixty fiery lashes in order to prevent future confusions between the deity and his angelic replica. Despite these reaffirmations, the boundaries between the deity and his angelic manifestation in the form of his *Shi^cur Qomah* or the divine name do not remain entirely unambiguous. The paradoxical nature of this angelic mediation of the divine name appears to be hinted at in the *Apocalypse of Abraham* through the depiction of Yahoel delivering a prayer to the deity, a hymn that now paradoxically includes his own name, "Yahoel."[37]

Praxis of the Voice

The identification of divine manifestation with the voice or the sound in the *Apocalypse of Abraham* underlines the importance of praise as a parallel process to

---

[34] Mettinger, *Dethronement of Sabaoth*, 124–25.

[35] *Apoc. Ab.* 10:4: "he took me by my right hand and stood me on my feet." Kulik, *Retroverting the Slavonic Pseudepigrapha*, 17.

[36] On the formative influence of the Yahoel lore on the figure of Metatron, see Scholem, *Jewish Gnosticism*, 51.

[37] *Apoc. Ab.* 17:7–13: "And I recited, and he [Yahoel] himself recited the song: O, Eternal, Mighty, Holy El, God Autocrat ... Eternal, Mighty, Holy Sabaoth, Most Glorious El, El, El, El, Yahoel." Kulik, *Retroverting the Slavonic Pseudepigrapha*, 23.

the aural expression of creation in relation to its Creator. Further, the authors of the text seem to view the praising of God as a mystical praxis that in many ways mirrors the visionary praxis of the *Kavod* paradigm. Scholars have previously observed the importance of aural invocation or "calling upon" in the *Shem* paradigm that had come to function as an act of actualization of the presence of God.[38] By invoking the deity (or more precisely the divine name) in praise, the practitioner "brings" the deity into existence,[39] summoning him from nonbeing into being, thus replicating the prototypical event of creation recounted in Genesis 1, where God himself brings everything into being by invoking the divine name.[40]

Time and again the angel Yahoel poses as a faithful adept of this mystical praxis of praise. The text defines him as the Singer of the Eternal One (*Apoc. Ab.* 12:4). He is exceptional both as a practitioner and as an instructor of this "aural mysticism," conveying the teachings of the praxis to various types of God's creatures, earthly as well as celestial. In *Apoc. Ab.* 10:8–9 he is described as the celestial choirmaster of the Ḥayyot:

> I am a power in the midst of the Ineffable who put together his names in me. I am appointed according to his commandment to reconcile the rivalries of the Living Creatures of the Cherubim against one another, and teach those who bear him [to sing] the song in the middle of man's night, at the seventh hour.[41]

This role can again be compared to the future office of Metatron, who often appears in the Hekhalot and *Shiʿur Qomah* accounts as the celestial choirmaster[42] conducting the liturgies of the Living Creatures.[43]

---

[38] Mettinger, *Dethronement of Sabaoth*, 125.

[39] The process of the constitution of the angelic or divine presence or the reconstitution of a human nature into a celestial one through the invocation of the divine name can be seen in the traditions about Moses' investiture with the divine name during his Sinai experience and Jesus' investiture with the divine name at his baptism. For a detailed discussion of these traditions, see Jarl Fossum, *The Name of God and the Angel of the Lord: Samaritan and Jewish Mediation Concepts and the Origin of Gnosticism* (WUNT 36; Tübingen: Mohr Siebeck, 1985), 76–112.

[40] In the Palestinian targumic tradition (*Targum Neofiti*; *Fragmentary Targum*) the divine command יהי uttered by God during the creation of the world is identified with the Tetragrammaton. For a detailed discussion of this tradition, see Fossum, *Name of God,* 80.

[41] Kulik, *Retroverting the Slavonic Pseudepigrapha*, 18. For an extensive discussion of the passages about the rivalries of the Ḥayyot in the *Apoc. Ab.* 10:8–9 and 18:8–10, see K. William Whitney, Jr., "Two Strange Beasts. A Study of Traditions Concerning Leviathan and Behemoth in Second Temple and Early Rabbinic Judaism" (Ph.D. diss., Harvard University, 1992), 94–96.

[42] On Metatron's role as the celestial choirmaster of the Ḥayyot, see Andrei A. Orlov, "Celestial Choirmaster: The Liturgical Role of Enoch-Metatron in 2 Enoch and the Merkabah Tradition," in idem, *From Apocalypticism to Merkabah Mysticism: Studies in the Slavonic Pseudepigrapha* (JSJSup 114; Leiden: Brill, 2007), 197–221.

[43] "One *ḥayyah* rises above the seraphim and descends upon the tabernacle of the youth whose name is Metatron, and says in a great voice, a voice of sheer silence: 'The Throne of Glory is shining.' Suddenly the angels fall silent. The watchers and the holy ones become quiet. They

Yahoel's expertise in heavenly praise does not seem to be limited to heavenly matters. In the apocalypse he is also depicted as the one who initiates a human visionary, the patriarch Abraham, into this mystical praxis of praising the deity, which serves here as an alternative practice to the vision mysticism.

> And he said, "Only worship, Abraham, and recite the song which I taught you."
> ... And he said, "Recite without ceasing." And I recited, and he himself recited the song. (*Apoc. Ab.* 17:5–7).[44]

Our previous remarks about the connections between the visionary and aural praxis make it intriguing that veneration of the deity is described in the *Apocalypse of Abraham* through the paradoxical formula of seeing/not seeing: "He whom you will see (*его же узриши*) going before both of us in a great sound of *qedushah* is the Eternal One who had loved you, whom himself you will not see (*самого же не зриши*)" (*Apoc. Ab.* 16:3).[45]

This ambiguous mixture of the paradigms of vision and voice can be seen in other parts of the text as well. For example, in the depiction of Abraham's fast in 12:2, two mystical practices appear to be mixed:

> And we went, the two of us alone together, forty days and nights. And I ate no bread and drank no water, because [my] food was to see the angel who was with me, and his speech with me was my drink. (*Apoc. Ab.* 12:1–2)[46]

Here the traditional motif found in the visionary accounts—viz., the motif of nourishment through the beholding of a celestial being, often in the form of the *Kavod*, that is especially famous in the later interpretations of Moses' story where he is often depicted as a being fed through the vision of God's *Shekhinah*—is paralleled with the motif of nourishment through the voice of the heavenly being, the angel Yahoel.[47]

---

are silent, and are pushed into the river of fire. The *ḥayyot* put their faces on the ground, and this youth whose name is Metatron brings the fire of deafness and puts it into their ears so that they could not hear the sound of God's speech or the ineffable name. The youth whose name is Metatron then invokes, in seven voices, his living, pure, honored, awesome, holy, noble, strong, beloved, mighty, powerful name" (Peter Schäfer et al., *Synopse zur Hekhaloth-Literatur* [TSAJ 2; Tübingen: Mohr Siebeck, 1981] 164). Another Hekhalot passage attested in *Synopse* §385 also elaborates the liturgical role of the exalted angel: "when the youth enters below the throne of glory, God embraces him with a shining face. All the angels gather and address God as 'the great, mighty, awesome God,' and they praise God three times a day by means of the youth" (*Synopse*, 162–63). The designation of Yahoel as the Singer of the Eternal One in *Apoc. Ab.* 12:4 is also intriguing. It again recalls the description of Metatron in the aforementioned account, where he is depicted as the leading singer of the heavenly host, the one who is able to invoke the divine name in seven voices.

[44] Kulik, *Retroverting the Slavonic Pseudepigrapha*, 22–23.
[45] Ibid., 22; Philonenko-Sayar and Philonenko, *L'Apocalypse d'Abraham*, 70.
[46] Kulik, *Retroverting the Slavonic Pseudepigrapha*, 19.
[47] David Halperin notes some similarities between the celestial nourishments of Abraham and Moses. He observes that "Moses also discovered that the divine Presence is itself nourishment

Also noteworthy is that in the *Apocalypse of Abraham* the praise seems to be understood as a sort of garment that envelops the formless deity, similar to the Merkabah tradition where the divine form is enveloped in the garment known as the *Ḥaluq* (חלוק), an attribute that underlines the anthropomorphic nature of the divine "extent." In contrast, in *Apoc. Ab.* 16:2–4 the deity is enveloped in the sound of angelic praise, a description that may serve to reaffirm the bodiless presence of the deity:[48]

> And he [Yahoel] said to me, "Remain with me, do not fear! He whom you will see going before both of us in a great sound of *qedushah* is the Eternal One who had loved you, whom himself you will not see. Let your spirit not weaken <from the shouting>, since I am with you, strengthening you." (*Apoc. Ab.* 16:2–4)[49]

The importance of angelic praise is highlighted also in the depiction of the divine throne in ch. 18, which draws on the imagery found in Ezekiel 1. One of the new details there, however, is the persistent emphasis on the symbolism of vocal praxis: in their portrayals of the Living Creatures (the *Ḥayyot*) and the Wheels (the *Ophannim*), the authors accentuate their role in the praising of the deity:

> And as the fire rose up, soaring higher, I saw under the fire a throne [made] of fire and the many-eyed Wheels, and *they are reciting the song*. And under the throne [I saw] four *singing* fiery Living creatures. (*Apoc. Ab.* 18:3)[50]

Thus, instead of emphasizing the role of the *Ḥayyot* as the foundation of the throne, which in the formative account found in the book of Ezekiel holds the divine presence/form, the Slavonic apocalypse stresses the praising functions of the Living Creatures depicted as "singing the divine presence."

"No Other Power of Other Form"

The most striking detail in the description of the divine throne in ch. 18, which radically differs from the Ezekielian account, is that at the climactic moment of the seer's encounter with the divine chariot—which also curiously appears to be missing a rider—the text does not give any indications of the presence of the anthropomorphic glory of God, which in Ezek 1:26 is described as דמות כמראה אדם.

---

enough. That is why Exod 24:11 says that Moses and his companions beheld God, and ate and drank. This means, one rabbi explained, that the sight of God was food and drink to them; for Scripture also says, In the light of the King's face there is life. . . . We might assume that the author of the *Apocalypse of Abraham* had such midrashim in mind when he wrote that 'my food was to see the angel who was with me, and his speech—that was my drink'" (*Faces of the Chariot*, 111).

[48] The concept of praise as a garment seems to be connected with the tradition of the investiture with the divine name discussed earlier in our article.

[49] Kulik, *Retroverting the Slavonic Pseudepigrapha*, 22.

[50] Ibid., 24.

Instead of the Ezekielian anthropomorphic "extent," the visionary encounters the already familiar voice in the midst of fire surrounded by the sound of the qĕdûšâ:

> While I was still standing and watching, I saw behind the Living Creatures a chariot with fiery Wheels. Each Wheel was full of eyes round about. And above the Wheels there was the throne which I had seen. And I was covered with fire and the fire encircled it round about, and an indescribable light surrounded the fiery people. And I heard the sound of their *qedushah* like the voice of a single man.[51] And a voice came to me out of the midst of the fire. (*Apoc. Ab.* 18:12–19:1)[52]

Polemics with the divine body traditions is then further developed in ch. 19, which can be considered the climactic point of the anticorporeal ideology of the apocalypse. Here the seer is allowed to take a final look at the upper firmaments so that he—and, more importantly, his audience—may be assured that no divine form is present there. The account detailing this final gaze is rather lengthy:

> And he [God] said, "Look at the levels which are under the expanse on which you are brought and see that on no single level is there any other but the one whom you have searched for or who has loved you." And while he was still speaking, and behold, the levels opened, <and> there are the heavens under me. And I saw on the seventh firmament upon which I stood a fire spread out and light, and dew, and a multitude of angels, and a power of the invisible glory from the Living Creatures which I had seen above. <But> *I saw no one else there.* And I looked from the altitude of my standing to the sixth expanse. And I saw there a multitude of *incorporeal spiritual angels,* carrying out the orders of the fiery angels who were on the eighth firmament, as I was standing on its suspensions. And behold, neither on this expanse was there *any other power of other form,* but only the spiritual angels, and they are the power which I had seen on the seventh firmament. (*Apoc. Ab.* 19:3–7).[53]

Intriguingly, the text repeatedly stresses the absence of any corporeal manifestation of the deity, in one instance even using the term "form" (Slav. *образ*):[54] "and behold, neither on this expanse was there any other power of other form (*образом силы иноя*)."[55]

---

[51] Halperin noted the paradigm shift from the visual plane to the aural plane: "Ezekiel's phrase 'like the appearance of a man,' becomes, in a concluding sentence, that plainly draws on the end of Ezek 1:28, 'like the voice of a man'" (*Faces of the Chariot,* 108).

[52] Kulik, *Retroverting the Slavonic Pseudepigrapha,* 24.

[53] Ibid., 24–25.

[54] The Slavonic word *образ* can be also translated as "type," "image," "icon," or "symbol." See Izmail Sreznevskij, *Материалы для словаря древнерусского языка по письменным памятникам* [Materials for a Dictionary of Old Russian Language](3 vols.; St. Petersburg: Russian Imperial Academy of Sciences, 1883–1912), 2:539–42.

[55] Kulik, *Retroverting the Slavonic Pseudepigrapha,* 25; Philonenko-Sayar and Philonenko, *L'Apocalypse d'Abraham,* 80.

Further, the text seems to deny even the presence of angelic "bodies" on the upper firmaments, constantly referring to angelic creatures found there as "incorporeal" (*бесплотныхъ*) or "spiritual" (*духовныхъ*) angels. What is important for our ongoing inquiry is that, according to the *Apocalypse of Abraham*, it is not a manifestation of the deity but the incorporeal angels who now represent "the power" (Slav. *сила*) that the seer beholds on the seventh firmament.

The Idol of Jealousy

The polemical "clash" between the *Kavod* and *Shem* ideologies reaches eschatological proportions in ch. 25, where God allows Abraham to behold the future temple polluted by the idol of jealousy:

> I saw there *the likeness of the idol of jealousy* (*подобие идола ревнования*), as *a likeness* (*подобие*) of a craftsman's [work] such as my father made, and its stature was of shining copper, and a man before it, and he was worshiping it; and [there was] an altar opposite it and youth were slaughtered on it before the idol. And I said to him, "What is this idol, and what is the altar, and who are those being sacrificed, and who is the sacrificer, and what is the beautiful temple which I see, art and beauty of your glory that lies beneath your throne?" And he said: "Hear Abraham! This temple and altar and the beautiful things which you have seen are my image of *the sanctification of the name of my glory* (*святительства имени славы моея*), where every prayer of men will dwell, and the gathering of kings and prophets, and the sacrifice which shall establish to be made for me among my people coming from your progeny. And the stature you saw is my anger, because the people who will come to me out of you will make me angry. And the man you saw slaughtering is he who angers me. And the sacrifice is the murder of those who are for me a testimony of the close of judgment in the end of the creation. (*Apoc. Ab.* 25:1–6)[56]

This description once again provides a graphic example of the polemical interaction between the traditions of the divine glory and the divine name, where the imagery of both trends becomes closely intertwined. In this pivotal passage, the earlier motifs that the readers encountered in the first section of the pseudepigraphon dealing with the idolatrous practices of Abraham's father become explicitly invoked. The figures similar to those made in the house of Terah are now installed in God's temple. This idolatrous practice of worship to the figure of shinning copper, labeled in the story as "a likeness (*подобие*) of a craftsman's work," seems to be cautiously invoking the language of "likeness" known from the Priestly theophanic paradigm exemplified in Gen 1:26 and Ezekiel 1. The idolatrous prac-

---

[56] Kulik, *Retroverting the Slavonic Pseudepigrapha*, 29; Philonenko-Sayar and Philonenko, *L'Apocalypse d'Abraham*, 92.

tices are then contrasted to the true worship, which is described in the now-familiar language of the *Shem* tradition. Here the future eschatological temple is portrayed as a dwelling place not for the abominable shining figure but for "the image of the *sanctification of the name of my [God's] glory (святительства имени славы моея)*, where *every prayer of men will dwell (в нюже вселится всяка молба мужьска)*."[57] It is apparent that the authors try to reinterpret the technical terminology of the *Kavod* tradition, merging it with the formulae borrowed from the *Shem* ideology. There is also no doubt that the authors' attitude to the anthropomorphic ideology remains polemical, which is shown unabashedly through labeling the shining figure as the idol of jealousy.

III. CONCLUSION

As has been shown, the *Apocalypse of Abraham* offers a complex mix of the *Kavod* and *Shem* conceptual developments, in which promulgation of the theology of the divine name and the praxis of the divine voice become linked with the theophanic imagery from the Priestly source, Ezekiel, *1 Enoch,* and some other Second Temple accounts. The consequences of this polemical encounter between two important revelatory trends appear to have exercised lasting influence on both traditions. The developments found in the Slavonic apocalypse should not be interpreted simply as a rejection of anthropomorphic theism through the aural paradigm of the divine name. Rather, they should be seen as an adaptation of Merkabah imagery to the framework of this aural paradigm, which has led to the construction of a new symbolic universe[58] in which two trends can coexist.[59] This synthesis is intriguing and might provide important insights for understanding the character of later Jewish mystical developments, where the traditions about the divine form and the divine name appear to undergo creative conflation. As has been mentioned, the protagonist of the later Hekhalot and *Shiʿur Qomah* accounts, the supreme angel Metatron, is often depicted in these materials as the celestial choirmaster, who instructs the Living Creatures on fitting ways of praising the deity. These later mystical traditions also portray him as יהוה הקטן,[60] the lesser manifestation of the

---

[57] Philonenko-Sayar and Philonenko, *L'Apocalypse d'Abraham*, 92.

[58] This new symbolic universe manifests itself, for example, in the depiction of the throne room with its paradoxical imagery reflecting the visual and the aural traditions.

[59] The synthetic nature of adaptations taking place in the Slavonic pseudepigraphon has been noticed previously by other scholars. Thus, John Collins observes that the *Apocalypse of Abraham* "belongs to the same general period as *4 Ezra* and *2 Baruch* and shares some of their concerns about theodicy. In place of the Deuteronomic tradition, which informs these books, however, the mystical tendency of the early Enoch books is taken up here" (*Apocalyptic Imagination*, 225).

[60] On Metatron's title יהוה הקטן, see Andrei A. Orlov, *The Enoch-Metatron Tradition* (TSAJ 107; Tübingen: Mohr Siebeck, 2005), 136–43.

divine name, the office that is reminiscent of the roles of Yahoel in the *Apocalypse of Abraham*.[61]

These later conceptual developments bring to mind Gershom Scholem's hypothesis about the existence of two streams that in his opinion constituted the background of the Metatron figure: one connected with Yahoel's figure and the other with the figure of the seventh antediluvian patriarch, Enoch.[62] The roles and offices of these two apocalyptic heroes, who can in many ways be seen as exemplars of the revelatory paradigms of the divine form and the divine voice, later became reconciled in the figure of the chief protagonist of the Merkabah lore. In view of these important developments attesting to the afterlife of the *Shem* and the *Kavod* trends in the later Hekhalot mysticism, the changes that take place in the *Apocalypse of Abraham* should not be underestimated. It is possible that the Slavonic apocalypse, in which the mystical praxis of the divine name was unfolded amid the familiar Merkabah imagery, can be seen as an important conceptual nexus where the traditions of the divine name become polemically engaged with the visionary Merkabah paradigm, thus anticipating the process of the gradual unification of both conceptual streams in the later Jewish mystical lore.[63]

---

[61] Collins notes that "in all, Jaoel bears striking resemblance to Metatron in Hekhalot literature. Metatron is 'the little Yahweh' (*3 En.* 12), whose name is like the name of God himself (*b. Sanh.* 38b)" (*Apocalyptic Imagination*, 228).

[62] The classic study by Gershom Scholem differentiates between two basic aspects of Metatron's lore that, in his opinion, were combined in rabbinic and Hekhalot literature. These aspects include the Enochic lore and the lore connected with the exalted figures of Yahoel and Michael. Scholem writes that "one aspect identifies Metatron with Jahoel or Michael and knows nothing of his transfiguration from a human being into an angel. The talmudic passages concerned with Metatron are of this type. The other aspect identifies Metatron with the figure of Enoch as he is depicted in apocalyptic literature.... When the *Book of Hekhaloth*, or *3 Enoch*, was composed, the two aspects had already become intertwined" (*Jewish Gnosticism*, 51).

[63] Kulik observes that the *Apocalypse of Abraham* can be seen as "representative of a missing link between early apocalyptic and medieval Hekhalot traditions" (*Retroverting the Slavonic Pseudepigrapha*, 1).

Job's Wives in the *Testament of Job*: A Note on the Synthesis of Two Traditions

MICHAEL C. LEGASPI
mlegaspi@creighton.edu
Creighton University, Omaha, NE 68178

When it comes to biblical heroes, biographical details fall into two categories. On the one hand, there are the few details provided explicitly in the biblical text. On the other hand, there are the many facts, episodes, and events that may be deduced from those few explicit details. In the case of Job, his biography is essential to his significance in biblical and subsequent religious tradition. That is, it is his life story *taken as a whole* that matters—and not merely his role or words in this or that affair (as with many judges and prophets, for example). With Job, then, the interest in biographical details would seem to be that much keener. One especially important yet under-reported figure is Job's wife. She appears briefly in Job 2:9 only to pose one question ("Are you still holding on to your integrity?") and to offer one bit of advice ("Curse God and die.").[1] Moreover, the presence of a wife (where one might expect her) among Job's second family in Job 42:12–17 is never indicated and is, at most, only implied. As a response to this paucity of information, a number of interpretive traditions grew up around the figures of Job and Job's wife.

There were, among ancient interpreters, two rather divergent traditions about the identity of Job's wife. One tradition—known from rabbinic commentary, the *Targum of Job*, and Pseudo-Philo—identifies the wife of Job with Dinah, the daughter of Jacob. A second tradition, witnessed principally in the Septuagint, identifies Job's wife with a wretched Arabian woman. The author of the *Testament of Job*, a Jewish composition from the first century B.C.E. or C.E., creatively combined both traditions in an attempt to offer a clearer understanding of Job's background, to provide a solution to lingering questions concerning his relation to ethnic Israel, and to elaborate on themes in the book of Job in a way that vindicates the role of women in Job's own moral athleticism.

---

[1] Literally, "bless God and die." The command to "bless God," instead of being a euphemism for cursing God, as most English translations suggest, may amount to a suggestion from Job's wife that Job bid farewell (i.e., "bless God") and accept his fate ("die").

71

I. Dinah, Wife of Job

What, ultimately, was the fate of Dinah, the daughter of Jacob? After the story of her encounter with Shechem ben Hamor and the subsequent destruction of all the males in the city of Shechem (Genesis 34), Dinah is not heard from again. Unlike her twelve brothers, whose life and times dominate the rest of Genesis and whose fortunes are foretold by Jacob in a dramatic deathbed scene (Genesis 49), Dinah disappears from the biblical text.[2] The question of Dinah's fate is only made keener by the fact that her well-being and prosperity after the Shechem incident cannot be assumed: as a "defiled" woman (Gen 34:13), Dinah's marital prospects must have seemed rather grim.[3] One rabbi, in addressing this question, puts the words of David's daughter Tamar in the mouth of Dinah ("Where will I carry my shame?" [2 Sam 13:13]) and posits that Simeon, in response to this cry of despair, married Dinah. Their offspring, Shaul, was then referred to as the son of a "Canaanite woman" (Gen 46:10) because Dinah had been defiled by a Canaanite.[4] A rather different, though not incompatible, outcome was envisioned by those interested in the identity of Joseph's wife, Asenath. Victor Aptowitzer has analyzed a complex of later traditions (fourth century C.E.) that make Dinah the mother of Asenath.[5] According to Aptowitzer, because Asenath was an Egyptian and the daughter of a "heathen priest," her distinguished place in biblical tradition had to be explained; one solution was to demonstrate that she was actually a descendant of Jacob.[6] Thus, many rabbinic sources claim that Asenath was the divinely protected offspring of Dinah and Shechem.

A third tradition, and the one most relevant here, is that Job married Dinah. We find a clear witness to this tradition in the *Targum of Job*. In its rendering of Job 2:9, the targum reads: "And Dinah his wife said to him, 'Are you steadfast in your integrity until now? Curse [lit., "bless"] the word of the Lord and die.'"[7] A more

---

[2] Dinah's name is mentioned in a genealogical notice in Gen 46:15.

[3] From the perspective of the biblical narrative, it is anachronistic to suggest that later laws concerning premarital sex (Exod 22:16–17) or intermarriage with foreigners (Deut 7:1–5) might in some way render Dinah's future precarious, but it is altogether reasonable to suggest that such laws informed early interpreters' perspectives on the story of Dinah. Thus, her future, from their vantage point, must have seemed uncertain.

[4] *Gen. Rab.* 80:11, trans. H. Freedman (*Midrash Rabbah* [ed. H. Freedman and Maurice Simon; London: Soncino, 1961], 743–44).

[5] Victor Aptowitzer, "Asenath, the Wife of Joseph: A Haggadic Literary-Historical Study," *HUCA* 1 (1924): 239–306.

[6] Ibid., 239, 242–43.

[7] David M. Stec has produced a critical edition of the text: *The Text of the Targum of Job: An Introduction and Critical Edition* (AGJU 20; Leiden: Brill, 1994). The English translation is my own.

emphatic witness to the "Dinah, wife of Job" tradition can be found in the first-century C.E. work *Liber antiquitatum biblicarum* of Pseudo-Philo. There we read:

> And Jacob dwelt in the land of Canaan, and Shechem the son of Hamor the Hurrite raped Dinah his daughter and humiliated her. And the sons of Jacob, Simeon and Levi, went in and killed the whole city of them by the sword; and they took their sister Dinah and went away from there. And afterward Job took her as a wife and fathered from her fourteen sons and six daughters; that is, seven sons and three daughters before he was struck down with suffering, and afterward seven sons and three daughters when he was healed. . . . And such as had been the names of the former, so were those of the latter. (*L.A.B.* 8:7–8)[8]

The passage is interesting in at least two ways. First, the author appears to have responded to the open-ended biblical description of Simeon and Levi's action ("They took their sister Dinah and went away from there" [Gen 34:26]) by supplying a destination: they took their unmarriageable sister to Job, a Gentile. In this way, then, the author addresses two concerns: the marital prospects of a defiled Dinah (have her marry exogamously) and the need to locate the figure of Job in Israelite history (have him marry into the family of Israel). Second, the author takes great pains to show in no uncertain terms that Dinah was Job's *only* wife. The careful enumeration of children, both before and after Job's ordeal, and the explicit reference to the reuse of names show an unmistakable effort to make Dinah, in terms of the book of Job, both the wife of the prologue (chs. 1–2) and the wife of the epilogue (42:7–17).

Thus, the author Pseudo-Philo presents a distinct version of the "Dinah, wife of Job" tradition—the version that asserts simply that Dinah was the wife of Job. Period. This rather flat identification of Dinah with the wife of Job was, as we will see, either unsatisfactory to other interpreters or inconsistent with other traditions about Job. Nevertheless, it still remains to ask how or why Dinah came to be associated with Job at all. Needless to say, these two figures are connected nowhere in the biblical text. The place to begin, as adumbrated above, is with the great desire on the part of early interpreters to locate Job in the history of Israel and, more specifically, in the time of the patriarchs.[9] But, given such a desire, why forge a substantive connection with *Dinah*? One interpretive concern, connected with the uncertain fate of Dinah herself, was for Dinah's marital prospects and, more generally, for her career as a biblical luminary. The marriage to Job addressed this by connecting her to a prominent yet pious Gentile. More than this, though, the asso-

---

[8] Daniel J. Harrington, "Pseudo-Philo," *OTP* 2:314.

[9] Although the rabbis speculated on many different time periods for Job (see, e.g., *b. B. Bat.* 15b), the *Targum of Job,* Pseudo-Philo, the *Testament of Job,* and the LXX all point to the time of the patriarchs. Moreover, Louis Ginzberg states that the older traditions about Job did indeed consider "him a contemporary of the patriarchs" and "in friendly relations toward them" (*The Legends of the Jews* [7 vols.; Philadelphia: Jewish Publication Society, 1968], 5:382 n. 3).

ciation of Job with Dinah may have something to do with a common Hebrew root in the story of Dinah and Shechem (Genesis 34) and in the prologue of Job (2:9):

> Some say that Job lived in the time of Jacob and married Dinah the daughter of Jacob. [The proof is that] it is written here [in the book of Job], *Thou speakest as one of the impious women* [נבלת] *speaketh* [Job 2:9], and it is written in another place [in connection with Dinah], *Because he had wrought folly* [נבלה] *in Israel* [Gen 34:7]. (*b. B. Bat.* 15b)[10]

Thus, these two occurrences of the root נבל served as a possible exegetical peg on which to hang the association between Job and Dinah—an association that early interpreters, for reasons we have suggested, were otherwise eager to make.

II. The Arabian Wife of Job Formerly Known as Jobab

There is a second tradition about the identity of Job's wife, which is witnessed principally in the Septuagint. According to this tradition, Job was an Edomite king named Jobab, and his wife was an Arabian woman.[11] The fullest explication of this tradition is witnessed in the LXX translation of Job. As is well known, the LXX version of Job is one-sixth shorter than the MT, but it is decidedly more expansive than the MT in two crucial places: in 2:9, where it supplies a fuller version of the speech of Job's wife (LXX 2:9a–e), and at the end of the book, where it supplies a colophon (LXX 42:17a–e). While the speech in 2:9 will figure importantly in later discussion, it is the latter passage that is relevant here:

> It is explained in the Syriac book that he, living in the land of Ausis on the borders of Edom and Arabia, once bore the name Jobab. He took an Arabian wife who bore a son named Ennon. His own father, though, was Zare, one of the sons of Esau, and his mother was Bosorra, such that [Job] was the fifth from Abraham. (LXX 42:17b–c)[12]

Though the Greek translator has rendered the place name Bozrah as a woman's name, Bosorra, it is clear that the source of the tradition is the Edomite king list in Gen 36:31–39 ("Jobab son of Zerah of Bozrah" [v. 33]). Again, Job is placed in the time of the patriarchs. Moreover, the similarity in the two names and the biblical tradition of renaming appear to have provided additional support for the Job-Jobab connection.[13]

---

[10] Trans. I. Epstein (London: Soncino, 1935), 75–76.

[11] This tradition is also attested in *T. Job* 1:1 ("Job, the one called Jobab") and in a fragment of Aristeas's work *Of the Jews*, which is preserved in the *Praeparatio Evangelica* of Eusebius (9.25.1–4: "Jobab, the one called Job").

[12] I have translated here the text of Alfred Rahlfs, *Septuaginta* (Stuttgart: Württembergische Bibelanstalt, 1935).

[13] Irving Jacobs suggests that the motif of "name change for converts," based on such bibli-

Most interesting, though, is the description of Job's wife as an Arabian woman. Given the fact that, unlike *Tg. Job* 2:9, LXX 2:9 does not supply the name of Job's wife and that the only other reference to her is as an unnamed "Arabian woman" (LXX 42:17c), it would seem that the Greek translator knows nothing of the "Dinah, wife of Job" tradition. But just as the Greek sources (Aristeas and LXX) do not appear to know the Dinah tradition, the rabbinic sources and targum that name Dinah do not appear to know the Job-Jobab tradition. Louis Ginzberg, however, includes the Job-Jobab tradition in his *Legends of the Jews*, thus creating the impression that this tradition was more widely known among Jewish interpreters.[14] Nevertheless, it is clear from the corresponding note that his sources for the tradition are merely the ones we have indicated (Aristeas, LXX).[15] It is only the *Testament of Job* that brings the "Dinah, wife of Job" and "Job-Jobab" traditions together.

III. Job and His Wives in the *Testament of Job*

How and why did the author of the *Testament of Job* bring the two traditions together? A brief summary of the *Testament* is in order. Gathering his family to himself while on his deathbed, Job offers counsel to his children and divides the inheritance. He also reviews the ordeal for which he is famous. In this retelling, Job's sufferings are brought on by Satan, who was retaliating against Job for destroying an idolatrous temple. The *Testament of Job* characterizes Job as the supreme moral athlete, the very embodiment of ὑπομονή ("endurance, patience"), who withstands Satan's provocations and, remaining steadfast, ultimately outlasts him. Job's wife, identified as a woman named Sitis, undergoes a parallel ordeal of her own, and Job's friends come to lament Job and question his sanity—but these things do not distract Job from his steadfast hope in the heavenly realm. He is restored, sees to his children's inheritance (including magical cords for his daughters), dies, and ascends (but not bodily) to heaven.

The *Testament of Job* opens with the following details:

---

cal examples as Abraham, "may have gained wide currency in the hellenistic-Jewish world" ("Literary Motifs in the Testament of Job," *JJS* 21 [1970]: 8). In Job's case the name change would have signaled a movement from "duality" (בב in יובב) to "monotheism" (initial א in איוב = the number 1) (p. 9 n. 36a).

[14] Ginzberg, *Legends of the Jews*, 2:231.

[15] Ibid., 5:384 n. 14. Additional support for the fact that rabbinic and proto-rabbinic sources were ignorant of (or avoided) the Job-Jobab tradition comes from *Gen. Rab.* 83:3. Here the precise verse that forms the basis of the Job-Jobab tradition ("and Jobab the son of Zerah of Bozrah reigned in his stead" [Gen 36:33]) is the subject of rabbinic commentary. Not only is there no mention of Job here, but the Edomite kings are seen principally from the perspective of a prophetic promise of judgment on Edom (see Isa 34:6). Clearly, the strong anti-Edomite sentiment expressed by the rabbis would have rendered the attempt to make Job an Edomite unlikely.

> The book of Job, the one called Jobab ... I, your father Job, am engaged in steadfastness, but you are a chosen and honored race from the seed of Jacob, your mother's father. I am from the sons of Esau, brother of Jacob, but your mother is Dinah, from whom I begot you. My former wife died a bitter death along with the other ten children. (1:1, 5–6)[16]

First, it must be said that the *Testament of Job* is clearly dependent on LXX Job.[17] Thus, it is hardly surprising that the author of the *Testament* would have known and used the Job-Jobab tradition from LXX 42:17a–e as he did. What is remarkable is his use of the Dinah tradition, since it seems to stand outside the scope of LXX traditions, and since there is, on the face of it, little to commend an exegetical link between Dinah and this Edomite king. The adoption of the Dinah tradition becomes even more interesting (and more unlikely) when one considers that the author of the *Testament of Job* knew and used a traditional speech that was already built into the LXX portrayal of Job's wife in LXX 2:9a–e:

> After a long time his wife said to him, "How long will you hold out, saying, 'Look, I will remain a little while longer, awaiting the hope of my salvation.' Well, your memory is already blotted from the earth. Your sons and daughters, the pains and labors of my womb—I toiled to raise them for nothing. Yet you yourself sit there among the rottenness of worms, spending the night in the open air, while I roam as a wandering worker, from house to house, awaiting sunset so that I may rest from the toils and pains which now oppress me. Come on, say some word against the Lord and die." (text from Rahlfs; my translation)

The traditions reflected in the LXX version of Job provide a fairly full portrait of Job's wife: she was an Arabian woman and an Edomite queen (LXX 42:17b–c) who hired herself out after Job's fall in order to provide for both of them (LXX 2:9a–e); hence, her cry of fatigue and exasperation ("How long will you hold out? ... say some word against the Lord and die." LXX 2:9d). The *Testament of Job* accepts and uses this portrait of Job's wife and, indeed, elaborates on it further by providing her with a name (Sitis) and describing how she begged and labored as a slave for many years in order to provide bread for Job and herself. As the *Testament* relates, Sitis

---

[16] I have translated here the critical text of Robert A. Kraft, Harold Attridge, Russell Spittler, and Janet Timbie (*The Testament of Job According to the SV Text* [SBLTT 5; Pseudepigrapha Series 4; Missoula, MT: Scholars Press, 1974]). I have chosen (with manuscript P) to read "Esau, brother of Jacob" rather than "Esau, brother of Nahor."

[17] In the introduction to his translation of the *Testament*, Russell Spittler summarizes: "Reliance of the testament on the Septuagint is clear. ... As yet unresolved is the complicated problem of the textual relations between the several Greek manuscripts of the Testament of Job and the textual growth of the Septuagint Book of Job" ("Testament of Job, A New Translation and Introduction," *OTP* 1:831). Another translator of the *Testament of Job*, Marc Philonenko, states plainly: "La version grecque du livre de *Job* est la source essentielle du *Testament de Job*. C'est cette version que l'auteur du *Testament* cite constamment et c'est à elle qu'il fait sans cesse allusion" ("Le Testament de Job: Introduction, traduction, et notes," *Sem* 18 [1968]: 10).

grew exhausted, sold her hair to Satan in exchange for bread, and, misled by Satan, told Job to give up his struggle. In the end, though, the *Testament of Job* describes Sitis's final vindication: she is granted a vision of her children crowned with splendor in heaven (*T. Job* 39–40) before she dies peacefully and is buried near her old house.

All of this, of course, has nothing to do with Dinah. Recall the flat identification of Dinah with the wife of Job that was attested in *Tg. Job* 2:9. Recall also that Pseudo-Philo took great pains to show that Dinah was the *only* wife of Job. The author of the *Testament of Job* knows these motifs and has great use for the "Dinah, wife of Job" tradition, as we will see, but he is also dependent on a rather different body of tradition about the wife of Job, the one attested in the LXX. The key move in the *Testament*, then, is the joining of both traditions, the Dinah tradition and the Sitis tradition. In order to reconcile the two, the author of the *Testament* proposes a creative and perhaps unique solution: he makes Dinah the *second* wife of Job.[18]

The MT does not give any indication that Job had two wives. It does not mention a wife at all in ch. 42, let alone whether the mother of the new children in Job 42:13 is to be identified with the wife of 2:9. At the same time, nothing in the biblical text precludes Job's having two wives. The author of the *Testament of Job* exploits precisely this possibility and is thus able to incorporate and utilize two separate traditions about Job's wife.

While the linking of such venerable traditions might be, for the early interpreter, a desirable thing in itself, it still remains to ask in what way the new "Dinah, second wife of Job" motif was especially useful. I believe that it solves a number of difficulties related to the book of Job and the earlier "Dinah, wife of Job" tradition. First, it saves Dinah embarrassment. She is neither the acrimonious, disloyal wife of MT 2:9 nor the exasperated, humiliated (but far more sympathetic) wife of LXX 2:9a–e. Neither characterization would seem to sit well with the only daughter of an esteemed patriarch.[19] The identification of Dinah as Job's second wife may also clarify two remarkable details from the epilogue of the book: the extraordinary beauty of Job's daughters and their unusual inheritance alongside their brothers. With regard to the former it seems that there might be another, submerged exegetical motif, "Dinah, the beautiful."[20] That is, Dinah became the object of Shechem's

---

[18] I have not come across any texts apart from the *Testament of Job* that explicitly identify Dinah as Job's *second* wife.

[19] The rabbis, however, appear to be divided over the issue of how pious Dinah really was. In *Gen. Rab.* 80:1 and 80:5, we find the view that Dinah's "going out" (Gen 34:1) had distinctly immoral overtones. Yet in 80:4, Rabbi Huna seems to view Dinah as a kind of missionary who converted Job.

[20] This is apparently the basis for the comment of Rabbi Berekiah in *Gen. Rab.* 80:5: Dinah's going out "may be compared to one who was holding a pound of meat in his hand, and as soon as he exposed it a bird swooped down and snatched it away."

desire because she was especially beautiful, and this helps explain the legendary beauty of Job's daughters in Job 42:15.

As for the unusual inheritance, it would seem that in chs. 46–53 the author of the *Testament of Job* has a rather different program for the explanation of the daughters' inheritance, identifying it with magical cords that enable angelic glossolalia and turn the heart toward heavenly things rather than with conventional property or land.[21] The Joban example of female inheritance when male heirs are available (Job 42:15) is unique in the Hebrew Bible. Perhaps, then, something like the redemption of Dinah is in view: she who was deprived of her marital rights (ויענה [Gen 34:2]) lives to see her own daughters blessed beyond all reasonable expectation.[22] Thus, the blessedness of Job's later life comes to include not only his own hyper-restoration but, fittingly, that of his wife as well.

By marrying Dinah, Job receives what is believed by the author of the *Testament* to be an inestimably valuable reward: he and his children are joined to the "chosen and honored" race, the Jews (*T. Job* 1:5). Job has proved his worthiness to join the Jews, and his marriage to Dinah is the way that his entrance into the covenant community is realized. The revision of the older "Dinah, wife of Job" motif thus permits an ethnic and religious contextualization of Job's ὑπομονή. Having distilled the moral content of the book of Job into a single virtue, ὑπομονή, the *Testament of Job* shows precisely what kind of ὑπομονή is worthy of emulation. In the *Testament*, endurance reinforces and sustains monotheistic zeal; more specifically, it has become the willingness to suffer persecution. This is clear in the *Testament*'s recasting of the Joban ordeal as a divinely sanctioned test that Job is made to undergo when Satan demands permission to get back at Job for destroying an idolatrous temple. If any biblical figure might have been taken for a non-Israelite moral exemplar, it is Job. The biblical book of Job makes no reference to Israel, Sinai, or Zion; it bears no apparent connection to essential Israelite religious traditions such as the Passover or the exodus. Yet the figure of Job, understood in the Hellenistic context of the *Testament of Job*, is not permitted to remain a model of generic ὑπομονή: Job suffers for righteous belief in the one God. Moreover, Job's ὑπομονή culminates in his second marriage to Dinah. The natural fulfillment of his earlier, pre-ordeal opposition to idolatry and of his heroic endurance, then, is

---

[21] Peter Machinist argues that the treatment of female inheritance in the *Testament of Job* is designed to "satisfy the dominant Biblical rule for male inheritance of the father's estate" while "satisfy[ing] the text of the Biblical book of Job that the daughters get an inheritance.... [S]ince these cords are of *heavenly* origin, they do not interfere with the worldly distribution" ("Job's Daughters and Their Inheritance in the Testament of Job and Its Biblical Congeners," in *The Echoes of Many Texts: Reflections on Jewish and Christian Traditions; Essays in Honor of Lou H. Silberman* [ed. William G. Dever and J. Edward Wright; BJS 313; Atlanta: Scholars Press, 1997], 76).

[22] ענה, when used in the *piel* to indicate sexual coercion, can refer more specifically to acts that render the victimized woman socially unfit for marriage (Deut 21:14; 22:29; 2 Sam 13:12, 14, 22, 32).

his incorporation into the "chosen and honored race" of the Jews. The telos of his ordeal is covenantal inclusion.

Finally, the "Dinah, second wife of Job" motif allows the author of the *Testament of Job* to develop useful characterizations of the women in Job's life. Both the dramatization of Sitis's plight and the hyper-restoration of Dinah are based on earlier textual traditions and exegetical motifs. In the pages of the *Testament,* they become the basis for an inclusive vision of piety, one that honors the moral athleticism of Job's wives. The "Dinah, second wife of Job" motif opened the way for the author of the *Testament* to develop the story of Job's first wife, Sitis. The elaboration of the story of Sitis, unlike that of Dinah, does not appear to address exegetical concerns in the epilogue of the book of Job. Rather, the story of her encounter with Satan, her begging for bread, and the shaving of her head simply reflects elements of the speech in LXX 2:9a–e. For example, as Pieter van der Horst has suggested, her very name may come from the Greek word σῖτος ("wheat," "bread") since the fall of Job necessitated her "roaming as a wandering worker" (LXX 2:9d) for their bread.[23] Many other details of *T. Job* 21–26 can, in a similar way, be connected with this speech. If the author of the *Testament* has used LXX 2:9a–e to develop the story of Sitis, he does not appear to have used the other LXX tradition about her, namely, her identity as an Arabian woman (LXX 42:17c). Nevertheless, the Arabian woman tradition, murky as it is, seems to have been just substantial enough to make the two-wives scheme possible. If it is taken seriously, it rules out the possibility that Dinah was the first wife. And if the "Dinah, wife of Job" tradition is jointly imported, it is only a small step to posit two wives rather than one.

A distinct progression is evident. The wife of Job in the MT is a nameless and bitter companion whose primary significance is to *intensify* the suffering of Job and throw his ὑπομονή into dramatic relief. The LXX offers a slightly more positive characterization: Job's wife is at least acknowledged as a sufferer in her own right. But in the *Testament of Job,* she becomes a full (though flawed) heroine: she receives a name, and her suffering becomes explicitly redemptive. Both she and her children reach heavenly glory. By making Dinah Job's *second* wife, the *Testament of Job* also draws on an earlier tradition that vindicates the ὑπομονή of Dinah herself. She who was violated and disgraced by Shechem did not, as the MT suggests, simply acquiesce and disappear from the scene; rather, Dinah survives her humiliation and perseveres. She goes on to marry Job and comes, eventually, to share in the restoration of his latter days, which—all sources agree—were even more blessed than the first.

---

[23] Pieter W. van der Horst, "Images of Women in the Testament of Job," in *Studies on the Testament of Job* (ed. Michael A. Knibb and Pieter W. van der Horst; SNTSMS 66; Cambridge: Cambridge University Press, 1989), 97.

A Neglected Rabbinic Parallel to the Sermon on the Mount (Matthew 6:22–23; Luke 11:34–36)

SINAI (TAMAS) TURAN
turan.st@gmail.com
Center of Jewish Studies at the Hungarian Academy of Sciences,
The Hebrew University, Jerusalem, Israel

One of the most difficult sayings in the Sermon on the Mount is the one about the light and the body (Matt 6:22–23):

> (22a) The lamp of the body is the eye. (22b) If, then, your eye is healthy/good, your whole body will be full of light. (23a) If, however, your eye is sick/evil, your whole body will be dark. (23b) If, therefore, the light which is in you is darkness —what darkness![1]

The ancient rabbinic parallel that I will present here is a partial one, a "loose" one. It does not solve the exegetical problems of the Gospel passage, nor does it challenge the main lines of its interpretation offered by NT scholarship—and yet it may help to illuminate the origins and nature of the imagery in this saying.

I

In *b. Ta'an.* 24a we read the following story:

> Once the House of the Patriarch ordained a fast and no rain fell. Thereupon Oshaiah the Younger, a colleague of the scholars, taught them: "If it was done

[1] The translation is taken from Hans Dieter Betz, *The Sermon on the Mount: A Commentary on the Sermon on the Mount, Including the Sermon on the Plain (Matthew 5:3–7:27 and Luke 6:20–49)* (Hermeneia; Minneapolis: Fortress, 1995), 437. Compare the parallel in Luke 11:34–36. Most of what I am going to say about this saying pertains to the Lukan parallel as well, so for the sake of brevity I will use the term "Sermon-saying" in an expanded way, including the Lukan parallel, unless specified otherwise. The translations of rabbinic texts are my own.

unwittingly, being hidden from the eyes of the assembly . . .'" (Num 15:24)—this can be compared to a bride who lives in her father's home. As long as her eyes are attractive, her body requires no examination; should, however, her eyes be ill-shaped, then her body requires examination. Thereupon the servants (of the Patriarch) came, put a scarf around his neck and started choking him. The people of the city cried out: Leave him alone; he insults us also, but since we see that whatever he does is for the sake of Heaven, we say nothing to him and we leave him alone—so you too leave him alone."[2]

The story reports an incident that happened, apparently, in Palestine. The identity of Oshaiah cannot be established with certainty; it is very likely, however, that he lived in the third century C.E.[3] Communal fasts, along with prayers and related rituals, were regularly held in times of drought, in order to urge the heavens to give rain.[4] Oshaiah makes a biting remark on the failed efforts of the Jewish patriarch's people (or of the patriarch, the "*Nasi*," himself) to bring rain, effectively saying that "the fish rots from the head."[5] The incident must be understood against the backdrop of the decline of patriarchal authority and the growing tensions between the patriarchal circles and the "sages."[6]

An important piece of information gets lost in the translation, almost unavoidably. Oshaiah's saying is introduced by the technical term תני ("he taught"), apparently indicating that all of what he says is a citation of an older, tannaitic source. In other words, his remark is presented as a tradition formulated in, or coming from, the first–second centuries C.E. approximately.[7] Some chronological uncertainties

---

[2] The translation follows the standard Vilna edition of the Babylonian Talmud, which reads: דבי נשיאה גזר תעניתא ולא אתא מטרא תני להו הושעיא זעירא דמן חבריא "והיה אם מעיני העדה נעשתה לשגגה" משל לכלה שהיא בבית אביה כל זמן שעיניה יפות אין כל גופה צריכה בדיקה עיניה טרוטות כל גופה צריכה בדיקה. אתו עבדי ורמו ליה אצוארריה סודרא וקא מצערין ליה אמרי להו בני מתא שבקוה דהא נמי מצער לן וכד חזינן דכל מילה דעביד לשום שמים עביד לא אמרינן ליה ולא מידי ושבקינן ליה אתון נמי שבקוה. For significant variant readings, see nn. 10, 20, 23 below.

[3] He is usually identified as a disciple of R. Yohanan; see Wilhelm Bacher, *Die Agada der palästinensischen Amoräer* (Strassburg: Trübner, 1899), 565; Hanoch Albeck, however, classes him among those whose chronology cannot be established beyond doubt (*Introduction to Talmudic Literature* [in Hebrew; Tel-Aviv: Dvir, 1969], 612). My translation follows Bacher's clarification of the term דמן חבריא (p. 551; cf. also Rashi's comment, ad loc., s.v., זעירא דמן חבריא).

[4] *M. Ta'an.*1:4–3:9; Str-B 4:82–87.

[5] This proverb is well attested in European and Near Eastern folklore, particularly in Mediterranean Jewish folklore; see Shirley L. Arora, "On the Importance of Rotting Fish: A Proverb and Its Audience," *Western Folklore* 48 (1989): 271–88, esp. 273–79.

[6] See Lee I. Levine, *The Rabbinic Class of Roman Palestine in Late Antiquity* (Jerusalem: Yad Ben-Zvi, 1989), 189; see also 122. For "choking/tormenting with a scarf," see *b. 'Abod. Zar.* 4a, where the same expression is used.

[7] The saying itself is cited in Hebrew (as tannaitic traditions generally are), clearly demarcated from the rest of the story, which is in Aramaic. A list of *baraithot* cited by Oshaiah in talmudic literature (all the others are introduced by תני) can be found in Michael Higger, *Otzar ha-baraithot* (in Hebrew; New York: De-bei Rabbanan, 1940), 3:360–62.

notwithstanding, I see no reason, textual or other, to doubt the basic historicity of the story or the tannaitic origins of the homily and—in particular—of the bride maxim.[8]

It is not so much the historical setting of Oshaiah's dictum that concerns us here as the simile he used. It is based on the notion of the eyes as primary markers of one's physical condition—as far as a bride is concerned. This notion can be properly seen as a physiognomic one. One has to bear in mind that, in ancient Jewish marriage law, certain bodily defects of the woman, unknown to the husband at the time of the betrothal or the marriage, had major legal implications.[9] The checking of certain bodily traits prior to marriage—by third parties—is mentioned in the early sources. *M. Ketub.* 7:8 discusses the preconditions necessary for the bridegroom/husband to make claims related to bodily defects of the bride/wife:

> The sages, however, say, that (such claims can be made) only in the case of defects on hidden (parts of the body); but in the case of defects on exposed (parts of the body), he can not make claims. And if there is a bath-house in that town, he can not make claims even about hidden defects, since he (is assumed to have had) examined her by his women relatives.

The role assigned to the eyes of the bride in Oshaiah's simile, therefore, is neither to indicate her overall state of health (as a sort of ancient "iridology") nor to reveal aesthetic qualities of her bodily shape, but primarily, it seems, to mark bodily defects.[10]

---

[8] One may think that Oshaiah (or some later "editor") presents this homily as a *baraitha*, "antedating" it and vesting it with added authority in order to mitigate the sharp and personal mark of the censure. I do not think that such a possibility in itself is sufficient to raise doubts about the tannaitic origins of the homily.

[9] See *m. Ketub.* 7:7 (= *m. Qidd.* 2:5); 7:8; *t. Ketub.* 7:8–10 (and Saul Lieberman, *Tosefta ki-Fshutah*, Pt. 6 [New York: Jewish Theological Seminary, 1967], 294–302, esp. 296 n. 55); *y. Ketub.* 7:9 (31c-d); *b. Ketub.* 75a–77a; see also *b. Qidd.* 41a. As stated explicitly in these sources, the blemishes involved in these laws are closely related to defects disqualifying priests from serving in the temple—which, in turn, are closely related to blemishes of animals that prevent them from being sacrificed (*m. Bek.* 7:1). The key term "blemish" (מום) itself, in these sources, belongs to sacrificial vocabulary; see Jacob Milgrom, *Leviticus 17–22: A New Translation with Introduction and Commentary* (AB 3A; New York: Doubleday, 2000), 1821–24, 1841–43.

[10] In *b. Taʿan.* 24a (cited above), "this can be compared to a bride *who lives in the house of her father*"; the words in italics here appear only in the sixteenth- or seventeenth-century Yemenite manuscript MS Yad Harav Herzog (in Jerusalem), in the earliest printed edition (Pesaro, 1516) and subsequent editions. This clause makes clear the connection with the context of *m. Ketub.*, where this distinction—whether she still lives (as a bride) in the parental house, or is actually married and lives already together with the husband—plays a role. "Blemish" (מום; see previous note) is used also in Cant 4:7.

Eyes played a prominent role in ancient Jewish "physiognomy" (*m. Bek.* 6:2–3, 8, 10, 12; 7:1–4; *b. Bek.* 43a–44a; Julius Preuss, *Biblical and Talmudic Medicine* [trans. and ed. Fred Rosner; New York: Hebrew Publishing Company, 1978], 259–69; trans. of *Biblisch-talmudische Medizin*

A close parallel to the relevant part of the above-mentioned simile can be found in Palestinian midrashic literature, in the standard editions of a rabbinic midrashic compilation on Canticles. This passage is worth citing, although its authenticity is doubtful:

> "Behind your plait" (Cant 4:1)—R. Levi said: If the eyes of a bride are ugly, her body requires examination, but if her eyes are attractive, her body does not require examination. And when this woman ties up her hair behind, this is an ornament to her. So when the great Sanhedrin sat behind the Temple, this was an ornament to the Temple. (*Cant. Rab.* 4.1)[11]

R. Levi, a third-century C.E. Palestinian master, famous for his contribution to *aggadah*, draws on the same essentially physiognomic aphorism, or "matchmaker's rule," that we met in the first rabbinic text—even in this "aesthetic context," explaining the verse from Canticles. The text, however, is fraught with textual and exegetical problems. Above all, it seems quite likely that the "matchmaker's rule" is a late medieval interpolation in the text.[12] It is also difficult to see how R. Levi's remark about the bride is connected to the biblical proof-text or to the subsequent comparison between the woman's "plaits" tied up and the Sanhedrin. There are no definite solutions to these problems.[13] Within the framework of the present article it

---

[Berlin: S. Karger, 1911]), as well as in Greek and Roman physiognomy (Hugo Magnus, *Das Auge in seinen ästhetischen und cultur-geschichtlichen Beziehungen* [Breslau: Kern, 1876], 45–47; Elizabeth C. Evans, "Galen the Physician as Physiognomist," *TAPA* 76 [1945]: 296; Maud W. Gleason, *Making Men; Sophists and Self-Presentation in Ancient Rome* [Princeton: Princeton University Press, 1995], 32, 55–58, 61–64, 68, 72, 77–78; [Ps.-]Aristoteles, *Physiognomonica* [trans. and commentary by Sabine Vogt, vol. 18 of *Aristoteles, Werke in deutscher Übersetzung;* Berlin: Akademie, 1999], 134–36, 475–76). See also Cant 1:15 and 4:1, where specific praises of the "bride" begin with the eye; see also nn. 13–14 below.

[11] The text in the standard printed editions (and, with minor variations, in the earliest printed editions—Pesaro [1519]; Constantinople [1520]; Venice [1545]) is as follows: "מבעד לצמתך" - אמר ר' לוי כל כלה שעיניה כעורות כל גופה צריך בדיקה ושעיניה יפות אין כל גופה צריך בדיקה והאישה הזאת כשמצמת שערה לאחוריה והוא תכשיט לה כך היתה סנהדרי גדולה יושבת אחורי בית המקדש והיא היתה תכשיט של בית המקדש.

[12] It is missing from the two manuscripts that contain this part of the midrash. Ms Vatican 76 reads: "הנך יפה רעיתי וכל ענינא כקדמית' מבעד לצמתך אמ"ר ועיני האש' הזאת כשמצמת שערה לאחוריה...". Ms Oxford, Bodl. 102 (Catal. Neubauer 164) reads: "הנך יפה רעיתי הנה יפה במצות מבעד לצמתך א"ר אליהו האשה הזאת מצמצמת שערה לאחוריה...". Both versions seem to be corrupt. The version in MS Vatican 76 contains a scribal remark ('וכל ענינא כקדמית) to the effect that comments brought in relation to the previous occurrence of this phrase (הנך יפה רעיתי; Cant 1:15) belong here as well. (My thanks are due to Dr. Tamar Kaddari for putting her copies of manuscripts of *Canticles Rabbah* at my disposal.) The text in question may have been transferred from sources other than certain textual witnesses of *b. Taʿan.*, including homilies on different verses of Canticles (see next note); no such source is known to me to date.

[13] The phrase "and when this woman . . ." seems to suggest that the two comments are closely connected—especially according to MS Vatican 76 and the early printed editions (see n. 11 above), which read here: "and the eyes of this woman, when (she) . . ." (. . . ועיני האשה הזאת כש). How-

is neither possible nor necessary to give an account of various possibilities in regard to textual corruptions and developments. In case the "matchmaker's rule" is an authentic part of the text, it is clear that it is meant as a comment on a biblical text rather than being derived from it. In other words, the physiognomic observation is utilized by the homilist as something well known to his "audience" (whatever that may have been) in order to explain a difficulty or to make a point about the biblical text.[14] It is not the "lesson" but the point of departure—similar to Oshaiah's remark in the Talmud.

II

There are similarities between this physiognomic maxim and the passage in the Sermon. I am not aware, however, of any mention of these rabbinic sources either in rabbinic or in NT scholarship that relates them to each other. In NT exegesis the rabbinic sources quoted above seem to have been overlooked not only by those who search for the origins of Jesus' saying in ancient Greek theories of vision and Hellenistic philosophical ethics, but also by those who emphasize the Jewish spiritual-literary background, in particular the ancient Jewish notions of the "good eye" and the "evil eye."[15] The last wave of scholarly work on the Sermon-saying,

---

ever, this phrase does not make much sense and may be a later insertion, a connecting phrase by a redactor or copyist. (An important sixteenth-century rabbinic scholar from Turkey, Judah Gedaliah, also proposed deleting the first word [אות אמת (Saloniki, 1565), 92a].) The "matchmaker's rule," on the other hand, would be a fitting comment on the previous part of the biblical verse, or on similar verses that praise the eyes of the bride (Cant 1:15; 5:12; 7:5), or on the verse that states: "there is no blemish in you" (4:7). The second comment fits the context and is attested by every primary textual witness. The biblical term *צמה is rendered by most translations as "veil" (see *HALOT* 3:1033), but in the present context the homilist himself makes clear that he understands it as a plait or braid.

[14] If the matchmaker's rule is in its "proper" place, we may point to two possible exegetical "problems" that may have served as the starting point for the remark: (1) Why does the text dwell specifically on the beauty of the eyes after the blanket admission of the "bride's" beauty (a type of problem that ancient rabbinic exegesis often felt the need to solve, in halakic as well as in aggadic contexts)? (2) Why do the compliments and praises begin with the eye (see also Cant 1:15)?

[15] The chief representative of the first approach is Betz (*Sermon*, 437–53). As for the second approach, see John Lightfoot, *A Commentary on the New Testament from the Talmud and Hebraica* (repr., Peabody, MA: Hendrickson, 1989), 2:156–57 (trans. of vol. 1 of *Horae hebraicae et talmudicae* {Cambridge: John Field & John Hayes, 1658]); Gerald Friedlander, *The Jewish Sources of the Sermon on the Mount* (London, 1911; repr., Library of Biblical Studies; New York: Ktav, 1969), 182–85; Str-B 1:431–33 (see also n. 18 below); Dale C. Allison, "The Eye Is the Lamp of the Body (Matthew 6.22–23 = Luke 11.34–36)," *NTS* 33 (1987): 61–83. Compare Betz's judgment: "The pre-Hellenistic parts of the Old Testament and Jewish literature offer no parallels" (*Sermon*, 449; and see a few more references in n. 213 there). The story is briefly discussed, although with inaccuracies, by Rivka Ulmer, *The Evil Eye in the Bible and in Rabbinic Literature* (Hoboken, NJ: Ktav,

heralded by an article by Hans Dieter Betz,[16] focuses on ancient theories of light, light imagery, and light speculation and takes the introductory sentence as the key for understanding the rest of the saying.[17]

The quoted sources draw our attention in a somewhat different direction that is almost entirely ignored in scholarly exegesis—the physiognomic aspects of the Gospel simile.[18] At the heart of both rabbinic traditions, it seems, lies a piece of proverbial wisdom, a popular maxim—a sort of matchmaking rule of thumb.[19] This essentially physiognomic-medical observation is apparently taken for granted in both rabbinic sayings. The rabbis applied this popular wisdom to various exegetical contexts and utilized it for different homiletic purposes. The story as presented in the Babylonian Talmud takes the biblical phrase "eyes of the assembly" metaphorically, referring to the leaders of the community—a frequent exegetical-homiletic twist in ancient rabbinic midrash[20]—while the text in *Canticles Rabbah*,

---

1994), 50 (a book which is a rich and useful collection of sources related to the eye). Passing reference is made there also to part of the Sermon-passage (Matt 6:22a) (pp. 33 n. 4; 41 n. 14) without establishing any connection between the two texts. The text from *b. Taʿan.* is actually cited in works with which NT scholars (esp. those studying the Sermon) would be familiar; see, e.g., Adolf Rosenzweig, *Das Auge in Bibel und Talmud: Ein Essay* (Berlin: Mayer & Müller, 1892), 19; Preuss, *Biblical and Talmudic Medicine*, 267.

[16] Hans Dieter Betz, "Matthew 6:22–23 and Ancient Greek Theories of Vision," in idem, *Essays on the Sermon on the Mount* (trans. L. L. Welborn; Philadelphia: Fortress, 1985), 71–87 (repr. from *Text and Interpretation: Studies in the New Testament, Presented to Matthew Black* [ed. Ernest Best and Robert McL. Wilson; Cambridge: Cambridge University Press, 1979], 43–56).

[17] Betz, "Matthew 6:22–23," 73, 85–86; Allison, "Eye Is the Lamp of the Body," 73; cf. Erich Klostermann, *Das Matthäusevangelium* (HNT; Tübingen: Mohr, 1926), 61. The studies of Betz and Allison, with slight modifications, found their way into the commentary literature: Betz, *Sermon*; W. D. Davies and Dale C. Allison, Jr., *A Critical and Exegetical Commentary on the Gospel According to Saint Matthew* (ICC; 3 vols.; Edinburgh: T&T Clark, 1988–97), 1:635–41. See also Thomas Zöckler, "Light within the Human Person: A Comparison of Matthew 6:22–23 and Gospel of Thomas 24," *JBL* 120 (2001): 487–99.

[18] The physiological-physical dimension of the simile, to be sure, was emphasized by scholars in the past; see, e.g., Günter Harder, "πονηρός, πονερία," *TDNT* 6:555–56. It is mentioned also by both Betz (*Sermon*, 450–51) and Allison ("Eye Is the Lamp of the Body," 76), connecting ancient theories of vision to physiological-medical ideas. It was only Str–B (1:431–32), however, that hinted at the "physiognomic" aspect to some extent, pointing (apropos of ἁπλοῦς) to sources pertaining to animal blemishes (an important branch of sacrificial "lore," technical knowledge of veterinary medicine or animal "physiognomy"; see n. 9 above) but not touching on issues of human physiognomy.

[19] Matthew 6:22a is characterized similarly by Betz (*Sermon*, 439, 450) and Allison ("Eye Is the Lamp of the Body," 62, 73).

[20] See *y. Hor.* 1:4 (46a); *b. Hor.* 5a–b; *Cant. Rab.* 1:64 (to Cant 1:15), and elsewhere. See also the Targum to Cant 4:9 and *passim*; see *The Targum of Canticles* (trans. and annot. Philip S. Alexander; ArBib 17A; Collegeville, MN: Liturgical Press, 2003), 130 n. 2. See also *b. B. Bat.* 4a, where two alternative versions of a saying (attributed to the sage Baba ben Buta, a contemporary

provided it is authentic, engages it in a symbolic-allegorical interpretation of a verse in Canticles. Next to the physiognomic maxim and its midrashic-exegetical use, the story in the Babylonian Talmud has a third level as well: Oshaiah's application of this exegetical remark in the given situation and his turning it against the patriarch. As noted before, the terminology suggests that the entire exegetical remark was known to him as a tannaitic tradition, and his contribution consists only of its "political" use and recontextualization (what we called the "third level").

Although the rabbinic rule pertains to "brides" (and by simple extension, to women: "as long as her eyes are attractive, her body requires no examination, etc."), the Sermon passage (Matt 6:22b–23a) addresses humans in general. Still, there is much similarity between these sayings, and this discrepancy can be explained by the marked popular-proverbial nature of the rabbinic dictum: such aphorisms, while aiming at general truths, have a predilection for concreteness and pointedness. The saying in the Sermon (perhaps inspired by a similar but "older" maxim) has a more explicit spiritual-philosophical bent than the rabbinic maxim, which in turn has, at first view, the character of applied, practical physiognomy. Even the latter, however, had a figurative, ethico-political meaning (or application) at an early stage—in all likelihood, in the first two centuries C.E. at the latest.

So when we ask, Does the rabbinic dictum talk about physical eyes? the answer is, Yes, it does. But, as is the case with the Sermon-saying, there is more than that. Already in the Bible, the semantic field of eyes and vision is very rich in figurative meanings; one has to take into account such meanings not only in the ethico-political direction (apropos of the Sanhedrin), but in the ethico-anthropological direction as well. Research on the Sermon made clear (almost 350 years ago) that the expression "nice eye" (עין יפה)—the term used in the rabbinic saying in the plural—has a figurative, ethical meaning in classical Hebrew (at least from tannaitic Hebrew and on),[21] similar to the expression "good eye" (עין טובה). The former

---

of Herod the Great) are cited, one referring to the sages and the holy temple as "the light of the World," the other referring to them as "the eye of the World"; and see n. 23 below. Note the difference between the text from *Canticles Rabbah*, "*if* the eyes of a bride are ugly..." (lit., "[the body of] every bride with ugly eyes...") and the version in *b. Taʿan.*, "*as long as* (or *when*) her eyes are attractive" (... כל זמן/בזמן שעיניה יפות); this latter version may well have been adjusted to fit the "political" context. Given the apparent antiquity and popularity of this understanding, one wonders whether the Gospel saying had, in its original setting, a similar political edge as well (directed against the "Pharisees"). While such a meaning is quite incompatible with the present context in Matthew, it seems plausible in the context in Luke (see below, p. 93 n. 31). For the problem of the original "context" of this saying (related, of course, to the problem of the Q source), see Conny Edlund, *Das Auge der Einfalt: Eine Untersuchung zu Matth. 6, 22–23 und Luk. 11, 34–35* (ASNU 19; Copenhagen: Munksgaard, 1952), 103–4; Zöckler, "Light within the Human Person," 487 n. 1.

[21] For examples, see Lightfoot, *Commentary on the New Testament*, 2:156–57; Str-B 1:834. See also, e.g., *Sifre Numeri* §110 on Num 15:21 (*Siphre D'Be Rav* [ed. H. S. Horowitz; Leipzig: G. Fock, 1917], 115) (an example cited already by Adolf Schlatter, *Der Evangelist Matthäus*

expression, in the plural, has also a physical meaning on top of the "ethical" one.[22] At a closer look, therefore, much of the difference between the practical-physical orientation of the rabbinic saying and the theoretical-ethical vein of the Gospel saying disappears. It is likely that the "eyes of the bride," in the rabbinic simile, are indicative not only of the physical state of the body but of character as well. So the moral of the popular saying (or rabbinic maxim) is something like this: the generosity or good-heartedness of the woman is indicative of good character in general, and, since she possesses these traits, her physical beauty (or the lack of it) is of secondary importance.[23] In the absence of such good character traits, however, at least she should be physically attractive.

[Stuttgart: Calwer, 1929], 223); t. Pe᾽ah 2:21; t. Ḥul. 9:11; t. Ḥal. 1:7; and dozens of other places. These expressions, in the singular, are used figuratively in biblical and rabbinic Hebrew, apparently without exception.

[22] One exception is *Deuteronomy Rabbah* (ed. S. Lieberman; Jerusalem: Wahrmann, 1940), 129, where the expression in the plural is used figuratively: יבא משה שעיניו יפות לברכן והוא יברך את ישראל; ... זה משה רבי׳ שעיניו יפות לברך את ישראל; but the parallel in *Tanḥuma* (ed. Buber), ברכה 1 (27b) reads: את בברכתו [!] זה משה שעיניו יפה ... יבא משה שעינו שעינו יפה ויברך את ישראל ... ישראל. For an early concrete-physical use of a similar phrase, in the plural, see יפה עינים (1 Sam 16:12; translated in the Targum as עינוהי יאין), and this became the standard expression in talmudic literature for "nice/attractive eyes" in the physical sense. In the Sermon-saying, ὀφθαλμός ἁπλοῦς, therefore, may be an equivalent of עין יפה/עינא יאיא; cf. Henry J. Cadbury, "The Single Eye," *HTR* 47 (1954): 74.

[23] Cf. *m. ᾽Abot* 2:9. A similar "ethical" interpretation is offered by R. Hanoch Zundel b. Yosef (nineteenth century) in his glosses titled *Yad Yosef*, printed in the standard editions of Jacob ibn Habib's ᶜ*Ein Yaᶜakov*, ad loc. (70a). R. Solomon Ephraim Luntschitz, in his commentary titled *Kli Yaqar* (Lublin, 1602; reprinted in later editions of the standard "Rabbinic" Bibles), on Gen. 24:14, interpreted our rabbinic saying in a similar way, in the context of the classic biblical story of matchmaking, the Eliezer–Rebekah episode. This interpretation of the rabbinic saying gives a further reason why the reading of all the manuscripts of *b. Taᶜan.*, the contradictory phrase "(if her eyes) aren't attractive" (אין עיניה יפות), is to be preferred over the reading "(if her eyes are) ill-shaped/bleary/narrow" (עיניה טרוטות/כעורות), which uses an antonym, a short, contrary term attested in the early printed editions of the Babylonian story (Pesaro [1516]; Venice [1521]; also reflected by the standard Vilna edition) and in the printed versions of *Canticles Rabbah*. (Contradictory terms are sometimes used as contrary terms in rabbinic literature [euphemistically, e.g., "unattractive" meaning "ugly"] and vice versa, so such considerations about variants are insufficient to declare a reading corrupt or inauthentic.) While the former phrase has a double meaning, the latter formulation (which I consider secondary) hardly has a meaning other than the aesthetic-physiological one (see, however, p. 92 below, at n. 29). The alternative phrase "her eyes are bad" (עיניה רעות), on the other hand, would be incompatible with the physiological meaning. Some later tradents or printers may have lost the original ambiguous sense and replaced the original phrase with a seemingly simpler one. Further support for a figurative meaning may be found in the biblical account itself, even raising the possibility that the saying is rooted in this story. *After* Eliezer pledges himself to choose a bride on the basis of his character test (Gen 24:14), the biblical story recounts that Rebekah appears on the scene and she is "beautiful" (Gen 24:15–16)—as if to hint, according to a hypothetical "rabbinic" reading at least, that Rebekah's generosity was a good "omen," a

III

Whether Matt 6:22b–23a (and Luke 11:34) is predicated on an indicative or "symptomatic" relation between the eye and the body (as a physiognomic model posits) or follows a rather causal pattern is an open question. This dilemma is intimately related to, although not identical with, the more immediate exegetical questions whether the phrases pertaining to the "eye" are used here in a concrete-physiological or a metaphorical-ethical sense, and whether the saying has a descriptive-philosophical or a prescriptive-ethical thrust. These dilemmas are real —at least translators of the Sermon into modern languages will admit this, having a hard time searching for equivalents for ambiguous phraseology in the original that conveys multiple messages.[24] Interpretive work, on the other hand, is much less affected by linguistic exigencies, and current research on the Sermon-saying, while demarcating the main alternatives of exegesis, in fact tries to synthesize

---

"symptom" of her physical beauty, as well as a "reward" for Eliezer (for using proper character criteria, as opposed to aesthetic ones); cf. *b. Taʿan.* 4a. An alternative scriptural support for the saying may be found in Gen 29:17, where the description of Leah's physical appearance relates only to the eyes, whereas Rachel is characterized in more general terms: "Leah had weak eyes, Rachel was shapely and beautiful." Although the connection between this verse and the physiognomic maxim (as in the previous case) is purely hypothetical, two things should be noted. First, according to some ancient and medieval opinions, the Hebrew adjective used for Leah's eyes (רכות) is synonymous with תרוטות/טרוטות (*t. Bek.* 5:3; *b. Bek.* 44a; Rashi ad loc.; cf. Preuss, *Biblical and Talmudic Medicine*, 266–67); for the early Jewish interpretation of the phrase, see Bernard Grossfeld, *Targum Neofiti I: An Exegetical Commentary to Genesis* (New York: Sepher-Hermon, 2000), 205–6. R. Samuel b. Meir, an important twelfth-century commentator, makes reference to the saying in *b. Taʿan.* in his comment on this verse. Second, rabbinic exegesis of this verse associates Leah's eyes with leadership of her descendants; see *b. B. Bat.* 123a. For talmudic maxims or proverbs with multiple meanings, see Heinrich (Hanoch) Ehrentreu, "Sprachliches und Sachliches zum Talmud," *Jahrbuch des Jüdisch-Literarischen Gesellschaft* 8 (1910): 4–13.

[24] See Betz's translation, quoted at the beginning of this article. The "symptomatic" and the "causal" patterns are implied, to some extent, by rendering the apodosis of the conditional sentences with the future or with the present tense, respectively. In the Lukan parallel, where the apodosis is in the present tense, most modern translations that I checked translate accordingly, which is close to the "symptomatic" pattern. In Matthew, which uses a future tense, most modern translations follow suit ("if your eye is . . . , your whole body will be/shall be . . ."), which suggests a "causal" pattern. It is not incidental that Klostermann, a chief proponent of the physical understanding of the eyes in the parable, translates the Matthean text in the present tense (*Das Matthäus-evangelium*, 60), as does Allison, who considers Luke to be closer to the original at this point too, and who argues for the "symptomatic" pattern ("Eye Is the Lamp of the Body," 71–72, 74–77); see also James M. Robinson et al., eds., *The Critical Edition of Q: Synopsis including the Gospels of Matthew and Luke, Mark and Thomas with English, German, and French Translations of Q and Thomas* (Hermeneia; Minneapolis: Fortress, 2000), 258–59. Betz himself translated the Matthean text in the present tense in his article ("Matthew 6:22–23," 72). In post-biblical Hebrew,

them.²⁵ Such interpretations may be corroborated and enriched by viewing both the Gospel saying and the rabbinic simile against the backdrop of physiognomic thinking. The mentioned dichotomies run in the blood of ancient physiognomy, which *is* a sort of synthesis of them. While it focuses on character, it operates mostly with physical traits. It is preoccupied with bodily symptoms and behavioral patterns, having at the same time a vested interest in improving human qualities and behavior.²⁶ In the particular context of the eye, the Sermon-saying, in my view, is an artful elaboration, partly at least, of markedly physiognomic notions, nurtured by biblical light imagery and Hellenistic light speculation, combined with ancient Jewish and Hellenistic ideas and figurative language related to the evil/good eye.²⁷

Without further relevant sources or data, it would be naïve and preposterous to think that either Jesus' saying influenced—directly or indirectly—the rabbinic simile or the other way around. Although the light symbolism is entirely absent from the rabbinic saying, the antithetic formulations concerning the "eye" and the "body" are common to both sayings, as well as the great significance—an indicative role, it seems—that they ascribe to the eye. Above all, these sayings share the same figurative and ambiguous phraseology: not only the Gospel saying but the rabbinic simile as well may have drawn on the metaphorical-ethical connotation of the term "eye" in a number of expressions (in addition to its metaphorical-political purport related to the "sages" and the "Sanhedrin") already in the initial stages of its formulation. Both texts can be seen as different rhetorical-homiletic applications of the same ancient popular physiognomic-ethical aphorism, which takes the eyes not as a "mirror of the soul" but rather as a mirror of the "body" and, figuratively, a mirror of the "character" or "spirit."

Postscript:
Finding Fault with the Eye in a Talmudic Jesus-Story

An intriguing story about Jesus in the Babylonian Talmud that puts the blame for Jesus' break with "rabbinic" or "mainstream" Judaism partly on his rabbi's harsh

---

already in the tannaitic corpus, סימן, a commonly used Greek loanword, denotes "mark" and "symptom" as well as "omen."

²⁵ Thomas W. Manson, *The Sayings of Jesus, as Recorded in the Gospels according to St. Matthew and St. Luke, Arranged with Introduction and Commentary* (1949; repr., London: SCM, 1971), 385; Betz, *Sermon*, 450–53; Allison, "Eye Is the Lamp of the Body," 76-78; Ulrich Luz, *Matthew 1–7* (Hermeneia; Minneapolis: Fortress, 2007), 332–34. For a survey of past scholarly opinions, see Edlund, *Das Auge der Einfalt*, 11–18, 103–17.

²⁶ That is why physiognomic observations are scattered in, and utilized by, ancient works of ethics and medicine as well as of rhetoric and aesthetics. These built-in dichotomies exist not only in Greek and Roman physiognomy, but—as I will argue elsewhere—in rabbinic "physiognomy" as well.

²⁷ For the ancient Near Eastern background of biblical and rabbinic notions about the "evil eye," see J. N. Ford, "'Ninety-Nine by the Evil Eye and One from Natural Causes,' KTU² 1.96 in

repudiation of him turns on an ill-fated remark about a woman's eye. The story in *b. Sanh.* 107b (and its parallel in *b. Soṭah* 47a) reports that R. Joshua ben Peraḥiah, on his way back to Jerusalem from Alexandria (where he fled from persecution) lodged in an inn, together with some of his students. He praises the place and the hospitality by using an ambiguous term: "how beautiful is this אכסניא (a Greek loanword, meaning 'inn' as well as 'hostess')! His disciple (Jesus) said to him: Master, her eyes are narrow (עיניה טרוטות)! He replied: Wicked person, it is such things that occupy your mind?!" Upon this incident, the master excommunicates Jesus, whose repeated attempts to appease his master are rejected—and as a consequence of another misunderstanding (of the master's "body language"), even a last-ditch effort fails.[28]

Some literary features are shared by this anecdote and the story in *b. Taʿan.*: (1) a central role assigned to eyes in describing a woman; (2) the use of the adjective טרוטות (in some textual witnesses of the *b. Taʿan.* text) in describing women's eyes; (3) the importance of ambiguous expressions in the narrative. The reader hardly misses the tragic colors and the literary sophistication of the narrative. My purpose here is merely to comment on the meaning and literary character of the remark on the woman's eyes in this particular anecdote about Jesus, and to argue, without presenting compelling evidence, that there may be even more tragedy or irony here than meets the eye. In line with the *Tendenz* of the story—its condoning attitude toward the disciple/Jesus and its emphasis on fatal misapprehension—it is possible to interpret the response of the disciple as a shrewd or ambiguous answer to the playful, intentionally provocative or unintentionally ambiguous remark (or question; see below) of the master. The narrative's emphatic mention of

---

Its Near Eastern Context," *UF* 30 (1998): 201–78 (with additions and corrections by the author in *UF* 32 [2000]: 711–16).

[28] The relevant part is as follows, according to the Vilna edition: קא אתא ואתרמי ליה ההוא אושפיזא עבדו ליה יקרא טובא אמר כמה יפה אכסניא זו אמר ליה רבי עיניה טרוטות אמר ליה רשע בכך אתה עוסק אפיק ארבע מאה שיפורי ושמתיה. Note the term טרוטות, which appears also in the *b. Taʿan.* story, according to the printed editions (see n. 23 above). The parallels (*y. Ḥag.* 2:2 [77d]; *y. Sanh.* 6:9 [23c]; see n. 30 below) mention only "a disciple," without mentioning Jesus, and the identification of the unnamed "disciple" with Jesus in the Babylonian Talmud is likely to be a relatively late development (see Stephen Gero, "The Stern Master and His Wayward Disciple: A 'Jesus' Story in the Talmud and in Christian Hagiography," *JSJ* 25 [1994]: 287–311, here 306–10). The mention of Jesus is attested at some point in the story by most textual witnesses of the Babylonian versions. For *b. Sanh.* 107b, see *The Sol and Evelyn Henkind Talmud Text Databank* (The Saul Lieberman Institute of Talmudic Research of the Jewish Theological Seminary, Version 5); for *b. Soṭah* 47a, see *The Babylonian Talmud, with Variant Readings . . .* , Tractate Sotah (II), ed. Abraham Liss (Jerusalem: Yad Harav Herzog–Institute for the Complete Israeli Talmud, 1979), 302–3. For critical discussions of this story, see Johann Maier, *Jesus von Nazareth in der talmudischen Überlieferung* (EdF 82; Darmstadt: Wissenschaftliche Buchgesellschaft, 1978), 114–29 (most of his conclusions about the historical development of these stories were anticipated by R. Travers Herford, *Christianity in Talmud and Midrash* [London: Williams & Norgate, 1903], 51–54; for a philological critique of Maier's treatment, see David Goldenberg, "Once More: Jesus in the

the repeated efforts of the disciple to conciliate his master intimates that there might have been some, at least partial, justification for his behavior (beyond mere begging for pardon, pointing out the disproportionate harshness of the punishment and the like). It suggests that the disciple/Jesus, too, has been misunderstood by his master—if not his words, then his intentions. The meaning of the adjective (passive participle) טרוטות in relation to the eyes is unclear, but it obviously describes, above all, a physical condition. Here it may also be understood, however, as a physiognomic code word referring to negative character traits, either concretely (envy, niggardliness),[29] or generally (in conformity with our interpretation of the b. Taʿan. saying). Traces of similar ambiguities, on the part of the master and/or the disciple, can be found in the Palestinian parallel story as well.[30] One should hardly miss a

---

Talmud," *JQR* 73 [1982]: 78–82); Gero, "Stern Master," 288–89, 303, 306; Peter Schäfer, *Jesus in the Talmud* (Princeton: Princeton University Press, 2007), 34–40. For parallels in the Jerusalem Talmud, see n. 29 below.

[29] There are good reasons to understand the passive participle טרוטות (spelled תרוטות in some textual witnesses, as well as in other texts) in the anecdote about Jesus as "flat" or "thin" or "narrow" (as translated above), describing the shape of the eye socket; cf. e.g., *m. Mid.* 2:5; see also Menahem Moreshet, *A Lexicon of the New Verbs in Tannaitic Hebrew* (in Hebrew; Ramat Gan: Bar-Ilan University Press, 1980), 393, and the literature cited there. A gloss in the medieval midrashic anthology *Yalqut Shimeoni* (to the Former Prophets, Kings II, *remez* 230) also understands the phrase this way: עיניה טרוטות–פי׳ סגורות מעט (ed. Dov Hyman and Yitzhaq Shiloni, Jerusalem: Mossad ha-Rav Kook, 1999), 530. The term "narrow eye" (עין צרה/צר עין) occurs frequently in rabbinic—already in tannaitic—literature. It is always used figuratively, almost synonymously with "evil/envious eye" (עינא בישא/עין הרע/עין רעה/רע עין); see, e.g., *t. Ḥal.* 1:7 (עינו צרה), where the parallel in *y. Ḥal.* 2:7 (58d) reads: רעה (עינו). See also Ulmer, *Evil Eye*, 15–20. (One may even read the disciple's words as a sort of slip of the tongue: instead of saying that the hostess was miserly or "narrow eyed" [צרת עינים/עיניה צרות; I am not aware of any Aramaic equivalent of this particular phrase], the disciple used an unequivocally physical term.) The proposed meaning of טרוטות may also fit the parallels in the Jerusalem Talmud (see n. 30 below), which use the word שוורה/שברה (perhaps related to שור/שורה ["wall, barrier, line, row"; *HALOT* 4:1453–54]). Based on Syriac, some scholars proposed the meaning "protruding eyes" (E. S. Rosenthal, *apud* Moshe Assis, "A Fragment of Yerushalmi Sanhedrin (5:1 [22c]–6:9 [23c])," *Tarbiz* 46 [1976/77]: 83; Gero, "Stern Master," 300 n. 34). Current psychological research confirms that round eyes are perceived as a sign for trust, while narrow eyes raise suspicion; Leslie A. Zebrowitz, *Reading Faces: Window to the Soul?* (Boulder, CO: Westview, 1997), 84–85. In the stories in *b. Taʿan.* and *Cant. Rab.* I translated the word טרוטות as "ill-shaped," because it seems to be secondary (see n. 23 above) and in those contexts conveys apparently a broader, less-specific negative meaning. The few other occurrences of this adjective in relation to the eye in ancient rabbinic literature, however, seem to retain a specific meaning, while standing for eye defects in general—to some degree, *pars pro toto*—in most of them; see *b. Ned.* 66b, *b. Šabb.* 31a. The meaning in the *b. Taʿan.* and *Cant. Rab.* contexts represents the last phase of a semantic extension.

[30] The relevant part of *y. Ḥag.* 2:2 (77d) reads (according to MS Leiden): פירש מייתי גו אילפא אמ׳ דכורה מרתה דביתא דקבלתא מה הוות חסירה אמ׳ ליה חד מן תלמידוי ר׳ עייניה הוות שברה אמ׳ ליה הא תרתיי גבך חדא דחשדתני וחדא דאיסתכלת בה מה אמרית יאיא ברווא לא אמרית אלא בעובדא וכעס עלוי ואזל. There is another version in *y. Sanh.* 6:9 (23c) published by Assis from a Genizah fragment ("Fragment of Yerushalmi"; the story is lacking in the printed versions and

further ambiguity in the story: the master's reference to the "hostess" may be taken to refer (both in the Babylonian story and in its Palestinian parallel) to Jerusalem—and what it stands for "politically." This is the third possible meaning of the term אכסניא/מרתה דביתא in these stories. The personification of "Jerusalem" as a woman was common in antiquity, and the introductory part of both stories in fact elaborates on this very symbolism. The remark of the disciple/Jesus can be seen as a play on this ambiguity—which may or may not have been intended by the master.[31] It is mostly these common words, with their multiple meanings, misused and/or misunderstood by the *dramatis personae*, that make up these stories. Here again, no "literary" dependencies can be proven, with any degree of certainty, between the Babylonian "Jesus" story, and the story in *b. Taʿan.* (or the Sermon-saying), even in regard to their use (in some textual witnesses) of the term טרוטות. But it seems that it is also not accidental that both talmudic stories single out the eyes in characterizing women's appearances, while alluding to nonphysical qualities as well.

MS Leiden), which reads as follows: פרש מייתי ליה גו אסרטה אמ׳ דכירה מרתה דבייתה דיאות קבלתן וחסידה [הוו]ת אמ׳ ל׳ חד מן תלמידוי חדא עיינה הוות שוורה אמ׳ ליה את גבך תרתי חדה דאסתכלת בה וחדה דחשדתני דאיסתכלית בה מה אמרית יאה ברייואה לא אמרית ואלא יאה בעובדה ואקפד עלוי ומית. Both versions are corrupt; for a discussion of various textual problems and different views of the relative textual value of the two versions, see Assis, "Fragment of Yerushalmi," 82–84; Gero, "Stern Master," 299–306. According to the version in *y. Ḥag.*, the disciple does not object to his master, but answers his ambiguous question: "What was lacking in the hostess?" In the version in *y. Sanh.*, the master says: "the hostess received us well/nicely and was kind," and his apologetic retort to the disciple's remark makes sense only if his previous words could have been understood also as referring to the woman's appearance (cf. Assis, "Fragment of Yerushalmi," 83). In both versions, the remark is made about the "eye," in the singular, which is reminiscent of the figurative usage of the terms עין רעה/צרה—also, characteristically, in the singular. The two interesting Christian parallels to our story (from the fifth–sixth centuries C.E.) adduced by Gero ("Stern Master," 292–97) are also not free, it seems, from similar ambiguities. In both anecdotes, a monk tests his disciple by praising a woman's appearance, while the disciple disagrees; and for his gazing at the woman the disciple is reproved by his master. In one story it is the disciple who makes reference to the fact that the woman is "one-eyed"; in the other version it is the master. This phrase might be influenced by NT usage with an ethical sense (Matt 18:9 and Mark 9:47; see Gero, "Stern Master," 296 n. 24, 298 n. 28, 300 n. 34) and may intimate that the bodily defect corresponds (as a divine or self-inflicted punishment) to Jesus' admonition. Alternatively, this reference may be related to the fact that according to ancient Near Eastern rules of etiquette, women were supposed to cover their faces in public, leaving out just one eye to see; see *y. Šabb.* 8:3 (11b); Saul Lieberman, *Tosefta ki-Fshutah*, Pt. 3 (New York: Jewish Theological Seminary, 1962), 128. In any case, the disciple did look at the woman (similar to the Palestinian and probably the Babylonian version of our story), so the reproach by the master is justified, even if the disciple's remark had this "ethical" overtone.

[31] This suggestion was made by Ernst Bammel with respect to the Babylonian story ("Christian Origins in Jewish Traditions," *NTS* 13 [1967]: 321–22). In my opinion, not only should his interpretation (of this issue at least) not be dismissed (*pace* Maier, *Jesus*, 116, 128; and Gero, "Stern Master," 290 n. 8), but it deserves serious consideration concerning the Palestinian story as well (see n. 20 above).

Important New Books from
Templeton Foundation Press

JESUS AND PSYCHOLOGY
Edited by Fraser Watts

For Christians, there is nothing more important than understanding the significance of the life and teaching of Jesus. This collaborative study shows how psychology is now providing important insights into the mind of Jesus, revealing the personality of Jesus himself and how he is portrayed, the psychological significance of his teaching, and the reasons why people read and understand the Bible differently. "Kudos to Fraser Watts and his Cambridge University colleagues . . . This is state-of-the-art scholarship."
—David G. Myers, co-author of
Psychology through the Eyes of Faith
$19.95, paperback / 978-1-59947-124-2

THE HISTORICITY OF NATURE
Essays on Science and Theology
By Wolfhart Pannenberg
Edited by Niels Henrik Gregersen

Known as one of the most outstanding theologians of the twentieth century, Wolfhart Pannenberg is also considered a great interdisciplinary thinker. Now, essays and articles on science and theology that are central to understanding his theories have been collected into one convenient volume.
$29.95, paperback / 978-1-59947-125-9

DIVINE ACTION
Examining God's Role in an Open and Emergent Universe
By Keith Ward

In an intellectual counterpoint to antispirituality arguments, philosopher, theologian, and scholar Keith Ward explores what is involved in the idea of creation and of particular divine actions in a world of scientific law and intelligibility. Briefly available in 1990 and out-of-print since then, for this new edition the author has added a new preface that reflects on the argument in light of the recent resurgence of naturalism in philosophy.
$19.95, paperback / 978-1-59947-130-3

Available at better bookstores
or order direct from our Web site:
www.templetonpress.org

TEMPLETON FOUNDATION PRESS
West Conshohocken, PA 19428

Rethinking Early Jewish–Christian Relations: Matthean Community History as Pharisaic Intragroup Conflict

ANDERS RUNESSON
runess@mcmaster.ca
McMaster University, Hamilton, ON, L8S 4K1, Canada

Anyone interested in the religio-ethnic identity and social location of the community/communities that produced the Gospel of Matthew must contend not only with multilayered composition but also with the complex reception history of this text.[1] While the Gospel was used by groups identifying themselves as Jew-

---

This study is a reworked version of a paper originally presented at the 2005 Calgary conference entitled "Common Judaism Explored: Second Temple Judaism in Context," held in honor of Ed Sanders on the occasion of his retirement from Duke University. I would like to thank the participants of the conference, especially Ed Sanders and Adele Reinhartz, for numerous suggestions that have improved the text. I am also grateful to Stephen Westerholm and Michael Knowles for reading and commenting on the penultimate draft. I alone am responsible for the conclusions drawn and any remaining errors.

[1] See the introductory statement regarding the early reception of Matthew by Graham Stanton, "Introduction: Matthew's Gospel in Recent Scholarship," in *The Interpretation of Matthew* (ed. Graham Stanton; 2nd ed.; Studies in New Testament Interpretation; Edinburgh: T&T Clark, 1995), 1–26, here 1: "Matthew's Gospel was more widely used and more influential in the early Church than any of the other Gospels." Stanton does not discuss the fact that this reception meant widely different uses and interpretations of Matthew. Note, however, that the first question he lists as the subject of discussion over the past twenty years is whether the author of Matthew was a Jew or a non-Jew (p. 2). Regarding the relationship between text and community, see the contributions in *The Gospels for All Christians: Rethinking the Gospel Audiences* (ed. Richard Bauckham; London: T&T Clark, 1998) and the debate between Bauckham and Philip Esler in *SJT* (Richard Bauckham, "Response to Philip Esler," *SJT* 51 [1998]: 249–53; Philip Esler, "Community and Gospel in Early Christianity: A Response to Richard Bauckham's Gospels for All Christians," *SJT* 51 [1998]: 235–48). The position taken here is that the gospel traditions and texts were transmitted and written down within—and served the needs of—specific communities as these groups interpreted their beliefs in specific cultural contexts and addressed specific problems and

ish, it also served the needs of people with a non-Jewish identity who actively opposed a Jewish understanding of "their" religion.[2] Interestingly, these two seemingly irreconcilable uses of the Gospel of Matthew are reflected in modern theories regarding the identity of the community behind the text: some scholars argue that Mattheans were well within the boundaries of "Judaism" (*intra muros*),[3] oth-

---

situations within those contexts, using the Jesus traditions as vehicles for those interpretations. This does not contradict the hypothesis that, in our case, the author may also have had a broader audience in mind than the most immediate one, hoping to influence Jews and Christ-believers of other dispositions.

[2] For a discussion of the use of Matthew by Jewish Christ-believers, see James Carleton Paget, "Jewish Christianity," in *Cambridge History of Judaism*, vol. 3, *The Early Roman Period* (ed. William Horbury et al.; Cambridge: Cambridge University Press, 1999). The early reception of Matthew before Irenaeus is treated by Édouard Massaux, *Influence de l'évangile de saint Matthieu sur la littérature chrétienne avant saint Irénée* (Universitas Catholica Lovaniensis, Dissertationes, Ser. 2, 42; Leuven: Leuven University Press, 1950; 2nd ed., 1986; Eng. trans., part 1, 1990). See also Helmut Koester, *Synoptische Überlieferung bei den Apostolischen Vätern* (TUGAL 65; Berlin: Akademie,1957); Wolf-Dietrich Köhler, *Die Rezeption des Matthäusevangeliums in der Zeit vor Irenäus* (WUNT 24; Tübingen: Mohr Siebeck, 1987); H. Benedict Green, "Matthew, Clement, and Luke: Their Sequence and Relationship," *JTS* 40 (1989): 1–25; For recent detailed studies of the reception of Matthew by church fathers after Irenaeus, see D. Jeffrey Bingham, *Irenaeus' Use of Matthew's Gospel in* Adversus Haereses (Traditio Exegetica Graeca 7; Louvain: Peeters, 1998); Jean-François Racine, *The Text of Matthew in the Writings of Basil of Caesarea* (New Testament in the Greek Fathers 5; Boston: Brill, 2004). A broader approach giving a range of comments by church fathers on Matthew, chapter by chapter, is found in Charles S. Kraszewski, *The Gospel of Matthew [To Euangelion kata Matthaion] with Patristic Commentaries* (Studies in the Bible and Early Christianity 40; Lewiston, NY: Edwin Mellen, 1999). Classical scholar Howard W. Clarke takes a general approach covering (selectively) two thousand years of interpretation of Matthew in his fascinating commentary *The Gospel of Matthew and Its Readers: A Historical Introduction to the First Gospel* (Bloomington: Indiana University Press, 2003). Among NT scholars, Ulrich Luz has been among the pioneers in his emphasis on the reception history of Matthew; see his multivolume commentary *Matthew: A Commentary* (Hermeneia; Minneapolis: Fortress, 1985–2006), as well as his *Matthew in History: Interpretation, Influence, and Effects* (Minneapolis: Fortress, 1994). See also his detailed study of Matt 25:31–46: "The Final Judgement (Matt 25:31–46): An Exercise in 'History of Influence' Exegesis," in *Treasures New and Old: Recent Contributions to Matthean Studies* (ed. David R. Bauer and Mark Allan Powell; SBLSymS 1; Atlanta: Scholars Press, 1996), 271–310.

[3] For *intra muros* opinions, see, e.g., Günter Bornkamm, "End-Expectation and Church in Matthew," in idem, Gerhard Barth, and Heinz Joachim Held, *Tradition and Interpretation in Matthew* (NTL; Philadelphia: Westminster, 1963), 15–51 (though he seems to have changed his mind in 1970: see "The Authority to 'Bind' and 'Loose' in the Church in Matthew's Gospel," reprinted in *Interpretation of Matthew*, ed. Stanton, 101–14), commented on by Donald Hagner, "The Sitz im Leben of the Gospel of Matthew," in *Treasures New and Old*, ed. Bauer and Powell, 27–68, here 35); Gerhard Barth, "Matthew's Understanding of the Law," in *Tradition and Interpretation in Matthew*, 58–164; W. D. Davies, *The Setting of the Sermon on the Mount* (Cambridge: Cambridge University Press, 1963); Schuyler Brown, "The Matthean Community and the Gentile Mission," *NovT* 22 (1980): 193–221; Alan Segal, "Matthew's Jewish Voice," in *Social History of*

ers that the author was a non-Jew writing for a community that had parted ways with the "synagogue" (*extra muros*).⁴ Within and between these two positions,

---

the Matthean Community: Cross-Disciplinary Approaches (ed. David L. Balch; Minneapolis: Fortress, 1991), 3–37, esp. 37: "But there was no uniformity in Judaism. . . . Thus we cannot say that Judaism uniformly dismissed Matthean Christians from their midst"; J. Andrew Overman, *Matthew's Gospel and Formative Judaism: The Social World of the Matthean Community* (Minneapolis: Fortress, 1990); idem, *Church and Community in Crisis: The Gospel According to Matthew* (New Testament in Context; Valley Forge, PA: Trinity Press International, 1996); Anthony Saldarini, *Matthew's Christian-Jewish Community* (Chicago Studies in the History of Judaism; Chicago: University of Chicago Press, 1994); David Sim, *Apocalyptic Eschatology in the Gospel of Matthew* (SNTSMS 88; Cambridge: Cambridge University Press, 1996); idem, *The Gospel of Matthew and Christian Judaism: The History and Social Setting of the Matthean Community* (Studies of the New Testament and Its World; Edinburgh: T&T Clark, 1998). For *extra muros* opinions, see Ulrich Luz, *Matthew 1-7: A Commentary* (rev. ed.; Hermeneia; Minneapolis: Fortress, 2007); idem, *The Theology of the Gospel of Matthew* (New Testament Theology; Cambridge: Cambridge University Press, 1995); Petri Luomanen, *Entering the Kingdom of Heaven: A Study on the Structure of Matthew's View of Salvation* (WUNT 2/101; Tübingen: Mohr Siebeck, 1998); Graham Stanton, "5 Ezra and Matthean Christianity in the Second Century," *JTS* 28 (1977): 67–83; idem, *A Gospel for a New People: Studies in Matthew* (Edinburgh: T&T Clark, 1992); Wayne A. Meeks, "Breaking Away," in *"To See Ourselves as Others See Us": Christians, Jews, "Others" in Late Antiquity* (ed. Jacob Neusner et al.; Scholars Press Studies in the Humanities; Chico, CA: Scholars Press, 1985), 93–115; Sean Freyne, "Vilifying the Other and Defining the Self," in *"To See Ourselves as Others See Us"*; Benno Przybylski, "The Setting of Matthean Anti-Judaism," in *Anti-Judaism in Early Christianity,* vol. 1, *Paul and the Gospels* (ed. Peter Richardson et al.; Studies in Christianity and Judaism 2; Waterloo, ON: Wilfrid Laurier University Press, 1986); Amy-Jill Levine, *The Social and Ethnic Dimensions of Matthean Salvation History* (Studies in the Bible and Early Christianity 14; Lewiston, NY: Edwin Mellen, 1988); cf. her recent contribution "Matthew's Advice to a Divided Readership," in *The Gospel of Matthew in Current Study: Studies in Memory of William G. Thompson, S.J.* (ed. David Aune; Grand Rapids: Eerdmans, 2001), 22–41, here 30: "the Gospel is, finally, a Christian, not a Jewish, text." It is not always easy to categorize scholars in either of these groups, *intra* or *extra muros* (I apologize to anyone who feels that he or she should have been placed in the other category). This difficulty probably has something to do with a not infrequent neglect among researchers to distinguish between the perspective of the Matthean community and that of the parent body (whether called "formative Judaism," "early rabbinic Judaism," or just referred to as "mainstream Judaism" or the like), as has been pointed out by Boris Repschinski, *The Controversy Stories in the Gospel of Matthew: Their Redaction, Form and Relevance for the Relationship between the Matthean Community and Formative Judaism* (FRLANT 189; Göttingen: Vandenhoeck & Ruprecht, 2000), 346–47. To this we shall return below.

⁴ See, e.g., K. W. Clarke, "The Gentile Bias in Matthew," *JBL* 66 (1947): 165–72; Samuel Sandmel, *A Jewish Understanding of the New Testament* (Cincinnati: Hebrew Union College Press, 1956; reprinted [with new preface], Woodstock: SkyLight Paths Publications, 2004); Poul Nepper-Christensen, *Das Matthäusevangelium: Ein judenchristliches Evangelium?* (ATDan 1; Aarhus: Universitetsforlaget, 1958); Georg Strecker, *Der Weg der Gerechtigkeit: Untersuchung zur Theologie des Matthäus* (1962; FRLANT 82; 3rd ed.; Göttingen: Vandenhoeck & Ruprecht, 1971); Sjef van Tilborg, *The Jewish Leaders in Matthew* (Leiden: Brill, 1972); David Flusser, "Two Anti-Jewish Montages in Matthew," *Imm* 5 (1975): 37–45; Lloyd Gaston, "The Messiah of Israel as Teacher of

there are numerous interpretations varying in both methodological approaches and conclusions.[5]

The purpose of the present study is to outline a social-scientific approach to the question of the nature and status of the group(s) that transmitted, redacted, and wrote down the traditions included in the Gospel. I shall begin by noting some problematic terms and categories that, in my opinion, confuse the discussion and may lead to inaccurate conclusions. After having identified the type of religion evidenced by the text and having related that religious type to the question of ethnic identity, I shall examine tensions between the Mattheans and Jewish society generally, on the one hand, and between Mattheans and Pharisees more specifically, on the other. In order to proceed, it will be necessary to reconstruct and analyze first-century institutions of importance to the Mattheans from a social-scientific perspective: we need a body to locate a soul.[6]

I will argue that, while Mattheans were initially part of the Pharisaic association, the community that authored the Gospel was in the process of leaving the larger collectivity after the war of 66–70 C.E. Tensions between the Mattheans and Jewish society generally seem to have been comparatively low, both before and after 70; relations between the Mattheans and other Pharisees, however, were more complex and negative, with tensions increasing drastically after 70 C.E. The final sections will provide detailed as well as more general arguments supporting this reconstruction of the Matthean community and its history. Essential to the present interpretation of the social location of the Mattheans is Ed Sanders's well-argued case for a "common Judaism" in first-century Jewish society, as well as his and others' insistence on the limited influence of the Pharisees in that society.[7]

---

the Gentiles: The Setting of Matthew's Christology," *Int* 21 (1975): 24–40; John P. Meier, *The Vision of Matthew: Christ, Church, and Morality in the First Gospel* (New York: Paulist, 1979); Michael J. Cook, "Interpreting 'Pro-Jewish' Passages in Matthew," *HUCA* 54 (1983): 135–46.

[5] Owing to divergent uses of terminology and different interpretations of how to apply social-scientific concepts and theories, it is not always easy to know where scholars stand in relation to each other. A brief discussion will therefore be given below, presenting the use of some key terms in the present study.

[6] It is common to use the metaphor of body and soul in discussions of sociology and the NT; the importance of reconstructing the institutional framework in which people lived and which provided the stage on which the players enacted their identities and conflicts is, however, not always given appropriate attention. In human societies, "the body" is, to a large degree, constructed with the help of various collectivities, institutions, which tend to determine the formation of identities and the development of conflicts.

[7] E. P. Sanders, *Judaism: Practice and Belief 63 BCE–66 CE* (London: SCM, 1992). Common Judaism is described generally as "what the priests and the people agreed on" (p. 47). The concept thus refers to beliefs and practices of individuals, "ordinary Jews," who did not belong to any specific party. This does not mean, however, that there would not have been considerable overlap between what ordinary Jews and people belonging to parties believed and practiced: such sim-

I. The Religio-Ethnic Identity of the Matthean Community

Theories regarding the religio-ethnic identity of the Mattheans are many and varied, from scholars who see their community as Jewish excluding non-Jews to those who argue for an exclusively non-Jewish community—and several positions in between.[8] Since it is human to think in categories and concepts, and these tend to create boxes limiting our horizons, it is necessary to address the question of terminology in order to take the discussion further.[9]

Most often, Matthean scholars speak of Matthean identity in terms of binary opposites, whereby *Jesus and the disciples/the Mattheans/Christianity/the church* are at one end of the spectrum, and *Jews/Israel/Judaism/the synagogue* at the other.[10] A close reading of the Gospel, however, suggests that such distinctions are not found in the text, but rather imposed on it from other ancient or modern sources. Once such false opposites are removed and authentic opposites mapped, many of the tra-

---

ilarities include the Pharisees (pp. 415–16, 451). See also Jacob Neusner ("The Formation of Rabbinic Judaism: Yavneh (Jamnia) from A.D. 70 to 100," *ANRW* 2.19.2 [1979]: 3–42), who similarly talks about a common Judaism, defining it by referring to three main elements: Torah, temple, and the "common and accepted practices of the ordinary folk—their calendar, their mode of living, their everyday practices and rites, based on these first two" (p. 21). For a critical discussion of common Judaism, see Martin Hengel and Roland Deines, "E. P. Sanders' 'Common Judaism,' Jesus, and the Pharisees," *JTS* 46 (1995): 1–70. On Pharisaic (lack of) influence, see Sanders, *Judaism*, 388–412, 448–51. Sanders refers to Morton Smith, Jacob Neusner, Shaye Cohen, and Martin Goodman as scholars sharing his "'low' view of the authority of the Pharisees" (p. 401). We may add the part of the entry "Φαρισαῖος" (*TDNT* 9) authored by Rudolf Meyer (pp. 11–35); see esp. p. 31, and note the emphasis on the heterogeneity of the Pharisaic movement (pp. 26–28, 35).

[8] For a selection of contributions, see nn. 3–4 above.

[9] The urgency of rethinking often misleading traditional terminology can hardly be overstated, and several scholars have analyzed how flawed ideas extend their lives and prevent more nuanced historical reconstructions by existing within certain key terms that will carry them right into the heart of scholarly analysis. See, e.g., Morton Smith, "Terminological Boobytraps and Real Problems in Second-Temple Judaeo-Christian Studies," in idem, *Studies in the Cult of Yahweh*, vol. 1, *Studies in Historical Method, Ancient Israel, Ancient Judaism* (ed. Shaye J. D. Cohen; Leiden: Brill, 1996), 95–103, esp. 101–3; Anders Runesson, "Particularistic Judaism and Universalistic Christianity? Some Critical Remarks on Terminology and Theology," *Journal of Graeco-Roman Christianity and Judaism* 1 (2000): 120–44; Paula Fredriksen: "Mandatory Retirement: Ideas in the Study of Christian Origins Whose Time Has Come to Go," *SR* 35 (2006): 231–46.

[10] "Synagogue" is usually treated as a phenomenon in the singular and as being in opposition to the "church." The "church," in turn, is often understood as an institution replacing "Israel," and so "Israel," third, is presented as something other than, and opposed to, Jesus and the disciples, with implications for the analysis of the community/-ies behind the text. Fourth, "Christianity" is often treated as if it were a homogeneous phenomenon and, as such, something that can be compared to and contrasted with "Judaism," which, fifth, is also understood in the singular.

ditional conclusions about the relationship between Mattheans and "others" in the Gospel are proved problematic.

Furthermore, the very terms "Jewish Christianity" and/or "Jewish Christians" must also be mentioned as problematic, since they tend to obscure what they intend to denote, namely, a belief in Jesus as the Messiah embodied in communities existing within the religious system of Judaism.[11] Anthony Saldarini and others have argued that the general term indicating this religious type should rather be Christian Judaism(s).[12] However, even if this is an improvement, "Christian" as a name for Christ-believers in the first century is problematic, since it carries with it many meanings from later centuries. In a forthcoming study, Mark Nanos and I have therefore suggested "apostolic Judaism" as a designation for this type of Christ-belief.[13] There is still a need, however, to go beyond such generalizing terms in the analysis of specific theological and halakic expressions *within* apostolic Judaism: thus, within the general category of apostolic Judaism we might refer to distinct types of Christ-centered Judaisms, one of which is, it will be argued, Matthean Judaism.[14]

---

[11] This was noted already by Johannes Munck, "Jewish Christianity in Post-Apostolic Times," *NTS* 6 (1960): 103–16. See also Brown, "Matthean Community," 208–9; Sim, *Christian Judaism*, 25 n. 67. "Religious system" refers to thought patterns and rituals within what can be defined as a "religion" (the term has nothing to do with "systematic theology"). "Type of religion" refers to a larger "family" of religions (cf. the concept of language families), which display important similarities. The relationship between "religious system" and "religious type" is defined in table 1 below.

[12] Saldarini, *Matthew's Christian-Jewish Community*. Before him, Gabriele Boccaccini made the same point (*Middle Judaism: Jewish Thought, 300 B.C.E. to 200 C.E.* [Minneapolis: Fortress, 1991]).

[13] Mark Nanos and Anders Runesson, *Paul and Apostolic Judaism* (in progress). As will be discussed in detail in the book, there are several advantages to this term, which, terminologically, parallels "Pharisaic Judaism," "Enochic Judaism" (cf. the recent study by David R. Jackson, *Enochic Judaism: Three Defining Paradigm Exemplars* [Library of Second Temple Studies 49; London/New York: T&T Clark, 2004]; see also Gabriele Boccaccini, *Beyond the Essene Hypothesis: The Parting of the Ways between Qumran and Enochic Judaism* [Grand Rapids: Eerdmans, 1998]), "rabbinic Judaism," etc. It should be noted that "apostolic Judaism" as a term, just as "Pharisaic Judaism," is not meant to indicate uniformity in beliefs, nor a developed supra-local authority structure among "apostolic Jewish" communities. Rather, it denotes a variant of Jewish religion within which Jesus is accepted—in different ways and with different implications—as the Messiah. See further below.

[14] This would solve the problem Sim (*Christian Judaism*) perceives in Overman's insistence on "Matthean Judaism" as the preferred term. It would also take seriously the specifics of the type of religion that is evidenced in Matthew, which should not be generalized to apply to all variants of apostolic Judaism. As to the general necessity of distinguishing and naming different Christ-believing groups in order to reflect these groups' self-perception, see, e.g., 1 Cor 1:12, where Paul mentions that his name, as well as Apollos's and Cephas's names, has been used by different factions among the Christ-believers to mark distinctive group identities.

Christ-centered Judaism should be distinguished from non-Jewish variants of Christ-centered religion, which, while not being part of the Jewish religious system, are nonetheless examples of "Adonayistic religion." The latter term functions well as a unifying category for all religious traditions, from antiquity until today, focusing practice and belief around the metaphors of God that originate with the Hebrew Bible and the communities that produced these texts.[15]

These observations indicate that, prior to addressing the identity of the community, it is essential to decide if the sacred of that community represents or describes a Jewish or non-Jewish religious perspective.

The first step is to discern the *pattern of religion* presupposed by the text.[16] The importance of analyzing the pattern of religion in order to identify a text as belonging within a certain religious system can hardly be overestimated, especially when dealing with processes in which groups are splitting up and boundaries are being modified. This includes not only theological aspects but also descriptions of practices performed on a day-to-day basis, such as keeping the Sabbath, purity laws, tithing, attending festivals, temple ritual, and so on. In terms of identity formation, these practices may turn out to be more important than any underlying theological motivations for their performance.[17] Furthermore, as James Carleton-Paget has argued, a praxis-oriented criterion for distinguishing Christ-centered Jewish texts ("Jewish-Christian" in Carleton-Paget's terminology) is more effective than a theological/ideological or ethnic criterion.[18] Combining an analysis of the theological pattern in Matthew's Gospel and a broader mapping of the practices endorsed by

---

[15] Cf. Anders Runesson, *The Origins of the Synagogue: A Socio-Historical Study* (ConBNT 37; Stockholm: Almqvist & Wiksell, 2001), 63, where I used the term "Yahwistic" in the same sense; cf. the use of "Yahwistic" by Gary Knoppers, "Mt. Gerizim and Mt. Zion: A Study in the Early History of the Samaritans and Jews," SR 34 (2005): 309–38.

[16] See E. P. Sanders, *Paul and Palestinian Judaism: A Comparison of Patterns of Religion* (London: SCM Press, 1979), 12–18.

[17] See Magnus Zetterholm, *The Formation of Christianity in Antioch: A Social-Scientific Approach to the Separation between Judaism and Christianity* (London/New York: Routledge, 2003). In his criticism of James D. G. Dunn's approach to the problem of the so-called parting(s) of the ways, Zetterholm writes: "While ideological aspects certainly played a vital part in the process, it seems more correct to assume that what Dunn describes as *the cause* of the separation process actually represents *the result* of the separation defined in ideological terms. The reason for this assumption is that *concrete cultural resources* (e.g., church architecture, symbolic practices, liturgical forms) are more likely to be the object of contention, while *abstract resources* (e.g., ideas, ideologies, values) are easier to manipulate and often function as strategically mobilized resources in conflicts over other kinds of resources" (p. 4). Zetterholm refers to F. Kniss, "Ideas and Symbols as Resources in Intrareligious Conflict: The Case of American Mennonites," *Sociology of Religion* 57 (1996): 7–23. See also the emphasis on practice in Sanders, *Judaism*.

[18] Carleton-Paget, "Jewish Christianity." See also Gerd Luedemann's discussion of Jean Daniélou and Marcel Simon in *Opposition to Paul in Jewish Christianity* (trans. M. Eugene Boring; Minneapolis: Fortress, 1989), 25–27.

the text will give us enough information to categorize it by and large as either Jewish or non-Jewish.[19]

This procedure, however, defines only the text, not the community. Jews in antiquity (as today) could and did choose different ways to worship—or not to worship at all—the God of Israel.[20] Likewise, diversity was true with regard to believers in Jesus, whether they were Jews or non-Jews. The neat division between Jews and non-Jews in Acts, and the invention of a specific type of Christ-belief for the latter, was most certainly not acknowledged by everyone, as shown by the Pauline correspondence. Non-Jews sometimes preferred expressing their beliefs within the Jewish religious system (see Gal 2:14; 5:3), others outside it (Acts' solution for non-Jewish converts), and Jews could also choose to live their faith as Gentiles (perhaps Hebrews can be quoted as an example of this position). Thus, an individual or group of non-Jewish ethnic background may well have composed or redacted a text that we would identify as Jewish.[21] We therefore need to ask an additional set of questions of the text in order to clarify the ethnic identity of the author(s).[22] Important here are aspects such as the general depiction and assessment of identifiable ethnic groups in the Gospel.

Space does not allow a full discussion applying this procedure to the Gospel of Matthew and the Mattheans: for this I will have to refer the reader to a forthcoming study.[23] It seems clear, however, that the type of religion represented in

---

[19] It is, thus, not enough to focus on some few isolated features such as alleged anti-Jewish statements, as, e.g., K. W. Clarke and Cook have done. See further below.

[20] For examples, see John M. G. Barclay, *Jews in the Mediterranean Diaspora: From Alexander to Trajan (323 BCE–117 CE)* (Berkeley: University of California Press, 1996).

[21] This is, e.g., Krister Stendahl's view on the author of the Gospel of Matthew, as he presented it in personal communication with the author, June 1997.

[22] The construction of ethnic identity is a complex process. For a general discussion, see Thomas H. Eriksen, *Ethnicity and Nationalism: Anthropological Perspectives* (London: Pluto, 1993). See also Jonathan M. Hall, *Ethnic Identity in Greek Antiquity* (Cambridge/New York: Cambridge University Press, 1997). A recent collection of essays relating the question of ethnicity to biblical texts is found in *Ethnicity and the Bible* (ed. Mark G. Brett; Biblical Interpretation 19; Leiden: Brill, 2002); for the purposes of the present study, see the articles by David Sim, "Christianity and Ethnicity in the Gospel of Matthew," 171–95; and Philip Esler, "Group Boundaries and Intergroup Conflict in Galatians: A New Reading of Galatians 5:13–6:10," 215–40, especially the methodological discussion on pp. 220–31. See also the discussion of ethnicity by Esler in *Conflict and Identity in Romans: The Social Setting of Paul's Letter* (Minneapolis: Fortress, 2003), 40–76. The most recent contribution to the discussion of ethnicity in relation to the claims of early Christ-believers is Denise Kimber Buell, *Why This New Race: Ethnic Reasoning in Early Christianity* (Gender, Theory, Religion; New York: Columbia University Press, 2005).

[23] Anders Runesson, *The Gospel of Matthew and the Myth of Christian Origins: Re-Thinking the So-Called Parting(s) of the Ways between Judaism and Christianity* (in preparation). This study gives a detailed analysis of the elaboration of divine judgment in the Gospel (as it relates to beliefs and practices) as well as the treatment of ethnic groups in the world of the text and the implications of both of these parameters for the ethnic identity of the community. For studies on Matthew

Matthew's Gospel is located within the Jewish religious system. The pattern of religion, analyzed by focusing on one of the fundamental structures of patterns of religion, the theme of divine judgment,[24] indicates a Jewish understanding of divine retribution, punishment, and reward, as opposed to Greco-Roman ideas about judgment.[25] Furthermore, the text accepts most of the practices central to Jewish identity, such as prayer (6:5-7), almsgiving (6:3-4), fasting (6:17-18), the Jewish law/the commandments (5:17-19; 19:17), dietary laws (15:1-20[26]) and other purity laws (8:4, 5-13;[27] 23:25-26), the Sabbath (12:1-14;[28] 24:20), festivals (Passover [26:2, 17-35]), tithing (23:23), the temple cult and practices connected with the temple, including the temple tax (5:23-24; 12:3-5; 17:24-27; 23:19-21),[29] and, most

---

and aspects of covenantal nomism, see, e.g., Benno Przybylski, *Righteousness in Matthew and His World of Thought* (SNTSMS 41; Cambridge/New York: Cambridge University Press, 1980); Kari Syreeni, *The Making of the Sermon on the Mount: A Procedural Analysis of Matthew's Redactoral Activity*, Part 1, *Methodology and Compositional Analysis* (AASF, Dissertationes 44; Helsinki: Suomalainen Tiedeakatemia, 1987). See also, more recently, Luomanen, *Entering the Kingdom of Heaven*.

[24] As is commonly acknowledged, in the NT the Gospel of Matthew emphasizes divine judgment more than any other text. In the author's perspective, the story of Jesus is understood only if and when God's judgment permeates and explains the teaching, events, and conflicts described.

[25] For a study of Greco-Roman thinking on divine judgment, see David Kuck, *Judgment and Community Conflict: Paul's Use of Apocalyptic Judgment Language in 1 Corinthians 3:5-4:5* (NovTSup 66; Leiden: Brill, 1992), 96-149. See also J. Gwyn Griffiths's wide-ranging study of divine judgment, arranged thematically according to ideas about judgment occurring in history and after death respectively, discussing, apart from Israel, Greek, Roman, Egyptian, Hittite, Babylonian, Iranian, and Indian traditions: *The Divine Verdict: A Study of Divine Judgment in the Ancient Religions* (SHR 52; Leiden: Brill, 1991). Recent studies on the judgment in Matthew include Daniel Marguerat, *Le jugement dans l'évangile de Matthieu* (Le Monde de la Bible; 2nd ed.; Geneva: Labor et Fides, 1995); Blaine Charette, *The Theme of Recompense in Matthew's Gospel*, (JSNTSup 79; Sheffield: JSOT Press, 1992); Sim, *Apocalyptic Eschatology*.

[26] Jewish food regulations are not rejected in Matt 15:1-20, which represents the author's reworked version of Markan material, where such regulations are explicitly rejected (Mark 7:19). This suggests that the Mattheans kept the dietary laws.

[27] Jesus never enters the house of the Roman centurion (καὶ λέγει αὐτῷ· ἐγὼ ἐλθὼν θεραπεύσω αὐτόν may be translated as a question: "should I come and cure him?"—so the Swedish translation of 1981, but not, e.g., NRSV, KJV, ASV). W. D. Davies and Dale C. Allison, Jr., read it as a question, comparing the story to Matt 15:21-28 (*A Critical and Exegetical Commentary on the Gospel According to Saint Matthew* [3 vols.; ICC; Edinburgh: T&T Clark, 1988-97], 2:21-22).

[28] Far from abolishing the Sabbath, this passage is a clear example of a discussion of the weightier things in the law: see especially vv. 5, 7, 12. The inviolability of the Sabbath is confirmed in Matt 24:20.

[29] The recognition of the temple is related to Matthew's view of Jerusalem as the holy city (Matt 4:5; 5:35; 27:53): the city receives its holiness from the temple. The holiness of the city is thus connected to the God of Israel and the temple, not the leadership, which is also, however, related

likely, circumcision.[30] As to religious type, then, we may locate Matthean religion in a table as represented on the following page.[31]

When one is analyzing the relationship between type of religion and ethnic identity, it is of some importance to note that, although non-Jewish characters such as the magi (2:1–12), the Roman centurion (8:5–13), and the Canaanite woman (15:21–28) are portrayed positively, these individuals are described as exceptions to the general rule, which is that non-Jews are and do everything that Mattheans should avoid (5:47; 6:7, 32; 18:17). The non-Jewish nations are, furthermore, explicitly prophesied to hate and persecute the disciples/Mattheans (24:9). Jews, however, are never generalized negatively in the same way (negative statements are limited to specific individuals and groups). In fact, all the good things that Mattheans should be and do are parts of Jewish life accepted by other Jews as well.[32] These and other features of the Gospel lead, in my opinion, to the conclusion that the group in which the Gospel originated was ethnically Jewish.[33] Figure 1 on p. 106 includes some examples that may serve as a comparison to highlight the position of the Mattheans.

---

to the city and the temple but as the caretakers of holy things. Indeed, Matthew's perspective is that some groups, which he connects with the temple and the city, were corrupt; they were bad servants, or shepherds (see, e.g., Matt 9:36), or tenants (Matt 21:33, 45) and have thus caused the destruction of both. Note the location of Matt 23:37–24:2 following directly after the criticism of the "scribes and Pharisees." See further below.

[30] Circumcision is not explicitly mentioned in the Gospel, but probably would have been if the Mattheans had rejected this custom, as they did with hand washing before meals (Matt 15:1–20), the use of oaths (Matt 5:33–37; 23:16–22), and divorce (except in the case of πορνεία: Matt 5:31–32; 19:1–12). Scholars arguing that circumcision was part of Matthean practice include Brown, "Matthean Community," 218; Roger Mohrlang, *Matthew and Paul: A Comparison of Ethical Perspectives* (SNTSMS 48; Cambridge/New York: Cambridge University Press, 1984), 44–45; A.-J. Levine, *Social and Ethnic Dimensions*, 183–85; L. Michael White, "Crisis Management and Boundary Maintenance: The Social Location of the Matthean Community," in *Social History of the Matthean Community*, ed. Balch, 211–47, here 241–42 n. 100; Anthony Saldarini, "The Gospel of Matthew and Jewish-Christian Conflict in Galilee," in *The Galilee in Late Antiquity* (ed. Lee I. Levine; New York: Jewish Theological Seminary, 1992), 23–38, here 25–26. (In his study *Matthew's Christian-Jewish Community*, however, Saldarini modifies his position somewhat, stating that "some [Gentiles] may have been circumcised, and some not" [p. 160]); Sim, *Apocalyptic Eschatology*, 208–9; idem, *Christian Judaism*, 251–55; idem, "Christianity and Ethnicity." See also the discussion in Davies and Allison, *Matthew*, 1:7–58.

[31] This categorization differs from several previous attempts at defining especially varieties of Christianity, e.g., Raymond E. Brown, "Not Jewish Christianity and Gentile Christianity but Types of Jewish/Gentile Christianity," *CBQ* 45 (1983): 74–79. Although this study is thought provoking, it suffers from not emphasizing the distinction between the Jewish and the non-Jewish religious systems.

[32] I have listed some such practices above.

[33] See the discussion and conclusion in Davies and Allison, *Matthew*, 1:7–58.

TYPE OF RELIGION						
Adonayistic Religions						**Non-Adonayistic Religions**
Jewish Religious System			Non-Jewish Religious Systems			[Greco-Roman Religions Traditions]
"Common Judaism"	Parties: Apostolic Judaisms and non-Apostolic Judaisms[34]		Non-Jewish Christianities	Samaritanism[35]	Islam[36]	
["What the priests and the people agreed on"[37]]	Pharisaic Judaism; Sadducean Judaism; Essene Judaism	Matthean Judaism; Paul	Ignatius; Irenaeus; Valentinians	Dositheanism	Shia; Sunni	

Table 1. The religious system within which we find the Gospel of Matthew, compared to other variants of Adonayistic religions

[34] This general distinction between Jewish believers in Jesus and "other parties" is adapted to the present study and is unsatisfactory as a general categorization, since it gives the impression that these other parties had things in common, which they did not necessarily have. More important, however, is that there were no neat divisions between these movements and parties, and considerable overlap could exist between the groups. See further below.

[35] Samaritans should be regarded not as a Jewish sect but as an independent interpretation of Israelite religion: see Runesson, *Origins of the Synagogue*, 388-94, and references there, especially the studies by J. D. Purvis and R. J. Coggins. See also Oskar Skarsaune, *In the Shadow of the Temple: Jewish Influences on Early Christianity* (Leicester: InterVarsity Press, 2002), 128: "Samaritanism was not Judaism, for the simple reason that the Samaritans did not recognize the true center." Cf. the conclusion of Martin S. Jaffee, *Early Judaism* (Upper Saddle River, NJ: Prentice Hall, 1997), 138: "These parallels and contrasts lead to an unavoidable conclusion; *the Samaritan's religious world is an example of a Judaic world that, in its own view as well as in the eyes of the Jews, is not part of Judaism*" (emphasis original). Jaffee discusses Samaritans under the heading "Israel but not Jews." For useful introductions to Samaritan history, religion, and culture, see *A Companion to Samaritan Studies* (ed. Alan D. Crown, Reinhard Pummer, and Abraham Tal; Tübingen: Mohr Siebeck, 1993); Robert T. Anderson and Terry Giles, *The Keepers: An Introduction to the History and Culture of the Samaritans* (Peabody, MA: Hendrickson, 2002).

[36] I have included Islam here since current debate on "the parting(s) of the ways" extends into the seventh century and beyond. Thus, according to some scholars, Judaism and Christianity had, in fact, not fully parted ways when Islam emerged on the historical scene. See *The Ways That Never Parted: Jews and Christians in Late Antiquity and the Early Middle Ages* (ed. Adam H. Becker and Annette Yoshiko Reed; Tübingen: Mohr Siebeck, 2003). This conclusion is dependent on how the metaphor "parting(s)" is defined; see, e.g., Judith Lieu, *Neither Jew nor Greek? Constructing Early Christianity* (Studies of the New Testament and Its World; London: T&T Clark, 2002), 11-29.

[37] Sanders, *Judaism*, 47.

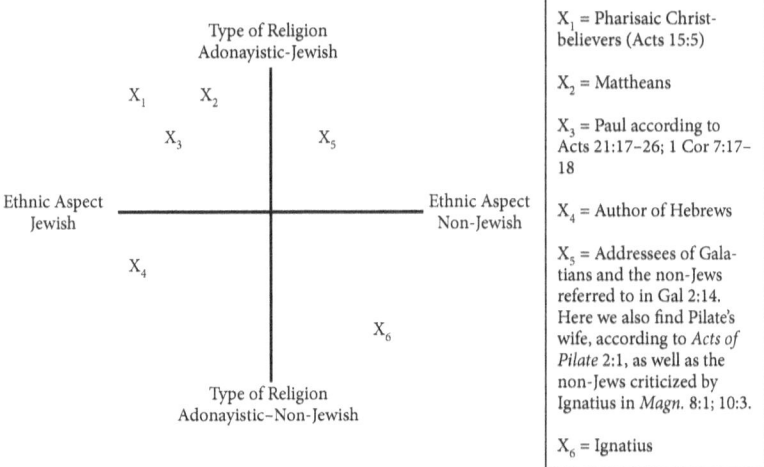

Figure 1. Mapping the relationship between type of religion and ethnic identity

These conclusions find support in several recent studies on Matthew, perhaps most emphatically in the work of David Sim.[38]

II. Place and Date

Our source material does not permit any firm conclusions with regard to the location of the transmission of traditions included in the Gospel of Matthew or to the production of the text as we have it today. The following places have been suggested in the last half century or so: Jerusalem/Palestine, Caesarea Maritima, Phoenicia, Alexandria, east of the Jordan, Edessa, Syria, Antioch.[39] Recently, however, several scholars have argued convincingly for the land of Israel—and, more

---

[38] In addition to the monographs cited above in nn. 23 and 29, see also Sim, "The Gospel of Matthew and the Gentiles," *JSNT* 57 (1995): 19–48; idem, "The 'Confession' of the Soldiers in Matthew 27:54," *HeyJ* 34 (1993): 401–24.

[39] For a discussion of possible locations, see Davies and Allison, *Matthew*, 1:138–47. Davies and Allison end up favoring Antioch, though being careful to point out the lack of evidence supporting this position. See also Graham Stanton, "The Origin and Purpose of Matthew's Gospel," in *ANRW* II.25.3 (ed. Hildegard Temporini and Wolfgang Haase; Berlin: Walter de Gruyter, 1985), 1889–1951, 1941–42. Several scholars reckon with two distinct stages in the life of the community, the first being located in Palestine and the second in Antioch, after the community moved there (because of the Jewish war). These two stages serve an explanatory purpose meant to solve assumed tensions within the Gospel, which, it is argued, occurred due to the change of location: cf., e.g., Brown, "Matthean Community." In my opinion, this is an unnecessary hypothesis, and the tensions within the Gospel can be explained more easily in other ways, as we shall see.

narrowly, Galilee.⁴⁰ Until we have further evidence, in my opinion the scales tip in favor of Galilee; a larger city such as Tiberias or, even more so, Sepphoris may well have provided the socioreligious setting that we see reflected in Matthew's Gospel.

In terms of dates, we need to distinguish between pre- and post-70 C.E. Matthean traditions.⁴¹ For the final text, I suggest, like the majority of scholars, a date in the 80s or 90s.⁴²

These conclusions, namely, that we are dealing with Jewish Christ-believers in a larger city in Galilee in the latter half of the first century, will serve as a basic point of departure for the reconstruction of the institutional setting and, by implication, for the analysis of the interaction between the Mattheans, the society in which they lived, and the groups that influenced the formation of their identity. In the following I shall treat social tensions (i.e., tensions between the Mattheans and Jewish society in general) separately from the conflicts these people experienced with spe-

---

⁴⁰ Overman, *Church and Community*, 16–19; he suggests Sepphoris or Tiberias. Eduard Schweizer suggests "Syria, or perhaps the neighbouring areas of Galilee" as the most probable supposition ("Matthew's Church," in *Interpretation of Matthew*, ed. Stanton, 149–77); Saldarini concludes that "[t]he Galilee, with its complex and cosmopolitan society and its tightly woven cultural network, could easily have supported the nascent rabbinic Jewish and Christian Jewish movements, as well as the other apocalyptic, priestly, messianic, revivalist, and revolutionary currents running through society" ("Jewish-Christian Conflict," 26–27); see also Segal, "Matthew's Jewish Voice," 26–29; Daniel J. Harrington, *The Gospel of Matthew* (SP; Collegeville, MN: Liturgical Press, Michael Glazier, 1991); Ekkehard W. Stegemann and Wolfgang Stegemann, *The Jesus Movement: A Social History of Its First Century* (Minneapolis: Fortress, 1999), 223–29. Aaron M. Gale concludes that Sepphoris is the best candidate (*Redefining Ancient Borders: The Jewish Scribal Framework of Matthew's Gospel* [New York: T&T Clark, 2005], 41–63).

⁴¹ Cf. the pre- and post-70 stages in the life of the Matthean community according to Brown, "Matthean Community." *Pace* Brown, however, the hypothesis that the community moved to Antioch after 70 is not needed to explain the text of the Gospel.

⁴² This is the position of the overwhelming majority of Matthean scholars, and any commentary may be consulted for detailed arguments (see, e.g., Davies and Allison, *Matthew*, 1:127–38, who list scholarly views since Grotius [!]). In the discussion of internal evidence, the Synoptic Problem has a primary place. If we do not accept Q (see Mark Goodacre, *The Case against Q: Studies in Markan Priority and the Synoptic Problem* [Harrisburg, PA: Trinity Press International, 2002]), Matthew would have to predate Luke, who would be using Matthew and Mark (this solution is, in my opinion, the only real competitor to the two-source hypothesis). Cf. the recent study by Benedict Viviano ("John's Use of Matthew: Beyond Tweaking," *RB* 111 [2004]: 209–37), in which he argues that the author of the Gospel of John knew Matthew, which would place Matthew in the 80s at the latest, if we accept a date for John in the 90s. Be that as it may, there are, in any case, several good arguments for placing Matthew in the late first century. One of the key passages always referred to is Matt 22:7, which is argued to convey knowledge of the destruction of Jerusalem. As to external evidence, quotations of or allusions to Matthew in early-second-century church fathers serve as a *terminus ante quem*. The following texts are listed by Davies and Allison and are usually part of the discussion: Ignatius, the *Didache*, Polycarp, the *Epistle of Barnabas*, the *Gospel of Peter*, and Justin Martyr. See also the discussion provided by scholars listed in n. 2 above.

cific groups. In order to do so, we need to reconstruct the first-century Jewish institutional setting and analyze Matthean attitudes to it. This will enable us to define the social status of the group in a two-step procedure.

III. Social Tensions, Common Judaism, and the Problem of the "Jewish Majority"

Much research on the Mattheans builds on the assumption that there existed a dominant group in Jewish society (variously identified as the Pharisees, "formative Judaism," "very early rabbinic Judaism," or just "the Jews" or "Judaism"), in relation to which the Mattheans would be described as a sect. Most often, regardless of the assumed location of the Mattheans, the Pharisees have been said to be extremely influential in society.[43] On the basis of careful analysis especially of Josephus, Sanders has argued convincingly against this majority view, and he is supported by an increasing number of scholars, though some variation exists regarding exactly how high or low the level of Pharisaic influence was.[44] The discussion has centered mostly on the pre-70 period, leaving aside the time when Matthew's Gospel was written down. Indeed, while older research tended to equate Pharisees and rabbis and claim a continuous and increasing influence of the Pharisees in the form of rabbinic Judaism after 70 C.E., more recent contributions have questioned such continuity in favor of more complex origins for rabbinic Judaism.

In this regard, Jacob Neusner's identification of a "formative Judaism"—an emerging coalition of different groups and individuals, predominantly Pharisees, priests, and landowners, evolving after 70 C.E.[45]—has played an increasingly important role in the discussion of the social context of the Mattheans.[46] The basic idea

---

[43] Proponents of a high level of influence of the Pharisees include Emil Schürer, Kaufman Kohler, Gedaliah Alon, and Louis Finkelstein, all mentioned by Steve Mason, "Pharisaic Dominance Before 70 CE and the Gospel's Hypocrisy Charge (Matt 23:2–3)," *HTR* 83 (1990): 363–81, here 363–64. Mason's article itself provides a renewed attempt at arguing for a pre-70 dominance of the Pharisees. See also Peter J. Tomson, *"If This Be from Heaven": Jesus and the New Testament Authors in Their Relationship to Judaism* (Biblical Seminar 76; Sheffield: Sheffield Academic Press, 2001), 50–55.

[44] See Mason, "Pharisaic Dominance," 363–67. There are basically three source groups available on the basis of which conclusions may be drawn: Josephus, the NT, and early rabbinic writings.

[45] Jacob Neusner has discussed formative Judaism in several publications. See, e.g., "Formation of Rabbinic Judaism"; and *Judaism: The Evidence of the Mishnah* (Chicago: University of Chicago Press, 1981).

[46] Cf. Saldarini, who states that Matthew is "probably responding to the leaders of an early form of rabbinic Judaism who were competing with him for the loyalties of the local Jewish Community" ("Jewish-Christian Conflict," 30–31 n. 22). See also Overman, who defines formative

is that, in order to explain the polemics of Matthew's Gospel, a dominant force in *society* needs to be postulated, against which the Mattheans compete for power and influence in the power vacuum created after the fall of the temple. Scholars therefore describe the Mattheans as a sect, using the broader definition of this term and focusing on the wider society in which a group exists, rather than any specific religious body from which another religious group would deviate.[47]

The question is, of course, whether such a majority existed in the last quarter of the first century. The general tendency in societies undergoing major turbulence, as the war of 66–70 certainly produced, seems to be that people who enjoyed privileged positions and political power before the devastation in one way or the other continue to exercise influence and power after it. Only rarely are political elites completely displaced.[48] There are, in fact, several problems with assuming an immediate rise to power of "formative Judaism."

It is quite possible that the Pharisaic movement experienced an influx of sympathizers after the war and that, as a result, the group took off in a certain direction, negotiating and modifying certain Pharisaic traditions and customs to the new situation. Already before 70 the Pharisees seem to have been home to a variety of

---

Judaism as a precursor to rabbinic Judaism, which came to dominate Judaism in late antiquity (*Formative Judaism*, 2). Sim concludes that formative Judaism "was certainly cohesive enough and sufficiently influential in *the society* of the Matthean community ... to stand as the parent body with which the evangelist and his group were in dispute" (*Christian Judaism*, 113–15; quotation from 115; my emphasis).

[47] The latter is the traditional focus for the definition of sect, going back to Ernst Troeltsch, *The Social Teaching of the Christian Churches* (2 vols.; Library of Theological Ethics; Louisville: Westminster John Knox, 1992), originally published in German in 1931. Most scholars who refer to Troeltsch point out the need to revise his concepts and categories. See Bryan R. Wilson, *Religion in Sociological Perspective* (Oxford: Oxford University Press, 1982), who distinguishes seven types of sects: coversionist, revolutionist, introversionist, manipulationist, thaumaturgical, reformist, and utopian. See also Bengt Holmberg, *Sociology and the New Testament: An Appraisal* (Minneapolis: Fortress, 1990), 108–10; Petri Luomanen, "The 'Sociology of Sectarianism' in Matthew: Modelling the Genesis of Early Jewish and Christian Communities," in *Fair Play: Diversity and Conflicts in Early Christianity; Essays in Honour of Heikki Räisänen* (ed. Ismo Dunderberg, Christopher Tuckett, and Kari Syreeni; NovTSup 103; Leiden/Boston: Brill, 2002), 109–14; Benton Johnson defines a sect as a group that rejects the social environment in which it exists, in contrast to "church," which refers to a group that accepts its social environment ("On Church and Sect," *American Sociological Review* 28 [1963]: 539–49). We shall return to this discussion below. On a general note, it must be emphasized that even if the sociological terminology in itself is heavily influenced by Christian culture, the four basic categories being "sect," "church," "denomination," and "cult," I use these terms strictly technically as sociological terms, without Christian content, to describe and categorize socioreligious phenomena.

[48] Cf., e.g., how Josephus managed to arrange not only for his survival after the war but also for a position from which he could continue to exercise influence. The same is true for Josephus's enemy Justus of Tiberias, who after the war became the secretary/historian of Agrippa II: see Tessa Rajak, *Josephus: The Historian and His Society* (Philadelphia: Fortress, 1984), 146.

subgroups, some of which, however, eventually left the movement.⁴⁹ Furthermore, it is probable that Pharisaism, as a result of these changes, eventually developed into what we know as rabbinic Judaism. What is not clear, however, is whether even fully developed rabbinic Judaism had an influential position in Jewish society before the sixth century or even later.⁵⁰ In other words, we know very little about the late first century that would enable us to talk about a powerful formative/early rabbinic Judaism in relation to which the Mattheans can be said to deviate. Saldarini was aware of this problem and therefore suggested that we are dealing with *local* influence of formative Judaism in the Galilean city where the Mattheans lived.⁵¹ It is not entirely apparent, however, whether he understands the Mattheans to be deviant in relation to a majority Judaism/Jewish society, or in relation to a specific leading group, which may or may not have had support among the majority of Jews. In any case, Saldarini defines the "leadership group" as a "reform/reformist movement." A quotation from his 1992 article on Matthew 23 is clarifying:

> In the late first century the very early rabbinic coalition was, like Matthew's group, a reform movement. They and Matthew were rivals for influence and access to power in the assemblies and other institutions of the Jewish community. Each sought not to form a new sect, but to gather the disparate groups and forms of Judaism into one fold. At this stage of Judaism's development, neither group was dominant in the Jewish community as a whole, but in Matthew's city or area the rabbinic group's program was more influential than Matthew's Jesus-centered Judaism.⁵²

---

⁴⁹ See Meyer, "Φαρισαῖος," 16–31. The basic point Meyer makes is well taken; however, some of his reconstructions display a somewhat optimistic approach to the many problems of the source material that is difficult to accept.

⁵⁰ See Shaye J. D. Cohen, *From the Maccabees to the Mishnah* (LEC 7; Philadelphia: Westminster, 1987), 221–24; idem, "The Place of the Rabbi in Jewish Society of the Second Century," in *Galilee in Late Antiquity*, ed. L. I. Levine, 157–71; Lee I. Levine "The Sages and the Synagogue in Late Antiquity: The Evidence of the Galilee," in *Galilee in Late Antiquity*, ed. L. I. Levine, 201–22. Seth Schwartz makes a convincing case for understanding the (re-)construction of Jewish identity as partly a result of the Christianization of the Roman Empire in late antiquity (*Imperialism and Jewish Society: 200 B.C.E. to 640 C.E.* [Jews, Christians, and Muslims from the Ancient to the Modern World; Princeton: Princeton University Press, 2001]). Schwartz does not, however, see the rabbis as being particularly influential in this process, and he dates their rise to prominence in the early Middle Ages. Elsewhere I have discussed the fact that the lack of rabbinic influence prior to this date is further evidenced in the art of several fourth-century and later synagogue buildings ("From Integration to Marginalization: Archaeology as Text and the Analysis of Early Diaspora Judaism" [in Swedish], *SEÅ* 67 [2002]: 121–44, here 125–26). See also my "Architecture, Conflict, and Identity Formation: Jews and Christians in Capernaum from the First to the Sixth Century," in *Religion, Ethnicity, and Identity in Ancient Galilee* (ed. Jürgen Zangenberg, Harold W. Attridge, and Dale B. Martin; WUNT 201; Tübingen: Mohr Siebeck, 2007), 231–57.

⁵¹ Cf. Sim, who addresses the same difficulty, but in relation to Antioch, where he believes the Mattheans belonged (*Christian Judaism*, 115).

⁵² Anthony J. Saldarini, "Delegitimation of Leaders in Matthew 23," *CBQ* (1992): 663–64.

It seems as if Saldarini here equates the Mattheans and "early rabbis" regarding their relationship to society at large: he labels both "reform movements" (according to Bryan R. Wilson's sevenfold definition of "sect," they would be defined as "reformist sects"[53]), one being more successful locally—but not universally—than the other. If I understand Saldarini correctly, his conclusion is that the (reformist) sect of "very early rabbis"/formative Judaism is the *local* leadership group in Jewish society defining the parent body in relation to which the Matthean reformist sect deviated. There is no direct connection between the Mattheans and the Pharisees; the tensions are created in a struggle over influence in society. If this is correct, the obvious question would be: If the early rabbis were a reformist sect, in relation to whom did they, in turn, deviate? At this point we need to take into account common Judaism, as described by Sanders, before 70 C.E., as well as discuss the institutional framework of first-century Jewish society.

There are no indications that common Judaism ceased to exist immediately after 70 C.E., and the reason for this is connected with the role and function of public institutions beyond the Jerusalem temple. Therefore, it is crucial to the following discussion that "synagogue" be defined.[54]

Despite some recent statements to the contrary,[55] the centrality of the synagogue(s) in first-century Jewish society cannot be doubted.[56] The problem lies rather in identifying the nature of the institution(s) referred to by synagogue terms.[57] In the first century, the term "synagogue" was not yet fixed to describe

---

[53] See Saldarini, "Jewish-Christian Conflict," 114.

[54] I refer the reader to my *Origins of the Synagogue*, ch. 3, for a full discussion. See also my "The Origins and Nature of the 1st Century Synagogue," *Bible and Interpretation*, July 2004, http://www.bibleinterp.com/articles/Runesson-1st-Century_Synagogue_1.htm.

[55] See, e.g., Howard Clark Kee, "The Transformation of the Synagogue after 70 C.E.: Its Importance for Early Christianity," NTS 36 (1990): 1–24 (reprinted in *The Evolution of the Synagogue: Problems and Progress* [ed. Howard Clark Kee and Lynn H. Cohick; Harrisburg, PA: Trinity Press International, 1999], 7–26); cf. Lieu, *Neither Jew nor Greek?* 25–26.

[56] See, e.g., Donald D. Binder, *Into the Temple Courts: The Place of the Synagogue in the Second Temple Period* (SBLDS 169; Atlanta: Society of Biblical Literature, 1999); Lee I. Levine, *The Ancient Synagogue: The First Thousand Years* (2nd ed.; New Haven: Yale University Press, 2005); Runesson, *Origins of the Synagogue*. See also James F. Strange, "Synagogue as Metaphor," in *Judaism in Late Antiquity*, part 3, *Where We Stand: Issues and Debates in Ancient Judaism*, vol. 4, *The Special Problem of the Ancient Synagogue* (ed. Alan J. Avery-Peck et al.; Leiden/New York: Brill, 2001), 93-120; idem, "Archaeology and Ancient Synagogues up to about 200 C.E.," in *The Ancient Synagogue: From Its Origins until 200 C.E.: Papers Presented at an International Conference at Lund University October 14–17, 2001* (ed. Birger Olsson and Magnus Zetterholm; Stockholm: Almqvist & Wiksell International, 2003), 37–62. For a comprehensive presentation of evidence of synagogues from the third century B.C.E. to 200 C.E., see Anders Runesson, Donald D. Binder, and Birger Olsson, *The Ancient Synagogue from Its Origins to 200 C.E.* (Ancient Judaism and Early Christianity 72; Leiden: Brill, 2008).

[57] It is clear that we are not, *contra* Kee ("Transformation"), dealing with informal gather-

only one type of institution: this is a later development that should not be read back into the first century. Συναγωγή, as well as other terms that were used synonymously, referred to two basic types of institution.[58] On the one hand, in the land of Israel synagogue terms could refer to a *public village or town assembly*, a kind of municipal institution, or the building in which the meetings of such an institution were held. The functions of this institution included, apart from political and judicial procedures, the public reading of Torah on Sabbaths. No specific group, such as the Pharisees or "early rabbis," was in charge of this institution, neither before 70 nor immediately after, and leadership could vary from place to place. Rather, individuals and groups could use public meetings to promote their own understanding of religious traditions and Jewish law, and how they should be implemented in contemporary society.[59]

The other kind of institution referred to by synagogue terms was of a voluntary-association type, similar to those that existed in Greco-Roman society generally, the *collegia*.[60] An example of this type of institution is found in Acts 6:9, where a "synagogue of the Freedmen" is mentioned.[61] These association synagogues provided a non-, or semipublic, institutional setting in which groups could maintain their specific religious and/or other identities. Philo reports that the Essenes had their own synagogue (*Prob.* 81); in the same way, the Pharisees and other Jewish

---

ings, as is shown, e.g., by the elaborate hierarchy of leadership indicated by titles used for individuals related to the synagogue: e.g., *archōn* (Josephus, *Vit.* 278, 294), *archisynagōgos* (Mark 5:22; *CIJ* no. 1404), *prostatēs* (*JIGRE* [*Jewish Inscriptions of Graeco-Roman Egypt: With an Index of the Jewish Inscriptions of Egypt and Cyrenaica* (Cambridge/New York: Cambridge University Press, 1992)], no. 24), *presbyteros* (Jdt 6:16; Luke 7:3–5), *gerōn* (Philo, *Hypoth.* 7.13), *grammateus* (Mark 1:22; *CPJ* no. 138), *nakoros* (*CPJ* no. 129), *hypēretēs* (Luke 4:20) or *archihypēretēs* (*CPJ* no. 138).

[58] I argue this case extensively and discuss the evidence in *Origins of the Synagogue*; see esp. ch. 3. For a list of synagogue terms and examples where they occur, see pp. 171–73. Cf. Cohen, who prefers a three-part distinction between forerunners to the later synagogue (*Maccabees*, 111–15).

[59] There are numerous general references in the Gospels to Jesus visiting, preaching, and healing in these synagogues. The judicial activities of public synagogues are mentioned, e.g., in Mark 13:9; readings and teaching of Torah are mentioned, e.g., in relation to the synagogues of Nazareth (Luke 4:16–30) and Capernaum (Mark 1:21–28). The closest modern institutional—and internal-architectural—parallel, excluding what we would call the religious component, would be the British parliament, thought of in local terms.

[60] For a thorough study of the *collegia* of Asia Minor, including discussion of synagogues and (Christian) congregations as examples of *collegia*, see Philip A. Harland, *Associations, Synagogues, and Congregations: Claiming a Place in Ancient Mediterranean Society* (Minneapolis: Fortress, 2003); note especially the categorization of different types of *collegia* (pp. 28–53). See also Peter Richardson, "An Architectural Case for Synagogues as Associations," in *Ancient Synagogue*, ed. Olsson and Zetterholm, 90–117.

[61] The Greek here is ambiguous. Either we are dealing with a synagogue of the Freedmen, which included members from Cyrene, Alexandria, Cilicia, and Asia, or the text refers to multiple synagogues. Apart from the synagogue of the Freedmen, we would then find, in Jerusalem, four more synagogues, serving the needs of Jews coming from the places mentioned.

groups, such as the Therapeutae (Philo, *De Vita Contemplativa*⁶²), would have made use of a similar institutional framework.⁶³

In addition to the synagogue(s), the Jerusalem temple and attitudes toward it must be taken into account, since the temple represented official religion in Jewish society before its destruction and continued to be a focal point for Jewish religious thinking. The temple was the center of the Jewish religious system as well as the heart of political affairs. The temple thus represented the state and "state religion"; therefore, it is crucial to analyze the attitudes of a specific group, or association synagogue, to the temple, since this will inform us about the distance perceived between the group in question and official religion, as well as about the nature of that distance.

The temple and the cult did not constitute a specific ideological force in society in the same way that the parties did: parties could be fighting each other, trying to influence political and religious events and structures in society, but still accept the cult and the authorities there.⁶⁴ The temple had its ideological extension and social base in common Judaism among "ordinary Jews," and the overlap between Pharisaic (and other groups') beliefs and practices and those of common Judaism indicates that we are dealing with a phenomenon closely related to what sociologists have called *civil religion*.⁶⁵ The fact that civil religion in the land of

---

[62] Two recent studies have argued forcefully, and successfully, that Philo did not invent this group but was describing an existing Jewish community: Joan E. Taylor, *Jewish Women Philosophers of First-Century Alexandria: Philo's 'Therapeutae' Reconsidered* (Oxford/New York: Oxford University Press, 2003); Mary Ann Beavis, "Philo's Therapeutai: Philosopher's Dream or Utopian Construction?" *JSP* 14 (2004): 30–42.

[63] See Runesson, *Origins of the Synagogue*. The Qumran community is also best understood as an association: see Matthias Klinghardt, "The Manual of Discipline in the Light of Statutes of Hellenistic Associations," in *Methods of Investigation of the Dead Sea Scrolls and the Khirbet Qumran Site: Present Realities and Future Prospects* (New York: New York Academy of Sciences, 1994), 251–67. Cf. Moshe Weinfeld, *The Organizational Pattern and the Penal Code of the Qumran Sect: A Comparison with Guilds and Religious Associations of the Hellenistic-Roman Period* (NTOA 2; Göttingen: Vandenhoeck & Ruprecht, 1986). As to descriptions of the later rabbinic group as a (professional) guild, see Jack N. Lightstone, *Mishnah and the Social Formation of the Early Rabbinic Guild: A Socio-Rhetorical Approach* (Waterloo, ON: Wilfrid Laurier University Press, 2002), esp. 183–200. Lightstone understands the rabbinic guild to have originated with "refugees from the Temple state's national bureaucracy and administration, who, having lost their institutional base, first tried to preserve and pass on their professional guild expertise" (p. 186).

[64] A conflict within the political and cultic establishment, however, could lead to separation of an association from the temple and thus from state religion and society at large, the obvious example being the Qumran community. See, e.g., the chart in Sanders, *Judaism*, 28. Other disputes over political and cultic control occurred with different outcomes: some would establish temples elsewhere, Leontopolis in Egypt being the most well known example. See Runesson, *Origins of the Synagogue*, 403–36.

[65] Of the four types of civil religion that have been identified, we are here dealing with a case where a particular religion and the state are not differentiated: see Clifford Geertz, "The Inte-

Israel was not dependent on an exact match with the administrative and political boundaries of the area after Herod I requires some comments.

While the different areas of the land were governed independently, all relating to Rome and the Roman presence in the land, in terms of *nation building*[66] Jerusalem and its cult played a major role for the national and religious identity of both "ordinary Jews" and the various parties. For the Jerusalem authorities, then, as well as for other groups, national identity extended beyond the immediate administrative and political borders resulting from Roman imperial[67] strategies after the reign of Herod I. This situation goes back to and is explained by the Hasmonean creation of an independent Jewish state covering roughly these areas.[68] The Hasmonean political strategy was to unify the country by nation building based on shared religious institutions and a centralized cult, a strategy that included forced conversion/circumcision of people in the annexed territories.[69] This provided a foundation for Herod to reconstruct the state/nation, and the notion among the Jewish inhabitants of a single religio-political identity was strong enough to survive the splitting up of the state into several administrative units.[70]

---

grative Revolution: Primordial Sentiments and Civil Politics in the New States," in *Old Societies and New States: The Quest for Modernity in Asia and Africa* (ed. Clifford Geertz; New York: Free Press, 1963), 105–57. For a discussion of other forms of civil religion, see Meredith B. McGuire, *Religion: The Social Context* (2nd ed.; Belmont, CA: Wadsworth, 1987), 163–64.

[66] "Nation building" refers to the construction of a sense of solidarity and identity as a collective defined by the limits within which the "state," defined as the organization developed to run everyday business relating to a country's internal and external affairs, operates.

[67] "Imperial"/"imperialism" as well as "colonial"/"colonialism" are terms often used interchangeably. For a discussion of this terminology, see, e.g., Ania Loomba, *Colonialism/Postcolonialism* (New Critical Idiom; London: Routledge, 1998), 1–7: "Like 'colonialism,' this concept [i.e., imperialism] too is best understood not by trying to pin it down to a single semantic meaning but by relating its shifting meanings to historical processes" (p. 4). Imperial interests and exercise of power do not require direct political rule over a nation. In this sense, Roman "imperialism" fits the situation in both the Galilee and Judea pre- and post-70 C.E., while "colonial" should be restricted to Judea under direct Roman rule from 6 C.E. onwards—and then, of course, from Hadrian onwards applying to both regions.

[68] Before Hasmonean expansion, the (secondary) state created by the Persians covered only Yehud/Judah: the national identity constructed around the Jerusalem temple at that time was limited to this province.

[69] This strategy was used by several of the Hasmonean rulers, according to Josephus: Hyrcanus (*A.J.* 13.257–58); Aristobulos I (*A.J.* 13.397); Alexander Janneus (*A.J.* 13.318–19).

[70] This does not mean that all areas and inhabitants of the state under Hasmonean or Herodian rule were Jewish: both Hasmonean and Herodian rule included territory that was not Jewish, and non-Jewish areas were distinguished from the Jewish in terms of how they were ruled: see E. P. Sanders, "Jesus' Galilee," in *Fair Play*, ed. Dunderberg et al., 3–41. The point made here is rather about the sense of identity in the Jewish population, which combines political, geographical, and ideological aspects, taken both from Scriptures read each Sabbath in the public assemblies and from recent and not so recent historical developments. The religious, or ideological,

Although the type of civil religion referred to above is, as Meredith McGuire notes,[71] a less obvious form of civil religion because of its close relationship to one religion, it fits Jewish society especially well after the formation of the parties. These parties, while being thoroughly convinced of the truth of their own distinctive interpretations, traditions, and customs, nevertheless accepted national religion as expressed in the Jerusalem cult. In other words, common Judaism had its sociological roots in the Hasmonean period as part of the revolutionaries' nation building, and it continued to have that function even after national independence and territorial unity had been lost.

To relate to civil religion was, therefore, to relate to national identity, and, by implication, to its ultimate ideal: the independence of a reunited state. For the parties and movements, most of which accepted civil religion,[72] wanting to influence Jewish life in any specific direction, this meant that they were also endorsing a specific political, or national, "program." Such acceptance of civil religion makes it difficult to speak of Pharisees (or, e.g., Sadducees) as a "sect" in the sense of the word used by Overman and Saldarini. These groups, on account of their acceptance of the Jerusalem cult and thus the religiously legitimate use of it by individuals other than their own members, should rather be understood as phenomena closer to the sociological category of *denomination*.[73] This does not mean that the Pharisees did not wish to reform society—on the contrary. But such a wish does not change the overall classification, or categorization, of the group. In the case of the Pharisees, therefore, it is better to talk about a *reform-oriented denomination*.[74]

Before relating the Mattheans to Jewish society and civil religion as evidenced in public institutions, we may summarize the above reconstruction of relevant institutions in the graph on the next page.

Analyzing the Mattheans and their relation to society, we need to assess the evidence of the Gospel text with regard to its attitudes to the temple and the public synagogues. Doing so, we shall continue to discuss the relationship between the Mattheans and other Jewish groups, understanding them as associations, and focusing on the Pharisees.

---

component of the vision of a unified nation is quite clear from the strategy of forced circumcision applied by the Hasmoneans (above n. 69).

[71] See n. 65 above.

[72] The Qumran community would be one obvious exception.

[73] I define *denomination* as pluralistic in terms of self-conceived legitimacy, and positive in terms of society tension. See McGuire, *Religion*, 119; cf. Loumanen's discussion of Overman and Saldarini in this regard ("Sociology of Sectarianism," 109–13). Luomanen correctly points out that it is misleading to designate the Pharisees as a sect (p. 124).

[74] The political aspirations of the Pharisees—and their failure to achieve the power and influence they aimed for—is described by Sanders, *Judaism*, 388–412.

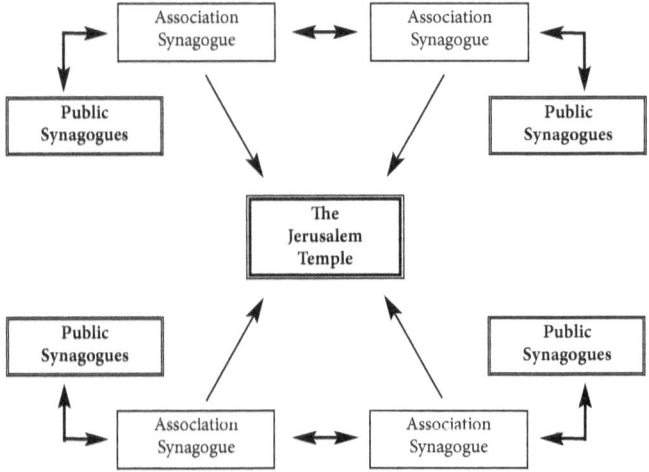

Figure 2. Reconstruction of the institutional framework of first-century Jewish society. Arrows indicate possible interaction between association synagogues and between associations and local as well as central public institutions.

The Gospel of Matthew indicates that its author and its immediate audience acknowledged the Jerusalem temple and its cult while the temple still stood, and continued to revere both Jerusalem and the temple after 70 C.E. (5:23–24; 12:3–5; 17:24–27). Jerusalem is the holy city before as well as after the death of Jesus (Matt 4:5; 5:35; 27:53), and there are no indications of any other event that would have changed this attitude. Contrary to the view of Saldarini,[75] the destruction of Jerusalem and the temple, of which the final redactor was aware, does not affect the holiness of, or respect for, the temple itself. Rather, the destruction is used to blame the leaders who had been appointed by God but who had used their position in ways contrary to God's purposes.[76] The city receives its holiness from the temple. The holiness of the city is thus connected with the God of Israel and the temple, not the leaders, who are also, however, related to the city and the temple but as the caretakers of things holy. Matthew's perspective is that some groups, which are connected with the temple and the city, were corrupt and acted as bad servants, or shepherds (see, e.g., 9:36), or tenants (21:33, 45), and had thus caused the disastrous destruction of both temple and city.

In relation to the Jewish state and state religion as represented by the temple, and thus civil religion, it seems as if the Mattheans were not taking a sectarian

---

[75] Saldarini, "Jewish-Christian Conflict," 33.

[76] This is why the temple needed to be cleansed (Matt 21:12–13). The fact that Jesus is regarded as something greater than the temple (12:6) is not meant to reduce the significance of the temple, but to enhance and emphasize the status and position of Jesus as God's Messiah.

stance. Indeed, by locating 23:37–24:2 directly after and thus in conjunction with the severe criticism of the Pharisees in ch. 23, the author in fact limits the responsibility of the Jerusalem leadership and attempts to transfer the guilt of the destruction of Jerusalem to the Pharisees, who, obviously, were not in charge of political affairs at the time. The same effect is aimed for when the author, alone among the Synoptics, introduces the Pharisees in the passion narrative after the death of Jesus. This creates the impression that the Pharisees were part of the leadership handing Jesus over to the Romans while, in fact, the "original" passion narrative lacks any references to the Pharisees.[77] In conclusion, the text indicates tensions between Jerusalem authorities (the chief priests, as well as references to Jerusalem as a metaphor for religio-political leadership) and the Mattheans, but these tensions are less emphatic than those between the Mattheans and the Pharisees. The political establishment—and thus the state—is not (most likely contrary to the attitude of the historical Jesus) the primary target of Matthean hostile rhetoric: the group referred to as Pharisees is.

Several scholars have pointed to the references to "their/your synagogue(s)," which have few parallels outside Matthew's Gospel,[78] arguing that this expression reflects a situation *extra muros*, or beyond "synagogue"/"Judaism," on the part of the Mattheans. However, locating these statements in their "body," the institutional setting of first-century Palestine, will yield a very different, indeed opposite, conclusion. In table 2 on the next page, I sort and summarize the passages in question and then comment on each instance of the expression.

First, it is clear that we cannot generalize the meaning of αὐτῶν in relation to synagogues. It is sometimes used to indicate public institutions in specific places that Jesus visited (4:23; 9:35; 13:54). That these institutions are public may be inferred from the fact that the reference is to large geographical areas or specific cities or villages: synagogues as public institutions represent the inhabitants of these places. When the reference is general, the evaluation is neutral; when the reference is specific (Jesus' hometown [13:54]), the evaluation is mixed or negative. One may conclude that the negative reaction is the exception and the neutral, nonhostile reaction is the rule. *Second*, supporting this conclusion is the fact that the general references to synagogues (without αὐτῶν [6:2, 5; 23:6]) indicate that the Mattheans regard the public synagogue as the normal or accepted place for worship in local

---

[77] In Matthew, the Pharisees disappear in 23:29 and reappear together with the chief priests in 27:62; Mark and Luke do not mention them at all after Mark 12:13 and Luke 19:39.

[78] The references in Mark 1:23, 39 are sometimes explained as non-Markan insertions, possibly by a copyist influenced by the Gospel of Matthew. See George Dunbar Kilpatrick, *The Origins of the Gospel According to St. Matthew* (Oxford: Clarendon, 1946), 111. Although this is a possibility, it is an unnecessary hypothesis since the meaning of "their" may shift both within Matthew, and between Matthew and Mark. Cf. the one instance in Luke 4:15, and see further below.

Activity	Verse	Text	"Their/your Synagogue(s)"	Reference	Neutral/ Negative
Teaching	4:23	Καὶ περιῆγεν ἐν ὅλῃ τῇ Γαλιλαίᾳ διδάσκων ἐν ταῖς συναγωγαῖς αὐτῶν καὶ κηρύσσων τὸ εὐαγγέλιον τῆς βασιλείας καὶ θεραπεύων πᾶσαν νόσον καὶ πᾶσαν μαλακίαν ἐν τῷ λαῷ.	X	Location	Neutral
Teaching	9:35	Καὶ περιῆγεν ὁ Ἰησοῦς τὰς πόλεις πάσας καὶ τὰς κώμας διδάσκων ἐν ταῖς συναγωγαῖς αὐτῶν καὶ κηρύσσων τὸ εὐαγγέλιον τῆς βασιλείας καὶ θεραπεύων πᾶσαν νόσον καὶ πᾶσαν μαλακίαν.	X	Location	Neutral
Teaching	13:54	καὶ ἐλθὼν εἰς τὴν πατρίδα αὐτοῦ ἐδίδασκεν αὐτοὺς ἐν τῇ συναγωγῇ αὐτῶν, ὥστε ἐκπλήσσεσθαι αὐτοὺς καὶ λέγειν· πόθεν τούτῳ ἡ σοφία αὕτη καὶ αἱ δυνάμεις;	X	Specific single location	Neutral/ Negative Mixed reaction
Worship and alms-giving	6:2	Ὅταν οὖν ποιῇς ἐλεημοσύνην, μὴ σαλπίσῃς ἔμπροσθέν σου, ὥσπερ οἱ ὑποκριταὶ ποιοῦσιν ἐν ταῖς συναγωγαῖς καὶ ἐν ταῖς ῥύμαις, ὅπως δοξασθῶσιν ὑπὸ τῶν ἀνθρώπων· ἀμὴν λέγω ὑμῖν, ἀπέχουσιν τὸν μισθὸν αὐτῶν.		General	Neutral
Worship and alms-givine	6:5	καὶ ὅταν προσεύχησθε, οὐκ ἔσεσθε ὡς οἱ ὑποκριταί, ὅτι φιλοῦσιν ἐν ταῖς συναγωγαῖς καὶ ἐν ταῖς γωνίαις τῶν πλατειῶν ἑστῶτες προσεύχεσθαι, ὅπως φανῶσιν τοῖς ἀνθρώποις· ἀμὴν λέγω ὑμῖν, ἀπέχουσιν τὸν μισθὸν αὐτῶν.		General	Neutral
Assembly (not specified)	23:6	φιλοῦσιν δὲ τὴν πρωτοκλισίαν ἐν τοῖς δείπνοις καὶ τὰς πρωτοκαθεδρίας ἐν ταῖς συναγωγαῖς		General	Neutral
Healing	12:9-10	Καὶ μεταβὰς ἐκεῖθεν ἦλθεν εἰς τὴν συναγωγὴν αὐτῶν· καὶ ἰδοὺ ἄνθρωπος χεῖρα ἔχων ξηράν. καὶ ἐπηρώτησαν αὐτὸν λέγοντες· εἰ ἔξεστιν τοῖς σάββασιν θεραπεῦσαι; ἵνα κατηγορήσωσιν αὐτοῦ.	X	Group or location	Negative
Punishment	10:17	Προσέχετε δὲ ἀπὸ τῶν ἀνθρώπων· παραδώσουσιν γὰρ ὑμᾶς εἰς συνέδρια καὶ ἐν ταῖς συναγωγαῖς αὐτῶν μαστιγώσουσιν ὑμᾶς·	X	Group	Negative
Punishment	23:34	Διὰ τοῦτο ἰδοὺ ἐγὼ ἀποστέλλω πρὸς ὑμᾶς προφήτας καὶ σοφοὺς καὶ γραμματεῖς· ἐξ αὐτῶν ἀποκτενεῖτε καὶ σταυρώσετε καὶ ἐξ αὐτῶν μαστιγώσετε ἐν ταῖς συναγωγαῖς ὑμῶν καὶ διώξετε ἀπὸ πόλεως εἰς πόλιν	X	Group	Negative

Table 2. The portrayal of "synagogues" and events in "synagogues" in the Gospel of Matthew

public contexts.[79] These synagogues are public since the rhetorical point in all passages is the public or open nature of the space referred to, where "hypocrites" play out their religious devotion in order to enhance their status among the people (6:2: synagogues and streets; 6:5: synagogues and street corners). In 23:6 "the scribes and the Pharisees" are said to use public space to boost their status in the eyes of people not belonging to their own group, be they "ordinary Jews," Mattheans, or members of other parties.[80]

We shall save the other passages for the discussion of Matthew's relationship to semipublic association synagogues and the Pharisees. For the purposes of the present section, we may now conclude that references in Matthew's Gospel to public synagogues support the point I noted above, namely: although tensions may exist in certain locations, the Mattheans recognized and interacted positively with public institutions. Indeed, the public synagogues provided an institutional and spatial setting in which the Mattheans carried out a mission to the people of the land.[81] The "crowds" in the Gospel of Matthew play an important role in this regard, as a literary character representing the object of Matthean missionary activities, that is, people not belonging to any specific parties, people whom we would call "ordinary Jews," adhering to common Judaism.[82] A literary analysis of their function in the narrative shows that extreme tensions between them and Jesus/the disciples are lacking. "The crowds" are not among the groups being judged in Matthew's Gospel. They are sometimes portrayed positively, sometimes less positively, but they are never condemned.[83] To be sure, certain places are judged col-

---

[79] The fact that the Mattheans are admonished to perform their *private* prayer at home does not invalidate this conclusion. On *public* prayer in synagogues, a disputed issue, see my *Origins of the Synagogue*.

[80] "Pharisees" are thus not said to operate the public synagogues, but to use them for promoting their own status in society.

[81] We shall return to the issue of mission below.

[82] For a recent, in-depth study of the crowds in Matthew, see J. R. C. Cousland, *The Crowds in the Gospel of Matthew* (NovTSup 102; Leiden/Boston: Brill, 2002).

[83] Great crowds followed Jesus (4:25; 8:1); Jesus has compassion on them, since they lack proper leadership (9:36; cf. 14:14); he preaches to them and heals them (5:1; 12:15; 19:2); they are astonished and praise the God of Israel for Jesus' ministry (7:28; 9:8, 33; 15:31; cf. 22:33), wondering whether he could be the Messiah ("the son of David" [12:23—in contrast to the reaction of the Pharisees, 12:24]; 21:9). The chief priests and the Pharisees are said to want to arrest Jesus, but they hesitate out of fear of the crowds, who regarded Jesus as a prophet (21:46; cf. 21:11), just as they had John the Baptist (21:26, exchanging Pharisees for elders; cf. 14:5). The sometimes ambivalent reactions of the crowds, as well as their suffering, are blamed on the lack of proper leadership (9:36). The accusations against the Pharisees and their scribes are framed as warnings directed to both the disciples and the crowds (23:1). It is sometimes argued that "the crowds" are portrayed as shifting their allegiance in the passion narrative, on account of their role in the arrest and trial of Jesus. However, the chief priests and the elders are said to plan to arrest Jesus in a way that would avoid upsetting the crowds (26:1–5), and "the crowds" arresting Jesus are specifically mentioned as being sent by the chief priests and elders (26:47), avoiding generalization. Indeed,

lectively (without references to "the crowds"), such as the cities of Chorazin and Bethsaida (Matt 11:21), and this would probably refer to encounters in public assemblies of these cities. The specificity in this case, however, should be compared to the general treatment of "the crowds" (and general references to public synagogues), which does not involve categorical rejection. Thus, as might be expected, depending on the local context, certain places would be less favorable to the messianic proclamation. This does not, however, mean a general rejection by the people who represent Jewish practice and belief more broadly—ordinary Jews—who interacted positively with Mattheans in public assemblies and other public places.

IV. GROUP TENSIONS: THE MATTHEANS AND THE PHARISEES

In sharp contrast to "ordinary Jews" and common Judaism, the Pharisees are repeatedly singled out for categorical condemnation in a way that leaves no room for exceptions. The threat of divine judgment is applied to its fullest extent, including both their removal as leaders (21:33–45; we shall return to the sense in which they would have been regarded as leaders) and their exclusion from the world to come (5:20). The intensity of the criticism of the Pharisees in Matthew's Gospel (as opposed to other NT texts[84]) has always attracted researchers' interest, resulting in

---

the crowds in the passion narrative seem to be representatives of people in the capital rather than the land as a whole, acting together with the leaders in a way that, in the author's eyes, condemns them both—the people of Jerusalem and the leaders together (switching to the inclusive λαός [27:25]). In other words, what the passion narrative shows are tensions between different areas of the land and the populations of those areas: whereas Galilee is home of and supports the prophet, would-be Messiah Jesus (with the exception of some specified towns; cf. Matt 11:20–24; 13:55–58), Jerusalem, from where the Messiah must rule the restored Israel, rejects him as the chosen one in order to protect its own—according to the author—corrupt, leadership. These tensions between a Galilean popular leader and the political establishment of the capital are most likely historical with regard to Jesus in the 30s. By inserting the Pharisees into the passion narrative (27:62) and in other ways connecting the Pharisees with the political leadership in Jerusalem, the Gospel of Matthew transfers the conflict—and the guilt—to apply also (and therefore more) to the Pharisees, thus extending, symbolically, the reach of Jerusalem's power and corruption geographically and chronologically to apply to Pharisees of the Galilee in the post-70 period of the Mattheans. A further piece of evidence supporting this hypothesis is the reference to Ἰουδαῖοι in Matt 28:15, which should be translated not "Jews" but "Judeans," referring to the geographical area. This may be a general reference, but since the Pharisees are introduced together with the chief priests in 27:62, it may well be that the author refers to Judean Pharisees, as opposed to his own Galilean community. For the presence of Pharisees in Galilee, see, e.g., Richard Horsley, "Conquest and Social Conflict in Galilee," in *Recruitment, Conquest, and Conflict: Strategies in Judaism, Early Christianity, and the Greco-Roman World* (ed. Peder Borgen et al.; Emory Studies in Early Christianity 6; Atlanta: Scholars Press, 1998), 129–68, here 157; Segal, "Matthew's Jewish Voice," 27. See further below.

[84] Cf. Wolfgang Reinbold, "Das Matthäusevangelium, die Pharisäer und die Tora," *BZ* 50

a variety of explanations as to possible reasons for such antagonism. For our purposes, it is important to locate this criticism within the institutional framework described above and to do a close reading of relevant passages taking into account insights from contemporary cross-culturally tested social-scientific and social-psychological theories. I begin with the former and then, distinguishing between pre- and post-70 C.E. periods in the life of the Matthean movement, identify their changing socioreligious location. As we shall see, in the words of L. Michael White, "[t]he tension of the Matthean community with other Jewish groups (or to be more precise, the Pharisees and 'their synagogues') was born of proximity rather than distance, of similarity rather than difference."[85]

The expression "their/your synagogue(s)" (see table 2 above) will provide us with information often neglected because of the lack of a careful definition of "synagogue." Beginning with Matt 12:9, it is possible that we have a reference to a Pharisaic association synagogue.[86] In 12:1–8, Jesus is debating with the Pharisees (v. 2), accusing them of not knowing the law (v. 5). He then enters "their synagogue" (v. 9) and heals a person. The people ("they") who ask Jesus whether it is right to heal on the Sabbath are clearly Pharisees, since (a) no other group has been introduced in the story since 12:2, (b) it is said to take place later on the same day as the debate in 12:1–8, (c) the topic of discussion is the same (the definition of "work" on the Sabbath), and (d) the conclusion of the episode is that "the Pharisees went out and conspired against him, how to destroy him" (v. 14). "The crowds" join Jesus only after he has left the synagogue and the area (ἀνεχώρησεν ἐκεῖθεν [v. 15]). This means that, according to Matthew, Jesus intentionally seeks out and relates to Pharisees in their own assembly building.[87] If this is correct, it is evidence of a specific association synagogue, belonging to a particular group, and the reaction is negative. This conclusion is strengthened by a consideration of the remaining passages on synagogues.

The author of the Gospel provides two passages that deal with punishment of followers of Jesus/Mattheans in, or through,[88] synagogues. Interestingly, both texts specify these synagogues as "their" or "your" synagogues: ἐν ταῖς συναγωγαῖς αὐτῶν in 10:17[89] and ἐν ταῖς συναγωγαῖς ὑμῶν in 23:34. Since these are the

---

(2006): 51–73, here 51: "Wie keiner anderer Text im Neuen Testament polemisiert das Matthäusevangelium gegen die Pharisäer."

[85] White, "Crisis Management," 241.

[86] See Runesson, *Origins of the Synagogue*, 355–57.

[87] This may be compared to the practice recorded in Matthew's Gospel to send "prophets, sages, and scribes" to the Pharisees, as witnessed by 23:34, a passage to which we shall return. Cf. Luke 7:36, where Jesus accepts an invitation to the home of a Pharisee who wants to eat together with him. In Matthew's Gospel, however, the initiative comes from Jesus.

[88] If ἐν is taken as instrumental; see Davies and Allison, *Matthew*, 2:183.

[89] It has been suggested that the mention of "Gentiles" in Matt 10:18 may be taken as an indication that this verse refers to a Diaspora situation. It is more likely, however, that the text is

only passages that deal with punishment in synagogues, and since 23:29 states that ὑμῶν in 23:34 refers to the Pharisees and their scribes,⁹⁰ 10:17 should be read from the perspective of 23:34, suggesting that αὐτῶν in 10:17 relates the synagogues in question to Pharisees. There are, then, two possible interpretations of these passages: (a) the term "synagogues" refers to Pharisaic association synagogues generally, or (b) the term refers to public synagogues in specific places where the Pharisees were influential and had power to affect the decisions of the public assemblies (cf. above on Matt 11:21; however, no Pharisees are mentioned in relation to these places).

In favor of alternative (a) the following can be said with regard to 10:17. We know that public synagogues functioned as local courts (which is the meaning of συνέδρια here).⁹¹ Matthew does not further define these courts by calling them "their" courts, as in the case of the synagogues three words later, and so implies a common judicial institution for Mattheans and those who accuse them. These courts, then, refer to judicial activities taking place in public synagogues. The next thing to note is that people referred to as ἄνθρωποι will be handing over followers of Jesus to these courts, which are public and not controlled by any specific group. These people are the same as those in charge of the synagogues mentioned: αὐτῶν refers to the nonspecific τῶν ἀνθρώπων, as does the subject implied in παραδώσουσιν. As we noted above, the parallel in 23:34 indicates that these people should be understood as Pharisees.⁹² Once the reader has finished the whole Gospel and knows about 23:34, the interpretive result with regard to 10:17 is twofold: first, the Pharisees are said to hand Christ-believers over to be judged in Jewish courts; second, it is prophesied that the Pharisees will flog Christ-believers in their own association synagogues. The latter point needs some elaboration.

Voluntary associations in the Greco-Roman world (including the land of Israel⁹³) made up their own rules and had the right to impose punishment in case

---

patterned on the passion of Jesus, who was first delivered to a Jewish council and then handed over to the governor (i.e., the Gentiles): see Davies and Allison, *Matthew*, 2:183. In addition, Matt 10:5–6 clearly sets the context for the passage: "Go nowhere among the Gentiles, and enter no town of the Samaritans, but go rather to the lost sheep of the house of Israel."

⁹⁰ While not all scribes would have been Pharisees, some would. I understand the combination of "scribes and Pharisees in the Gospel of Matthew to refer to scribes who belonged to the Pharisaic party; this does not exclude the existence of scribes outside of that community. On scribes, see Sanders, *Judaism*, esp. 179–82. See also Neusner, "Formation of Rabbinic Judaism," 39, referred to by Luomanen, "Sociology of Sectarianism," 123.

⁹¹ See Binder, *Into the Temple Courts*, 445–49; Levine, *Ancient Synagogue*, 143, 395–96.

⁹² The general warning Προσέχετε δὲ ἀπὸ τῶν ἀνθρώπων, rather than a specific warning against the Pharisees, is motivated by the fact that the passage begins within the Jewish people but extends beyond it to non-Jews. The warning cannot, then, be limited to a specific group or people.

⁹³ It is somewhat ironic that one of the groups that isolated itself most from outside influences, the sect at the Dead Sea, shows very clear signs of outside influences in their organizational pattern; see further n. 95 below.

of disobedience to those rules.⁹⁴ In terms of the relationship between members and the association, on the one hand, and the public courts of society, on the other, it would have been a punishable offense for a member who had been attacked or beaten by another member of the association to turn to public courts and sue the offender. The victim was required first to consult the leaders of the association (in the case of the *Iobaccoi*, the priest or the arch-bacchus), who would then settle the case and prescribe appropriate punishment (cf. Matt 18:15–18). The punishments in an association would vary according to the character of the offense, but would almost always range from fines and/or expulsion for certain time periods to permanent expulsion from the association.

As I noted above, there were several associations in first-century Jewish society, the organizational pattern of which was adopted by the parties described in Josephus, Philo, and other sources. A comparison between the organization and the penal codes of the Qumran community and Greco-Roman associations strongly supports the conclusion that we are to understand the Qumranites, too, as an association.⁹⁵ In the same way, the Pharisees would have had their own penal codes within their association synagogues. The question with regard to the passages under discussion, Matt 10:17 and 23:34, is whether flogging (the term used in both passages is μαστιγόω [cf. LXX Deut 25:1–3]) could be a punishment imposed by an association. No evidence in favor of such punishment exists with regard to any known voluntary associations in the Greco-Roman world.⁹⁶ However, as Deut 25:1–3 indicates, it would be a type of punishment fitting the context of public courts (cf. *m. Mak.* 3:12).

Does this mean that Matt 10:17 and 23:34 refer to public institutions, despite everything said up to this point against this interpretation (and its sociopolitical implications)? I think not. Matthew uses hyperbole—and does it "symmetrically." In 23:34 we are told that Jesus says that he will send prophets, sages, and scribes to the Pharisees and their scribes, and, as a result, the latter will "kill and crucify" some of these learned people. Others will be flogged "in their synagogues." We know that execution/crucifixion was a punishment that could be imposed only by

---

⁹⁴ The most famous and fullest description of penal codes in associations is the statutes of the *Iobaccoi* (Athens, 176 C.E.), translated by Wilhelm Dittenberger in *SIG*; translation provided in Weinfeld, *Organizational Pattern*, 51–54.

⁹⁵ So Klinghardt, "Manual of Discipline"; cf. Weinfeld, *Organizational Pattern*, esp. Appendix E, 71–76, his response to Lawrence Schiffman, *Sectarian Law in the Dead Sea Scrolls: Courts, Testimony, and the Penal Code* (BJS 33; Chico, CA: Scholars Press, 1983). Unfortunately, Klinghardt argues that the identification of the Qumranites as an association contradicts their categorization as a sect. Associations could have different views on society; some of them would qualify as sects, others as denominations. The designation "association" does not dictate the "content," but rather the (organizational) "form." This is further evidenced in Roman imperial treatment of different *collegia*, some of which were banished while others, old enough to have proven their loyalty to the empire, were allowed to continue business as usual.

⁹⁶ I am grateful to Philip Harland for discussions of this issue.

the Roman imperial power. Yet Matthew, in order to increase the guilt of the Pharisees, turns them into the executioners, thus transforming them into the likeness of the (political) authorities in Israel's history who, according to the Hebrew Bible, executed prophets sent to them (23:29–33). In order to achieve this portrait and transfer of guilt, the author has to make use of images of Israel's past political authorities as well as of the current Roman authorities and their power to impose the capital punishment. Then he has to transfer this power—not to Jewish political authorities of his own time (which would have been the chief priests) but to the nonofficial group he has selected as primary target, the Pharisees. The result, obviously, has nothing to do with sociohistorical or political realities in the late first century.

Step 2 is to transfer the power to impose a punishment that *was* possible in Jewish society (in the public courts), flogging,[97] to the same group—the Pharisees. In this way, Matthew achieves a connection, as complete as it can be on all levels of (unjust) punishment, between a contemporary group without judicial power in society and the prophet-killing political authorities of the Hebrew Bible. This allows the author to state in 23:35–36 that the Pharisees and their scribes shall be held responsible for all unjust punishment throughout Israelite history (including, by implication, punishments that may be imposed on Mattheans by Roman authorities!). Again, this carefully planned rewriting of history, which fuses it with the present, has nothing to do with sociopolitical realities either before or immediately after 70 C.E.

If we return to Matt 10:17, the pattern becomes clear. "Their synagogues" indeed refers to Pharisaic associations, but the punishment mentioned is taken from another judicial context in order to increase the guilt of the Pharisees. What was considered possible in Israel's past history in terms of punishment in Jewish society was, in the first century, divided up between two political bodies, the Jewish courts and Roman imperial legislation. The author of Matthew fuses these two judicial contexts, creating an image for his own time reflecting earlier Israelite society, and then substitutes the Pharisees for the political leaders of his time.

It would seem, therefore, that despite the author's creative use of Israelite history when interpreting his own time, the historical fact was that the Pharisaic synagogues ("their/your synagogues" in 10:17 and 23:34) *did have judicial power* over the Mattheans, even if punishments were less severe than the Gospel wants us to believe. This situation created, and explains, the frustration the Mattheans—contrary to other groups in the Jesus movement who were not involved institutionally with the Pharisees—felt with the Pharisees, a frustration that permeates the Gospel from beginning to end and results in repeated and violent rhetorical attacks. Indeed, one of the keys to the origins of the Gospel of Matthew and the Matthean community lies in this observation. If the Mattheans did not belong within the Phari-

---

[97] See Davies and Allison, *Matthew*, 2:182–83.

saic associations, these extreme tensions would be difficult to explain sociologically. At the same time, however, some passages seem to indicate that a schism between some Mattheans and the Pharisaic associations had occurred when the Gospel was written down and redacted. In light of this, the hypothesis I am proposing unfolds as follows:

The Mattheans were urban-based[98] Pharisees who became convinced, most likely after the death and resurrection of Jesus had been proclaimed to them by missionaries, that Jesus of Nazareth was Israel's Messiah,[99] confirming their Pharisaic belief in the resurrection of the dead as well as their hope for a restored Israel.[100] Seeing their hopes soon to be fulfilled, they formed a movement within Pharisaism that engaged in a mission to "ordinary Jews," proclaiming that the end of the present age—and the suffering it implied—was near.[101] Doing so, they constantly referred to holy scripture, accepted as such by the wider movement, but subjected it to a specific interpretation.[102]

---

[98] See Stegemann and Stegemann, *Jesus Movement*, 227–28. I would, however, think of an urban context of somewhat larger size than they suggest for several reasons, among which are language and evidence of a mixed population.

[99] Even if there may have been people within the movement that had met Jesus, the urban setting suggests a lack of direct continuity, since Jesus focused his ministry and missionary activity on rural areas.

[100] This was before the consolidation of believers of Jesus in a single group with a supralocal leadership organization: at this time, many Christ-believers belonged within other parties and did not interpret their new beliefs as necessitating the creation of a new association. People previously not belonging to an association, however, most likely joined together forming new associations in an early stage of the history of the Jesus movement (cf. the Jerusalem-based group referred to by Paul in Galatians, and by the author of Acts, which seems to have achieved a leading position by the middle of the first century).

[101] Rituals specific to the Christ-believers, such as the Eucharist (Matt 26:26-29—regardless of whether this was celebrated on a weekly or an annual cycle), would have been performed in meetings that did not involve non-Christ-believers. It is not uncommon for subgroups within larger groups to develop/maintain rituals not practiced by the majority; for different types of subgroups and possible relationships between subgroup and larger collectivity, see n. 109 below. We see a similar phenomenon when Pharisees and other groups—but not the Qumranites—develop rituals practiced only by their own group (in their associations) but not to the exclusion of participation in the Jerusalem temple cult. The same pattern is found in Acts 2:46, where the distinction between temple worship and worship in private homes is described not as mutually exclusive but as complementary.

[102] In this way, one could say that the reform movement was "conservative" in that it focused on traditions, of which they claimed they had the true interpretations, as opposed to wholly new phenomena that would override shared traditions. In the same way, Jesus becomes a teacher like those of the Pharisees and their scribes, with the difference that he would be the only one. In Matthew's Gospel the emphasis is on knowing the traditions and interpreting them correctly: see Matt 9:13; 12:3–7; 21:16, 42; 22:29, 31. See Freyne, "Vilifying the Other," 120–21. Jesus' teaching takes on the same importance, since his instruction is indispensable both for interpreting the sacred texts and for knowing the truth about what was happening in the Mattheans' own time (see

Every reform movement causes tension to appear within the larger collectivity. The larger Pharisaic community remained unconvinced about the identification of this—now dead—individual as the Messiah, which caused open conflicts in public synagogues as well as internal strife between messianic believers and the majority. With the destruction of the Jerusalem temple in 70 C.E., probably predicted by the historical Jesus or, in any case, predicted by the earlier Markan communities, to whose Gospel traditions the Mattheans had access, the majority of Mattheans experienced tremendous "real-life evidence" that the coming kingdom was within reach. This spurred a never-before-witnessed missionary outreach on the part of the majority of the Matthean reform movement.[103] This movement ultimately expanded beyond the Jewish people, since, at the dawn of the new age, the Gentiles must come to Zion.[104] Previously, by contrast, more "theoretical" eschatological expectations had anticipated non-Jews coming to the people of God and their Messiah of their own accord.[105]

This development within the Matthean reform movement happened coterminously with an increased influx of people to the wider Pharisaic denomination. These sympathizers and new members were most likely, as described by Neusner,[106] landlords and priests, who were of a relatively high status in Jewish society. Thus, they had less interest in a radical movement proclaiming the imminent coming of the end; the Mattheans, on the other hand, at this stage likely recruited more people from the lower strata of society.[107] The result was increased tension within the Pharisaic associations, based on both ideological and social factors. Together these factors created a schism in which the majority, but not all,[108] of the Mattheans left

---

Matt 7:24–29 [cf. Prov 10:25]; 24:35)—two aspects, past and present, old and new, that are inseparably interwoven. Indeed, a Matthean is best identified as a scribe combining new and old (13:52: "Therefore every scribe who has been trained for the kingdom of heaven is like the master of a household who brings out of his treasure what is new and what is old"). One must also note that, for the Mattheans, acknowledging Jesus' teaching in and of itself will help no one: "only the one who does the will of my Father in heaven" will enter the kingdom (Matt 7:21; cf. v. 24).

[103] Thus, the common assumption that the missionary zeal and eschatological expectations were intense in the beginning of the movement and then faded is turned on its head.

[104] See Terrence Donaldson, "Proselytes or 'Righteous Gentiles'? The Status of Gentiles in Eschatological Pilgrimage Patterns of Thought," *JSP* 7 (1990): 3–27.

[105] Matthew 2:1–12; 8:5–13; 15:21–28. These passages display a consistent centripetal movement toward the people of Israel and its Messiah, Jesus, as opposed to the centrifugal force of the so-called Great Commssion in 28:19–20.

[106] Neusner, "Formation of Rabbinic Judaism."

[107] See Stegemann and Stegemann, *Jesus Movement*, 227–29, 230, and the social pyramid chart, 232.

[108] When a reform movement within a denomination parts from the parent body, those who leave will not be able to convince all members of the movement to go with them. See the example noted by Philip Esler (*Community and Gospel in Luke-Acts: The Social and Political Motivations of Lucan Theology* [SNTSMS 57; Cambridge: Cambridge University Press, 1987]), 53,

the Pharisaic denomination and became, in relation to the Pharisees, a *sect*.[109] This group, whom we may call the separatists, authored and redacted the Gospel of Matthew as we have it today.[110] The reason why they wrote it was basically twofold: to consolidate their own emerging association, providing a foundation for their particular identity, and to attempt to convince Mattheans who had remained within the Pharisaic association to join them.

These reasons explain the polemic and exaggerations regarding possible punishments Mattheans may suffer within the Pharisaic association, as discussed above. They also account for the relationship between Matt 23:1–3 and the rhetorical attacks that follow:[111] the author, a former member of the Pharisees, a scribe with a modified self-understanding, takes as the point of departure the shared and long-held conviction and self-definition that the Pharisees sit on Moses' seat. It is likely that this was an expression used by pre-70 Pharisees, including Mattheans. In the new situation experienced by the separatists, such acknowledgment was probably intended to gain the sympathies of the Mattheans still within the Pharisaic association before introducing the complete and final delegitimation of the (non–Christ-believing) Pharisees using ad hominem arguments and accusing them of perverting rituals and customs that they all shared (e.g., making use of/wearing

---

where 10 percent of the members of a reform movement remained within the parent body as the others left; see also the discussion in Holmberg, *Sociology*, 102–3. A main reason for the schism could be indicated in Matt 23:13, where Pharisees and the scribes are said to "lock people out of the kingdom of heaven": this may refer to an active attempt by leading Pharisees to prevent people—including other Pharisees and sympathizers—from joining the Matthean reform movement.

[109] Thus the focus on community building and the establishment of rules for the new association (Matthew 18; cf. the transfer of leadership in Matthew's version of the parable of the vineyard, including the concluding comments, adding the Pharisees [21:33–46]). See Dennis Duling, "The Matthean Brotherhood and Marginal Scribal Leadership," in *Modelling Early Christianity: Social Scientific Studies of the New Testament in Its Context* (ed. Philip Esler; London: Routledge, 1995), 159–82; and Richard Ascough, "Matthew and Community Formation," in *Gospel of Matthew in Current Study*, ed. Aune, 96–126. I would emphasize, however, that the Matthean association, *pace* Ascough (p. 125), is, at the time of the writing of the Gospel, still in the process of formation. Important to note regarding the definition of "sect" is that the more traditional understanding going back to Troeltsch, focusing on relationships between (religious) groups rather than between groups and society at large (see n. 46 above) is, *pace* Overman and Saldarini, better suited for the analysis of the Matthean community. See the similar position in Luomanen, "Sociology of Sectarianism," based on Rodney Stark and William Sims Bainbridge, *A Theory of Religion* (New York: Peter Lang, 1987). (I do not, however, agree with Luomanen on the characterization of the Mattheans as a cult movement [pp. 129–30].) See the discussion in Esler, *Community and Gospel*, 46–70.

[110] This means that within our Gospel are preserved not only non-Matthean traditions from before 70 C.E. (from Mark and Q, if Q is accepted) but also Matthean traditions antedating the war.

[111] There is an almost endless flow of articles and sections in books that attempt to solve this problem. One of the best studies, including a comprehensive discussion of most theories, is Mark Alan Powell, "Do and Keep What Moses Says (Matthew 23:2–7)," *JBL* 114 (1995): 419–35.

phylacteries and fringes [23:5]; attending public synagogues [23:6]; tithing [23:23]; pronouncing oaths in relation to the temple [23:16–21; but cf. 5:33–37]). The reference to the "outside" that Pharisees are said to make look righteous (23:28) may also be an indication of halakic positions shared by Mattheans and other Pharisees.[112]

The repeated assertions that the Pharisees who do not acknowledge Jesus as the Messiah are not going to be part of the coming kingdom (23:33, 36; cf. 5:20) are meant as a warning to Mattheans remaining within the Pharisaic denomination that they have nothing to gain and everything to lose by choosing to stay. Indeed, leaving means joining those who have the keys to the kingdom (Matt 16:18–19) and the power to exclude others from "what really matters."

These assertions show that the Matthean separatists had left the Pharisees and, in relation to them, constitute a *sect*. Joachim Wach has described the coexistence of conflicting orientations within the same collectivity—what he terms *ecclesiolae in ecclesia*—and identifies three basic types: *Collegium pietas, Fraternitas*, and the *Order*.[113] Common to all types, apart from the fact that they most often try to reform the larger collectivity, is the acceptance of a dual standard of religiosity, one for "the masses" and one for the virtuosi. While we find such a position in pre-70 Matthean tradition (Matt 19:16–22),[114] the denunciation of Pharisees combined with repeated condemnations resulting in their ultimate exclusion show that a schism had taken place at the time of final redaction.[115] Indeed, the definitive accusation that the Pharisees are guilty of all innocent blood in the history of Israel, the

---

[112] The lawlessness of the inside is the opposite of the law-abiding of the outside; that is, there is agreement on the basic halakic requirements that take the form of external signs of identity. This does not mean acceptance of all Pharisaic customs by the separatists. For example, Matt 15:1–9 retains the basic criticism of Mark's Gospel (7:1–13), even though disagreeing with Mark's conclusion (Mark 7:23; Matt 15:20).

[113] Joachim Wach, *Sociology of Religion* (Chicago: University of Chicago Press, 1944), 173–86; cf. McGuire, *Religion*, 127–29. These groups may be described as sectarian or cultic dissenters within a *church* or *denomination*.

[114] Other passages indicating an intra-Pharisaic location include, e.g., Matt 13:52 (identifying the Mattheans as scribes) and 23:34 (showing signs of their being actively involved in trying to reform the Pharisaic denomination). To this should be added the evidence of shared institutional context discussed above. In terms of virtuoso religion in Matthew's Gospel, see the comments on celibacy (19:10–12) and perfection (5:38). The author's attitude to "sinners and righteous" is also stated as avoiding premature judgment and allowing for a *corpus mixtum* (13:24–30; cf. 22:11–14). Contrary to the example of 19:16–22, however, the sinners are, ultimately, not going to enter the kingdom.

[115] I take the inclusivity of Matt 5:17–19 to be addressed to Mattheans still remaining in the Pharisaic association, expressing willingness to modify their religious outlook. The exclusion of Pharisees from the kingdom in 5:20 serves as a warning aimed at preventing such adjustment. In addition, it assures them that the separatists uphold a strict law observance, despite the type of Gentile mission in which the latter are now involved (28:19–20).

implicit claim that they are to blame for the destruction of Jerusalem (23:35–24:2), their insertion into the passion narrative (27:62), implying that they took an active part in the arrest, trial, and death sentence of Jesus, as well as the institutional evidence of the first stages of a separate Matthean association (ch. 18; 21:33–46) strongly suggest that the separatists, while having belonged to the Pharisees, had, at the time of the final redaction of the Gospel,[116] parted ways with them.

On the basis of the above considerations, one must recognize the diversity of traditions in the Gospel and distinguish among different Matthean groups, each displaying its own perspective and interpretation of the traditions.[117] In this regard, time is a crucial factor, and the events of 70 C.E. play an important role for the transforming (eschatological) identity of the Mattheans. These Christ-believers at first existed as a "little church within the church," with the goal of reforming the Pharisaic denomination but focusing their mission on "ordinary Jews." Their group likely included prosperous people and their retainers.[118] This should not surprise us, since, sociologically, a *denomination*, the nature of the larger collectivity of which the Mattheans were a part, tends to attract people who are well established

---

[116] A Pharisaic origin for the Mattheans has been suggested by, e.g., Freyne, "Vilifying the Other," 138. See also Reinhart Hummel, *Die Auseinandersetzung zwischen Kirche und Judentum in Matthäusevangelium* (2nd ed.; BEvt 33; Munich: Kaiser, 1966).

[117] On the plurality of Matthean communities—but without the conclusions drawn here—see Graham Stanton, "The Communities of Matthew," *Int* 46 (1992): 379–91. See also Elaine M. Wainwright, *Shall We Look for Another? A Feminist Rereading of the Matthean Jesus* (Bible and Literature Series; Maryknoll, NY: Orbis Books, 1998), 41–45. Although my conclusions differ from Wainwright's in many regards, her insistence on and sensitivity to different voices in Matthew's Gospel are a valuable contribution to the interpretation of the Mattheans and their text. I have emphasized two basic communities, the split occurring after 70, constituting the institutional frames within which interpretations of Jesus traditions were made. However, we must not overlook the fact that *within* these two communities, respectively, we must reckon with some diversity. This does not mean that every tradition would have come from a separate (Matthean) community, only that the Matthean material is best explained by not theorizing about too homogeneous a setting in which it was kept, transmitted, and redacted. Other communities, consisting mainly of non-Jews, would soon adopt Matthew's Gospel as their preferred text, a fact that should make us even more cautious about postulating too much regarding possible readers of Matthew. In the monograph mentioned above (n. 23), *The Gospel of Matthew and the Myth of Christian Origins*, I deal in more detail with different layers in the Gospel and the criteria used for distinguishing pre- and post-70 layers.

[118] See Stegemann and Stegemann, *Jesus Movement*, 230 (they do not, however, distinguish between different periods in the life of the Mattheans). As to the Mattheans' status within the denomination, according to Rodney Stark's definition of *cult* (*The Rise of Christianity: How the Obscure, Marginal Jesus Movement Became the Dominant Religious Force in the Western World in a Few Centuries* [San Francisco: HarperSanFrancisco, 1997], 33), Mattheans before 70 would have constituted *cultic type dissent* (introducing a new aspect but referring conservatively to shared traditions), *within* the Pharisaic denomination.

in society. However, at this stage the Mattheans also included some people from lower social strata.[119]

As a result of the socioeconomic changes brought about by the war,[120] the majority of people in the *sect* separating itself from the larger collectivity (and from Mattheans choosing not to follow them) would have been from nonelite lower-stratum groups, which partly explains the egalitarian emphasis of the final redaction of the Gospel (see 18:1–4; 23:8–11).[121] In addition to the increased intensity of eschatological expectations, the separatists brought about, as a result of the former, a change in missionary strategies, introducing an active Gentile mission.[122]

The post-70 changes, both social and theological, resulted in the fierce polemic in Matthew's Gospel against the Pharisees.[123] Taken out of its sociohistorical context and applied to the Jewish people as a whole, this polemic has had disastrous consequences in the history of Jewish–Christian relations. Originally, however, the denunciation of the (non–Christ-believing) Pharisees was meant for the ears of Mattheans and "ordinary Jews," whom the separatists hoped would join their community now when the end of time was nearer than it was when they had first embraced a faith in Jesus of Nazareth as the risen Messiah.[124]

---

[119] Stegemann and Stegemann, *Jesus Movement*, 230, 232.

[120] Regarding socioeconomic changes as reasons for sects to emerge, see McGuire, *Religion*, 131.

[121] For characterization of the social status of sect members, see Stark, *Rise of Christianity*, 33; also McGuire, *Religion*. See the discussion of egalitarianism among Mattheans in Ascough, "Matthew and Community Formation," 99; see also Duling, "Matthean Brotherhood."

[122] On the question whether this mission included the circumcision of male converts, affirming that this was likely the case, see Brown, "Matthean Community," 218; A.-J. Levine, *Social and Ethnic Dimensions*; Anthony Saldarini, "Jewish-Christian Conflict"; idem, *Matthew's Christian-Jewish Community*; Sim, *Apocalyptic Eschatology*; idem, *Christian Judaism*.

[123] The negative stereotyping and slander of the "Pharisees" in Matthew have been analyzed by several scholars. One important insight is that the offensive language used by the author was not unusual in antiquity and may thus have been regarded as less offensive by the ancients than it seems to us today. See, e.g., Luke Timothy Johnson, "The New Testament's Anti-Jewish Slander and the Conventions of Ancient Polemic," *JBL* 108 (1989): 419–41; Moshe Weinfeld, "The Charge of Hypocrisy in Matthew 23 and in Jewish Sources," *Imm* 24/25 (1990): 52–58; Benedict Viviano, "Social World and Community Leadership: The Case of Matthew 23:1–12, 34," *JSNT* 39 (1990): 3–21; Saldarini, "Delegitimation"; Margaret Davies, "Stereotyping the Other: The 'Pharisees' in the Gospel According to Matthew," in *Biblical Studies/Cultural Studies: The Third Sheffield Colloquium* (ed. J. Cheryl Exum and Stephen D. Moore; JSOTSup 266; Sheffield: Sheffield Academic Press, 1998), 415–32. See also James D. G. Dunn, "Pharisees, Sinners, Jesus," in *The Social World of Formative Christianity and Judaism: Essays in Tribute to Howard Clark Kee* (ed. Jacob Neusner et al.; Philadelphia: Fortress, 1988), 264–89. Regardless of the level of offensiveness, however, it is clear that the author of the Gospel targets the Pharisees as the enemy par excellence, even above the political establishment that, historically, decided to hand Jesus over to the Romans.

[124] Sociologically, this phenomenon is similar to what we see in John Chrysostom's extreme polemic against the Jews. It is quite clear that this polemic was meant to be heard by Christ-

V. Concluding Remarks

Few scholars, with some notable exceptions,[125] have understood the Matthean communities as Pharisaic communities. Indeed, a glance at any presentation of the history of scholarship of the NT will show that the Pharisees (often equated with "Judaism") have been presented as the absolute opposite of the Jesus movement (or "Christianity"), which, in turn, is most often understood as a homogeneous entity. Still, in addition to the evidence discussed above regarding Matthew's Gospel, there are clear indications in the ancient sources, supported by social-scientific theories based on contemporary empirical studies, that suggest a much more complex situation with considerable overlap between and within Jewish movements in the first century, including the Jesus movement and the Pharisees.

We know from Acts 15:5 that in the late first century there were Pharisees who, without leaving their identity or institutional belonging behind, had accepted a belief in Jesus as the Messiah.[126] Indeed, according to Acts, Paul never ceased to regard himself a Pharisee (Acts 23:6).[127] It seems that the earliest Jesus movement was rather loosely joined together institutionally. It included Christ-believers who retained their basic group identity and institutional affiliation but related in dif-

---

believers, who did not perceive their identity as Christians to exclude participation in activities provided by the synagogue. By delegitimizing the group that attracted members of his church, Chrysostom hoped to establish his own institution as the only viable alternative for Christ-believers and to prevent "dual memberships." See Robert L. Wilken, *John Chrysostom and the Jews: Rhetoric and Reality in the Late Fourth Century* (Transformation of the Classical Heritage 4; Berkeley: University of California Press, 1983). See also Leonard V. Rutgers, "Archaeological Evidence for the Interaction of Jews and Non-Jews in Late Antiquity," *AJA* 96 (1992): 101–18, here 115–16.

[125] See the conclusion by Wolfgang Roth, "To Invert or Not to Invert: The Pharisaic Canon in the Gospels," in *Early Christian Interpretation of the Scriptures of Israel: Investigations and Proposals* (ed. Craig A. Evans and James A. Sanders; JSNTSup 148; Sheffield: Sheffield Academic Press, 1997), 59–78, here 76: "One seeks Matthew among Jesus-affirming Pharisees, much like Saul of Tarsus or Nicodemus of Jerusalem. His (still intra-Pharisaic) polemic is at times stinging, betraying a passionate involvement." See also Freyne, "Vilifying the Other," 138, who suggests a Pharisaic origin for the Mattheans.

[126] Acts 15:5: Ἐξανέστησαν δέ τινες τῶν ἀπὸ τῆς αἱρέσεως τῶν Φαρισαίων πεπιστευκότες λέγοντες ὅτι δεῖ περιτέμνειν αὐτοὺς παραγγέλλειν τε τηρεῖν τὸν νόμον Μωϋσέως. While the passage recounts an event taking place in the middle of the first century, the author, writing in the late first century, seems to have no problem with the fact that some Pharisees were believers in Jesus, remaining within a group in which the majority would not share that belief.

[127] Note the present tense: ἐγὼ Φαρισαῖός εἰμι, υἱὸς Φαρισαίων, περὶ ἐλπίδος καὶ ἀναστάσεως νεκρῶν [ἐγὼ] κρίνομαι. I believe that this self-understanding attributed to Paul reflects his own view, and, consequently that Phil 3:5–11 should not be read as contradicting a Pharisaic identity, but rather as emphasizing the importance of Jesus as Christ transcending specific group identities, without necessarily abolishing them.

ferent ways to an independent leadership body located in Jerusalem, which functioned as a centripetal force for the formation of a messianic identity (cf. Gal 2:9). It is important to distinguish between the self-perception of the Christ-believers who remained within their original associations, on the one hand, and the perspective of those sharing institutional affiliation with them but who did not accept Jesus as the Messiah. A Christ-believing Pharisee may or may not have been accepted as a Pharisee by other Pharisees, depending on which particular Pharisaic group we are dealing with. The tensions that would follow as Christ-believers established themselves as "subgroups" within larger groups, or associations, would lead to strife and, undoubtedly, suffering on the part of the minorities, eventually resulting in schisms between the parent body—in our case the Pharisees—and the reform movements.

The Pharisees themselves, in existence since the Hasmonean period (Jonathan [161–143 B.C.E.]), whom we have defined sociologically as a denomination, had among them diverse groups that at times exhibited schismatic tendencies.[128] It was similar with the rabbinic movement. This diversity calls into question the (anachronistic) tendency among many scholars to understand christology to be the distinguishing factor behind intragroup tensions that resulted in the parting of ways between people who originally belonged within the same institutional context. The career of Rabbi Akiva in the rabbinic movement is telling, especially when compared to the story of the fate of Rabbi Eliezer. The former was ridiculed by some for his support of Bar Kokhba as the Messiah, but he still remained a celebrated authority in the rabbinic community; the latter was excommunicated as a result of a dispute with the majority over a halakic issue (b. B. Meṣiʿa 59a–59b). In other words, it seems indeed that halakah was more central for Jewish identity than dogma. If christology is of prime importance in our own time in the shaping of separate Jewish and Christian identities, we must nevertheless acknowledge that social location and identity formation may have functioned quite differently within the institutional framework of Jewish society in the first centuries of the Common Era.

In conclusion, the Gospel of Matthew provides us with early evidence not only of an inner-Jewish parting of the ways, but of an inner-Pharisaic split between groups, a process very different in character from the developments that much later would lead to the establishment of "Christianity" as a religion independent of "Judaism." Indeed, the use of the Gospel of Matthew by non-Jewish Christ-believers as a resource in that later process of identity formation is a fascinating and hermeneutically complex problem that deserves further study.

---

[128] See the discussion above and Meyer, "Φαρισαῖος."

Cannibalistic Language in the Fourth Gospel and Greco-Roman Polemics of Factionalism (John 6:52-66)

J. ALBERT HARRILL
jharrill@indiana.edu
Indiana University, Bloomington, IN 47405

This essay names the elephant in the room around which scholarly interpreters of John 6:52–66 have long been tiptoeing with their overly circumspect discussions of the eucharistic imagery in the passage. That elephant is cannibalism, of course, and ignoring it leaves fundamental exegetical questions about this famous *crux interpretum* unanswered and even unasked. What specific connotations did the idiom of cannibalism have in the ancient Mediterranean world? Why did the Johannine author (or redactor) ascribe cannibalistic language to Jesus in a specific scene of factionalism? Did it draw on a recognizable topos familiar from the wider Greek and Roman culture and not just from the Hebrew Bible alone?[1] What nongustatory

An earlier version of this essay was read at the Johannine Literature Section of the SBL annual meeting in Washington, D.C., in November 2006. I am grateful to the participants in that session for their questions; to David Brakke, Maud Gleason, Turid Karlsen Seim, Steve Weitzman, and the anonymous referees of this journal for suggestions and criticism; and to Bart Ehrman and Dale Martin for supporting the project at a crucial stage of its conception. The completion of this article was made possible by a summer research grant and a semester faculty fellowship from Indiana University. I also thank Weston Jesuit School of Theology for library access as a Visiting Scholar in summer 2005.

[1] In the OT, drinking animal blood is a ritual abomination (Gen 9:4; Lev 3:17; Deut 12:23). The metaphor of cannibalism is used, albeit rarely, with reference to hostile action (Ps 27:2; Zech 11:9), a curse for Torah disobedience (Jer 19:9; cf. Gal 5:15), and the animalization of corrupt rulers (Mic 3:2–3), but none of these passages figures explicitly in the Johannine text under study (on Genesis 9, see p. 150 below). Previous commentators note some of these citations but only to emphasize their irrelevance to the meaning of John 6; see Raymond E. Brown, *The Gospel according to John: Introduction, Translation, and Notes* (2 vols.; AB 29, 29A; Garden City, NY: Doubleday, 1966, 1970), 1:284. An exception is the unpersuasive thesis of Herman C. Waetjen, that the

133

messages about community maintenance and regeneration could such talk of cannibalism have conveyed? What connection did anthropophagy have for ancient audiences to articulate community dissent, party division, or even civil war?

An exclusive focus on "sacramentalism" has framed the kinds of questions previous commentators have brought to John 6, a preoccupation that has often been concerned more about the theological controversies between Protestants and Catholics than about the text itself.[2] Exegetes have debated the "sacramental tradition" of the Lord's Supper in John 6, and many have repeated the standby interpolation hypothesis of Rudolf Bultmann's "ecclesiastical redactor," to "solve" the crux.[3] One view holds that the cannibalistic language has antidocetic intent.[4] But, as is well known, John's narrative departs from the Synoptic Gospels on, among other things, precisely this point: the Lord's Supper is never instituted in the Gospel of John. The exegetical debate on John 6 goes, therefore, back and forth rehashing old proposals without a resolution in sight.[5] We should recognize the sterility of cur-

---

"irony" of John 6 follows Micah 3 in criticizing "hierarchical structures" of society for cannibalizing (victimizing) the poor and marginalized (*The Gospel of the Beloved Disciple: A Work in Two Editions* [New York: T&T Clark, 2005], 219–20).

[2] Jo-Ann A. Brant, *Dialogue and Drama: Elements of Greek Tragedy in the Fourth Gospel* (Peabody, MA: Hendrickson, 2004), 155.

[3] The best history of scholarship is Paul N. Anderson, *The Christology of the Fourth Gospel: Its Unity and Disunity in the Light of John 6* (Valley Forge, PA: Trinity Press International, 1997). See also Rudolf Bultmann, *The Gospel of John: A Commentary* (trans. G. R. Beasley-Murray; Philadelphia: Westminster, 1971), 234–37; C. H. Dodd, *The Interpretation of the Fourth Gospel* (Cambridge: Cambridge University Press, 1953), 338–39; Raymond E. Brown, *An Introduction to the Gospel of John* (ABRL; New York: Doubleday, 2003), 229–34; idem, *John*, 1:284–87, 291–92; Herbert Leroy, *Rätsel und Missverständnis: Ein Beitrag zur Formgeschichte des Johannesevangeliums* (BBB 30; Bonn: P. Hanstein, 1968), 109–24; James D. G. Dunn, "John VI—A Eucharistic Discourse?" *NTS* 17 (1970–71): 328–38; C. K. Barrett, *Essays on John* (Philadelphia: Westminster, 1982), 37–49; R. Alan Culpepper, *Anatomy of the Fourth Gospel: A Study in Literary Design* (FF New Testament; Philadelphia: Fortress, 1983), 197; Maarten J. J. Menken, "John 6:51c–58: Eucharist or Christology?" in *Critical Readings of John 6* (ed. R. Alan Culpepper; Biblical Interpretation Series 22; Leiden: Brill, 1997), 183–204: repr. from *Bib* 74 (1993); John M. Perry, "The Evolution of the Johannine Eucharist," *NTS* 39 (1993): 22–32; and Michael Labahn, *Offenbarung in Zeichen und Wort: Untersuchungen zur Vorgeschichte von Joh 6,1–25a und seiner Rezeption in der Brotrede* (WUNT 2/117; Tübingen: Mohr Siebeck, 2000), 68–80.

[4] The best discussion is Udo Schnelle, *Antidocetic Christology in the Gospel of John: An Investigation of the Place of the Fourth Gospel in the Johannine School* (trans. Linda M. Maloney; Minneapolis: Fortress, 1992), 194–210. The eucharistic interpretation does not depend on the antidocetic interpretation, however: see Menken, "John 6:51c–58," 198; and Brown, *John*, 1:lxxvi–lxxvii.

[5] On the extent of the debate, see Culpepper, *Critical Readings*; and Andrew McGowan, *Ascetic Eucharists: Food and Drink in Early Christian Ritual Meals* (Oxford Early Christian Studies; Oxford: Clarendon, 1999), 236–37 (with discussion of Rev 17:2–6). Virtually all studies assume that the Eucharist is the only meaning of the cannibalistic language; see, most recently, Susan Hylen, *Allusion and Meaning in John 6* (BZNW 137; Berlin/New York: de Gruyter, 2005), 33–39,

rent debates on the redaction-critical issues and on the place of the sacraments in the Fourth Gospel.

The passage deserves reexamination. It provides the strangest exchange between Jesus and his Jewish interlocutors in the Fourth Gospel. In a series of dialogues that collapse into monologues, the Johannine Jesus provides warrants for his midrash on the Bread from Heaven that turn the factionalism of bewildered grumbling (ἐγόγγυζον) among "the Jews" (John 6:41–43) into an open fight (ἐμάχοντο) (6:52) in the synagogue at Capernaum (6:59).[6] The speech culminates in a pronouncement bewildering to the audience:

> So Jesus said to them, "Very truly, I tell you, unless you eat the flesh [ἐὰν μὴ φάγητε τὴν σάρκα] of the Son of Man and drink his blood [πίητε αὐτοῦ τὸ αἷμα], you have no life in you. Those who eat my flesh [ὁ τρώγων μου τὴν σάρκα] and drink my blood [πίνων μου τὸ αἷμα] have eternal life, and I will raise them up on the last day; for my flesh is true food and my blood is true drink. Those who eat [τρώγων] my flesh and drink [πίνων] my blood abide in me, and I in them." (6:53–56)

The whole dialogue is a virtual parody of a revelation discourse: what is revealed is Jesus' utter incomprehensibility. Even Jesus' own followers fail to understand what their prophet-messiah is requiring of them, which escalates the divisive fray. Jesus asks his disciples whether "this saying" (ὁ λόγος οὗτος) offends them too (6:60–61). The reaction of the respondents could imply that they may simply not comprehend what Jesus is requiring, but the context makes clear that they hear Jesus saying something literally obscene (disgusting to the senses): to indulge in cannibalism by consuming *his* flesh and blood. The offense of the saying triggers the decision by "the Jews" to kill Jesus (cf. 7:1; 5:18) and the desertion of "many disciples" (6:66). This scene is one of factionalism. In this context, the forms of speech that would normally provide warrants for a particular kind of instruction (midrash) serve solely to emphasize Jesus' strangeness as the Other. This parody of a traditional epiphany belongs to the Fourth Gospel's regular subversion and reinterpretation of familiar symbolism. Indeed, subversion of familiar symbolism is *the* principal strategy of the Fourth Gospel.[7]

190–94; Mira Stare, *Durch ihn Leben: Die Lebensthematik in Joh 6* (NTAbh n.s. 49; Münster: Aschendorff, 2004), 192–225; and Jane S. Webster, *Ingesting Jesus: Eating and Drinking in the Gospel of John* (Academia Biblica 6; Leiden: Brill, 2003), 152–53.

[6] Peder Borgen, *Bread from Heaven: An Exegetical Study of the Concept of Manna in the Gospel of John and the Writings of Philo* (rev. ed.; NovTSup 10; Leiden: Brill, 1981); Wayne A. Meeks, "The Man from Heaven in Johannine Sectarianism," in idem, *In Search of the Early Christians: Selected Essays* (ed. Allen R. Hilton and H. Gregory Snyder; New Haven: Yale University Press, 2002), 66–67: repr. from *JBL* 91 (1972); John Ashton, *Understanding the Fourth Gospel* (Oxford: Clarendon Press, 1991), 200; Anderson, *Christology*, 206–8.

[7] Meeks, "Man from Heaven," 65–66; and idem, "Equal to God," in idem, *In Search of the Early Christians*, 102: repr. from *The Conversation Continues: Studies in Paul and John in Honor of J. Louis Martyn* (ed. Robert T. Fortna and Beverly Roberts Gaventa; Nashville: Abingdon, 1990).

I argue that the cannibalistic language in John 6 draws on the Greco-Roman polemics of factionalism. By offering a previously overlooked cultural context in which to read the imagery in the Fourth Gospel, I take a wholly new approach to the problem of John 6 that promises to break through the current exegetical impasse. I should make clear a methodological point about my use of literary parallels. My thesis does not claim that the ancient sources analyzed below had any direct influence on the author of John's Gospel. Rather, the parallels sketch the logic or "ideology" with which the literary representation of John 6:52–66 lies in tension. By *ideology*, I mean language that colludes with, supports, and makes use of the current structures of authority and domination that a particular community uses to construct and maintain its social "reality" and in which people can participate even if the collusion is not altogether conscious.[8]

The charge of the cannibal in "our" midst signaled for ancient audiences a recognizable Greek and Roman condemnation of domestic rebels and internal conspirators. The first section below examines this charge of anthropophagy in Greek and Roman literature. Anthropophagy functioned in ancient polemics to brand an opponent or faction in terms of the Other who overturned not only the state but also the norms of language itself. The second section integrates this evidence into an analysis of Josephus's *Jewish War*, which provides a Jewish example of factionalism described with the same topoi. A third section applies these findings to an exegesis of John 6. While derived from the ritual language of early Christian eucharistic practices, anthropophagy proved especially useful to the author because it also celebrated the very cultural idiom of factionalism that defined John's community. The Johannine author revaluated the cultural taboo of cannibalism in positive terms as a means of self-definition for his community, to throw outsiders off the scent and to weed out those insiders "who did not believe" (6:64).

I. Anthropophagy: A Greco-Roman Cultural Idiom of Factionalism

Anthropophagy served Greek and Roman culture as a traditional way of thinking about threats to society.[9] Ancient writers warned that factionalism among citizens had the power to overturn the value system within which people think and to destroy the normal linguistic and semantic world. A common Greek term for this

---

[8] Dale B. Martin, *The Corinthian Body* (New Haven: Yale University Press, 1995), xii–xiii, xiv–xv; J. Albert Harrill, *Slaves in the New Testament: Literary, Social, and Moral Dimensions* (Minneapolis: Fortress, 2006), 3.

[9] Andrew McGowan, "Eating People: Accusations of Cannibalism against Christians in the Second Century," *JECS* 2 (1994): 441.

phenomenon was στάσις, but proper analysis of the term lies in its *use* in Greek society, not in its philology or lexical word study.[10] Indeed, a range of vocabulary expressed the phenomenon of factional strife, including σχίσμα (as in John 7:43; 9:16; 10:19), without differentiation.[11] Anthropophagy articulated a "poetics" of consumption, in which the human became the beast. The cultural code correlated diet with particularly Greek structural fears about civic stability: the savagery of "the raw" may overturn the civilization of "the cooked."[12]

This idiom goes back to Homeric epic. The metaphor of "blood" (αἷμα) in the *Iliad* increasingly compares warriors to bestial, blood-hungry predators.[13] Simile and narrative correspond as *fighting* and *eating* become indistinguishable on the level of diction, the war descending into factionalism, an essentially cannibalistic enterprise. The blood-eating imagery increases—with the figure of the predatory wolf—as heroic participation in the communal pre-battle ritual meal decreases. Agamemnon's brutal fighting style is "as wolves, who tear flesh raw, in whose hearts the battle fury is tireless, who have brought down a great horned stag in the mountains, and then feed on him, till the jowls of every wolf run red/bloody with blood" (Homer, *Il.* 16.156–59).[14] The war-god Ares thirsts for human blood, and the effects of his anthropophagic hunt reduce warriors to carrion animals belching up clotted

---

[10] M. I. Finley, "Athenian Demagogues," *Past and Present* 21 (1962): 6. Standard studies include Andrew Lintott, *Violence, Civil Strife and Revolution in the Classical City, 750–330 BC* (Baltimore: Johns Hopkins University Press, 1982), 34–81, 90–96 and passim; Hans-Joachim Gehrke, *Stasis: Untersuchungen zu den inneren Kriegen in den griechischen Staaten des 5. und 4. Jahrhunderts v. Chr.* (Vestigia, Beiträge zur alten Geschichte 35; Munich: Beck, 1985); Olivier Aurenche, *Les groupes d'Alcibiade, de Léogoras et de Teucros: Remarques sur la vie politique athénienne en 415 avant J.C.* (Collection d'études anciennes; Paris: Belles Lettres, 1974), 9–41; Lily Ross Taylor, *Party Politics in the Age of Caesar* (Sather Classical Lectures 22; Berkeley: University of California Press, 1949); cf. Paul Mikat, *Die Bedeutung der Begriffe Stasis und Aponia für das Verständnis des 1. Clemensbriefes* (Arbeitsgemeinschaft für Forschung des Landes Nordrhein-Westfalen, Geisteswissenschaften 155; Cologne: Westdeutscher Verlag, 1969).

[11] On the vocabulary's range and its lack of differentiation, see the excellent studies of Margaret M. Mitchell, *Paul and the Rhetoric of Reconciliation: An Exegetical Investigation of the Language and Composition of 1 Corinthians* (HUT 28; Tübingen: Mohr Siebeck, 1991), 70–80; and L. L. Welborn, "Discord in Corinth: 1 Corinthians 1–4 and Ancient Politics," in idem, *Politics and Rhetoric in the Corinthian Epistles* (Macon, GA: Mercer University Press, 1997), 1–42: repr. from *JBL* 106 (1987). See also Joseph Roisman, *The Rhetoric of Conspiracy in Ancient Athens* (Berkeley/Los Angeles: University of California Press, 2006), 2–7.

[12] On the alimentary metaphor, see Charles Segal, "The Raw and the Cooked in Greek Literature: Structure, Values, Metaphor," *CJ* 69 (1973–74): 289–308; and Athenaeus, *Deipn.* 660d–661d.

[13] Tamara Neal, "Blood and Hunger in the *Iliad*," *CP* 101 (2006): 15–33, whose excellent analysis informs my discussion throughout this paragraph.

[14] Trans. in ibid., 24 (full context, pp. 23–27). See also Margaret Graver, "Dog-Helen and Homeric Insult," *Classical Antiquity* 14 (1995): 48–49.

blood.[15] Achilles' rage, the central concern of the poem, becomes explicit cannibalism in his angry wish to carve up Hector's flesh and to eat it raw (22.346–48).[16] By the later books of the poem, therefore, the insatiable appetite for human blood no longer serves as a metaphor for fighting fury but self-consuming rage. Rather than displaying the war's heroism, the unfolding αἷμα motifs ultimately convey the war's pointless savagery and destruction.[17]

For factionalism's effects on semantic meaning, we find the classic expression in Thucydides' narrative of the savage, three-year στάσις on the island of Corcyra during the Peloponnesian War. According to Thucydides, factionalism contaminates all social interaction down through the very core of language itself.[18] People in the grip of civic dissension distort linguistic conventions by exchanging "the conventional value [ἀξίωσις] of words in relation to the facts [τὰ ἔργα], according to their own perception of what was justified" (Thuc. 3.82.4).[19] Thucydides claims not that the rebels and conspirators actually changed the *meanings* of words (which, in any case, would hardly persuade crowds to their side), but that they gave a more or less plausible redescription of ἔργα within the existing vocabulary. They changed the verbal "evaluation" (ἀξίωσις) of phenomena, which means that they distorted moral judgments. The collapse of νόμοι enabled the revolutionaries in oaths, legal processes, and political slogans to assign "good" values to norms of action previously condemned as vice. In his analysis, Thucydides draws on Greek ethical theory that articulates immorality not in terms of mere decline or degeneration but rather by the figure of inversion. The inversion of verbal "transvaluation" belongs to a set of interrelated elements within the Thucydidean topos that includes tyranny, the subordination of justice to self-interest, rampant criminality, violent unrestraint, and bloodthirstiness.[20]

---

[15] Neal, "Blood and Hunger," 27–30. Neal argues convincingly that the war-god identifies himself with humans in the epic poem, and so the imagery is indeed cannibalism.

[16] Edith Hall, *Inventing the Barbarian: Greek Self-Definition through Tragedy* (Oxford Classical Monographs; Oxford: Clarendon, 1989), 27.

[17] Neal, "Blood and Hunger," 30–33.

[18] Simon Swain, "Law and Society in Thucydides," in *The Greek World* (ed. Anton Powell; London: Routledge, 1995), 551–57; David Cartwright, *A Historical Commentary on Thucydides* (Ann Arbor: University of Michigan Press, 1997), 155–57; June W. Allison, *Word and Concept in Thucydides* (American Philological Association American Classical Studies 41; Atlanta: Scholars Press, 1997), 167 n. 9.

[19] Trans. in Jonathan J. Price, *Thucydides and Internal War* (Cambridge: Cambridge University Press, 2001), 39.

[20] The best commentaries are Simon Hornblower, *A Commentary on Thucydides* (2 vols.; Oxford: Clarendon, 1991), 1:466–91; Allison, *Word and Concept*, 163–87; Price, *Thucydides*, 6–78; and John Wilson, "'The Customary Meanings of Words Were Changed'—Or Were They? A Note on Thucydides 3.82.4," *CQ* 32 (1982): 18–20 (contra John T. Hogan, "The ἀξίωσις of Words at Thucydides 3.82.4," *GRBS* 21 [1980]: 139–49). On inversion, see Lowell Edmunds, "Thucydides' Ethics as Reflected in the Description of Stasis (3.82–83)," *HSCP* 79 (1975): 73–92; cf. Nicole

Thucydides' depiction of that *stasis* at Corcyra connects to his description of anthropophagy in a previous episode, the cannibalism during the siege at Potidaea (Thuc. 2.70.1). This Greek topos of siege cannibalism also enters Roman rhetoric as a declamatory theme, the disgust (*fastidium*) at which satirists exploited.[21] It bears close affinities to depictions of civil and familial breakdown in Greek tragedy, such as Euripides' *Bacchae*, which dramatizes the disrupted body politic feeding off itself through the Dionysian σπαραγμός (ritual dismembering) and ὠμοφαγία (eating of raw flesh).[22] Thucydides' narrative of the dissension at Corcyra is important for our study of the Fourth Gospel because Jesus' cannibalistic talk of John 6:52–56 presents a corresponding inversion of verbal evaluations in a similar episode of communal dissension and factionalism.

The description in Thucydides also has a striking parallel in Plato's *Republic*. Devoting an entire section to the effects of political constitutions on language, Plato envisages the turmoil that democracy brings to the soul of a developing youth. False and arrogant words (λόγοι) and opinions (δόξαι) from demagogues revalue basic human qualities to the point that vices masquerade as virtues, parading in public as if in a procession (insolence, anarchy, extravagance, and cowardice). The onslaught of wanton speeches praising these vices ignites both a faction and a counterfaction (στάσις δὴ καὶ ἀντίστασις) in the youth's soul, which eventually erupts (Plato, *Resp.* 8.559d–560e). Plato argues that the revolution in the city from oligarchy to democracy initiates a tyrannical breakdown of language itself.[23] The philosopher compares the horrifying effects of factionalism to its very prototype—the Arcadian mountaintop mysteries of Zeus on Mount Lycaon—and so uses *ritual* as a point of Otherness (Plato, *Resp.* 8.565d–566a). The covert rites have inevitably lycanthropic properties that conjure in Greek society the dangerous Other who normally lurks

---

Loraux, "La guerre civile grecque et la représentation anthropologique de monde à l'envers," *RHR* 212 (1995): 299–326.

[21] Robert A. Kaster, "The Dynamics of Fastidium and the Ideology of Disgust," *TAPA* 131 (2001): 158–59; Nicola Biffi, "*Sueta insuetaque vesci*: Verifica di un *topos*," *Invigilata Lucernis* 10 (1998): 35–57; H. D. Rankin, "'Eating People Is Right': Petronius 141 and a Trope," *Hermes* 97 (1969): 381–84; William S. Anderson, "Juvenal Satire 15: Cannibals and Culture," in *The Imperial Muse: Ramus Essays on Roman Literature of the Empire* (ed. A. J. Boyle; Berwick, Australia: Aureal, 1988), 203–14; Richard McKim, "Philosophers and Cannibals: Juvenal's Fifteenth Satire," *Phoenix* 40 (1986): 58–71.

[22] J. Peter Euben, *The Tragedy of Political Theory* (Princeton: Princeton University Press, 1990), 135–36. Cf. John H. Finley, "Euripides and Thucydides," in idem, *Three Essays on Thucydides* (Loeb Classical Monographs; Cambridge, MA: Harvard University Press 1967), 33, repr. from *HSCP* 49 (1938). On the cultic terms, see Charles Segal, *Dionysiac Poetics and Euripides' "Bacchae"* (Princeton: Princeton University Press, 1982), 23–26, 33, 48–49, and passim; and Hans-Josef Klauck, *The Religious Context of Early Christianity: A Guide to Graeco-Roman Religions* (trans. Brian McNeil; Studies of the New Testament and Its World; Edinburgh: T&T Clark, 2000), 109–11.

[23] Allison, *Word and Concept*, 170–71; Hornblower, *Thucydides*, 483.

safely on the savage periphery: *ritual* places the cannibalistic monster in the civilized center.[24] For Plato, the hidden but certain Arcadian rites describe figuratively the hidden but certain threat that a "protector of the people" poses to the *polis*: the demagogue inevitably transforms into a cannibalistic tyrant through the seductive "rituals" of a democratic constitution. Cannibalism thus belongs to ancient polemics against rival forms of government and community self-definition.

These themes recur in Roman polemics against factionalism. One example is the invective against domestic enemies that mask *bellum civile* as a *foreign war* in order to recast an internal opponent as an external Other: not as a *civis* but as a *hostis*; from an authentic Roman to a bestial *monstrum*.[25] Importantly, this invective charges an opponent with anthropophagy—or at least a "cannibal eye." In his speeches against Mark Antony, Cicero brands Antony with a tyrannical appetite for citizen blood: "he gorged himself with the blood of citizens" (Cicero, *Phil.* 2.59); "you had tasted, or rather had drunk deeply, the blood of citizens" (*Phil.* 2.71). Seneca repeats the same theme when he brands Antony an "enemy of the state" (*hostis rei publicae*), filled with un-Roman vices, and "thirsting for blood" (Seneca, *Ep.* 83.25). Plutarch comments sardonically that while some supporters welcomed Antony with Bacchic processions hailing him as "Dionysus," most of the crowd understood him to be the "Eater of Raw Flesh" that the hail named him (Plutarch, *Vit. Ant.* 24.4). The "cannibalistic eye" appears in Valerius Maximus as a device within the topos *de crudelitate* to condemn the cruelty of the Roman dictator Sulla: "Another sign of his insatiable savagery: he had the severed heads of the victims, still all but retaining expression and breath, brought into his presence, so that he could chew them with his eyes, since it was forbidden to do so with his mouth" (Val. Max. 9.2.1).

The invective of cannibalism invoked a central motif in Greek and Roman literary imagination—the tyrant as the inverted Other. The theme went back to the Lycaon story in Plato's *Republic*, was enacted in the popular theme of Atreus and Thyestes on the tragic stage, and frequently was depicted through the imagery of carrion animals (wolves, hawks, vultures).[26] Anthropophagy emerges, therefore, as a fundamental trope in polemics against factionalism and tyranny.

---

[24] On this phenomenon, see David Frankfurter, *Evil Incarnate: Rumors of Demonic Conspiracy and Ritual Abuse in History* (Princeton: Princeton University Press, 2006), 76–85, and passim.

[25] Michèle Lowie, *Horace's Narrative "Odes"* (Oxford: Clarendon, 1997), 149–50. Related is the theme of *bellum civile* as gladiatorial combat; see Carlin A. Barton, *The Sorrows of the Ancient Romans: The Gladiator and the Monster* (Princeton: Princeton University Press, 1993), 36–39, and passim.

[26] Lucan, *Bel. civ.* 1.327–33; Varius Rufus, *Thyestes*; Seneca, *Thyestes*; Ovid, *Met.* 6.527–28; Statius, *Theb.* 8.71–74 and 757–66; Diodorus Siculus 22.3.5 and 34/35.12; Plutarch, *Mor.* 556d; Heraclitus, *Ep.* 7 (*First-century Cynicism in the Epistles of Heraclitus* [ed. Harold W. Attridge; HTS 29; Missoula, MT: Scholars Press, 1976], 74–75); Tacitus, *Hist.* 3.39.1; Plautus, *Trin.* 101–2; Cicero,

The polemics target conspirators in particular as tyrannical cannibals. Such monstrous traitors were said to lurk in "our" midst to feed on the body politic, often literally, in a ritual meal that inverted normal eating. Livy's narrative of the Bacchanalian "conspiracy" (*coniuratio*) in 186 B.C.E., for example, expands the allegations to fit just such a stereotype (Livy 39.8–39). Livy piles up an accumulation of inversions (cacophonous rites, orgy, ecstatic behavior, ritual murder that implies dismemberment, cannibalism) to evoke horror at a bestial subculture of ritual atrocity right in the heart of the Roman Republic.[27] As in Plato's polemics against democracy, Livy's polemics against the Bacchanalia use *ritual* as a point of Otherness. In addition, Livy's account is a *literary* construction: "a little drama about the son of a good family, his wicked step-father, and his freed-woman mistress with a heart of gold, a plot reminiscent of the plays written in Greece in the Hellenistic period and imitated by Plautus."[28] The Senate's "sudden" discovery of Bacchanalia, its objection being rooted in the cult's "crimes of immorality," and the entire event as a "conspiracy" are fictions that Livy creates, as we know from the methodological control of the documentary evidence (the actual Senatorial decree of 186 B.C.E.) that mentions none of these details.[29] The examples show that an ancient author's use of cannibalism for the polemics of factionalism does not require a high level of civil conflict or an actual context of warfare.

Phil. 11.8; *Pis.* 38; and *Sest.* 71. See also Matthew Leigh, "Varius Rufus, Thyestes and the Appetites of Antony," *Proceedings of the Cambridge Philological Society* n.s. 42 (1996): 171–97; Denis C. Feeney, *The Gods in Epic: Poets and Critics of the Classical Tradition* (Oxford: Clarendon, 1991), 221, 360–61; Brian S. Hook, "Tyranny and Cannibalism: The Thyestes Theme in Greek and Roman Literature" (Ph.D. diss., Duke University, 1992); Leonard Barkan, *The Gods Made Flesh: Metamorphosis and the Pursuit of Paganism* (New Haven: Yale University Press, 1986), 24–27, 92; Ruth Parkes, "Men from Before the Moon: The Relevance of Statius *Thebiad* 4.275–84 to Parthenopaeus and his Arcadian Contingent," *CP* 100 (2005): 364–65; Eleni Manolaraki, "A Picture Worth a Thousand Words: Revisiting Bedriacum (Tacitus *Histories* 2.70)," *CP* 100 (2005): 262; Ittai Gradel, "Jupiter Latiaris and Human Blood—Fact or Fiction?" *Classica et Mediaevalia* 53 (2002): 248–51 (on "emperor vampires"). On the "cannibal eye" and its Roman context, see Shadi Bartsch, *The Mirror of the Self: Sexuality, Self-Knowledge, and the Gaze in the Early Roman Empire* (Chicago: University of Chicago Press, 2006), 115–52.

[27] McGowan, "Eating People," 431; Frankfurter, *Evil Incarnate*, 103; Mary Beard, John North, and Simon Price, *Religions of Rome*, vol. 1, *A History* (Cambridge: Cambridge University Press, 1998), 91–97; Jean-Marie Pailler, *Bacchanalia, la répression de 186 av. J.-C. à Rome et en Italie: Vestiges, images, tradition* (Bibliothèque des Ecoles Françaises d'Athènes et de Rome 270; Rome: Ecole Française de Rome, 1988), 21–24, 523–96. On the vocabulary of conspiracy, see Victoria Emma Pagán, *Conspiracy Narratives in Roman History* (Austin: University of Texas Press, 2004), 10–14.

[28] Beard, North, and Price, *Religions of Rome*, 1:92.

[29] John A. North, "Religious Toleration in Republican Rome," *Papers of the British School at Rome* n.s. 44 (1976): 1–12.

Another narrative target of the polemics of tyrannical cannibalism is Catiline (L. Sergius Catilina), who is said to have attempted a coup d'état with senatorial confederates to seize power throughout Italy in 67–66 and 63 B.C.E. But, as with Livy's narrative of the Bacchanalia, we must remember that many details existed only in the mind of the authors. Cicero, who exposed the plots, took the controversial step of executing the chief conspirators without a trial. His details and characterizations, especially of the first Catilinarian "conspiracy" (ca. 67–66 B.C.E., a likely fiction), are more rhetorical than historical.[30]

For later Roman authors, the earliest full source of the subsequent "Catiline story" was Sallust's *Bellum Catilinae* (*De Catilinae coniuratione*). Borrowing direct details from Thucydides' account of the *stasis* at Corcyra, Sallust analyzes the Catilinarian conspiracy as the pathology of moral decline that attends civil strife.[31] He describes the conspiracy as a "civil war," to be sure, but equivocates on whether the anthropophagic details are true or stereotyped invective. According to Sallust, Catiline compelled his confederates in crime to take an oath by passing "around bowls of human blood mixed with wine [*humani corporis sanguinem vino permixtum in pateris circumtulisse*]." Sallust continues, "Others thought that these and many other details were invented by men who believed that the hostility which afterwards arose against Cicero would be moderated by exaggerating the guilt of the conspirators whom he had put to death. For my own part I have too little evidence for pronouncing upon a matter of such weight" (Sallust, *Bell. Cat.* 22; Rolfe, LCL).

From the innuendo found in Sallust, the Catiline story grew from simple, alleged blood drinking to outright human sacrifice and ritual cannibalism (Plutarch, *Cic.* 10.2–4). Catiline "imposed the obligation of taking a monstrous oath. For he sacrificed a boy, and after administering the oath over his entrails [σπλάγχνα], ate them in company with the others" (Dio Cassius 37.30.3). Cast in the role of a Tantalus/Atreus/Lycaon, Catiline created not a new religious system but an inversion of familiar Roman rites, a monstrous pact through an inverted *sacramentum* (military oath). The invective of anthropophagic συσπλαγχνεύειν alienates Catiline and his confederates from the very people and community that once gave them identity as Romans.[32] Such alienation appears also in the ritual murder

---

[30] H. H. Scullard, *From the Gracchi to Nero: A History of Rome 133 BC to AD 68* (5th ed.; London: Methuen, 1982), 105–10, 423 n. 2, 424–25 n. 8.

[31] Thomas Francis Scanlon, *The Influence of Thucydides on Sallust* (Bibliothek der klassischen Altertumswissenschaften n.s. 2/70; Heidelberg: Carl Winter, 1980), 99–125, and passim.

[32] For other versions, see Florus 2.12.4; Tertullian, *Apol.* 9.9; Minucius Felix, *Oct.* 30.5. See also McGowan, "Eating People," 431–33; J. Rives, "Human Sacrifice among Pagans and Christians," *JRS* 85 (1995): 72–73; Albert Henrichs, "Pagan Ritual and the Alleged Crimes of the Early Christians: A Reconsideration," in *Kyriakon: Festschrift Johannes Quasten* (ed. Patrick Granfield and Josef A. Jungmann; 2 vols.; Münster: Aschendorff, 1970), 1:22, 33–35; Thomas N. Habinek, *The Politics of Latin Literature: Writing, Identity, and Empire in Ancient Rome* (Princeton: Princeton University Press, 1998), 71–72, 80–81; Pagán, *Conspiracy Narratives*, 33–34; Benjamin Isaac, *The Invention of Racism in Classical Antiquity* (Princeton: Princeton University Press, 2004), 208.

and cannibalistic communion of brigands, a plot formula of outlaw behavior cultivated in the ancient Greek novels,[33] as well as in stories of anthropophagic night-witches.[34] Among the most dreadful images in Roman imagination, cannibalism signaled a society falling into internal sedition and a city taken (*urbs capta*) from within, a familiar topos that drew on the literary precedent of Thucydides.[35]

II. Anthropophagy: Also a Jewish Cultural Idiom of Factionalism

Ancient Jews shared the Greek and Roman ideology that condemned factionalism in the language of cannibalism. Flavius Josephus serves as an example of a Jew using this classical theme in connection with Judean society. His *Jewish War* sets the revolt within Rome's own internal disorders (ἐν Ῥωμαίοις μὲν ἐνόσει τὰ οἰκεῖα) (*J.W.* 1.4–5), when "civil strife broke out [ἐστασιάσθη] among the Jews" and "the tyrants [οἱ τύραννοι] rose to power with their mutual feuds" (1.23–24). Indeed, "στάσεως τοῖς δυνατοῖς Ἰουδαίων" places *factionalism* in the first words of the narrative after the prologue (1.31). Josephus explains, "For [my country] owed its ruin to civil strife [στάσις οἰκεία], and that it was the Jewish tyrants [τύραννοι] who drew down upon the holy temple the unwilling hands of the Romans and the conflagration" (1.10; see also 5.257). Josephus uses a range of terms besides στάσις, many grouped together, to sound civil discord (e.g., 4.131–32; 4.375–76: διχόνοια ἔρις, τὸ φιλόνεικον, αἵρεσις, πόλεμος ἐμφύλιος [Greek equivalent to *bellum civile*]). Josephus tells the story of the Jewish War apologetically, as a civil war, and in terms of a universal pattern conforming to Flavian-era historiography.[36]

---

[33] Achilles Tatius, *Leuc. Clit.* 3.15; Lollianos, *Phoinikika* B.1 recto (*Ancient Greek Novels: The Fragments* [ed. Susan A. Stephens and John J. Winkler; Princeton: Princeton University Press, 1995], 338–39, 350–52); Jack Winkler, "Lollianos and the Desperadoes," *JHS* 100 (1980): 155–81. Related is the *misoxenia* motif in ancient Greek stock accusations against Jews engaging in ritual cannibalism; see Peter Schäfer, *Judeophobia: Attitudes toward the Jews in the Ancient World* (Cambridge, MA: Harvard University Press, 1997), 62–65.

[34] E.g., the night-witch Erichtho in Lucan, *Bel. civ.* 589–623. Erichtho's anthropophagy fleshes out a central theme of Lucan's epic—that civil war inverts all cultural norms, especially those of language and religion; see C. A. Martindale, "Three Notes on Lucan VI," *Mnemosyne* ser. 4/30 (1977): 375–87; and Jamie Masters, *Poetry and Civil War in Lucan's "Bellum Civile"* (Cambridge Classical Studies; Cambridge: Cambridge University Press, 1992), 179–215.

[35] See G. M. Paul, "*Urbs Capta*: Sketch of an Ancient Literary Motif," *Phoenix* 36 (1982): 150–51; and Elizabeth Keitel, "Principate and Civil War in the *Annals* of Tacitus," *AJP* 105 (1984): 306–25.

[36] Steve Mason, "Of Audience and Meaning: Reading Josephus' *Bellum Judaicum* in the Context of a Flavian Audience," in *Josephus and Jewish History in Flavian Rome and Beyond* (ed. Joseph Sievers and Gaia Lembi; JSJSup 104; Leiden: Brill, 2005), 71–100; idem, "Figured Speech

The pattern locates the first fight of civil discord to be the *family row*, in which participants faced off, especially along generational lines, in the space all shared and all called home.[37] The hostility escalated to the breaking point of turning kin and friends into strangers and enemies:

> Beginning in houses [πρῶτον μὲν ἐν οἰκίαις], this party rivalry [τὸ φιλόνει-κον] first attacked those who had long been bosom friends; then the nearest relations severed their connexions and joining those who shared their respective views ranged themselves henceforth in opposite camps. Faction [στάσις] reigned everywhere; and the revolutionary and militant party overpowered by their youth and recklessness the old and prudent. The various cliques began by pillaging their neighbors, then banding together in companies they carried their depredations throughout the country; insomuch that in cruelty and lawlessness the sufferers found no difference between the compatriots and Romans, indeed to be captured by the latter seemed to unfortunate victims far the lighter fate. (*J.W.* 4.132–34; Thackeray, LCL, alt.)

In this passage, the emphasis shifts from the particular to the generic as the narrative expands its description more widely, over the entire region. Presenting the family row as generic and typical of all conflicts, everywhere, treats the particular aberration as symptomatic of the pathology of factionalism universal to human nature. In this way, Josephus stylizes the events of his narrative to a predictable, overarching scheme recognizable and so understandable to his Greco-Roman audience.[38]

The scheme points to the inversion of language itself, as we saw in Thucydides' account of Corcyra and in the Roman conspiracy and *bellum civile* literature. According to Josephus, in addition to inverting the family and its patron-client relations, the Jewish War inverted the way the rebels used language. Likely echoing Plato's "parade of vices" (*Resp.* 8.559d–560e), Josephus crafts a calculated

---

and Irony in T. Flavius Josephus," in *Flavius Josephus and Flavian Rome* (ed. Jonathan Edmondson, Steve Mason, and James Rives; New York: Oxford University Press, 2005), 267–68; Gottfried Mader, *Josephus and the Politics of Historiography: Apologetic and Impression Management in the "Bellum Judaicum"* (Mnemosyne Sup. 205; Leiden: Brill, 2000), 53–54. On Josephus and his contemporary writers of the Flavian age, helpfully complicating the question of what is "Jewish" and what is "Roman," see Steve Weitzman, "Josephus on How to Survive Martyrdom," *JJS* 55 (2004): 230–45.

[37] I borrow the term *family row* from the insightful analysis of Ashton, *Understanding the Fourth Gospel*, 151 and 159.

[38] Mader, *Josephus and the Politics*, 49, 69–73; see also 56–66 on the *mundus inversus* (μεταβολή) scheme generally. Josephus's audience included Jews as well, and Josephus used also biblical prophetic typology, notably, the Jeremianic theme of sin, repentance, and divine punishment (ibid., 8–9, 35). See also A. M. Eckstein, "Josephus and Polybius: A Reconsideration," *Classical Antiquity* 9 (1990): 175–208, which responds to Shaye J. D. Cohen, "Josephus, Jeremiah, and Polybius," *History and Theory* 21 (1982): 366–81.

polemic against the Zealots: "For you parade your unspeakable crimes and contend daily to see who can be the worst, making an exhibition of vices as though they were virtues" (J.W. 5.414–15). "In short," the historian charges, "they boasted of their audacious crimes as if they were benefactors and saviors of the city" (4.146). "You protest of being tyrant-ridden," concurs an Idumean leader in the narrative, "and hurl a charge of despotism against the victims of your own tyranny! Who could stomach your hypocritical words ... contradicted by the facts?" (4.278–79). The Zealots rename neutrality as hostility, invert virtue and vice, and reframe the norms of language itself. Verbal transvaluation becomes increasingly prominent with the arrival of Josephus's *bête noire* in Jerusalem, the rebel leader John of Gischala (4.121–282).[39] This invective against "semanticide" has the important function of "reversing the reversals"—countering the specific rebel claims by turning them on their head—to show the real truth to be the exact opposite of what the rebels assert.

In his excellent analysis, Gottfried Mader explains the narrative device:

> Whenever ... catchwords are used by the Zealots in self-justification or to attack their opponents, they are reported by Josephus in a manner calculated to expose them as ὀνόματα εὐπρεπῆ, fraudulent λόγοι at variance with ἔργα; and finally the theme of verbal distortion culminates in a grand Thucydidean-type antilogy at 4.236–282 ... where it is both dramatized and subjected to a penetrating theoretical analysis. The function and strategy of the ὀνόματα εὐπρεπῆ system in Josephus could be described thus: first he shows the Zealots to be willfully manipulating words to promote their own devious ends (this is a typical symptom of *stasis*), then he himself deploys polemical reversal as a "corrective" to their distortions—reversing the reversals, as it were. In this sense his own polemic is predicated on the Thucydidean analysis (*stasis* leading to general reversal) and derives apparent legitimacy through that affiliation.[40]

Important for our study of the Fourth Gospel, the polemical Othering of the Jewish splinter factions involves cannibalistic imagery. Josephus brands the opponents as bestial monsters (non-Jews, even nonhumans) who eat the raw flesh and gulp down the warm blood of the very fellow citizens they claim to protect. He envisages them as carrion animals: "The entire city was the battleground for these conspirators and their rabble, and the people were being torn in pieces like some huge carcass [δῆμος ὥσπερ μέγα σῶμα διεσπαράσσετο]" (J.W. 5.27–28). The brigands (λῃσταί) became like brute beasts "divorcing soul from body," and "continued like dogs to maul the very carcass of the people [νεκρὸν τὸν δῆμον ὥσπερ κύνες ἐσπάραττον]" (5.526). When the Zealots imprisoned the wife of a rival rebel leader, her husband (Simon of Gioras) advanced to the walls of Jerusalem

---

[39] For a full analysis, see Mader, *Josephus and the Politics*, 55–103. On the historical figure, see U. Rappaport, "John of Gischala: From Galilee to Jerusalem," *JJS* 33 (1982): 479–93.

[40] Mader, *Josephus and the Politics*, 74.

"like some wounded beast [καθάπερ τὰ τρωθέντα τῶν θηρίων]. Any who ventured outside the city gates to gather herbs or firewood, old people without arms, [Simon] seized and tortured to death. In his boundless rage he was almost gnawing their very corpses [νεκρῶν γευόμενος τῶν σωμάτων]" (4.540–42).

Food became so scarce in the besieged Jerusalem that if the partisans "found anyone with food they snatched it away and swallowed it, dripping with the wretched man's blood. By now they were actually fighting each other for the loot; and I have little doubt that if capture had not forestalled it, their utter bestiality would have made them get their teeth into the very corpses [δ᾽ ὑπερβολὴν ὠμότητος γεύσασθαι καὶ τῶν νεκρῶν]" (J.W. 6.372–73).[41] "We should not be far wrong," writes Josephus, "if we described this as a faction within a faction, like a maddened beast [καθάπερ θηρίον λυσσῆσαν] driven by lack of other food to devour its own flesh [ἐπὶ τὰς ἰδίας ἤδη σάρκας ὁρμᾶν]" (5.2–5).[42] The language casts the factional leaders, especially Simon of Gioras and John of Gischala in the classical topos of the "cannibalistic" tyrant.[43]

In a scene parallel to that of Catiline in Sallust, Josephus exposes the abomination of cannibalistic rituals in the conspiracy: "When a man had been stripped by Simon he was sent to John [of Gischala]; when someone had been plundered by John, Simon took him over. They drank to each other's health in the blood of their countrymen and divided the carcasses of the wretches between them [ἀντιπρούπινον δ᾽ ἀλλήλοις τὸ αἷμα τῶν δημοτῶν καὶ τὰ πτώματα τῶν ἀθλίων διεμερίζοντο]."[44] By using human blood to seal an oath to do the evil of sedition, the act inverts the oath (ὅρκος) motif and reveals the wider pattern of verbal anarchy in the narrative.[45] Although as rivals for power they crossed daggers, Simon and John "were united [ὁμόνοια] in their crimes" (5.440–41). Those crimes included ransacking houses of the rich, murdering men, raping women for sport, and drinking down their spoils with blood (μεθ᾽ αἵματός τε τὰ συληθέντα κατέπινον), an "insatiable passion for looting" (4.560–61). To the bitter end, these

---

[41] Trans. G. A. Williamson, *The Jewish War/Josephus* (rev. E. Mary Smallwood; Penguin Classics; New York: Penguin Books, 1981), 367–68.

[42] Ibid., 287.

[43] For Josephus on the rebel leaders as "tyrants," see *J.W.* 1.27–28; 2.448–49, 626; 4.158, 166, 172, 258, 396–97, 401, 564, 566–67; 5.169–70, 439; 6.98, 129, 143, 228.

[44] On the connection to Catiline, see H. St. J. Thackeray, *Josephus, The Jewish War* (2 vols.; LCL; Cambridge, MA: Harvard University Press, 1927–29), 1:548; 2:27, 62–63; Paul, "*Urbs Capta*," 154; Tessa Rajak, *Josephus: The Historian and His Society* (2nd ed.; London: Duckworth, 2002), 160–61; Thomas Grünewald, *Bandits in the Roman Empire: Myth and Reality* (trans. John Drinkwater; London: Routledge, 2004), 202 n. 64; and Mason, "Figured Speech," 272–73.

[45] Mader, *Josephus and the Politics*, 89, 94. Cf. Herodotus 4.62, 64, 70; and Claude Rawson, "Narrative and the Proscribed Act: Homer, Euripides and the Literature of Cannibalism," in *The History and Philosophy of Rhetoric and Political Discourse* (ed. Kenneth W. Thompson; 2 vols.; Lanham, MD: University Press of America, 1987), 2:99 n. 63.

leaders and their "war party" did everything possible "to feed on the public miseries [ἐσθίειν ἐκ τῶν δημοσίων κακῶν] and to drink the city's life-blood [τὸ τῆς πόλεως αἷμα πίνειν]" (5.344). The use of cannibalistic language is not merely sensationalist but points to a set piece of invective that brands a factional leader as the barbarian, tyrannical Other, who mutilates the body politic. Jews, Romans, and Greeks thus all shared this ideology of internal war.[46] Indeed, the metaphor of cannibalism for the predatory fury of the Zealots and other rebels recalls Achilles' taunt to carve up Hector's flesh and eat it raw (Homer, *Il.* 22.346–48).[47]

As the narrative progresses, the insatiable appetite for human blood in besieged Jerusalem no longer serves as a metaphor for the rebel's fury but becomes a literal abomination: Mary bat Eleazar of Bethezuba cooks up her baby for the conspirators (*J.W.* 6.201–19).

> At once the rebels were upon her and, scenting the unholy odour, threatened her with instant death unless she produced what she prepared. Replying that she had reserved a goodly portion for them also, she disclosed the remnants of her child. Seized with instant horror and stupefaction, they stood paralyzed by the sight. She, however, said, "This is my own child, and this is my handiwork. Eat, for I too have eaten. Show yourselves to be not weaker than a woman, or more compassionate than a mother. But if you have pious scruples and shrink from my sacrifice, then let what I have eaten be your portion and the remainder also be left for me." At that they departed trembling, in this one instance, cowards, though scarcely yielding even this food to the mother. The whole city instantly rang with the abomination, and all, picturing the horror of it, shuddered as though they had perpetrated it themselves. (6.209–13; Thackeray, LCL, alt.)

Although initially ignorant of the stew's contents, and horrified at their virtual act of cannibalism, the rebels nonetheless "scarcely yielded even this food to the mother." Their deep implication in the mother's crime is clear. The picture of the female in bestial frenzy dismembering her own child for food evokes Bacchic *sparagmos* familiar from Greek and Roman tragedy.[48] Not an isolated showpiece of

---

[46] Mader, *Josephus and the Politics*, 135–46; Shaye J. D. Cohen, *Josephus in Galilee and Rome: His Vita and Development as a Historian* (Columbia Studies in the Classical Tradition 8; Leiden: Brill, 1979), 70–74, 87–89, 93, 241; Maud Gleason, "Mutilated Messengers: Body Language in Josephus," in *Being Greek under Rome: Cultural Identity, the Second Sophistic and the Development of Empire* (ed. Simon Goldhill; Cambridge: Cambridge University Press, 2001), 68, 70–74.

[47] Honora Howell Chapman, "'By the Waters of Babylon': Josephus and Greek Poetry," in *Josephus and Jewish History*, ed. Sievers and Lembi, 132. Although the specific words are not necessarily Homeric vocabulary, Chapman finds enough intertextual echoes to argue that Josephus links the fall of Jerusalem and the fall of Troy.

[48] Honora Howell Chapman, "Spectacle and Theater in Josephus' Bellum Judaicum" (Ph.D. diss., Stanford University, 1998), 58–120; eadem, "'Myth for the World': Early Christian Reception of Cannibalism in Josephus *Bellum Judaicum* 6.199–219," in *SBLSP* 39 (2000): 363–70; and eadem, "'By the Waters,'" 140–43. Cf. recent works arguing that the Fourth Gospel uses tragic

theater, however, the spectacle of impiety links the theme of cannibalism developed throughout the narrative to the pivotal atrocity of the war, the destruction of the Jerusalem temple. Following the divine will of God, the Roman general Titus declares that because the Jews prefer sedition to concord (peace to war, famine to plenty and prosperity), he decides to "bury this abomination of infant cannibalism [τὸ τῆς τεκνοφαγίας μύσος] beneath the ruins of their country" (J.W. 6.216-17).[49]

In all these passages, Josephus shares the Greek and Roman ideology that describes factionalism in the language of cannibalism.[50] He presents the Jewish War as a *stasis*, not as a national or provincial rebellion against Rome, and "Others" the rebels (and his opponents)—John of Gischala, Simon of Gioras, and the Zealots—as renegades from Judaism (tyrants, conspirators, cannibals). Josephus, therefore, provides evidence of the theme, used in ancient Judaism, being part of wider Mediterranean culture. NT exegetes have overlooked the importance of this evidence for illuminating the strange exchange between Jesus and his Jewish interlocutors in John 6:52-66. Leon Morris, for example, declares, "References to drinking blood are rare in Jewish literature. Josephus once [sic] says, 'It was still possible to feed upon the public miseries and to drink of the city's life-blood' (*Bell.* 5.344). But this sheds no light on the present passage."[51] The section below indicates otherwise. The Greco-Roman polemics of factionalism, with its imagery of cannibalism, provides an overlooked ancient context in which to interpret both the presence and the function of the cannibalistic language in John 6:52-66.

---

themes from Greek dramatic models for character portrayal: Brant, *Dialogue and Drama*; and George L. Parsenios, "'No Longer in the World' (John 17:11): The Transformation of the Tragic in the Fourth Gospel," *HTR* 98 (2005): 1-21.

[49] For further discussion, see Chapman, "'Myth for the World,'" 360-63; eadem, "Spectacle and Theater," 108-11, and passim; Mader, *Josephus and the Politics*, 133-46; Gleason, "Mutilated Messengers," 74-75; and cf. Burton L. Visotzky, "Most Tender and Fairest of Women: A Study in the Transmission of Aggada," *HTR* 76 (1983): 403-18. Despite Josephus's claim to "describe an act unparalleled in the history of either the Greeks or the barbarians" (J.W. 6.199-200), *teknophagia* circulated widely as a wartime topos of horror: Josephus, *Ant.* 13.345-47; Philo, *Praem.* 134-35 (reference to Thyestes' cannibalism); Herodotus 3.11; Lev 26:29; Deut 28:52-59; 2 Kgs 6:25-29; Jer 19:9; Ezek 5:9-10; Lam 2:20; 4:10; Bar 2:2-3. Cf. *L.A.B.* 25.9 (*OTP* 2:335-36); *1 En.* 7.4-6 (*OTP* 1:16); and Manfred Oeming, "'Ich habe einen Greis gegessen': Kannibalismus und Autophagie als Topos der Kriegsnotschilderung in der Kilamuwa-Inschrift, Zeile 5-8, im Alten Orient und im Alten Testament," *BN* 47 (1989): 90-106.

[50] Note Ashton, *Understanding the Fourth Gospel*, 184: "all human speech, even the most inspired, draws instinctively upon a high stock of models lodged in the individual's memory and immediately available to him in the appropriate circumstances."

[51] Leon Morris, *The Gospel according to John* (rev. ed.; NICNT; Grand Rapids: Eerdmans, 1995), 335 n. 132.

III. Anthropophagy in the Fourth Gospel: The Revaluation of Cannibalism

Factionalism is a main theme of the Fourth Gospel. The author introduces it in the first public act of Jesus, the temple conflict at Passover season (John 2:13–20). In the scene, Jesus talks back to "the Jews" (presumably, the authorities) in language that they construe as a rally for civil war, λύσατε τὸν ναὸν τοῦτον—the destruction of the temple by its own people (2:19). Later, in the context of another festival, Jesus' brothers warn about the appearance of conspiracy: "for no one who wants to be widely known acts in secret [ἐν κρυπτῷ ποιεῖ]. If you do these things, show yourself to the world" (7:4). But Jesus nonetheless goes up to Jerusalem, in defiance of the warning, "not publicly but (as it were) in secret [ἐν κρυπτῷ]" (7:10). The fact that Jesus keeps his movements in Jerusalem secret divides the festival crowds into pro and contra factions who mutter quietly because of their fear of "the Jews," shorthand for the authorities (7:11–13). At the temple once more, Jesus provokes a division (σχίσμα) in the crowd (7:30–31, 40–44); again we find the explicit diction of factionalism. Jesus' healing the blind man divides an entire neighborhood (9:9) and causes a σχίσμα among the Pharisees (9:16). Jesus' subsequent speech on the Good Shepherd only worsens the factionalism, throwing "the Jews" into a σχίσμα once again (10:19–21).[52]

This factionalism results repeatedly from a misunderstanding on the part of Jesus' interlocutors. Jesus' temple outburst calls for destruction, "but he was speaking of the temple of his body" (2:21). The division of the crowds over Jesus' secret movements during the Festival of Booths arises from misunderstanding his claim to depart "where you will not find me" as a plan of escape into the Diaspora (7:33–36), and his citation of Scripture as a self-condemnation of his origins (7:37–43). When Jesus repeats his exit plan, the Jews misconstrue it as his intention to commit suicide (8:22). The enigma of his Good Shepherd παροιμία throws many of the Jews into total confusion and into calls not to listen anymore to such a person "out of his mind" (10:20). The Johannine Jesus provokes the misunderstandings in his audience deliberately, through the device of double entendre, which is common in the Fourth Gospel (3:7–15, 31–38; 11:11–13).

Cannibalism was one of the prime images of factionalism in ancient Mediterranean culture and is the key image of John 6. John 6 contains both a miracle (6:1–14) and a dialogue (6:22–51) about hunger. The saying reinforces the radical reworking of OT models in the midrash on the Bread from Heaven, and it repeats

---

[52] On the passage and its context, see John Ashton, *Studying John: Approaches to the Fourth Gospel* (Oxford: Clarendon, 1994), 131–32; and David Brakke, "Parables and Plain Speech in the Fourth Gospel and the *Apocryphon of James*," *JECS* 7 (1999): 192–202.

the feeding of the five thousand in a way that "the Jews" cannot comprehend. Concerning OT models, the saying may also play on Genesis 9, where humans are allowed to eat flesh but not drink the blood because the blood is the life (Gen 9:4). The Johannine author quite possibly reworks this Noahide dietary motif to suggest that Jesus has restored the antediluvian way of eating in the same way that Jesus also revives the manna given to Israel in the wilderness.[53] As a narrative piece, John 6 moves from OT concepts familiar to the Jews to something monstrous, subverting their symbols and traditions.[54] In a traditional OT tale of famine, the inverted figure of the cannibal emerges.

The plausibility of any hypothesis depends upon its ability to explain the evidence,[55] in our case, the reason why the Fourth Gospel presents cannibalistic language in a context of factionalism. The charge of cannibalism was a commonplace in polemics against factionalism, and the synagogue authorities who faced the religious dissent of what would become the Johannine community likely Othered such messianic sectarians as "cannibals." My argument thus participates in the general consensus of those scholars who understand the Fourth Gospel to function as a "two-level drama," in which the murderous hostility between Jesus and "the Jews" refers not to the situation of the historical Jesus but to the late-first-century experience of the author's community being expelled from one of the emerging synagogues. The social history admitted here is, therefore, unabashedly based on the pioneering work of J. Louis Martyn (now in its third edition), to which scholars have made some qualifications and important nuances.[56]

To be sure, ongoing scholarly discussions have brought recent challenges to this consensus.[57] Although such scholars often claim that their critique offers a

---

[53] I owe this exegetical insight to my Hebrew Bible colleague Steve Weitzman.

[54] On the movement of John 6 as a narrative piece, see Meeks, "Man from Heaven," 67.

[55] I borrow the apt phrasing of Ashton, *Understanding the Fourth Gospel*, 108–9 n. 102.

[56] J. Louis Martyn, *History and Theology in the Fourth Gospel* (3rd ed.; NTL; Louisville: Westminster John Knox, 2003), 40, 46–66; all subsequent citations are to this edition. See ibid., 60 n. 69, 61–62 n. 75, 147 n. 6. See also D. Moody Smith, "The Contribution of J. Louis Martyn to the Understanding of the Gospel of John," foreword to Martyn, *History and Theology*, 7–8, 20–22; Wayne A. Meeks, "Breaking Away: Three New Testament Pictures of Christianity's Separation from the Jewish Communities," in idem, *In Search of the Early Christians*, 116–23: repr. from *"To See Ourselves as Others See Us": Christians, Jews, "Others" in Late Antiquity* (ed. J. Neusner and E. S. Frerichs; Scholars Press Studies in the Humanities; Chico, CA: Scholars Press, 1985); and Ashton, *Understanding the Fourth Gospel*, 107–11, 229–32.

[57] Judith Lieu, "Temple and Synagogue in John," *NTS* 45 (1999): 51–69; R. Bieringer, Didier Pollefeyt, and F. Vandecasteele-Vanneuville, eds., *Anti-Judaism and the Fourth Gospel* (Louisville: Westminster John Knox, 2001); Colleen M. Conway, "The Production of the Johannine Community: A New Historicist Perspective," *JBL* 121 (2002): 479–95; Robert Kysar, *Voyages with John: Charting the Fourth Gospel* (Waco: Baylor University Press, 2005), 237–45; and Raimo Hakola, *Identity Matters: John, the Jews and Jewishness* (NovTSup 118; Leiden: Brill, 2005). One recent volume even celebrates the so-called scholarly fall of Martyn's "two-level" drama as a vindication of John A. T. Robinson's revisionist theory—as a "one-level" drama, the Fourth Gospel can serve

more nuanced and complex picture of the protracted process of separation, many commit a methodological error. They assume too quickly that the theory rests entirely upon the *birkat ha-minim* (in the *Eighteen Benedictions*) to explain the expulsion from synagogues.⁵⁸ Such a critique is not valid and distracts attention from the real issue of social history, as Wayne Meeks writes:

> It is time to recognize that the *birkat ha-minim* has been a red herring in Johannine research. Not only do questions remain about its date and the earliest form of its writing—not to mention questions of where and when it would have been effective after it was promulgated—the more fundamental issue for interpreting John 16:2 and John 9's depiction of the healed blind man's expulsion is whether these scenes have anything to do with the way the *birkat ha-minim* would have worked in practice. John does not speak of people who do not go to synagogue services because they cannot conscientiously say the prayers. It speaks of being put out of the synagogue. All we have to assume is that the ἄρχοντες of the Jewish community in John's location had simply made up their minds to get rid of these trouble-making followers of a false Messiah.⁵⁹

The social process that the Fourth Gospel portrays does not require the formality that the *birkat ha-minim* implies. Nor does the theory make claims beyond the local community to which the Johannine Christians belonged.⁶⁰

---

as a primary witness to the historical Jesus (Francisco Lozada Jr. and Tom Thatcher, eds., *New Currents through John: A Global Perspective* [SBLRBS 54; Atlanta: Society of Biblical Literature, 2006], referring to John A. T. Robinson, *The Priority of John* [ed. J. F. Coakley; Oak Park, IL: Meyer-Stone, 1985]). Citing only the first edition of Martyn's book, Michael Labahn accepts but qualifies the expulsion theory as reflecting controversies over Sabbath observance in John's tradition that were unrelated to the *birkat ha-minim* (*Jesus als Lebensspender: Untersuchungen zu einer Geschichte der johanneischen Tradition anhand ihrer Wundergeschichten* [BZNW 98; Berlin: de Gruyter, 1999], 34–41, 305–77, 467).

⁵⁸ See, e.g., Hakola, *Identity Matters*, 41–86.

⁵⁹ Meeks, "Breaking Away," 123.

⁶⁰ But many scholars persist in following this red herring to argue against the expulsion theory for wholly theological (confessional) reasons. As the editors of one major volume admit, the theological hermeneutics of Jewish–Christian relations should control biblical exegesis: "Martyn's reconstruction runs the risk of blaming the representatives of Judaism single-handedly for the separation" (R. Bieringer, Didier Pollefeyt, and F. Vandecasteele-Vanneuville, "Wrestling with Johannine Anti-Judaism: A Hermeneutical Framework for the Analysis of the Current Debate," in *Anti-Judaism*, ed. Bieringer et al., 25). I understand the historical difficulty in actually *knowing* who said, or acted, maliciously "first," or even whether anyone (other than the author) was vicious to other groups. My acceptance of the expulsion theory in no way endorses Christian theologies that use the Fourth Gospel's anti-Jewish language as a pretext to blame "the Jews" for starting the invective (on the theological concern, see Adele Reinhartz, "Love, Hate, and Violence in the Gospel of John," in *Violence in the New Testament* [ed. Shelly Matthews and E. Leigh Gibson; New York: T&T Clark International, 2005], 120). But theology should never control biblical exegesis, even for the noblest of aims. On the hermeneutical tension between biblical criticism and theological debate, see Harrill, *Slaves in the New Testament*, 165–92. I thank Jennifer Knust for advice here.

Even detractors of the expulsion theory who acknowledge the red herring of the *birkat ha-minim* nonetheless persist in arguments that misunderstand the fundamental issue. Adele Reinhartz, for example, claims that two passages in John 11 and 12 should exert more hermeneutical control over the interpretation of the Fourth Gospel than the explicit mention of the expulsion from the synagogue in the text (the hapax ἀποσυνάγωγος [9:22; 12:42; 16:2]). Reinhartz explains that Mary and Martha are associating themselves with Jesus but have clearly not been excluded from the Jewish community (11:1–44), and, later, that Jews are said to be "deserting" rather than "being expelled" from the synagogue (12:11).[61] But this critique misunderstands the fundamental point of the expulsion theory. The issue is not the *association* of Jewish believers with Jesus but the *declaration* by a certain number of those believers publicly that Jesus was ἴσος τῷ θεῷ ("equal to God"), υἱὸς τοῦ θεοῦ ("son of God"), and θεός ("God").[62] The narrative makes a distinction between Jews who come to Jesus in belief and those who believe *and subsequently endure*. The expulsion theory envisions a dynamic, fluid situation in which a low-level commitment to Jesus as a "prophet" was tolerated for some time. A spiraling escalation of claims on each side—"Moses or Jesus" (9:28–29), "equal to God" (5:18)—led to a clear rupture. In such a situation, it is likely that some of Jesus' adherents left the synagogue of their own accord ("deserted") while others were expelled.[63]

Nicodemus is the paradigmatic figure for the first type of believer (3:1–21), who comes to belief in Jesus, because of the signs (σημεῖα), but to whom Jesus does not entrust himself (2:23–25). The narrative makes clear that not all so-called believers are true (abiding): "Then Jesus said to the Jews who had believed in him, 'If you continue in my word, you are truly my disciples'" (8:31–32). The true disciple must "continue" in the faith. Those who come superficially, because of the signs, Jesus rejects as from "your father the devil" (8:42–47, at v. 44). Those "many Jews who were deserting and were believing in Jesus" (12:11; see also 11:45–46) were coming to Jesus *on account of* the greatest σημεῖον in the Gospel (next to the resurrection itself), the raising of Lazarus (11:1–44). Rumors about the high number of these anonymous believers flare up among the Jewish leaders (Pharisees) in the alarmist hyperbole, "Look, the world has gone after him!" (12:19). These the Johannine Jesus separates from himself as he separates darkness from light, and himself from ὁ κόσμος. In John's Gospel, the term κόσμος means what alienates and even

---

[61] Adele Reinhartz, *Befriending the Beloved Disciple: A Jewish Reading of the Gospel of John* (New York: Continuum, 2001), 42–53; and eadem, "'Jews' and Jews in the Fourth Gospel," in *Anti-Judaism*, ed. Bieringer et al., 223.

[62] See Meeks, "Equal to God."

[63] On the fluid situation of missionary and polemical interaction with a strong Jewish community whose piety accorded very great importance to Moses, see Wayne A. Meeks, *The Prophet-King: Moses Traditions and the Johannine Christology* (NovTSup 14; Leiden: Brill, 1967), 292–95, and passim.

"hates" (μισεῖ) Jesus and his followers (17:14, 16; cf. 18:36). "If the world [ὁ κόσμος] hates you," Jesus explains to his disciples, "be aware that it hated me before it hated you. If you were of the world [ἐκ τοῦ κόσμου], the world would love you as one of its own [τὸ ἴδιον]. Because you are not of the world [ἐκ τοῦ κόσμου], but I have chosen you out of the world [ἐκ τοῦ κόσμου]—therefore the world hates you" (15:18-19).

In sum, any interpretation of John 6 must take seriously its overarching theme of "enduring" and "falling away." The author contrasts the perishable manna that the Jewish ancestors ate in the wilderness (Exodus 16; Psalm 78), along with the flesh of the quail supplied at twilight (Exod 16:12-13; Ps 105:40), with the enduring ("true") food and drink of Jesus' flesh and blood (6:55). Jesus tells his interlocutors not simply "to believe" but to endure: "Do not work for the food that perishes, but for the food that endures for eternal life" (6:27). The emphasis on endurance identifies the community with Jesus, the "true vine" (15:1) of which Christians are branches.[64] Such talk plays on the ancient ideology that cannibalism feeds on the body politic—the community. Believers must consume only *Jesus'* flesh and blood. Just as Jesus is the "true light" (1:9), the "true vine" (15:1), and the one sent by the "true God" (17:3), Jesus' flesh and blood are the only "true" food and drink (6:32, 55). In this way and smarting from their synagogue expulsion, the Johannine sectarians appropriated "cannibalism" from its negative polemics of factionalism into a positive affirmation of community self-definition, thus turning the tables on the invective for those who endured.

John 6:52-66 may also draw on eucharistic language, but not in a simplistic, passive fashion.[65] To be sure, early Christian traditions of the Eucharist would have supported the positive appropriation of "cannibalism" in the Johannine circle. But if we move the scholarship on the cannibalistic language in John 6:52-66 beyond the limited hermeneutical framework of "sacramentalism" and the "ecclesiastical" (read "Roman Catholic") redactor as the only possible sources of the passage's language, we open an entirely new avenue of investigation into the text and its cultural context.

That avenue leads us to ask whether any ancient group would have positively appropriated normally negative connotations of invective.[66] In fact, we do have the

---

[64] On the vine symbolism for discipleship, see Craig R. Koester, *Symbolism in the Fourth Gospel: Meaning, Mystery, Community* (2nd ed.; Minneapolis: Fortress, 2003), 270-77.

[65] The verbal, stylistic, and thematic agreements between John 6:51-58 and 1 Cor 10:2-3 (also 1 Cor 10:16-17, 21; 11:23-29) suggest that the author of the Fourth Gospel may have drawn on an early Christian oral tradition that associated eucharistic and manna traditions in a way similar to the formulations that came down to Paul; see Peder Borgen, "John and the Synoptics," in idem, *Early Christianity and Hellenistic Judaism* (Edinburgh: T&T Clark, 1996), 121-57; repr. from *The Interrelations of the Gospels: A Symposium Led by M.-É. Boismard, W. R. Farmer, F. Neirynck, Jerusalem 1984* (ed. David L. Dungan; BETL 95; Leuven: Leuven University Press, 1990). On the eucharistic parallels between John 6:12 and *Did.* 9.4, see Meeks, *Prophet-King*, 94-96.

[66] I leave aside Paul's positive appropriation of invective in 2 Cor 10:10; on this example,

example of one movement in antiquity that appropriated abuse against it for positive self-definition—the Cynics. Diogenes the Cynic, for example, willingly accepted the invective "dog" (κύων/κύνων). "When Plato styled him a dog," reports his biographer, "he replied, 'Quite true! [ναί],' for I come back again and again to those who have sold me" (Diog. Laert. 6.40; also 6.61, and passim). The Cynic Epistles confirm that this particular doxographic tradition reflects actual social practice. Much of the paraenesis in the Cynic Epistles calls on (especially, new) Cynics "not to fear the name" (τὸ ὄνομα), to continue enduring such invective "robustly" (σφοδρῶς), and to "make full use of the name of κυνισμός" to those outside the movement.[67] By accepting the abusive nickname "dog" willingly, the Cynics demonstrated their fondness for using animal wildlife as behavioral paradigms of living "according to nature." Such was the sport that the Cynics made out of the invective that they experienced socially.

This jesting rose to performance art in the flouting of sexual and dietary taboos, acting like "dogs." Traditions circulated that Diogenes made a habit out of eating meat raw in public, which ultimately lead to his end when he gnawed into a tainted Octopus raw (Diog. Laert. 6.34 and 76). Importantly, Diogenes is even reported to have endorsed cannibalism, as a "natural" way of eating in the ideal, by writing his (no longer extant) play *Thyestes* (Diog. Laert. 6.73). And at least one of the Cynic Epistles, addressed to "the so-called Greeks," jests that the corpses of executed criminals (on the cross and on the rack) have no good use "except to eat as the flesh of sacrificial victims" (εἰ μὴ ὥσπερ ἱερείων σάρκας ἐσθίειν), a paraenetic harangue on the immorality of non-Cynics, who ignore what nature teaches, for the movement's self-definition.[68] The topos of cannibalism invoked the barbarian wildness of the Scythians, a famous Cynic icon. The Cynics turned the normally negative connotations of cannibalism into a positive icon of their movement's *autarkeia* ("self-sufficiency"), *parrhēsia* ("bold speech"), and freedom from cultural conventions.[69] They thus provide an example of an ancient group appropriating

---

see Harrill, *Slaves in the New Testament*, 35–57; and idem, "The Slave Still Appears: A Historiographical Response to Jennifer Glancy," *BibInt* 15 (2007): 216–18.

[67] *Crates Ep.* 16 and 21; *Diogenes Ep.* 27 (*The Cynic Epistles: A Study Edition* [ed. Abraham J. Malherbe; SBLSBS 12; Missoula, MT: Scholars Press, 1977], 67, 71, 119). See also the positive appropriation of κύων as "heaven's κύων" to assuage a father's distress at his son joining a movement disparaged with such abuse (*Diogenes Ep.* 7) (Malherbe, *Cynic Epistles*, 99). In this analysis, I understand that the Cynics differed among themselves over accepting their antisocial and misanthropic reputations; on Cynic diversity, see Abraham J. Malherbe, "Self-Definition among Epicureans and Cynics," in *Jewish and Christian Self-Definition*, vol. 3, *Self-Definition in the Greco-Roman World* (ed. Ben F. Meyer and E. P. Sanders; Philadelphia: Fortress, 1982), 48–59.

[68] *Diogenes Ep.* 28 (Malherbe, *Cynic Epistles*, 121). This Cynic topos may inform Trimalchio's satire of cannibalism in Petronius, *Sat.* 141; see Albert Henrichs, *Die Phoinikika des Lollianos: Fragmente eines neuen griechischen Romans* (Papyrologische Texte und Abhandlungen 14; Bonn: R. Habelt, 1972), 70 n. 78.

[69] John L. Moles, "Cynic Cosmopolitanism," in *The Cynics: The Cynic Movement in Antiq-*

invective against itself positively, an action that the Johannine community also may have taken.

The Fourth Gospel's overarching message is one of "alienation." The devices that convey this message include inversion and polemical irony. The narrative appropriates many motifs and symbols from their traditional meaning and revalues them in a way *precisely to offend* the Jewish interlocutors. For example, John introduces motifs familiar from Jewish tradition only to subvert each by redirecting the symbol to an exclusive application to Jesus—ascent to heaven (1:51; 3:13; 6:62), living water (4:10; 7:37–39), Moses "lifting up" the serpent (3:14; 8:28; 12:32–34), Abraham's children (8:31–58), the manna from heaven (6:31–42), the light of Genesis (1:4–9; 3:19–21; 8:12; 9:5; 12:35–36, 46), the paschal lamb (1:29, 36). The positive appropriation of cannibalistic language, therefore, fits an overall exegetical pattern of Johannine irony, subversion, and polemic.[70]

As many scholars have pointed out, the "teachings" of the Johannine Jesus offer riddling and obscure speech that cause confusion and division in the audience, pitting the insider against the outsider. Much of the first half of the Gospel (esp. John 5–10) adopts a polemical tone of dissent, conspiracy, and rebellion.[71] The episode of Jesus' healing the blind man triggers a neighborhood/family row (9:8–9) and a Pharisaic σχίσμα (9:16), leading the "disciples of Moses" to revile the disciples of Jesus (9:27–28), a drama epitomizing the estrangement of the Johannine community "from the synagogue" (a people ἀποσυνάγωγος).[72] Moreover, the

---

uity and Its Legacy (ed. R. Bracht Branham and Marie-Odile Goulet-Cazé; Berkeley/Los Angeles: University of California Press, 1996), 112, 117; James Romm, "Dog Heads and Noble Savages: Cynicism before the Cynics?" in *Cynics*, ed. Branham and Goulet-Cazé, 122–23; Derek Krueger, "The Bawdy and Society: The Shamelessness of Diogenes in Roman Imperial Culture," in *Cynics*, ed. Branham and Goulet-Cazé, 226–27; Sarah Rappe, "Father of the Dogs? Tracking the Cynics in Plato's *Euthydemus*," *CP* 95 (2000): 291–93; Michel Onfray, *Cynismes: Portrait du philosophe en chien* (Paris: Bernard Grassett, 1990), 99–114; Ragnar Höistad, *Cynic Hero and Cynic King: Studies in the Cynic Conception of Man* (Lund: C. Bloms, 1948), 145–46. The Cynic ideal of ἀνθρωποφαγία entered Stoic traditions about the wise; see Richard Bett, *Sextus Empiricus, Against the Ethicists (Adversus Mathematicos XI)* (Oxford: Clarendon, 1997), 32, 207–9, 265; and Paul A. Vander Waerdt, "Zeno's *Republic* and the Origins of Natural Law," in *The Socratic Movement* (ed. Vander Waerdt; Ithaca: Cornell University Press, 1994), 300–301. Cf. F. Gerald Downing, *Cynics and Christian Origins* (Edinburgh: T&T Clark, 1992), 50, 173–74; and the response by McGowan, *Ascetic Eucharists*, 73–75.

[70] On John's use of irony as a weapon, see Paul D. Duke, *Irony in the Fourth Gospel* (Atlanta: John Knox Press, 1985), 39–41 and 149–50, but without analysis of John 6.

[71] On the polemical tone in the first half of John and its background in Jewish–Christian debate that created the Johannine community, see Ashton, *Understanding the Fourth Gospel*, 150.

[72] Ashton, *Studying John*, 121. On religious dissent in Palestinian synagogues as the crucible that forged the Johannine community's self-definition, see Ashton, *Understanding the Fourth Gospel*, 124–59, 171–79; and Meeks, "Breaking Away." Cf. Daniel Boyarin, "The Ioudaioi in John and the Prehistory of 'Judaism,'" in *Pauline Conversations in Context: Essays in Honor of Calvin J.*

raising of Lazarus causes a literal parting of the ways, with "many of the Jews" coming to join Mary's belief in Jesus, but some of the others going to join the Pharisees' accusation of Jesus. The "chief priests and the Pharisees" call a meeting of the Sanhedrin, in which they invoke the visual description (*ekphrasis*) of war's aftermath (the destruction that the Romans would do to "our holy place and our nation") to justify Jesus' execution (11:45–53). These episodes highlight Jesus as the cause of rebellion and *stasis*.[73]

The Jesus-inspired division of a Jewish community may have been a local crisis, but the Gospel represents it in totalized, cosmic terms, a theme that fundamentally belongs to the ancient literary imagination of anthropophagy and which may very likely have used *ritual* as a point of Otherness.[74] The polemics of cannibalism functioned to alienate dissidents outside the civilized (orderly) world (οἰκουμένη, κόσμος). In John, the alienation's cosmic dimensions include also accusations of demonology (10:20). Interestingly, the Johannine Jesus fires this cosmic representation of Otherness back upon "the Jews" themselves (8:44–49), which turns the tables on what we might call hate language. We should interpret the cannibalistic language in John 6:52–66 in the social context of this firing back and forth of invective between the synagogue authorities and the sectarian Johannine community.

The originally negative sense of anthropophagy remained useful for the Johannine community, however. Jesus warns his followers to beware "the wolf" (ὁ λύκος) that tears the shepherd's throat out and "snatches up" (ἁρπάζει) and scatters "the sheep" (John 10:12–13, 28).[75] The saying conceptualizes danger in terms close to lycanthropy (cf. Matt 7:15; Acts 20:29). Trying to snatch people back into the fold, "the Jews" will prey on the Johannine community even after its expulsion. Other folklore-like tales besides that of the wolf further this warning. The menace of the thief (ὁ κλέπτης) and the robber (ὁ λῃστής) represent related manifestations of danger also affiliated with predatory wildlife in the ancient literary imagination. Such terms recur in Josephus's characterization of John of Gischala, Sallust's portrait of Catiline, Cicero's invective against Mark Antony, and Plato's myth of Lycaon. The combination of these terms in John's Gospel produces a similar context in which an anthropophagic imagery is expected. The wolf in John 10 supports the negative or derogatory connotations of anthropophagy already familiar to ancient audiences.

The semantics of cannibalism, therefore, reflect John's characteristic use of

---

Roetzel (ed. Janice Capel Anderson, Philip Sellew, and Claudia Setzer; JSNTSup 221; Sheffield: Sheffield Academic Press, 2002), 216–39.

[73] John 11:48 is likely a reference to the Jewish War. On the *ekphrasis* of war's aftermath, see Manolaraki, "Picture Worth a Thousand Words."

[74] On ritual as a point of Otherness, see Frankfurter, *Evil Incarnate*, 8. The ritual would, of course, be the Eucharist.

[75] See Ashton, *Studying John*, 122, 127–29.

private language (*Sondersprache*, as German scholars say) throughout the Gospel. Such sectarian discourse gave legitimacy to the estrangement and degradation that the community experienced. A product of a "cognitive minority," the private language affirmed the community's feelings of Otherness and alienation from the world.[76] Jesus' cannibalistic language also provokes a fight (ἐμάχοντο) among "the Jews" (6:52) while he teaches it "in the synagogue" (6:59), causing dissent ("grumbling," γογγύζουσιν) in his own camp (6:61; cf. 6:41). "Many" (πολλοί) followers of Jesus defect from the group (6:66) because the saying is "too hard" to accept (6:60). The anthropophagic saying of the Johannine Jesus functions in an antimissionary way, to steer outsiders away from the community and to encourage unworthy insiders to leave.[77]

IV. Conclusion

Anthropophagy appears in both Greek and Roman polemics of factionalism. The proverbial anthropophagy of the tyrant inverts the citizen to create the barbarian Other in ancient ethnography, a recognizable topos in classical culture and society. Homeric warriors who were reducing themselves to bloodthirsty carrion animals embody this monstrousness. Thucydides describes the transvaluation of words endemic to the pathology of *stasis* as an exemplar of its type. Plato depicts the tyrant "passing" between the human and the beast as the ritual anthropophagy of the Lycaon myth.

As invective, the charge of cannibalism functions to Other an opponent. In the literature of their enemies, the Bacchanals, Catiline, and Mark Antony become vicious "cannibals." Cicero, Seneca, Plutarch, and Valerius Maximus employed the topos in literature, while actors portrayed the popular theme on the tragic stage. From the standpoint of the socially dominant, the trope depicts would-be con-

---

[76] Leroy, *Rätsel*, 51–67; Ashton, *Understanding the Fourth Gospel*, 451; Meeks, "Man from Heaven," 55–59, 74–79. On "cognitive minorities," see Peter L. Berger, *A Rumor of Angels: Modern Society and the Rediscovery of the Supernatural* (rev. ed.; New York: Anchor Books, 1990), 6–7; and Ashton, *Understanding the Fourth Gospel*, 212.

[77] The new situation of factionalism even among disciples may represent a later insertion, but the author himself may have done the redaction, one of the many stages in the Gospel's composition over time (Ashton, *Understanding the Fourth Gospel*, 200–201). On Johannine riddles, see ibid., 110–11, 189–90; and Brakke, "Parables and Plain Speech," 188–89, 194. The scholarly appeal to "antilanguage" amounts to the same interpretation, only in jargon: Bruce J. Malina and Richard L. Rohrbaugh, *Social-Scientific Commentary on the Gospel of John* (Minneapolis: Fortress, 1998), 7–11; and Jerome H. Neyrey, *An Ideology of Revolt: John's Christology in Social-Scientific Perspective* (Philadelphia: Fortress, 1988), 143–45. See also Norman R. Petersen, *The Gospel of John and the Sociology of Light: Language and Characterization in the Fourth Gospel* (Valley Forge, PA: Trinity Press International, 1993), 89–108.

spirators as political cannibals on the body politic. The imagery was among the most dreadful in ancient literary imagination. Flavius Josephus serves as an example of an ancient Jew participating in this literary imagination. His *Jewish War* argues that the rebels distort language as monstrous tyrants, who drink the blood of their fellow citizens and tear Jewish society apart like a great carcass. Their abomination leads Mary of Bethezuba to cook up her baby for the conspirators, an act that seals their doom and causes the Jerusalem temple's destruction.

Although Mary of Bethezuba and Josephus's other Jewish rebels remain God-condemned monsters in the *Jewish War*, the Jewish rebels of the Fourth Gospel turn their revolt into a badge of honor marking their birth "from above" (John 3:7) as "children of light" (12:36; cf. 3:19). It is part of the proper separation of "light" from "darkness" (1:5). Importantly, the Gospel of John does not change the cannibalistic *meaning* of the words: the command to "eat my flesh" (φάγητε τὴν σάρκα) and "drink my blood" (πίητε τὸ αἷμα) still means cannibalism (6:52–57).[78] Rather, John's Gospel gives a redescription of the cannibalistic motif within the existing vocabulary and redirects it exclusively to Jesus. The revaluation of cannibalism belongs to the revaluation of traditional symbols in the Fourth Gospel generally.

The Fourth Gospel provides a fascinating entrée into the ancient debate over factionalism from a standpoint not favoring concord—the "losing side" that embraces its alienation—which is something of a rarity. By appropriating the charge of cannibalism positively for sectarian self-definition, John deviates from the classical discourse of anthropophagy in rejecting the *negative* ideology about factionalism diffused throughout the ancient Mediterranean. The inversion stands very close to the verbal transvaluation that Greco-Roman literature depicts as typical for factious, seditious bands. The concept comes from the traditional association of cannibalism and factionalism in ancient literary imagination. It also may come from a need for the Johannine community to respond to the increasing hostility of the emerging synagogue authorities toward religious dissenters in the varieties of Judaism in Palestine (and throughout the Diaspora). In any case, Jesus' cannibalistic talk in the Fourth Gospel functions to divide insiders and outsiders. For John, such division is good and the very purpose for which Christ came into "the world" (3:19–21).

[78] I leave aside the lexical debate over the supposed shift in Greek terminology, most of which is beside the point; ἐσθίω (John 6:53) and τρώγω (6:54) are interchangeable: see C. Spicq, "τρώγειν: est-il synonyme de φαγεῖν et d'ἐσθίειν dans le Nouveau Testament?" *NTS* 26 (1979–80): 414–19; C. K. Barrett, *The Gospel according to St. John: An Introduction with Commentary and Notes on the Greek Text* (2nd ed.; Philadelphia: Westminster, 1978), 299; Menken, "John 6:51c–58," 195–96. The point is to study the concept, not the word; see Ashton, *Understanding the Fourth Gospel*, 515; and Finley, "Athenian Demagogues," 6.

Table Fellowship and the Translation of 1 Corinthians 5:11

JONATHAN SCHWIEBERT
jschwieb@artsci.wustl.edu
Washington University, St. Louis, MO 63130

In a commonsense reading of 1 Cor 5:11, Paul adds insult to injury:

But now I am writing to you not to associate with anyone who bears the name of brother or sister who is sexually immoral or greedy, or is an idolater, reviler, drunkard, or robber. *Do not even eat with such a one.* (NRSV; emphasis mine)

As William F. Orr and James Arthur Walther put it, "The dissociation is drastic: there is to be no table fellowship."[1] This gloss captures a commonsense approach to Paul's prohibition "not to eat with such a person." Refusing to eat with someone is, it would seem, an extreme form of exclusion, a "drastic" instance of refusing to "associate" with that person. However, commonsense notions about ancient texts are frequently misleading, especially when they remain unexamined.[2] In this case, modern ideas about table fellowship may be exerting an unwarranted influence on translators and interpreters of the text.

---

[1] William F. Orr and James Arthur Walther, *I Corinthians: A New Translation, Introduction, with a Study of the Life of Paul, Notes, and Commentary* (AB 32; Garden City, NY: Doubleday, 1976), 192.

[2] I have been unable to locate a single study or commentary that argues for, rather than assumes, the traditional rendering of μηδέ as "not *even*" in this clause. Two commentators from the late nineteenth century, Frédéric L. Godet and Wilhelm Meyer, debate whether μηδέ should be taken to introduce "a matter of less gravity" (Godet, *Commentary on Paul's First Epistle to the Corinthians* [2 vols.; trans. A. Cusin; Edinburgh: T&T Clark, 1889–90], 1:274) or a "klimatische" example of general shunning (Meyer, *Handbuch über den ersten Brief an die Korinther* [Kommentar über das Neue Testament; Göttingen: Vandenhoeck & Ruprecht, 1888], 154–55), in the interests of deciding whether Communion can be intended in the prohibition. The problem still vexes Gordon D. Fee, *The First Epistle to the Corinthians* (NICNT; Grand Rapids: Eerdmans, 1987), 226.

The translation of the clause in question hinges on what BDF terms a "negative correlative," μηδέ. The Pauline text reads as follows:[3]

νῦν δὲ ἔγραψα ὑμῖν μὴ συναναμίγνυσθαι ἐάν τις ἀδελφὸς ὀνομαζόμενος ᾖ πόρνος ἢ [κτλ.] . . . τῷ τοιούτῳ μηδὲ συνεσθίειν.

The major translations (NASB, NIV, NJB, NKJV, New Living Translation [NLT], RSV) and commentators agree in rendering μηδέ in the last clause of this sentence as "not *even*," or its equivalent.[4] In this translation, δέ carries an exceptional force that is usually associated with καί. Although μηδέ indeed can, in certain cases, convey the sense "not *even*," the question here is whether this exceptional force is warranted in 1 Cor 5:11.

This verse is not singled out for attention in BDF, which claims that οὐδέ/μηδέ "remains the same as in classical" (§445). According to Herbert Weir Smyth, then, the default sense of οὐδέ/μηδέ in classical usage is "*and not, nor*" (§2163A), although δέ in this compound word can mean "*and, even, also,* or *but*" (§2930), as context and usage may require.[5] BAGD agrees, listing as the primary sense "*and not, but not, nor* continuing a preceding negation (almost always w. μή)," and listing "*not even*" for more specialized constructions (BAGD, s.v. μηδέ).

Under what circumstances, then, does μηδέ tend to take the stronger sense "not even"? The construction μή . . . μηδέ alone does not resolve the matter (see Smyth §2932; BAGD, μηδέ 1; and examples in the following paragraph); additional

---

[3] NA²⁷; punctuation modified. No textual variants affect the argument of this article.

[4] The following commentators (in addition to Orr and Walther, *I Corinthians*) are representative of a much larger sampling. Despite their chronological range and methodological differences, all simply assume the rendering "not even" without argument: Archibald Robertson and Alfred Plummer, *A Critical and Exegetical Commentary on the First Epistle of St Paul to the Corinthians* (ICC; New York: Charles Scribner's Sons, 1911), 107; Hans Conzelmann, *1 Corinthians: A Commentary on the First Epistle to the Corinthians* (trans. James W. Leitch; Hermeneia; Philadelphia: Fortress, 1975), 95; Fee, *1 Corinthians*, 226; Simon J. Kistemaker, *Exposition of the First Epistle to the Corinthians* (New Testament Commentary; Grand Rapids: Baker, 1993), 170–71; Richard B. Hays, *First Corinthians* (Interpretation; Louisville: John Knox, 1997), 87; J. Paul Sampley, "The First Letter to the Corinthians," *NIB* 10:848. A partial exception (F. W. Grosheide) will be discussed below. So too even Wayne A. Meeks, *The First Urban Christians: The Social World of the Apostle Paul* (New Haven: Yale University Press, 1983), 103, 130; Dennis E. Smith, *From Symposium to Eucharist: The Banquet in the Early Christian World* (Minneapolis: Fortress, 2003), 203; and Gerald Harris, "The Beginnings of Church Discipline: 1 Corinthians 5," *NTS* 37 (1991): 6, 10–11. These last three continue to assume "not *even*," despite insightful arguments in which exclusion from the table clearly emerges as a substantial consideration. On unity at table in Corinth, see Matthias Klinghardt (*Gemeinschaftsmahl und Mahlgemeinschaft: Soziologie und Liturgie frühchristlicher Mahlfeiern* [Tübingen: Francke, 1996], 294–95, 299–301, 330–31); he does not discuss 1 Cor 5:1–13.

[5] Herbert Weir Smyth, *Greek Grammar* (1916; rev. Gordon M. Messing; Cambridge, MA: Harvard University Press, 1956).

factors must be in play. According to BDF, "If οὐδέ (μηδέ) stands at the beginning of the whole sentence or follows an οὐ (μή) within the same clause, it means 'not even'" (§445). Neither rule holds for 1 Cor 5:11. As examples, BDF offers Mark 3:20 (ὥστε μή . . . μηδέ, in which what follows ὥστε μή is an infinitive that requires what follows μηδέ for completion); Mark 8:26 (μηδέ introducing a prohibition with the subjunctive); and Matt 6:15 (οὐδέ introducing an apodosis in which "not *even*" would be an overtranslation).[6] None of these constructions parallels the μή . . . μηδέ of 1 Cor 5:11. The examples Smyth offers for οὐδέ/μηδέ in the sense "not even," however, present the same kinds of constructions: a single verb with οὐ . . . οὐδέ (Sophocles, *Trachiniae* 280), which agrees with the second part of the rule in BDF §445 cited above, and a negated infinitive (with οὐ) completed by a clause introduced by οὐδέ (Xenophon, *Anabasis* 6.6.25), which is similar to Mark 3:20. In these cases οὐδέ (μηδέ) is said to "resume a preceding οὐ" (Smyth §2939). The μηδέ in 1 Cor 5:11 does not "resume" the earlier μή in an analogous way. Finally, BAGD offers, as instances of "not even," Mark 2:2 (ὥστε μηκέτι . . . μηδέ, again where what follows μηδέ completes a prior infinitive); Eph 5:3 (μηδέ introducing a prohibition); the first two verses given by BDF (Mark 3:20; 8:26); and 1 Cor 5:11. Neither Mark 2:2 nor Eph 5:3, however, offers any kind of warrant for rendering μηδέ as "not *even*" in 1 Cor 5:11.

On the other hand, BAGD offers many examples where μηδέ in μή . . . μηδέ is best rendered in keeping with the rubric "*and not, but not, nor* continuing a preceding negation (almost always w. μή)." For example, Mark 13:15, which reads μὴ καταβάτω μηδὲ εἰσελθάτω, "let him not go down nor enter," is very close in construction to 1 Cor 5:11: μὴ συναναμίγνυσθαι . . . μηδὲ συνεσθίειν. Similarly, John 14:27; Rom 6:12–13; and Heb 12:5 (citing Prov 3:11 LXX) all employ μή . . . μηδέ with an imperative in each clause, and clearly mean "do not . . . *nor*" in these cases. Even closer to 1 Cor 5:11, two negated *infinitives* depending on a verb of speech (παραγγέλλω; λέγω) are normally connected by μή . . . μηδέ, in each case with the sense "not . . . *nor*" (Acts 4:18; 1 Tim 1:3–4; 6:17; Acts 21:21).

The instances given in the preceding paragraph provide an important clue for 1 Cor 5:11: Paul, employing indirect speech to remind the Corinthians (or interpret for them) what he had previously written, introduces two "commands" in the requisite infinitive mood: "I wrote to you that you must not associate with . . . nor eat with such a person."[7] The closest NT examples offered for μηδέ in the lexicon,

---

[6] Matthew 6:15: ἐὰν δὲ μὴ ἀφῆτε τοῖς ἀνθρώποις, οὐδὲ ὁ πατὴρ ὑμῶν ἀφήσει τὰ παραπτώματα ὑμῶν (NA²⁷). The sense "neither" is adequate for this οὐδέ. BAGD (correctly) leaves Matt 6:15 out of its list of instances of "not even."

[7] The sense of νῦν δὲ ἔγραψα is moot here; even if one were to take this expression to mean "Now I am writing . . ." (as, e.g., Fee, *1 Corinthians*, 224), Paul would thereby be introducing indirect speech. On the above rendering, however, see Conzelmann, *1 Corinthians*, 95, 102, and n. 81; cf. BAGD, s.v. νῦν 2; Smyth §2924.

including Paul's own usage in Rom 6:12–13, strongly favor a translation of "and not, nor" in a μή . . . μηδέ construction involving (a) a negated infinitive or imperative in each clause; and (b) a verb introducing indirect discourse. In 1 Cor 5:11 we have both.

The experts in grammar are in agreement, then (BAGD's categorization of 1 Cor 5:11 aside), that "and not, nor" is the normal sense of μηδέ, unless a stronger sense is demanded by certain constructions absent from 1 Cor 5:11. In other words, "not *even*" is, in grammatical terms, an overtranslation of the passage and should be avoided unless it simply makes no sense to render the term as "and not, nor." If we adhere to grammar, leaving commonsense assumptions aside, the translation should be something like this:

> As it is, I wrote to you not to associate—if someone (nom.) who is called a brother should be a *pornos* (nom.) . . .—nor to eat with such a person.

Or simply,

> —do not eat with such a person.

In this rendering, by implication, Paul regards "do not eat" as a prohibition that is on the same level as, and intimately connected to, "do not associate with." In 1953, F. W. Grosheide came to the same grammatical conclusion: "*with such a one not to eat* is coordinate with *not to keep company*." However, he could not make sense of this coordination: "*Not to eat* implies that not keeping company together is stronger than not eating together. The former speaks of regular intercourse which includes eating together, the latter refers to having a meal together, not including regular intercourse." To this tortured reasoning, as if grasping at straws, Grosheide adds, "In a time in which hotels were not numerous private hospitality was indispensable, and thus eating together could most easily occur."[8] Neither remark clarifies the matter.

Yet, despite Grosheide's befuddlement, the grammatical conclusion that the two commands are coordinate, that not eating with someone is parallel to, comparable to, and conceptually linked with not associating with someone, can indeed be understood in an ancient context. In fact, this grammatical conclusion is not only possible but is even likely in view of the social significance of meals in the ancient world. In first-century Mediterranean cultures, as in many non-Western cultures today, eating with someone is a form of social approval.[9] For such cultures, the act

---

[8] F. W. Grosheide, *Commentary on the First Epistle to the Corinthians* (NICNT; Grand Rapids: Eerdmans, 1953), 129–30.

[9] On this richly documented topic, one might begin, for example, with the largely anecdotal *Consuming Passions: The Anthropology of Eating*, by Peter Farb and George Armelagos (Boston: Houghton Mifflin, 1980), esp. the prologue and chs. 5, 8, and 10; see also the fine ethnographic analysis of Arjun Appadurai, "Gastro-Politics in Hindu South Asia," *American Ethnologist* 8 (1981): 494–511; and Mary Douglas's classic essay "Deciphering a Meal," in *Myth, Symbol and Culture*

of "eating with" (συνεσθίειν) does not so much symbolize as *embody* or *enact* common cause, kinship, acceptance, among other things.[10] Refusing to eat with a certain person would embody the opposite: rejection or exclusion.[11]

For its part, the verb "to associate with" (συναναμίγνυσθαι) likewise has a strong concrete or embodied meaning. Moreover, Margaret M. Mitchell has shown that the verb often concerns "associations" in the political sense.[12] As such, the term seems to have in view corporate rather than one-on-one "mingling."[13] For example, Philo uses the term to express the distance between the "customs" of the Jews and those of the other nations, with whom "they do not mix" (*Mos.* 1.278 [LCL]). Plutarch similarly uses the term of an army "joined" (συνανεμίχθησαν) by civilians (*Phil.* 21 [LCL]). Josephus uses the exact verbal form that we find in 1 Cor 5:9, 11 in a similar corporate sense: a centurion was not to let an unknown soldier "mingle" (συναναμίγνυσθαι) with his company (*Vita* 242). The verbal form appears also in 2 Thess 3:14 and confirms the point: "mark [pl.: σημειοῦσθε] such a person, not to associate with [συναναμίγνυσθαι] him, that he may be shamed."[14] Here again the group (not an individual) is shunning someone. Moreover, like idleness in 2 Thessalonians 3, offending practices that call for this corporate exclusion can be surprising: abusive speech (i.e., λοιδορία) and drunkenness stand out in 1 Cor 5:11, and both are suggestive of indecorous behavior at meals (cf. 11:20–22).

(ed. Clifford Geertz; New York: Norton, 1971), 61–81, which emphasizes the "messages" sent by food behavior.

The leading areas of research for Greco-Roman food ways are summarized nicely (and advanced) by Peter Garnsey, *Food and Society in Classical Antiquity* (Key Themes in Ancient History; Cambridge/New York: Cambridge University Press, 1999); see esp. ch. 9, "You Are with Whom You Eat."

[10] See, e.g., Klinghardt, *Gemeinschaftsmahl und Mahlgemeinschaft*, 155–58, on κοινωνία in common meals (including in Pauline communities). Note also Smith, *From Symposium to Eucharist*, 114–15, on the *stibas* (rustic dining couch) and its symbolic force for the *Iobakchoi*.

[11] Note the Qumran covenanters' practice of excluding the errant from meals (e.g., 1QS 8:23–24); the relevant texts, with sensible discussion, are covered by Heinz-Wolfgang Kuhn, "A Legal Issue in 1 Corinthians 5 and in Qumran," in *Legal Texts and Legal Issues: Proceedings of the Second Meeting of the International Organization for Qumran Studies, Cambridge, 1995; Published in Honour of Joseph M. Baumgarten* (ed. Moshe Bernstein et al.; STDJ 23; Leiden: Brill, 1997), 495–96, 499.

[12] Margaret M. Mitchell, *Paul and the Rhetoric of Reconciliation: An Exegetical Investigation of the Language and Composition of 1 Corinthians* (Louisville: Westminster John Knox, 1991), 113–16, 229–30; her point is that Paul wants to attain the right "mix" that will achieve "concord."

[13] Fee suggests that the verb carries the sense of close contact (*1 Corinthians*, 222); Conzelmann, however, prefers "associate with" (*1 Corinthians*, 99 n. 56). Sampley adopts the translation "mingle" but without necessarily implying intimate, one-on-one contact (*1 Corinthians*, 849).

[14] The translation "have nothing to do with him" (RSV, NJB, NRSV ["them"]) is probably too sweeping, in view of v. 15. The prohibition may again have common meals in mind (cf. 2 Thess 3:11–13).

Wayne A. Meeks comes close to what I have in mind: "To shun the offender, especially at common meals—the Lord's Supper and others—would be an effective way of letting him know that he no longer had access to that special fellowship indicated by use of the term brother."[15] Meeks makes the exclusion from the meal a *metaphor* for the actual exclusion. That is an understatement, in my view, since the meal is the locus for inclusion or exclusion itself—where it actually happens. Similarly, Dennis Smith writes, "The act of excluding the immoral person, defined as 'the old yeast,' is described in terms of a metaphor of sharing a festival meal: . . . (5:8). Indeed, the act of exclusion comes to focus especially at the communal meal: . . . (5:10–11) [sic]."[16] This too is an understatement: the reason exclusion "comes to focus" here is that eating with someone in antiquity in and of itself carried social force, although that aspect of eating no longer exists in the realm of common sense. As Mitchell aptly puts it, "those who perform immoral acts . . . are excluded from table fellowship, and therefore from unity with the group"—or, rather, they are *thereby* excluded from it.[17]

Exclusion from table fellowship, so far from being an extreme measure that Paul commands for some "drastic" effect, is actually integral to exclusion from the group as such. An overtranslation of μηδέ, dictated by modern commonsense notions but grammatically unwarranted, makes the *substance* of the exclusion into an insulting metaphorical gesture.

---

[15] Meeks, *First Urban Christians*, 130. See also W. Harold Mare, *1 Corinthians* (Expositor's Bible Commentary 10; Grand Rapids: Zondervan, 1976), 220 (he also assumes "not even"): "In sharing in a common meal Christians show their union with one another." "Show" is, again, an understatement for "enact" or "embody."

[16] Smith, *From Symposium to Eucharist*, 203.

[17] Mitchell, *Paul and the Rhetoric of Reconciliation*, 230. She does not comment on the translation of 1 Cor 5:11.

τοῦτο πρῶτον γινώσκοντες ὅτι in 2 Peter 1:20 and Hellenistic Epistolary Convention

STANLEY E. PORTER
princpl@mcmaster.ca
McMaster Divinity College, Hamilton, ON L8S 4K1, Canada

ANDREW W. PITTS
andrewwp@gmail.com
McMaster Divinity College, Hamilton, ON L8S 4K1, Canada

---

[19] καὶ ἔχομεν βεβαιότερον τὸν προφητικὸν λόγον, ᾧ καλῶς ποιεῖτε προσέχοντες ὡς λύχνῳ φαίνοντι ἐν αὐχμηρῷ τόπῳ, ἕως οὗ ἡμέρα διαυγάσῃ καὶ φωσφόρος ἀνατείλῃ ἐν ταῖς καρδίαις ὑμῶν, [20] τοῦτο πρῶτον γινώσκοντες ὅτι πᾶσα προφητεία γραφῆς ἰδίας ἐπιλύσεως οὐ γίνεται·

In a recent issue of *JBL*, Terrance Callan argues against a general consensus among commentators that ἐν ταῖς καρδίαις ὑμῶν in 2 Pet 1:19 modifies the previous verb ἀνατείλῃ.[1] He suggests instead that ἐν ταῖς καρδίαις ὑμῶν modifies what follows in 1:20, τοῦτο πρῶτον γινώσκοντες ὅτι. He insists that "[t]here is no obstacle to understanding ἐν ταῖς καρδίαις ὑμῶν as modifying the following participle." Since prepositional phrases in 2 Peter are often placed before the verb, Callan suggests, "Other things being equal, it is almost as likely that a prepositional phrase will precede the verb it modifies as that the phrase will follow the verb." Callan's interpretation leads him to conclude that, instead of speaking of an internal reality, in 2 Pet 1:20 "the παρουσία is simply a physical event, as elsewhere in 2 Peter, and ἐν ταῖς καρδίαις ὑμῶν specifies the locus of the knowing

---

[1] Terrance Callan, "A Note on 2 Peter 1:19–20," *JBL* 125 (2006): 143–50; quotations in this paragraph from 148.

that 1:20 speaks about." However, despite the proposed contextual consistency, this analysis fails to take into consideration the formalized nature of the language and the syntactic configurations typically associated with this type of phrasing. The first clause in 2 Pet 1:20 parallels conventions used in ancient Hellenistic letters for disclosure. A comprehensive search of disclosure formulas in the NT, as well as a survey of papyrological evidence, reveals that these formulas have fairly regular syntactic configurations and that, when an adjunct (e.g., a prepositional phrase) is used in a disclosure formula, it does not modify the knowing verb. This amounts to a significant syntactic obstacle for Callan's proposed interpretation.

Although the disclosure formula (an epistolary convention expressing the author's desire that the audience know something) has abundant currency in the Greco-Roman and NT epistolary tradition, it has received surprisingly little attention from NT scholars. T. Y. Mullins, in his treatment of disclosure formulas in the NT, proposes four essential formal elements: (1) θέλω, (2), a noetic verb in the infinitive, (3) the person addressed, and (4) information.[2] This formulation is clearly too stringent, since it cannot account for the development of the formula in the Hellenistic period[3]—the exclusive use of θέλω also rules out several legitimate instances of the formula.[4] It is no coincidence that all of Mullins's examples come from after 100 C.E. One would not necessarily gather this from reading his article, since he does not provide dates for the papyri he cites, but all of his examples come from later in the Roman period.[5] What Mullins refers to as a disclosure formula is really a full, more formulaic version of a literary form that had begun to develop much earlier in an imperatival and participial form during the Ptolemaic period.[6]

---

[2] T. Y. Mullins, "Disclosure, A Literary Form in the New Testament," *NovT* 7 (1964): 44–50, here 46; he is followed by Peter T. O'Brien, *The Epistle to the Philippians: A Commentary on the Greek Text* (NIGTC; Grand Rapids: Eerdmans, 1991), 82; idem, *Introductory Thanksgivings in the Letters of Paul* (NovTSup 49; Leiden: Brill, 1977), 201–2; and E. Randolph Richards, *The Secretary in the Letters of Paul* (WUNT 2/42; Tübingen: Mohr Siebeck, 1991), 204.

[3] On development, see John L. White, *Light from Ancient Letters* (FF; Philadelphia: Fortress, 1984), 207–8; on the full formula, see MM, 127.

[4] For example, βούλομαι is often used. See *P.Oxy.* XIV 1680.12–13; *P.Köln* V 238.2–3; *P.Stras.* I 35.2–3; cf. also Phil 1:12 for a NT example.

[5] Mullins, "Disclosure," 47–48; these include (with dates added): *P.Oxy.* VI 937 (third cent. C.E.), *P.Oxy.* VIII 1155 (104 C.E.), *P.Oxy.* IX 1185 (about 200 C.E.), *P.Oxy.* XII 1481 (early second cent. C.E.), *P.Oxy.* XII 1493 (late third or early fourth cent. C.E.), *P.Oxy.* XIV 1670 (third cent. C.E.), *P.Oxy.* XIV 1683 (fourth cent. C.E.), *P.Oxy.* XIV 1770 (late third cent. C.E.), *P.Oxy.* XIV 1773 (third cent. C.E.), *P.Giss.* 11 (118 C.E.), *P.Giss.* 13 (116–120 C.E.), *P.Lond.* II 411 (259 C.E. [?]), *P.Lond.* II 414 (259 C.E. [?]), *P.Lond.* II 417 (259 C.E. [?]), and *P.Lond.* III 973 (third cent. C.E. [?]). For the Oxyrhynchus papyri, see B. Grenfell and A. Hunt, *The Oxyrhynchus Papyri* (London: Egypt Exploration Society, 1898–1948); for the Giessen papyri, see O. Eger, E. Koremann, and P. M. Meyer, *Griechische Papyri im Museum des Oberhessischen Geschichtsvereins zu Giessen* (Leipzig: Teubner, 1910–12); for the London papyri, see F. G. Kenyon and H. I. Bell, *Greek Papyri in the British Museum: Catalogue with Texts* (1893–1917; repr., 3 vols.; Milan: Cisalpino-Gollardica, 1973).

[6] Jeffrey T. Reed attributes the morphological and literary differences in the formula to

That it was an established epistolary convention before it reached its fuller expression with the knowing verb in the infinitive (no. 2 above), a verb for desire (no. 1 above), and a pronominalized referent (no. 3 above) is clear from the consistency with which it occurs in more abbreviated forms in the body opening and body closing in a large number of letters dating from one to three hundred years before the turn of the millennium and the persistence of these expressions thereafter.[7]

John L. White's analysis of the disclosure formula is more convincing. His formulation builds around knowing verbs and various formal features used in association with them. He lists five discrete expressions of the formula:

1. The full disclosure formula: γινώσκειν σε θέλω ὅτι . . .
2. The imperative form: γίνωσκε ὡς or γίνωσκε ὅτι . . .
3. The motivation for writing: γέγραφα (οὖν) σοι ὅπως ἂν (or ἵνα) εἰδῇς.
4. "Know" in the perfect indicative: οἶδες ὅτι . . . or οἶδα ὅτι . . .
5. The verb for "know" in the participial form (usually the perfect participle): εἰδώς (or εἰδότες) ὅτι . . .[8]

---

politeness and variation between letter types. According to Reed, the full forms are preferred in business letters and the shorter imperative forms are used in personal letters (*A Discourse Analysis of Philippians: Method and Rhetoric in the Debate over Literary Integrity* [JSNTSup 136; Sheffield: Sheffield Academic Press, 1997], 212). See also John L. White, "Introductory Formulas in the Body of the Pauline Letter," *JBL* 90 (1971): 93. While this may be the case (there are more full formulas in business letters than in private), the most important factor contributing to variation between the imperative and the full formula seems to be developmental and chronological rather than literary and contextual. Distribution of various expressions according to letter type has to be seen as a phenomenon that happened later in the Hellenistic period.

[7] In the body opening: *P.Mich.* I 10 (257 B.C.E.): ὑπογέγραφά σοι τῆς παρὰ Σωσιπάτρου ἐλθούσης μοι ἐπιστολῆς τὸ ἀντίγραφον, ὅπως εἰδῶς . . . ; *P.Mich.* I 32 (185/161 B.C.E.): γνώριζε ἡμᾶς παραγεγενημένους . . . ; *P.Paris* 47 (152 B.C.E.): γίνωσκε ὅτι πιράσεται . . . ; *P.Tebt.* II 408 (3 C.E.): ἐπιστάμενος πῶς σε τίθεμαι κὲ φιλῶ, παρακαλῶ σε . . . ; in the body closing: *P.Cair.Zen.* V 59804 (258 B.C.E.): γέγραφα οὖν σοι ὅπως ἂν εἰδῇς; *P.Col.* III 6 (257 B.C.E.): γίνωσκε δέ, ὡς ἄν . . . ; *P.Yale* I 36 (232 B.C.E.): γινώσκων ὅτι. . . . For additional examples, see John L. White, *The Form and Function of the Body of the Greek Letter: A Study of the Letter-Body in Non-Literary Papyri and in Paul the Apostle* (SBLDS 2; Missoula, Mont.: Society of Biblical Literature, 1972), 11–15.

[8] White, *Form*, 11; idem, "Introductory Formulas," 93; see also idem, *Light*, 204–5, 207–8. Reidar Aasgaard offers a similar formulation, but a bit more stringent: "(1) a particle, indicating a contrast to or a consequence of the preceding: γάρ or δέ, (2) often a verb denoting will (sometimes stated negatively: οὐ), (3) those addressed: you, ὑμᾶς, (4) an address in the vocative [sic], always ἀδελφοί, (5) what is disclosed: introduced by ὅτι, περί, or the like" ('*My Beloved Brothers and Sisters!': Christian Siblingship in Paul* [JSNTSup 265; London: T&T Clark, 2004], 278; see also idem, "'Brotherly Advice': Christian Siblingship and New Testament Paraenesis," in *Early Christian Paraenesis in Context* [ed. J. Starr and T. Engberg-Pedersen; BZNW 125; Berlin/New York: de Gruyter, 2004], 237–65, here 248–49). This analysis is interesting since, contra Aasgaard, scholars generally agree that the feature of address is optional (see White, "Introductory Formu-

For White there is a mixture of morphological and literary-based expressions of the formula.⁹ The advantage of this analysis is that it takes lexical content as the basis for the formula and therefore exhibits sensitivity to its development and flexibility. Given the morphological orientation of White's analysis, the subjunctive should perhaps also be accounted for—it often occurs in the purpose-for-writing formula but is found in other formulas as well. Although the formulation suggested by White accounts for more data than Mullins's criteria,¹⁰ White's analysis is probably too broad in that it seems to include statements that do not disclose information to the audience or that do not embody the dialogic nature of communication in an epistolary context. So, with the addition of a criterion that requires that legitimate instances of the formula occur in second person discourse and disclose or affirm information with respect to the addressees, White's analysis offers a suitable framework for identifying disclosure formulas in the NT and in the epistolary papyri.¹¹

Disclosure formulas take a variety of syntactic combinations in the NT. The most frequent configuration occurs in the abbreviated or shorter disclosure formulas that use only a predicator and a subordinating conjunction (usually ὅτι, ἵνα, or ὅπως).¹² The subject is rarely realized within the formula, and negative parti-

---

las," 93; Mullins, "Disclosure," 46; David E. Aune, *The New Testament in Its Literary Environment* [LEC 8; Philadelphia: Westminster, 1987], 188). Colossians 2:1 is a NT example in which all elements of the full formula are present but the element of address is missing. Multiple examples can be accumulated from the papyri. It should also be noted that numerous examples in the papyri use word forms other than ἀδελφοί in the address role, but Aasgaard seems concerned exclusively with NT instances of the formula. See also Klaus Schäfer, *Gemeinde als 'Bruderschaft': Ein Beitrag zum Kirchenverständnis des Paulus* (Europäische Hochschulschriften 23/333; Frankfurt a.M.: Peter Lang, 1989), 322–23.

⁹ Reed (*Discourse Analysis*, 211–12) follows White's analysis, emphasizing the full formula, the purpose for writing formula, and the imperatival formula.

¹⁰ Mullins claims in a later article ("Formulas in New Testament Epistles," *JBL* 91 [1972]: 382–83) that White's assertion ("Introductory Formulas," 93) that there is a two-component version of the formula that is quite common is off base, since White does not provide examples from the papyri. Mullins insists instead that his four/five-component formulation accounts for the only legitimate instances of the formula. Yet White does provide several examples of all five expressions of the formula he proposes in a later publication (see White, *Form*, 11–15). We add several examples to this list in our analysis above which further disconfirm Mullins's account (see n. 7 above).

¹¹ This framework is used as the basis for selecting the disclosure formulas that figured into the searches displayed below.

¹² The syntactic terminology we use here is slightly more nuanced than traditional subject–verb–object–indirect object terminology, but it is relatively straightforward. By *Subject* we mean the explicit grammatical subject of the finite verb; by *Predicator* we mean the verbal element or process of the clause; by *Complement* we mean the word or group of words that complements the *Predicator* (e.g., most accusatives); by *Adjunct* we mean the word or group of words that modifies the *Predicator* by indicating the circumstances associated with the process (e.g., prepositional phrases, most datives); and by *address* we mean the component that directs attention to a particular participant(s).

cles often occur as adjuncts. There is a notable amount of consistency, however, in which elements are typically realized within the clause, especially compared to the various configurations that occur in the clause that the disclosure formula introduces. The Predicator, Predicator–Complement and Predicator–Adjunct (with a negative particle in the Adjunct)[13] are the standard syntactic configurations in the NT formulas, all of which are typically followed by a subordinating conjunction. The dominance of patterns that reflect abbreviated versions of the formula are what we would expect to find in the NT, which was written around the time that the full formula was just beginning to gain currency. The same combinations can also occur with the added element of address, usually ἀδελφοί. However, in some instances the addressees as a whole (Phil 4:15) or a particular group within the discourse audience (Jas 4:4) can be addressed. While the most common adjunct is a negative particle, other items appear in the adjunct as well, including demonstratives and—on occasion—prepositions. Disclosure formulas occurring in the NT with an adjunct are listed in the chart below.

Knowing Verb	Adjunct	Text
γινώσκω (6x)	πρῶτον	2 Pet 1:20; 2 Pet 3:3
	ἐν τούτῳ	1 John 3:16, 24; 4:13; 5:2
ἐπιγινώσκω (2x)	ἕως τέλους	1 Cor 1:13–14
	οὐκ	2 Cor 13:5
ἀγνοέω (6x)	οὐ	Rom 1:13; 11:25; 1 Cor 10:1; 2 Cor 1:8; 1 Thess 4:13
	περί	1 Cor 12:1
οἶδα (15x)	οὐκ	Rom 6:16; 11:2; 1 Cor 3:16; 5:6; 6:1–19 (6x); 9:13, 24; Jas 4:4
	περί	1 Cor 8:1, 4

Prepositions rarely occur in the adjuncts of disclosure formulas, and when a preposition is present, it never modifies the knowing verb directly. In the series of ἐν τούτῳ phrases in John, ἐν modifies τούτῳ and τούτῳ is cataphoric, referring to the following clause. Similarly, in 1 Corinthians 8, περί serves as a prelude to the knowledge that the statement introduces, not as a direct qualification of οἶδα. There are no uncontestable instances of a disclosure statement in the NT in which there is a preposition in the adjunct modifying the knowing verb.

---

[13] These configurations refer to the components present in the clause, not to their order or number of occurrences.

In the papyri, the syntactic configurations are a bit more rigid. There are the standard Predicator and Predicator–Complement configurations, but very few formulas take an adjunct and, like the formulas in the NT, they do not seem to take prepositions in the adjunct modifying the knowing verb. The abundance of the full formula in later papyri causes the Predicator–Complement structure to dominate. As in the NT, some formulas use a negative particle in the adjunct (e.g., *P.Oxy.* IV 745.6), and others use περί as a prelude to the information that is being introduced by the statement—but these are not frequent.

Although interpreters of 2 Pet 1:20 do not in general show familiarity with epistolary disclosure formulas, some have recognized the formulaic nature of the language.[14] Karl Matthias Schmidt sees the formula in 1 Peter as a reflection of *Kundgabeformel*, as we see in Ezra 4:12, 13; 5:8 and *2 Bar.* 79:1; 82:2; 85:1,[15] but the construction here does not align directly with any of those found in Ezra or the *Syriac Apocalypse of Baruch*. E. I. Robins is also off base in identifying the phrase as a quotation formula.[16] J. N. D. Kelly comes closer when he recognizes that "the stereotype expression"[17] makes prepositional modification of the knowing verb unlikely, but he is still far from identifying the statement as a disclosure formula. Callan, however, dismisses Kelly's remarks since he "does not explain why he thinks ... 'the stereotype expression' make[s] this [prepositional modification of the knowing verb] construal unlikely."[18]

The opening clause of 2 Pet 1:20 (τοῦτο πρῶτον γινώσκοντες ὅτι . . .) is the participial version of the formula White identifies, and it has parallels in both the NT and the papyrological epistolary material. This instance of the formula occurs in the body middle of the letter and is used with a demonstrative pronoun (τοῦτο), functioning cataphorically, and an ordinal adverb (πρῶτον). Both here and in 2 Pet 3:3, where the same expression of the formula occurs, the function of the adverb is formulaic, indicating the conventionalized nature of the language.[19] The ὅτι introduces the information associated with the content verb (γινώσκοντες): "no prophetic Scripture comes from someone's individual interpretation." The traditional interpretation of the verse, therefore—which understands the παρουσία in 2 Pet 1:19 as an internal reality, owing to the modification of

---

[14] Richard J. Bauckham, *Jude, 2 Peter* (WBC 50; Dallas: Word Books, 1983), 228.

[15] Karl Matthias Schmidt, *Mahnung und Erinnerung im Maskenspiel: Epistolographie, Rhetorik, und Narrativik der Pseudepigraphen Petrusbriefe* (Herders biblische Studien 38; Freiburg: Herder, 2003), 300.

[16] E. I. Robins, *Studies in the Second Epistle of St. Peter* (Cambridge: Cambridge University Press, 1915), 33–35.

[17] J. N. D. Kelly, *The Epistles of Peter and of Jude* (HNTC; New York/Evanston: Harper & Row, 1969), 322.

[18] Callan, "Note," 144.

[19] See Bauckham, *Jude*, 228.

ἀνατείλῃ by ἐν ταῖς καρδίαις ὑμῶν—seems to be sustained by the syntax and literary character of the language.

The syntactic configuration of the formula in 2 Pet 1:20 is not unusual. It occurs in an embedded participial clause with an adverb and demonstrative pronoun in its adjunct. Our investigation yielded no solid examples of disclosure formulas in the epistolary papyri or in NT letters that have a prepositional phrase in their adjunct modifying the knowing verb. This seems to be a point that Callan's study overlooked. His thesis proceeds from the assumption that "[t]here is no obstacle to understanding ἐν ταῖς καρδίαις ὑμῶν as modifying the following participle."[20] But the formulaic expression of the language appears to be precisely such an obstacle. While the disclosure formula is flexible in many ways (morphologically, functionally, etc.), it nevertheless has a fixed syntactical pattern that does not admit of this type of modification. Callan's argument that his reading makes better sense of the passage notwithstanding, it seems that there are significant difficulties with understanding the knowing verb in the formula in 1 Pet 1:20 to be modified by the preceding prepositional phrase when this verse is read in light of the Hellenistic epistolary tradition, since no parallel examples (either in the NT or the papyri) have been confirmed.

[20] Callan, "Note," 148.

CAMBRIDGE

Outstanding Scholarship

The Cambridge History of Christianity
Volume 3: Early Medieval Christianities, c.600-c.1100
Edited by
Thomas F. X. Noble and Julia M. H. Smith
Cambridge History of Christianity
$195.00: Hb: 978-0-521-81775-2: 880 pp.

The Story of Joy
From the Bible to Late Romanticism
Adam Potkay
$99.00: Hb: 978-0-521-87911-8: 318 pp.

The First English Bible
The Text and Context of the Wycliffite Versions
Mary Dove
Cambridge Studies in Medieval Literature
$99.00: Hb: 978-0-521-88028-2: 332 pp.

The Psalms of Lament in Mark's Passion
Jesus' Davidic Suffering
Stephen Ahearne-Kroll
Society for New Testament Studies Monograph Series
$95.00: Hb: 978-0-521-88191-3: 254 pp.

Cosmology and Eschatology in Hebrews
The Settings of the Sacrifice
Kenneth L. Schenck
Society for New Testament Studies Monograph Series
$95.00: Hb: 978-0-521-88323-8: 232 pp.

The Origins of Judaism
From Canaan to the Rise of Islam
Robert Goldenberg
$70.00: Hb: 978-0-521-84453-6
$22.99: Pb: 978-0-521-60628-8: 312 pp.

Disability in the Hebrew Bible
Interpreting Mental and Physical Differences
Saul M. Olyan
$80.00: Hb: 978-0-521-88807-3: 200 pp.

A Primer on Ugaritic
Language, Culture and Literature
William M. Schniedewind and Joel H. Hunt
$80.00: Hb: 978-0-521-87933-0
$39.99: Pb: 978-0-521-70493-9: 242 pp.

Prices subject to change.

www.cambridge.org/us/ **CAMBRIDGE UNIVERSITY PRESS**

JBL 127, no. 1 (2008): 173-194

Hierarchy, Prophecy, and the Angelomorphic Spirit: A Contribution to the Study of the Book of Revelation's *Wirkungsgeschichte*

BOGDAN G. BUCUR
bucurb@duq.edu
Duquesne University, Pittsburgh, PA 15282

Thanks to the work of scholars such as Ulrich Luz and Dale C. Allison, Jr., *Wirkungsgeschichte* (usually rendered into English as "reception history") has come to be regarded as a necessary part of biblical scholarship.[1] Recent years have seen the publication of a volume on Revelation in the Ancient Christian Commentary on Scripture series, as well as of a book, authored by Judith Kovacs and Christopher Rowland, on the reception of Revelation in Christian tradition.[2]

In what follows, I propose an interpretation of several passages in Revelation that deal with πνεῦμα and prophecy. I explore the possible fusion of horizons between the views expressed in the book of Revelation at the end of the first cen-

---

I am grateful to Dr. William Kurz, S.J., Dr. Andrei Orlov (both of Marquette University), and especially to Dr. Charles Gieschen (of Concordia Theological Seminary) for their helpful critique at various stages of the draft.

[1] Ulrich Luz, *Matthew: A Commentary* (Hermeneia; Minneapolis: Augsburg Fortress, 1989–); idem, *Matthew in History: Interpretation, Influence, and Effects* (Minneapolis: Fortress, 1994); idem, "The Contribution of Reception History to a Theology of the New Testament," in *The Nature of New Testament Theology: Essays in Honour of Robert Morgan* (ed. Christopher Rowland and Christopher Tuckett; Malden, MA: Blackwell, 2006), 123–35; Dale C. Allison, Jr., *Studies in Matthew: Interpretation Past and Present* (Grand Rapids: Baker Academic, 2005). Aside from Allison's studies of specific Matthean passages, see the programmatic essay in that volume entitled "Reading Matthew through the Church Fathers" (pp. 117–31).

[2] William C. Weinrich, ed., *Revelation* (Ancient Christian Commentary on Scripture, New Testament 12; Downers Grove, IL: InterVarsity, 2005); Judith Kovacs and Christopher Rowland, *Revelation: The Apocalypse of Jesus Christ* (Malden, MA: Blackwell, 2004).

173

tury, the views of certain second-century writers, in particular Clement of Alexandria, and, to a certain degree, the views of today's scholars on Revelation. The witness of Clement is extremely valuable because he is very self-conscious in committing to writing certain oral traditions inherited from earlier authoritative, even charismatic, teachers, whom he refers to as "the elders." This is especially true of the surviving portions of his *Hypotyposeis*—the *Excerpta ex Theodoto, Eclogae propheticae* and the *Adumbrationes*.[3] It is generally admitted that in these works the voice of the elders is heard more often and more clearly than in other Clementine writings.[4]

I argue that Revelation exemplifies an archaic "angelomorphic" pneumatology similar to the one discernible in other early Christian writings, one that occurs in tandem with Spirit christology, within a theological framework still marked by binitarianism.[5] I will clarify my use of "Spirit christology" and "binitarianism" at a

---

[3] Clement of Alexandria's work known as the *Hypotyposeis* did not survive as such. Aside from the passages preserved by later patristic writers, scholars count as among surviving portions of the *Hypotyposeis* the *Excerpta ex Theodoto* and the *Eclogae propheticae*, together with the *Adumbrationes*. This was argued in the nineteenth century by Christian K. J. von Bunsen, *Analecta Antenicena* (orig. ed. London, 1854; repr., Aalen: Scientia, 1968), 1:159, 163–65. Definitive proof came with Pierre Nautin's study "La fin des *Stromates* et les *Hypotyposeis* de Clément d'Alexandrie," *VC* 30 (1976): 268–302. The thesis has also been adopted by Alain le Boulluec, the editor of Clement for Sources chrétiennes. See le Boulluec, "Extraits d'oeuvres de Clément d'Alexandrie: La transmission et le sens de leur titres," in *Titres et articulations du texte dans les oeuvres antiques: Actes du colloque international de Chantilly 13–15 décembre 1994* (ed. Jean-Claude Fredouille et al.; Paris: Institut d'Études Augustiniennes, 1997), 287–300, esp. 289, 292, 296, 300; idem, "Pour qui, pourquoi, comment? Les 'Stromates' de Clément d'Alexandrie," in *Entrer en matière: Les prologues* (ed. Jean-Daniel Dubois and Bernard Roussel; Paris: Cerf, 1998), 23–36, esp. 24 n. 10.

[4] Paul Collomp, "Une source de Clément d'Alexandrie et des Homélies Pseudo-Clémentines," *RevPhil* 37 (1913): 19–46; Wilhelm Bousset, *Jüdisch-christlicher Schulbetrieb in Alexandria und Rom: Literarische Untersuchungen zu Philo und Clemens von Alexandria, Justin und Irenäus* (Göttingen: Vandenhoeck & Ruprecht, 1915), 248–64; Georg Kretschmar, *Studien zur früh-christlichen Trinitätstheologie* (BHT 21; Tübingen: Mohr, 1956), 68 and n. 3; Jean Daniélou, "Les traditions secrètes des Apôtres," *ErJb* 31 (1962): 199–215, here 214; Christian Oeyen, "Eine frühchristliche Engelpneumatologie bei Klemens von Alexandrien," *IKZ* 55 (1965): 102–20; 56 (1966): 27–47; Wolf-Dieter Hauschild, *Gottes Geist und der Mensch: Studien zur frühchristlichen Pneumatologie* (BEvT 63; Munich: Kaiser, 1972), 79 and n. 10; Henning Ziebritzki, *Heiliger Geist und Weltseele: Das Problem der dritten Hypostase bei Origenes, Plotin und ihren Vorläufern* (BHT 84; Tübingen: Mohr Siebeck, 1994), 121.

[5] Charles A. Gieschen, *Angelomorphic Christology: Antecedents and Early Evidence* (AGJU 42; Leiden: Brill, 1998), 6: "Ignorance concerning the influence of angelomorphic traditions has also plagued scholarship on early Pneumatology ... the same or similar angelomorphic traditions also influenced teaching about the Holy Spirit." See also the dense but necessarily brief survey of early Jewish and Christian examples of angelomorphic pneumatology in Gieschen, *Angelomorphic Christology*, 114–19. For angelomorphic pneumatology in early Christianity, see Oeyen, "Eine frühchristliche Engelpneumatologie"; Bogdan G. Bucur, "The Son of God and the Angelomorphic Holy Spirit: A Rereading of the *Shepherd's* Christology," *ZNW* 98 (2007): 121–43;

later point. As for "angelomorphic," this term, coined by Jean Daniélou, is now widely used by scholars writing on the emergence of christology.[6] I follow Crispin Fletcher-Louis's definition and use it "wherever there are signs that an individual or community possesses specifically angelic characteristics or status, though for whom identity cannot be reduced to that of an angel."[7] The virtue of this definition is that it signals the use of angelic *characteristics* in descriptions of God or humans, while not necessarily implying that the latter are angels *stricto sensu*.

I. Early Christian Commentaries on Revelation

The earliest surviving commentaries on Revelation is that of Victorinus of Poetovio, composed around 258–260.[8] The works by Melito and Hippolytus did not survive; a few scholia are ascribed to Origen.[9] There is, however, much that can be learned about the exegesis of Revelation prior to Hippolytus and Origen. It is certain, for instance, that a passage in the scholia ascribed to Origen finds an exact match in *Strom*. 4.25.156.[10]

It appears that Clement of Alexandria's notes on Revelation (as well as on the *Apocalypse of Peter*) were part of the eighth book of the *Hypotyposeis*.[11] It is not

---

idem, "Revisiting Christian Oeyen: 'The Other Clement' on Father, Son, and the Angelomorphic Spirit," VC 61 (2007): 381–413.

[6] Jean Daniélou, *The Theology of Jewish Christianity* (French ed. 1958; London: Darton, Longman & Todd, 1964), 146; Richard Longenecker, "Some Distinctive Early Christological Motifs," NTS 14 (1968): 529–33; Robert Gundry, "Angelomorphic Christology in Revelation," SBLSP 33 (1994): 662–78; Loren T. Stuckenbruck, *Angel Veneration and Christology: A Study in Early Judaism and in the Christology of the Apocalypse of John* (WUNT 2/70; Tübingen: Mohr Siebeck, 1995); Peter R. Carrell, *Jesus and the Angels: Angelology and the Christology of the Apocalypse of John* (SNTSMS 95; Cambridge/New York: Cambridge University Press, 1997); Crispin Fletcher-Louis, *Luke-Acts: Angels, Christology and Soteriology* (WUNT 2/94; Tübingen: Mohr Siebeck, 1997); Gieschen, *Angelomorphic Christology*; Darrell D. Hannah, *Michael and Christ: Michael Traditions and Angel Christology in Early Christianity* (WUNT 2/109; Tübingen: Mohr Siebeck, 1999).

[7] Fletcher-Louis, *Luke-Acts*, 14–15; similarly Gieschen, *Angelomorphic Christology*, 4, 349.

[8] Martine Dulaey, ed. and trans, *Victorin de Poetovio: Sur L'Apocalypse et autres écrits* (SC 423; Paris: Cerf, 1997), 15.

[9] Constantine I. Dyobouniotes and Adolf von Harnack, *Der Scholien-Kommentar des Origenes zur Apokalypse Johannis* (TU 38.3; Leipzig: Hinrichs, 1911), 21–44; C. H. Turner, "The Text of the Newly Discovered Scholia of Origen on the Apocalypse," JTS 13 (1912): 386–97; idem, "Document: Origen, Scholia in Apocalypsin," JTS 25 (1924): 1–15. Origen's scholia have been translated into French by Solange Bouquet and published in the volume *L'Apocalypse expliquée par Césaire d'Arles: Scholies attribuées à Origène* (Paris: Desclée de Brouwer, 1989), 167–203.

[10] The text of Scholion 5 (Dyobouniotes and von Harnack, *Scholien-Kommentar des Origenes*, 22) is identical to that of *Strom*. 4.25.156.

[11] Von Bunsen, *Analecta Antenicena*, 1:164; Theodor Zahn, *Forschungen zur Geschichte des*

clear whether Cassiodorus, who commissioned a Latin translation of this work, possessed only excerpts of the *Hypotyposeis* dealing with some of the catholic epistles (since he only mentions Clement's commentaries on these NT writings), or whether he not only took care to "purge" the *Hypotyposeis* of "offensive" ideas, as he does admit, but also thought it best to leave out certain passages, such as, for instance, the scholia on Revelation.[12] In any case, the *Adumbrationes* consist only of scholia to 1 Peter, 1–2 John, and Jude.

We are fortunate, however, to possess Cassiodorus's commentary on Revelation, contained in his *Complexiones*. To the degree that passages in Cassiodorus's commentary reflect the theology present in the *Adumbrationes*, the commentary may represent views that go back to Clement and the "elders."

II. The "Seven Spirits" of Revelation and the Second-Century Πρωτόκτιστοι

Revelation refers several times to a mysterious group of "seven spirits" (1:4; 3:1; 4:5; 5:6). The first of these occurrences is also the most important one, because it places the seven spirits in the initial greeting: "grace and peace" are said to come from God, and from the seven spirits, and from Jesus Christ.

The structure of the phrase (καὶ ... καὶ ... καὶ) suggests that "the seven spirits before his [God's] throne" are one among three coordinated entities. The blessing with "grace and peace" is suggestive of a divine origin.[13] The three must, then, in some way stand for the divinity (cf. 2 Cor 13:14, "The grace of the Lord Jesus Christ, and the love of God, and the communion of the Holy Spirit, be with you all").[14] This is why it seems most likely that the mention of the "seven spirits" corresponds to the expected reference to the Holy Spirit. In other words, the author's expression "seven spirits" would designate what the early church more often referred to as "Holy Spirit."

---

neutestamentlichen Kanons und der altkirchlichen Literatur, vol. 3, *Supplementum Clementinum* (Erlangen: Andreas Deichert, 1884), 156.

[12] According to Zahn (*Supplementum Clementinum*, 136–37, 153), Cassiodorus was aware of the fact that Clement had commented on the OT and NT (e.g., *Inst. Div. litt.*, Praef.), but he possessed only Clement's notes on the catholic epistles.

[13] Pace Joseph Michl, *Die Engelvorstellungen in der Apokalypse des hl. Johannes* (Munich: Max Hueber, 1937), 155–56. Michl tries to escape the difficulty by interpreting the blessing with "grace and peace" coming from the angels as "eine Spendung im uneigentlichen Sinne" (p. 156). On the other hand, he adduces a number of Jewish and Christian texts in which angels appear to hold a certain exalted status in their relations with humans. The difficulty of Rev 1:4, however, is due to the fact that angels appear to be placed on the same level as the Father and the Son.

[14] See also the list of passages illustrating Paul's "soteriological trinitarianism" in Gordon D. Fee, *God's Empowering Presence: The Holy Spirit in the Letters of Paul* (Peabody, MA: Hendrickson, 1994), 839–42.

According to Edmondo F. Lupieri, Revelation's use of a "Satanic triad" composed of the dragon, the beast, and the false prophet (16:13; cf. ch. 13) suggests the existence of a similar triadic structure in the opposite, divine world.[15] In the cautious words of Lupieri, with the greeting in Revelation "John is developing some kind of (pre-)Trinitarian thinking."[16] Whether one chooses to term it a "grotesque" Trinity or one that is "quite orthodox" depends on whether one considers this theology in its proper context, which is that of Jewish apocalyptic traditions appropriated by early Christians.[17]

On the other hand, the angelic traits of the seven spirits are quite obvious. In fact, Revelation also mentions "the seven stars" held by the Son of Man, which are said to represent "the seven angels" (1:20), and "the seven angels before the throne" (8:2). Pierre Prigent argues that the seven spirits are different from the seven stars, because they are mentioned separately in Rev 3:1 ("he who has the seven spirits of God and the seven stars . . .").[18] However, since both "stars/ angels" and "spirits" are well-defined groups (*the* seven stars, *the* seven angels, *the* seven spirits), the simplest solution is to admit that we have here symbolic references to the same reality, which the author conveyed by recourse to the language of angelic worship before the divine throne.[19] The seven are placed before the divine throne, clearly subordinated to Christ (seven eyes of the Lord, seven stars in his hand, seven horns of the Lamb), ever contemplating the divine Face, offering up the prayers mounting from below and passing on the illumination that descends from above. These are standard elements in the depiction of angelic intercession, contemplation, and service.

To make sense of all of the above, patristic as well as modern-day commentators have outlined the following alternatives: (a) Revelation connects the seven spirits/eyes/lamps of the Lord (Zech 3:9; 4:10) with the rest/tabernacling of the seven spiritual gifts (Isa 11:2; Prov 8:12–16); (b) Revelation connects the seven spirits/eyes/lamps of the Lord (Zech 3:9; 4:10) with the seven angels of the presence (Tob 12:15; *1 En.* 90:20–21). The latter is a minority position, although it has notable defenders.[20]

---

[15] Edmondo F. Lupieri, *Commentary on the Apocalypse of John* (Italian Texts and Studies on Religion and Society; Grand Rapids: Eerdmans, 2006), 103.

[16] Ibid., 102.

[17] These are the terms used by R. H. Charles (*A Critical and Exegetical Commentary on the Revelation of St. John* [2 vols.; ICC; Edinburgh: T&T Clark, 1920], 1:xii; cf. 1:12) and Gregory Dix ("The Seven Archangels and the Seven Spirits: A Study in the Origin, Development, and Messianic Associations of the Two Themes," *JTS* 28 [1927]: 248).

[18] Pierre Prigent, *Commentary on the Apocalypse of St. John* (Tübingen: Mohr Siebeck, 2001), 117.

[19] Lupieri, *Commentary on the Apocalypse*, 102–3, 136; David E. Aune, *Revelation* (3 vols.; WBC 52A–C; Dallas: Word Books, 1997), 1:33.

[20] Charles, *Revelation*, 1:11; Michl, *Engelvorstellungen*; Aune, *Revelation* 1:33–35; Gieschen, *Angelomorphic Christol-ogy*, 264–65; Gottfried Schimanowski, *Die himmlische Liturgie in der Apokalypse des Johannes* (WUNT 2/154; Tübingen: Mohr Siebeck, 2002), 118. Among patristic writers, this explanation is implied by Cyprian (*Exhortation to Martyrdom, to Fortunatus* 11) and

The exegetical impasse is evident. Patristic authors from the fifth century onward are overcautious, trying to avoid any interpretations that would fall short of doctrinal orthodoxy.[21] Many modern exegetes tend to juxtapose the two solutions, rarely daring to eliminate either possibility.[22] Both solutions have significant strengths and weaknesses: the first one accounts for the number seven and the position in the greeting; the second accounts for the undeniable angelic traits of these seven spirits. However, neither is able to integrate the advantages of the alternative interpretation, and so both are still open to criticism.[23]

Could the theology of second-century writers shed some light on this matter? Even though we possess no direct reference to Rev 1:4 (and related verses), several passages in Clement suggest that the Alexandrian did hold a specific view about the passages in Revelation dealing with the seven spirits.

---

favored by Oecumenius and Arethas, echoing statements by Irenaeus and Clement of Alexandria (see the discussion below).

[21] I rely on the fragments from patristic commentaries provided in Albin Škrinjar, "Les sept esprits: Apoc. 1, 4; 3, 1; 4, 5; 5, 6," *Bib* 16 (1935): 2–24; Henry Barclay Swete, *The Apocalypse of St. John: The Greek Text with Introduction, Notes and Indices* (3rd ed.; London: Macmillan, 1909), 5–6; Michl, *Engelvorstellungen*, 113–34. Andrew of Caesarea and Arethas present both alternatives and note the tentative character of the angelic solution ("one could consider the spirits as angels"). Oecumenius and Andrew of Caesarea agree that the expression "before the throne" in 1:4 suggests inferiority in status, and therefore should not be interpreted as a reference to God; nevertheless, Oecumenius interprets 5:6 as a reference to the seven gifts of the Spirit. Andrew of Caesarea states that the expression "who is, and was, and is to come" refers to Father, Son, and Holy Spirit; thus, he manages to find *both* the Trinity *and* the angels in 1:4. Karl Schlütz (*Isaias 11:2 [Die sieben Gaben des Heiligen Geistes] in den ersten vier christlichen Jahrhunderten* [Münster: Aschendorff, 1932], 34) has shown that a connection between Isa 11:2 (the seven gifts of the Spirit) and Zech 4:10 (the seven lamps) was an established topos in patristic exegesis.

[22] Eduard R. Schweizer (*Spirit of God* [Bible Key Words 9; London: Adam & Charles Black, 1960], 105–6) simply juxtaposes the religio-historical perspective ("from the point of view of the history of religion, they are simply the seven archangels"), and the traditional theological point of view, according to which the seven spirits "represent the Spirit of God in its fullness and completeness." Aune (*Revelation*, 1:34) is exhaustive in his references but very reserved in advocating the identification between the seven spirits and the principal angels.

[23] Equating the seven spirits with the seven gifts of the Holy Spirit of Isa 11:2 does not explain the resulting "double blessing" (why is the Holy Spirit dispensing grace and peace if he is *already* designated by his *gifts*?), or the awkward conflation of personal traits (being in service before the throne, blessing the church), and impersonal traits (the Spirit as spiritual gifts), or the facts that, despite being "seven" and "before the throne," the seven spirits and the seven angels are not the same. Moreover, critics point out that the overwhelming majority of greetings in apostolic epistles mention "grace and peace" from the Father and the Son (Michl, *Engelvorstellungen*, 151; for a list of greetings in the NT, see Aune, *Revelation*, 1:26–27), and that a trinitarian interpretation of the greeting in Revelation is derived from "later conceptualization of God" (Aune, *Revelation*, 1:34). On the other hand, we have 2 Cor 13:14 ("The grace of the Lord Jesus Christ, the love of God, and the communion of the Holy Spirit be with all of you") and the trinitarian baptismal formula, both of which suggest that a reference to the Holy Spirit would have been the likely intention of Rev 1:4.

In some of his texts (e.g., *Excerpta* 10–11; 27; *Eclogae* 51–52; 56) Clement furnishes a detailed description of the hierarchical structure of the spiritual universe. This celestial "hierarchy," if the anachronism is acceptable, features, in descending order, the Face, the seven first created angels, the archangels, finally the angels.[24] The orienting principle (ἀρχή) of the hierarchy is the "Face of God," which Clement, like other early Christian writers, identifies as the Logos, the Son (*Excerpta* 10.6; 12.1; *Paed.* 1.57; 1.124.4; *Strom.* 7.58; Tertullian, *Adv. Prax.* 14). The first level of celestial entities contemplating the Face consists of the seven πρωτόκτιστοι, celestial beings "first created." These *protoctists* are numbered with the angels and archangels, who are their subordinates; on the other hand, they are bearers of the Name and, as such, are called "gods" (*Adumbrationes in 1 Jn* 2:1; *In Juda* 5:24). Clement equates the seven *protoctists* with "the seven eyes of the Lord" (Zech 3:9; 4:10; Rev 5:6), the "thrones" (Col 1:16), and the "angels ever contemplating the Face of God" (Matt 18:10) (*Strom.* 5.6.35; *Eclogae* 57.1; *Excerpta* 10). The *protoctists* are seven, but they are simultaneously characterized by unity and multiplicity; "their liturgy," says Clement, "is common and undivided" (*Excerpta* 10.3; 11.4). In relation to Christ, they present the prayers ascending from below; on the other hand, they function as "high priests" of the archangels, just as the archangels are "high priests" of the angels, and so forth (*Excerpta* 27.2).

Here we find a definite echo of biblical and pseudepigraphic traditions about the highest angelic company (Ezek 9:2–3; Tob 12:15; *1 En.* 20; 90:21),[25] which will also surface in later rabbinic writings.[26] Among the Christian texts available to

---

[24] The term "hierarchy" was coined centuries later by the anonymous author of the Pseudo-Areopagitic corpus. Nevertheless, the multistoried cosmos that characterizes apocalyptic writings such as the *Ascension of Isaiah*, *2 Enoch*, or the *Epistula Apostolorum* can also be labeled "hierarchical." Moreover, there are some surprising similarities between the Clementinian and Dionysian "hierarchies." See in this respect Bousset, *Jüdisch-christlicher Schulbetrieb*, 179 n. 1; Utto Riedinger, "Eine Paraphrase des Engel-Traktates von Klemens von Alexandreia in den Erotapokriseis des Pseudo-Kaisarios?" *ZKG* 73 (1962): 253–71, esp. 262; Alexander Golitzin, *Et introibo ad altare Dei: The Mystagogy of Dionysius Areopagita, with Special Reference to Its Predecessors in the Eastern Christian Tradition* (Analekta Vlatadon 59; Thessalonica: Patriarchal Institute of Patristic Studies, 1994), 265.

[25] In the *Prayer of Joseph* Israel ranks higher than the seven archangels, as chief captain and first minister before the face of God. In *Jubilees*, the angels of the presence are "first created" (*Jub.* 2:2; 15:27). Other relevant passages are *T. Levi* 3:5; 4:2; *T. Judah* 25:2; 1QH 6:13. See also James C. VanderKam, *The Book of Jubilees* (Guides to Apocrypha and Pseudepigrapha; Sheffield: Sheffield Academic Press, 2001), 87–89, 126–27; Gieschen, *Angelomorphic Christology*, 124–51; Dix, "Seven Archangels."

[26] According to *3 En.* 10:2–6, Metatron is exalted above the "eight great princes" who bear the divine Name. *Pirkê de Rabbi Eliezer*, a work composed around 750 C.E. but incorporating material going back to the Pseudepigrapha, speaks about "the *seven angels which were created first*," who are said to minister before God within the Pargod (*The Chapters of Rabbi Eliezer the Great According to the Text of the Manuscript Belonging to Abraham Epstein of Vienna* [trans. Gerald Friedländer; New York: Hermon 1965], iv, 23).

Clement, the *Shepherd of Hermas* knows of a group of seven consisting of the six "first created ones" (πρῶτοι κτισθέντες) who accompany the Son of God as their seventh (*Vis.* 3.4.1; *Sim.* 5.5.3). There can be no question, however, that Revelation offered an even more explicit source mentioning the seven spirits before the divine throne.

Is it possible to connect Clement's statements on the seven *protoctists* with the seven spirits of Revelation? I think we can answer in the affirmative. The following elements are certain: (a) Ancient and modern exegetes agree that Rev 1:4 is intended as a reference to the seven spirits/eyes/lamps of the Lord in Zech 3:9; 4:10. Clement also connects his *protoctists* with Zech 3:9 and Isa 11:2–3 (LXX) (*Excerpta* 10; *Eclogae* 57.1; *Strom.* 5.6.35). (b) Arethas (ca. 860–940), who is writing on Revelation on the basis of earlier commentaries (Andrew of Crete, 660–740; Oecumenius, ca. 550–600), affirms that both Irenaeus and Clement saw in Rev 1:4 a reference to the seven angels, and Arethas regards this explanation as the more probable.[27] These two elements could, in theory, mean that Clement is drawing on several biblical passages from the Old and New Testaments, but not on Revelation, and that Arethas simply does not know what he is talking about.[28] But the reference to Irenaeus finds a counterpart in the *Demonstration of the Apostolic Preaching*.[29] Irenaeus's tenuous connection between the seven heavens and the seven spirits is echoed with greater clarity in Victorinus's treatise *De Fabrica Mundi* 7–8, where "the seven heavens" correspond to "the seven spirits," and, among many other things, to "the seven angels."[30] Arethas's information on Clement is even more

---

[27] Michl (*Engelvorstellungen*, 113–14) argues that Arethas tells us only that Irenaeus and Clement *knew* of a group of seven principal angels, without connecting this theological opinion with the exegesis of Revelation. However, by mentioning this opinion to explain the seven-angel interpretation of Rev 1:4, Arethas is at least saying that they *would have* read the passage in this way and derived their teaching from it. To impose upon patristic writers a separation between exegetical and theological options does violence to their thinking.

[28] This is the interpretation of Škrinjar, "Les septs esprits," 4–6, 14, 21.

[29] *Dem.* 9 (St. Irenaeus of Lyons, *On the Apostolic Preaching* [trans. John Behr; Crestwood, NY: St. Vladimir's Seminary Press, 1997], 45–46): "But this world is encompassed by seven heavens, in which dwell <innumerable> powers and angels and archangels.... Thus the Spirit of God is <active [in] manifold [ways]> and seven forms of service were counted by Isaias the prophet resting upon the Son of God ... for he says, 'The Spirit shall rest upon him' ... [quotation from Isa 11:2–3]. Hence, the first heaven ... is that of wisdom; and the second, after it, [that] <of> understanding...." Irenaeus continues to list all seven "spirits" and concludes with the following: "From this pattern Moses received the seven-branched candlestick, since he received the service as a pattern of heaven."

[30] "To those days [the seven days of creation] correspond also seven spirits.... Their names are those spirits that rested upon the Christ of God, as is given assurance in the prophet Isaiah. ... Therefore, the highest heaven [is that] of wisdom, the second [is that] of understanding.... Behold! the seven horns of the lamb, seven eyes of God, seven spirits, ... seven golden lamps, ... seven angels, ... seven weeks completed in Pentecost, ... the lamp with seven orifices, the seven columns in the house of Solomon ..." (translation mine, on the basis of the Latin text in SC 423, 145–46).

certainly deduced from actual Clementine texts. Given Clement's familiarity with the idea that "the whole world of creatures ... revolves in sevens" and that "the first-born princes of the angels (πρωτόγονοι ἀγγέλων ἄρχοντες), who have the greatest power, are seven" (*Strom.* 6.16.142–43), and given that he goes so far, as I have noted above, as to interpret the "angels of the little ones" in Matt 18:10 as a proof text for the seven *protoctists*, it would be quite awkward for him to neglect the explicit groups of seven spirits and angels in Revelation. Finally, a passage from the scholia on Ps.-Dionysius by John of Scythopolis links the seven supreme angels of Revelation and those of Clement's *Hypotyposeis*.[31]

Cassiodorus's commentary on Revelation seems indebted to the *Adumbrationes* on precisely the point under discussion: the blessing "from the seven spirits" (Rev 1:4) is said to come from the seven archangels mentioned in Tob 12:15.[32] We may therefore be reasonably certain that this was Clement's interpretation of the seven spirits in Revelation. Moreover, given what has been said earlier about the indebtedness of the *Hypotyposeis* to earlier Christian teachers, this was most likely the prevalent interpretation of the seven angels in the second century.

III. Seven Angels or Angelomorphic Pneumatology?

I noted that the angelic traits of the seven spirits in Rev 1:4 are undeniable. It appears that Revelation illustrates the same use of πνεῦμα terminology to designate angelic beings that scholars have shown to be widespread in the Hebrew Bible, in the LXX and various authors of the Alexandrian Diaspora, in the Qumran writings, as well as in early Christianity.[33] In the OT, the *locus classicus* is Isa 63:9–10. Here the agent of the exodus is referred to neither as "angel" nor as "pillar of cloud," but as "holy spirit." In the NT, aside from the designation of *evil* angels as (impure) "spirits," the equivalence of "spirit" and "angel" is implicit in Heb 12:9 ("Father of spirits") and Acts 8:26, 29, 39, where Philip's guide is successively described as "angel of the Lord," "spirit," and "spirit of the Lord." In Revelation, πνεῦμα is used twice for evil angels (16:13–14; 18:2). But as the chart on the next page shows, πνεῦμα can also designate a good angel:

---

[31] Λέγει δὲ πρεσβυτέρους ἀγγέλους ὁ θεῖος Ἰωάννης ἐν τῇ Ἀποκαλύψει, καὶ ἑπτὰ εἶναι τοὺς πρώτους ἐν τῷ Τωβίᾳ ἀνέγνωμεν καὶ παρὰ Κλήμεντι βιβλίῳ ε΄ τῶν Ὑποτυπώσεων (*PG* 4:225, 228).

[32] ... *a septem angelis qui ... sicut in libro Tobiae Rafael angelus dixit, unus sum ex septem angelis ...* (*Complexiones* 2 [113]); *ante quem erant septem spiritus, id est angeli dei* (*Complexiones* 8 [117]). Text in Roger Gryson, ed., *Variorum auctorum commentaria minora in Apocalypsin Johannis* (CCSL 107; Turnhout: Brepols, 2003), 113–29. The numbers in brackets indicate the page number in this volume.

[33] Arthur E. Sekki, *The Meaning of Ruach at Qumran* (SBLDS 110; Atlanta: Scholars Press, 1989), 145–71; John R. Levison, "The Angelic Spirit in Early Judaism," *SBLSP* 34 (1995): 464–93; Bucur, "Rereading of the *Shepherd's* Christology."

Revelation 14:13	Revelation 19:9
And I heard <u>a voice from heaven saying</u>, "Write this: *Blessed are the dead who from now on die in the Lord!*" "Yes," <u>says the Spirit</u> [the initial locutor, the voice], "they will rest from their labors, for their deeds follow them."	And <u>the angel</u> <u>said</u> to me, "Write this: *Blessed are those invited to the marriage supper of the Lamb!*" And <u>said he</u> to me [the initial locutor, the angel] "These are true words of God!"

Both passages are examples of the so-called promise-to-the-victor, a type of statement that occurs fairly often in Revelation. In both passages, an initial declaration is repeated and confirmed by the same heavenly locutor. The difference consists only in the fact that we read "spirit" in 14:13, and, respectively, "angel" in 19:9. Yet in light of the similarities of structure and content, and given the interchangeability of the terms "angel" and "spirit" in early Jewish and Christian texts, I judge this to be another example of πνεῦμα terminology in the service of angelology.[34]

On the other hand, as I have argued, the pneumatological content of Rev 1:4 is equally undeniable. Lupieri finds additional support for this view by pointing to the dualism between the sevenfold Spirit and the sevenfold demonic power (Rev 12:3; 13:1).[35]

Just as for Clement, who on the one hand equates the seven *protoctists* with the "thrones" of Col 1:16 and "the angels of the little ones" of Matt 18:10 but on the other hand refers to them as "heptad of the Spirit" (*Paed.* 3.12.87), the seven angelic spirits of Revelation occupy an area of confluence between angelology and pneumatology. These two realities—angelic imagery and pneumatological content—need not be viewed as mutually exclusive. They can be fused by appealing to a new descriptive category: "angelomorphic pneumatology." Here I follow the convention of using the term "angelomorphic" to denote the angelic *characteristics* of an individual or community, whereas the latter's *identity* cannot be reduced to that of an angel or angels.[36]

---

[34] So also Gieschen, *Angelomorphic Christology*, 266–68.

[35] Lupieri, *Commentary on the Apocalypse*, 136: "We are to understand that whenever the Spirit comes forth in human history... it must be sevenfold, in contrast to the Satanic dominion. That this dominion is in fact sevenfold is shown by the fact that the various demonic beasts always have seven heads, which in its turn probably reflects Satan's dominion over the seven periods into which the duration of this world seems to be divided.... The sevenfold pattern of the Spirit's interventions thus probably indicates the constant presence of the Spirit throughout the duration of human history."

[36] Fletcher-Louis, *Luke-Acts*, 14–15; similarly Daniélou, *Jewish Christianity*, 118. See also

IV. BINITARIANISM AND SPIRIT CHRISTOLOGY IN REVELATION

A definition of the operating concepts is in order at this juncture. For the purpose of this essay, "Spirit christology" refers to the use of πνεῦμα terminology to designate Christ in numerous pre-Nicene texts and authors.[37] The term "binitarianism" points to a bifurcation of the divinity, which, however, maintains the monotheistic framework.[38]

It is my contention that despite what seems to be a trinitarian opening (Rev 1:4–5), Revelation remains determined by a binitarian framework, concerned to present the divinity as a binitarian reality: God and his Son. On this second point, second-century writings can again provide some insight into the theology of Revelation. It is generally accepted that on the way from the use of trinitarian formulas to a mature trinitarian theology, these formulas coexisted with a certain binitarian orientation.[39] Such early Christian binitarianism is often the result of an unclear or even nonexistent distinction between the Son and the Spirit; in other words, binitarianism and Spirit christology are two aspects of the same phenomenon.[40]

---

the remark of Lupieri: "perhaps the fact that there are seven spirits is the result of John's reflection on *the angelic nature of the Spirit*" (*Commentary on the Apocalypse*, 103 [emphasis added]).

[37] For a rich survey of texts, see Manlio Simonetti, "Note di cristologia pneumatica," *Aug* 12 (1972): 201–32, esp. 230–31.

[38] The Jewish traditions investigated by Alan F. Segal (*Two Powers in Heaven: Early Rabbinic Reports about Christianity and Gnosticism* [SJLA 25; Leiden: Brill, 1977]) are examples of binitarianism; see also Daniel Boyarin, *Border Lines: The Partition of Judaeo-Christianity* (Divinations; Philadelphia: University of Pennsylvania Press, 2004), 112–27. One may find such "binitarian" elements echoed in the religious philosophies of Philo and Numenius. Binitarianism is not dualism: "neither the apocalyptic, mystical, nor Christianized Judaism affirmed two separate deities. They understood themselves to be monotheistic. . . . Only radical gnosticism posited two different and opposing deities" (Segal, "Dualism in Judaism, Christianity and Gnosticism: A Definitive Issue," in idem, *The Other Judaisms of Late Antiquity* [BJS 127; Atlanta: Scholars Press, 1987], 13).

[39] See, in this respect, Friedrich Loofs, *Theophilus von Antiochien Adversus Marcionem und die anderen theologischen Quellen bei Irenaeus* (TU 46; Leipzig: Hinrichs, 1930), 114–205; H. E. W. Turner, *The Pattern of Christian Truth: A Study in the Relations between Orthodoxy and Heresy in the Early Church* (Bampton Lectures 1954; London: Mowbray, 1954), 133–36; Raniero Cantalamessa, *L'omelia in S. Pascha dello Pseudo-Ippolito di Roma: Ricerche sulla teologia dell'Asia Minore nella seconda metà del II secolo* (Milan: Vita e pensiero, 1967), 171–85; Harry A. Wolfson, *The Philosophy of the Church Fathers* (3rd ed., rev.; Structure and Growth of Philosophic Systems from Plato to Spinoza 3; Cambridge, MA: Harvard University Press, 1970), 177–256; Salvatore Lilla, *Clement of Alexandria: A Study in Christian Platonism and Gnosticism* (Oxford: Oxford University Press, 1971), 26, 53; Simonetti, "Note"; Christopher Stead, *Philosophy in Christian Antiquity* (Cambridge: Cambridge University Press, 1994), 155–56.

[40] Kretschmar, *Trinitätstheologie*, 115–16; Waldemar Macholz, *Spuren binitarischer Denkweise im Abendlande seit Tertullian* (Diss., Halle 1902; Jena: Kämpfe, 1902); Loofs, *Theophilus*,

Who is "God" in the Book of Revelation? The specific indicators are abundantly present in the text: the divine name, the divine throne, the fact of receiving worship. All three indicators point to the same theological view: God and, associated with God, the Son or Lamb. The bearer of the divine name is the Father (1:4, 8; 4:8, 11, 17; 15:3; 16:7, 14; 19:6, 15; 21:22).[41] Yet as Gieschen has shown extensively, Revelation also attributes the divine name to the Son.[42] This is especially noteworthy in 1:8 ("'I am the Alpha and the Omega,' says the Lord God, who is and who was and who is to come, the Almighty").[43] The divine throne is occupied jointly by the Father and the Lamb (5:6), and the Lamb is associated in various ways with the worship received by God.[44] There is no indication of a third enthroned entity being associated with the Father and the Son as bearer of the name or as recipient of worship. Within this binitarian framework, the Spirit appears at the same time indis-

---

114–205; Joseph Barbel, *Christos Angelos: Die Anschauung von Christus als Bote und Engel in der gelehrten und volkstümlichen Literatur des christlichen Altertums: Zugleich ein Beitrag zur Geschichte des Ursprungs und der Fortdauer des Arianismus* (1941; Fotomechanischer Nachdruck mit einem Anhang; Bonn: Peter Hanstein, 1964), 188–92.

[41] The fact that "He–Who–Is" functions as a stand-in for Yhwh explains why the writer refuses to subject the name to the rules of declination in Rev 1:4. According to Prigent (*Commentary*, 15), "it is impossible to suppose that . . . it was not deliberate, especially since the same expression is repeated later (1:8; 4:8; 11:17; 16:5) with the same persistence in making a noun out of the imperfect form of the verb 'to be.' . . . [T]he titles of the eternal God cannot be subjected to temporal vicissitudes, and consequently to the laws of noun declension. The God in question is one who can only act as subject."

[42] Gieschen, "The Divine Name in Ante-Nicene Christology," *VC* 57 (2003): 115–57, esp. 131–34; idem, *Angelomorphic Christology*, 253–55.

[43] Sean McDonough (*YHWH at Patmos: Rev. 1:4 in Its Hellenistic and Early Jewish Setting* [WUNT 2/107; Tübingen: Mohr Siebeck, 1999], esp. 195–231) has provided erudite proof that "the designations in Rev 1:8 are . . . derived from three variations of the name Yhwh" (p. 200), namely, Iaô/Yhwh Elohim, and Yhwh Sabaoth (p. 218). Aune (*Revelation*, 1:55–59) suggests connections with both Hellenistic revelatory magic and Jewish alphabet symbolism. Martin McNamara found that the passage "is perfectly paralleled in TJI Dt 32, 39 and in this text alone of those available to us. . . . It is not to be excluded that the Apocalypse is directly dependent on TJI Dt 32, 39 in its use of it, although it is possible that both texts are dependent on the same early liturgical tradition" (*The New Testament and the Palestinian Targum to the Pentateuch* [AnBib 27; Rome: Pontifical Biblical Institute, 1966], 112). In any case, whether the author of Revelation draws on Jewish or Greek traditions, or perhaps on a typically Hellenistic fusion of both, he is also subjecting preexisting formulas to his own theological views. His eschatological perspective dictates an original modification of the third member of the *Dreizeitenformel* from "who will be" to "who will come" (so Ben Witherington III, *Revelation* [New Cambridge Bible Commentary; Cambridge/ New York: Cambridge University Press, 2003], 75).

[44] Revelation 5:13–14 ("blessing, honor and glory" are given to God and to the Lamb); 7:10 (God and the Lamb receive the acclamation of the martyrs); 14:4 (God and the Lamb receive the self-offering of the martyrs as "first fruits" of humankind); 20:6 (God and Christ receive priestly service from those who are worthy and reign together with them); 21:22–23; 22:5 (the Lamb is or embodies the divine glory and light).

solubly linked to the worshiped second person ("seven horns of the Lamb," "seven eyes of the Lord," "seven stars in the Lord's hand"), and strictly subordinated to it ("the seven holy spirits before the throne").

V. "Spirit" in Revelation

Revelation never uses the expression "holy spirit." The instances in which the author uses πνεῦμα can be divided into the following categories: πνεῦμα as "breath" of life (11:11; 13:15); πνεῦμα for evil angels (16:13, 14; 18:2); ἐν πνεύματι as an indicator of the visionary ecstatic state (1:10; 4:2; 17:3; 21:10); πνεῦμα at the closing of the seven letters: "listen to what the Spirit says to the churches" (2:7); the seven πνεύματα (1:4; 3:1; 4:5; 5:6); "the spirit of prophecy" (19:10); "the God of the spirits of the prophets" (22:6); πνεῦμα in association with the heavenly church, "the bride" (22:17).

I have already discussed the case of the seven spirits in Revelation. Of the remaining categories, the following are irrelevant for a discussion about the pneumatology of Revelation: πνεῦμα as life-giving "breath," πνεῦμα for the "evil angels," and the expression ἐν πνεύματι to denote an ecstatic state.[45] At this point it is necessary to explore the use of πνεῦμα in the closing section of the seven letters (chs. 2–3). I shall discuss the remaining references in the section on prophecy.

There is a precise parallelism between the function of Christ and that of the "spirit" as described in the introductory and final parts of the seven letters. The letters are framed by an opening announcement of what Christ proclaims (τάδε λέγει ὁ . . . [completed with descriptions of Christ drawn from ch. 1]), and a final exhortation to hear what the Spirit says (τὸ πνεῦμα λέγει). It is clear that the parallelism is intentional and that the author consciously and consistently introduces a functional overlapping between "Christ" and "Spirit."[46] Unfortunately, commen-

---

[45] I take "breath of life" to mean simply the vital force that characterizes that which is biologically alive, as opposed to dead matter. The designation of evil angelic beings as evil "spirits" implicitly eliminates any reference to the Holy Spirit. For the expression "in the spirit," see Richard Bauckham, "The Role of the Spirit in the Apocalypse," *EvQ* 52 (1980): 66–73. The phrase seems to have functioned in early Christian literature as a technical designation of the inspired state of prophets. In such cases (e.g., *Did.* 11.7–9), "the primary reference is . . . not the source of inspiration, but the phenomenon of ecstatic speech" (Bauckham, *The Climax of Prophecy: Studies on the Book of Revelation* [Edinburgh: T&T Clark, 1993], 151). In the case of Revelation, Bauckham believes that "γενέσθαι ἐν πνεύματι . . . is probably to be taken as both phenomenological and theological, denoting both the visionary as such and the Spirit's authorship of it" (p. 152). I agree with Aune, whose dense excursus dedicated to the formula "in the spirit" concludes that "ἐγενόμην ἐν πνεύματι is best rendered as 'I fell into a trance'" (*Revelation*, 1:83). Prigent holds the same position (*Commentary*, 128).

[46] Revelation 2:1—2:7; 2:8—2:11; 2:12—2:17; 2:18—2:29; 3:1—3:6; 3:7—3:13; 3:14—3:22.

tators sometimes evade the difficulty by restating the obvious, or they resort to convenient dogmatic "shortcuts," simply bypassing the exegetical trouble zone: "Christ speaks through the Spirit."[47]

Given the prophetic-visionary character of Revelation 2–3, "spirit" is most likely connected to the reality of prophetic experience (cf. 1 John 4:1–3).[48] From this point on, scholarly opinions begin to diverge. Some take "Spirit" as a christological title, derived from the act of Christ's inspiring the prophet: "the Spirit is none other than . . . the Ascended Christ in his role of speaking to the Church."[49] Others hold the opposite position:

> it is not that the Spirit is identical to the exalted Lord, but that the exalted Lord speaks to the Churches by . . . the Spirit of prophecy. . . . When the spirit of prophecy comes upon him, John speaks of himself as being, or becoming, "in the Spirit" (ἐν πνεύματι).[50]

In other words, "listen to what the Spirit says" would be shorthand for "listen to what Christ says through *the one who was in the spirit*."

As can be seen, the divergence can be reduced to the issue of whether "Spirit" should be relegated to Christ or to the seer. Whatever the case, it is obvious that πνεῦμα here is not unambiguously "the Holy Spirit."[51] The first position, advocating a christological use of "Spirit," seems more plausible because it better accounts for the Christ—Spirit parallelism, noted above, and also because it offers the simpler solution, in comparison to the exegetical acrobatics required to transform τὸ πνεῦμα λέγει into ἐν πνεύματι λέγει. Similarly to Pauline literature, Revelation

> indicates by the word "spirit" the mode in which the Lord exists . . . the power in which he encounters his Church. . . . When Christ is seen in terms of his role for the Church and of his works of power within the Church, he can be identified

---

[47] E.g., "the seven messages are . . . equated with the words of the exalted Christ" (Bauckham, "Role of the Spirit," 73); "the author is emphasizing the close relation of the Spirit with the exalted Christ" (Aune, *Revelation*, 1:123); "the Spirit speaks as Christ and Christ as the Spirit" (Gieschen, *Angelomorphic Christology*, 269).

[48] According to R. W. L. Moberly ("'Test the Spirits': God, Love, and Critical Discernment in 1 John 4," in *The Holy Spirit and Christian Origins: Essays in Honor of James D. G. Dunn* [ed. Graham N. Stanton, Bruce W. Longenecker, and Stephen C. Barton; Grand Rapids: Eerdmans, 2004], 298–99), "John's concern is here with the discernment of that which purports to belong to the realm of God, that is 'spirit(s)'. So his basic injunction is clear: 'Do not believe every spirit,' that is, do not be gullible, credulous, or unthinking in the spiritual realm, but rather 'test the spirits' to see whether claims to be from God are indeed justified."

[49] Schweizer, *Spirit of God*, 105.

[50] F. F. Bruce, "The Spirit in the Apocalypse," in *Christ and Spirit in the New Testament: In Honour of C. F. D. Moule* (ed. Barnabas Lindars and Stephen S. Smalley; Cambridge: Cambridge University Press, 1973), 340, 339. So also Bauckham, *Climax of Prophecy*, 160–61.

[51] Contra Charles Brütsch (*La clarté de l'Apocalypse* [Geneva: Labor et Fides, 1966], 58), who does not even debate the matter: "l'Esprit: *indubitablement*, le Saint-Esprit" (emphasis added).

with the Spirit; but insofar as Christ is also Lord over his own power, he can be distinguished from that power, just as "I" can always be distinguished from the power which goes out from me.[52]

The intimate relation between Christ and the Spirit in early Christian theological reflection (the Fourth Gospel and the Pauline corpus) has been described in various ways by scholars.[53] The identity between the experience of Christ and the experience of the Spirit has been termed "dynamic," "functional," "experiential," "existential," or "immanent"—meaning that, from the perspective of the Christian, the experience of the Spirit *is* the experience of Christ, which *is* the experience of God the Father. Disagreement occurs only when this type of experiential identity is pushed further to describe the theological relation between Christ and Spirit. Some scholars conclude that the terms are fully interchangeable, and they implicitly question the trinitarian reference to the three terms "God," "Christ," and "Spirit"; others forcefully argue against this identification.[54]

I think it is important to recall that we use "binitarianism" and "Spirit christology" to designate the widespread incongruence, in early Christian writings, between theological discourse, on the one hand, and the liturgical, communal, and mystical experience that this discourse recounts, on the other. In the words of H. E. W. Turner, "Christians lived Trinitarianly before the doctrine of the Trinity began to be thought out conceptually."[55] With this theological disclaimer spelled out clearly, I return to the phrase τὸ πνεῦμα λέγει. My judgment is the following: (a) the hypothesis of Spirit christology in Revelation has the advantage of accounting for the functional and experiential overlap between the "Christ" and "Spirit"; (b) this hypothesis does not allow us to speculate about a personal identification between Christ and the Holy Spirit; (c) this hypothesis seems verified by the similar phenomenon in the Pauline corpus and in other early Christian texts, most notably the *Shepherd of Hermas*; (d) finally, I subscribe to Mehrdad Fatehi's overall thesis that the identification between the concept of "Spirit of God" in the OT

---

[52] Schweizer, *Spirit of God*, 60.

[53] Mehrdad Fatehi, *The Spirit's Relation to the Risen Lord in Paul: An Examination of Its Christological Implications* (WUNT 2/128; Tübingen: Mohr Siebeck, 2000). For the Gospel of John, see Gary M. Burge, *The Anointed Community: The Holy Spirit in the Johannine Tradition* (Grand Rapids: Eerdmans, 1987), 137–49.

[54] Fatehi (*Relation*, 23–43) provides an overview of scholarly opinions on the subject, ranging from Hermann Gunkel and Adolf Deissmann, to James D. G. Dunn and Gordon Fee, and many others.

[55] H. E. W. Turner, *Pattern of Christian Truth*, 474; see also 134–35: "If, however, there is a persistent tendency in the early centuries to interpret the Christian doctrine of the Godhead in a bi-personal rather than in a tri-personal manner... [t]here is no reason to believe that those who worked normally with a Binitarian phrasing in their theology were other than Trinitarian in their religion. There is no trace, for example, of an alternative Twofold Baptismal Formula."

and the "Spirit of Christ" in the NT is ultimately christologically motivated, since it identifies Christ as divine.[56]

As noted earlier, scholars of Revelation often speak about the "functional" or "experiential" overlap between Christ and Spirit. In what follows I shall offer a more detailed examination of this topic by discussing the phenomenon of prophecy. I shall argue that, similar to the *Shepherd of Hermas* and Clement of Alexandria, Revelation views the Spirit-experience as a direct influx of the Logos mediated by the *angelic* spirit.

VI. THE PHENOMENON OF PROPHECY IN REVELATION

> Then he [the angel] said to me, Write: "Blessed [are] those who are called to the marriage supper of the Lamb!" And he said to me, These are the true sayings of God. And I fell at his feet to worship him. But he said to me, See [that you do] not [do that!] I am your fellow servant, and of your brethren who have the testimony of Jesus. Worship God! For the testimony of Jesus is the spirit of prophecy, ἡ γὰρ μαρτυρία Ἰησοῦ ἐστιν τὸ πνεῦμα τῆς προφητείας. (Rev 19:9–10)

Scholarly interpretations of Rev 19:10 vary, most notably on the issue of whether the genitive Ἰησοῦ is objective or subjective.[57] I judge that the more probable meaning of μαρτυρία Ἰησοῦ is "the witness borne by Jesus Christ." This is suggested by the fact that one of Christ's fundamental designations in Revelation is "witness" (1:5; 3:14), and especially by the correspondence between the first mention of "witness of Jesus" in 19:10 and "the commands of this book" in 22:9. See the chart on the next page.

---

[56] Indeed, as Fatehi repeatedly affirms, no mediatorial figure among the so-called exalted, angelomorphic patriarchs is ever presented as having the same relation to the Spirit that the OT affirms of God and his Spirit. An older formulation of this thesis can be found in Max Turner, "The Spirit of Christ and 'Divine' Christology," in *Jesus of Nazareth: Lord and Christ; Essays on the Historical Jesus and New Testament Christology* (ed. Joel B. Green and Max Turner; Grand Rapids: Eerdmans, 1994), 413–36.

[57] For a survey of positions, see Aune, *Revelation*, 3:1038–39. Cf. the similar debate over the phrase πίστις Χριστοῦ in Rom 3:22, 26; Gal 2:16, 20; 3:22; Phil 3:9; Eph 3:12. The option for subjective genitive is a significant minority position: Morna D. Hooker, "Πίστις Χριστοῦ," *NTS* 35 (1989): 321–42; Richard B. Hays, *The Faith of Jesus Christ: The Narrative Substructure of Galatians 3:1–4:11* (2nd ed.; Grand Rapids: Eerdmans, 2002). Revelation's μαρτυρία Ἰησοῦ and the Pauline πίστις Χριστοῦ are both treated in Ian G. Wallis, *The Faith of Jesus Christ in Early Christian Traditions* (SNTSMS 84; Cambridge/New York: Cambridge University Press, 1995), 65–127, 169–72. In his survey of patristic treatments of the topic (pp. 175–212), Wallis shows that after figuring prominently in pre-Nicene literature, "the paradigmatic significance of Jesus' faith . . . was a casualty of the movement towards establishing Christ's divinity" (p. 212).

Revelation 19:10	Revelation 22:8-9
And I	Now I, John, saw and heard these things. And when I heard and saw,
fell at his feet to worship him.	I fell down to worship before the feet of the angel who showed me these things.
But he said to me, "See [that you do] not [do that!] I am your fellow servant, and of your brethren	Then he said to me, "See [that you do] not [do that.] For I am your fellow servant, and of your brethren the prophets, and of those
who have **the testimony of Jesus.** Worship God!" For the testimony of Jesus is the spirit of prophecy.	who keep **the words of this book.** Worship God!"

The meaning of Rev 19:10 must bear some relation to the visionary's error of worshiping the *angelus interpres*. It may well be that the clause "angels are only fellow servants" functioned as a corrective in the polemic against angel worship.[58] Yet the attempt to worship the angel occurs after an emphatic declaration about the authority of the "true sayings"—very likely the book of Revelation itself. Thus, as some scholars have argued, the theme of angelic worship and its correction are only secondary and subservient to a more important theme: "John's purpose was ... perhaps, to claim for his brothers a certain primacy in the affairs of churches."[59] Read in this way, the passage makes perfect sense in the context of early church debates about the status and authority of prophets, or the polemics concerning the criteria of true versus false prophecy.

---

[58] This mirror reading is confirmed by texts documenting that the veneration of angels was not uncommon in Second Temple Judaism and early Christianity: Tob 12:16–22; Col 2:18 ("worship of angels," although the meaning is not unambiguous); *Mart. Ascen. Isa.* 7:21–23; 8:4–5; *Apoc. Zeph.* 6:13–15.

[59] Martin Kiddle, *The Revelation of St. John* (1940; London: Hodder & Stoughton, 1963), 449; Hanna Roose, *"Das Zeugnis Jesu": Seine Bedeutung für die Christologie, Eschatologie und Prophetie in der Offenbarung des Johannes* (Texte und Arbeiten zum neutestamentlichen Zeitalter; Tübingen: Francke, 2000), 202–8; Prigent, *Commentary*, 529–33. The fact that the divine authority of the book is a crucial theological theme for Revelation becomes evident when 19:10 is read in conjunction with 1:1 and 22:6. For the importance of Christian prophetic circles in Revelation, see Jan Fekkes III, *Isaiah and the Prophetic Traditions in the Book of Revelation: Visionary Antecedents and Their Development* (JSNTSup 93; Sheffield: JSOT Press, 1994), 40–41, 49–58; and David E. Aune, "The Prophetic Circle of John of Patmos and the Exegesis of Revelation 22.16," *JSNT* 37 (1989): 103–16, esp. 108–11.

It seems, then, that "the spirit of prophecy" in Rev 19:10 refers not to the person of the Holy Spirit, or a heavenly agent ("spirit" as angelic being) but to the charisma of the prophets. Additional proof can be gleaned from 22:6. It is interesting to consider the various readings of this verse:

(a)	the Lord God of the spirits	of the		prophets	sent his angel
(a′)	the Lord God of the spirits	of the	holy	prophets	sent his angel
(b)	the Lord God	of the	holy	prophets	sent his angel
(c)	the Lord God of the spirits and	of the		prophets	sent his angel

Obviously, the textual variation reflects a process of interpretation: (a) and (b) agree in that they both refer not to the Holy Spirit but to the receptive faculty of the prophets.[60] The (b) version, lacking πνεῦμα, makes the very same point. As for (a′), it seems to combine elements of both: "spirits" from (a) and "holy" from (b). Overall, these versions represent fundamentally the same understanding of the text, as opposed to a different one witnessed by (c). The latter understands πνεύματα as distinct entities, separate from the prophets.

This manuscript variation recalls Num 16:22, where the MT has אל אלהי הרוחת לכל בשר ("O God, God of the spirits of all flesh"), thus presenting God as master over all life-endowed creatures, while the LXX reads Θεὸς Θεὸς τῶν πνευμάτων καὶ πάσης σαρκός ("O God, God of the spirits and of all flesh"). It seems evident that the LXX turns the text into a statement about God as master of two categories of beings—"spirits," on the one hand, and humans, on the other. There is overwhelming evidence that this reworking is in accordance with a semantic evolution of *rûaḥ* toward what has been called "the angelic spirit."[61]

Returning to version (c) of Rev 22:6, and bearing in mind the established tradition of designating God's sovereignty over the celestial realm by the formula "Lord of spirits" (*1 En.* 37:2; 39:12) or "Father of spirits" (Heb 12:9), I believe it is legitimate to conclude that this version understands "spirits" as angelic beings subject (together with the prophets) to God.

One thing we may affirm about πνεύματα in Rev 22:6 is that, whether it refers to an anthropological reality (a, a′) or to angelic beings (c), it does not designate the Holy Spirit. While this conclusion may close one chapter of the discus-

---

[60] Prigent notes that "the expression is also used by Paul (1 Cor 12:10, 14:32) to designate the prophetic gift, the ability to prophesy" (*Commentary*, 635). Cf. Swete: "they are the natural faculties of the Prophets, raised and quickened by the Holy Spirit, but still under human control, and standing in creaturely relation to God" (*Apocalypse*, 303); Isbon Beckwith: "the divinely illumined spirits of the prophets are meant" (*The Apocalypse of John: Studies in Introduction with a Critical and Exegetical Commentary* [New York: Macmillan, 1919], 772); Witherington: "John . . . has in mind not the Holy Spirit but human spirits of the prophets" (*Revelation*, 279). According to Aune (*Revelation* 3:1182), "the psychic faculty of individual prophets rather than to the Spirit of God."

[61] Levison, "Angelic Spirit," 475.

sion, it opens up another important problem: in the absence of a reference to the Holy Spirit, what is the understanding of prophecy in this verse? I shall address this question shortly after considering one last passage:

> I, Jesus, have sent my angel to testify to you these things in the churches. I am the Root and the Offspring of David, the Bright and Morning Star." The Spirit and the bride say, "Come!" And let him who thirsts come. Whoever desires, let him take the water of life freely. (Rev 22:16–17)

If it is true that no use of the singular πνεῦμα has so far proven to refer to the Holy Spirit, it is unlikely that the writer would have suddenly included such a reference in the final chapter of his book.[62] Once again, πνεῦμα stands for something other than the Holy Spirit.

The dialogical setting of the passage, possibly bearing liturgical echoes, places "spirit" and "church" on the same side—namely, the earth—and Christ on the opposite side, in heaven: Christ makes the statement to which, on earth, the Spirit and the church give their response.[63] In this case, it does make good sense to consider that πνεῦμα and "bride" are collective terms for "prophets" and "saints":

> *pneuma* is . . . the Spirit of prophecy, the Spirit of the prophetic order; "the Spirit and the Bride" is thus practically equivalent to "the Prophets and the Saints" (16:6, 18:24). The Christian prophets, inspired by the Spirit of Jesus, and the whole Church . . . respond as with one voice to the Lord's great announcement.[64]

It would be wrong, however, to assume a strict division between the realms of the church, on earth, and Christ, because any response or appeal to Christ, whether private or corporate, is made under divine influence. "Spirit" is a perfect metonymy for "prophets" precisely because the prophet is never a prophet by his or her own power.

I return, therefore, to the question raised above: in the absence of a reference to the Holy Spirit, what is the understanding of prophecy in this verse? The answer to this question lies, I suggest, in the formulas employed by the opening and closing chapters of Revelation: "The revelation . . . sent and signified by his angel to his servant John" (Rev 1:1); "I, Jesus, have sent my angel to testify to you these things for the churches." (Rev 22:16). Commenting on διὰ τοῦ ἀγγέλου αὐτοῦ (Rev 1:1), Lupieri notes, "That the first manifestation of God toward humanity is of an angelic

---

[62] I insist on "singular," because I take the seven spirits as an angelomorphic reference to the Holy Spirit.

[63] Prigent notes that "one can hardly avoid describing [this dialogue] as liturgical" (*Commentary*, 645). For the liturgical setting of Revelation, see Fekkes, *Prophetic Traditions*, 42, with abundant references; Prigent, *Apocalypse et liturgie* (CahT 52; Neuchâtel: Delachaux et Niestlé, 1964).

[64] Swete, *Apocalypse*, 310; Kiddle, *Revelation*, 456.

nature superior to all others makes plain that there is a pyramidal angelic hierarchy."[65] If this type of inspiration is what characterizes prophecy (and the writer clearly considers himself not only a fellow minister of the angels but also one among his brothers, the prophets [22:9]), and if "spirit" is used in Revelation to designate angelic beings, then the following hypothesis can be put forth: prophecy is Christ's illumining and revelatory action upon the prophet, performed through the mediation of the angel, or rather the angelomorphic Spirit.[66]

This conclusion should not be surprising, because a similar understanding of prophecy occurs in another major apocalyptic work of early Christianity, the *Shepherd of Hermas* (Herm. Mand. 11), and in Clement of Alexandria's *Eclogae* and *Adumbrationes*:

> *The heavens proclaim the glory of God* (Ps 18:2). By "heavens" are designated in manifold ways both "the heavens" pertaining to distance and cycle [= the sky], and the proximate operation [ἐνέργεια προσεχής] of the first-created angels, which pertains to covenant. For the covenants were wrought [ἐνηργγήθησαν] by the visitation of angels, namely those upon Adam, Noah, Abraham, and Moses. For, moved by the Lord, the first-created angels worked in [ἐνήργουν εἰς] the angels that are close to the prophets, as they are telling the "glory of God," (namely) the covenants. But the works accomplished by the angels on earth also came about for "the glory of God," through the first-created angels. So, (the following) are called "heavens": in a primary sense, the Lord; but then also the first-created [angels]; and with them also the holy persons (that lived) before the Law, as well as the patriarchs, and Moses and the prophets, and finally the apostles. (*Eclogae* 51–52)

It is clear that the explanations above presuppose Clement's hierarchical worldview, described earlier. Prophecy occurs when the Logos moves the first rank of the *protoctists*, and this movement is transmitted from one level of the angelic hierarchy down to the next. The lowest angelic rank, which is the one closest to the human world, transmits the "movement" to the prophet. Following the logic of the text, one could say that the prophet represents the highest level in the human hierarchy. As noted earlier, Revelation may have intended, among other things, to claim for the prophets "a certain primacy in the affairs of churches."[67]

Through a sort of telescoping effect, the first mover—the Logos—is simultaneously far removed from the effect of prophecy and immediately present. This principle of "mediated immediacy" becomes evident when Clement says that Jude refers the action of a lower angel ("an angel near us") to a superior angelic entity,

---

[65] Lupieri, *Commentary on the Apocalypse*, 98.
[66] See Gieschen, *Angelomorphic Christology*, 265 n. 66, 266–67: the *angelus interpres*, as well as the "voice" of Rev 1:10, and the seven angels before the throne are ways of speaking about the Holy Spirit.
[67] Kiddle, *Revelation*, 449.

the archangel Michael;[68] or when "Moses calls on the power of the angel Michael through an angel near to himself and of the lowest degree (*vicinum sibi et infimum*)" (*Adumbrationes* in 1 John 2:1).

In this light, it is possible to see how Clement understands the traditional statements about the Logos speaking in the prophets ἁγίῳ πνεύματι: the prophet experienced the presence and message of the Logos by receiving the "energy" of the proximate angel.

The view expressed in Clement's *Adumbrationes* fits rather well with the notion of prophecy in Revelation outlined above. Nevertheless, aside from the "normal" sequence Christ–angelomorphic spirit–prophet, Revelation also speaks of the visionary being commanded to address his prophetic word to the angels of the seven churches. This detail, "a written message destined for an angelic rather than a human audience" comes, according to Lupieri, "from the Enochic tradition."[69] Ultimately, however, the recipients of the messages are the congregations. Since the mediators of these messages are the prophets, and given the intimate link between the prophet and the inspiring agent—namely, the angelomorphic sevenfold spirit, since "John mentions the *seven* churches precisely for having *seven* angels to whom he can write"[70]—the messages are said to be addressed to the "angels of the churches." I suggest that they represent a summons to the prophets to exercise their charisma by relaying the respective messages to their congregations.

VII. Conclusions

Reading Revelation in light of second-century writings such as the *Shepherd of Hermas* or Clement's *Excerpta*, *Eclogae*, and *Adumbrationes* has led to highlighting the following three elements: (a) a multilevel cosmos populated by an angelic hierarchy, dominated by the seven angels "first created"; (b) a theological framework that is fundamentally binitarian, even though certain "(pre)-trinitarian" elements are undeniably present; (c) a theory of angelic interaction according to which communication between the divine and the human world is passed on— "channeled," as it were—from Christ to the *protoctists* and further down along the angelic hierarchy until it reaches the highest representative of the Christian community—not the bishop, as some centuries later in Ps.-Dionysius's *Hierarchies*, but the prophet, as in the *Shepherd of Hermas*, the *Ascension of Isaiah*, and Clement's *Hypotyposeis*.

---

[68] "'When the archangel Michael, disputing with the devil, was arguing over the body of Moses.' This confirms the *Assumption of Moses*. 'Michael' here designates the one who argued with the devil through an angel close to us" (*Adumbrationes* in Jude 9).

[69] Lupieri, *Commentary on the Apocalypse*, 115.

[70] Ibid., 98.

There can be no question that Revelation's group of seven spirits/angels before the divine throne (1:4; 3:1; 4:5; 5:6; 8:2) echoes angelological speculations common in Second Temple Judaism. It is equally true, however, that the traditions about the highest angelic company underwent considerable modifications. One example in this regard is the subordination of the *protoctists* to the Son of God: Zechariah's "eyes of the Lord" (Zech 4:10) are reinterpreted as the seven horns and eyes of the Lamb (Rev 5:6), and, "since the lesson of the vision is 'not by might nor by power but by the Spirit' (Zech 4:6), the lamps of the lampstand, the eyes of the Lord, are his Spirit."[71] Revelation illustrates the continuation in early Christianity of the Second Temple tradition about the seven principal angels and its reworking in the service of pneumatology.[72]

I have also argued that these views are, by the standards of today's biblical exegesis, legitimate readings of Revelation. Whether they correspond to the intentions of Revelation's author must remain an issue of debate.

[71] Bauckham, "Role of the Spirit," 76.

[72] Bauckham ("Role of the Spirit," 66) goes so far as to say that "the prominence of the Spirit is one of the characteristics which mark the Apocalypse out from the category of apocalyptic works in which its literary genre places it."

Slaves in the New Testament
Literary, Social, and Moral Dimensions
J. ALBERT HARRILL

"Harrill combines wide-ranging knowledge of ancient sources with a sharp eye for the jugular of a text. The result is that rare thing in biblical scholarship, genuinely fresh insights into an old question. A book both delightful and disturbing, Slaves in the New Testament demolishes a card house of wishful thinking about early Christian views on slavery. Everyone who believes that the Bible has something to say about moral issues needs to pay attention."

— WAYNE A. MEEKS, Woolsey Professor Emeritus of Biblical Studies, Yale University

978-0-8006-3781-1
360 pp paper $25.00

FORTRESS PRESS
An imprint of Augsburg Fortress

At bookstores or call 1-800-328-4648 fortresspress.com

New from T&T Clark!

The Fourth Gospel and the Quest for Jesus
Modern Foundations Reconsidered
Paul N. Anderson

New in paperback!

"Paul Anderson's *Fourth Gospel and the Quest for Jesus* clearly enters a dialogue between gospel studies and historical Jesus studies that is critically entrenched and opinionated. Anderson is well aware of the battle lines and carefully navigates between them, not ignoring them, and is able to cordially offer a better way. This reviewer thinks he does this well. There is much to appreciate in his approach. He clearly wants to participate in the discussion, a long-standing discussion, and help bring together distinct aspects of the same dialogue. In a way, Anderson has come to the rescue of an underdog who is being bullied and outnumbered three-to-one." — Review of Biblical Literature

PB 978 0 567 03330 7 • $49.95 • 256 Pages
January 2008 • Library of New Testament Studies, vol. 321 • T&T Clark

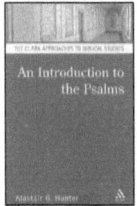

An Introduction to the Psalms
Alastair G. Hunter

"*An Introduction to the Psalms* is a refreshingly different addition to many introductions already available. Alastair Hunter brings to this study a wealth of experience in teaching and research, and has the gift of addressing traditional questions about the origin and use of the psalms in a perceptive and original way. Students thinking about the psalms for the first time will find here a useful map to help them discover un-chartered territory; and those who have journeyed through the psalms many times before will find many new vistas and unexpected places of interest." — Susan Gillingham, Worcester College, Oxford University

PB 978 0 567 03028 3 • $19.95 • 168 Pages
March 2008 • T&T Clark Approaches to Biblical Studies • T&T Clark

John and Empire
Initial Explorations
Warren Carter

In this significant and innovative contribution, Warren Carter explores John's Gospel as a work of imperial negotiation in the context of Ephesus, capital of the Roman province of Asia. Carter employs multiple methods, rejects sectarian scenarios, and builds on other Christian writings and recent studies of diaspora synagogues that combined participationist lifestyles with observance of distinctive practices to argue that imperial negotiation was a contested issue for late first-century Jesus-believers.

PB 978 0 567 02840 2 • $39.95 • 432 Pages
March 2008 • T&T Clark

These books are available from fine booksellers,
or direct from Continuum 1.800.561.7704
www.continuumbooks.com • www.tandtclarkblog.com

T&T Clark is an imprint of
the Continuum International
Publishing Group

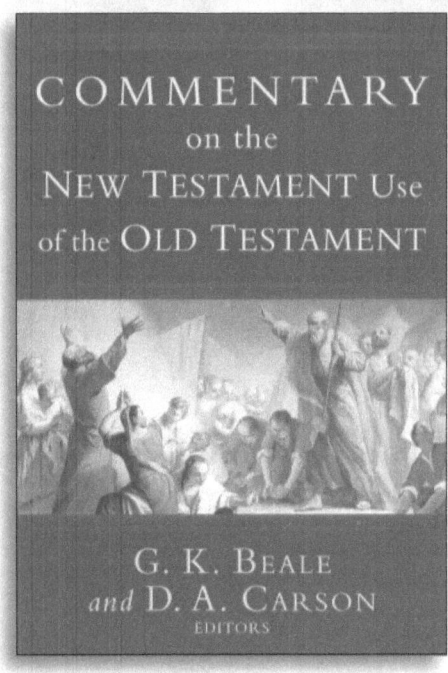

Announcing a New Series for the Classroom

ΠΑΙΔΕΙΑ paideia

Commentaries on the New Testament
Mikeal C. Parsons and Charles H. Talbert, Series Editors

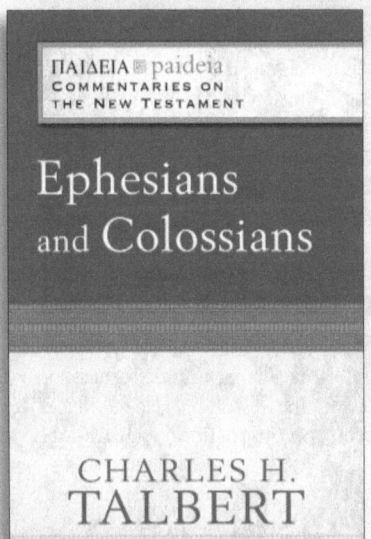

Ephesians and Colossians
Charles H. Talbert
9780801031281 • 320 pp. • $24.99p

"Talbert initiates Baker Academic's new Paideia series, which promises a fresh approach beneficial especially to beginning students but of value to the more advanced as well, with an accessible, user-friendly commentary on Ephesians and Colossians. Talbert's contribution shines forth as a concise yet comprehensive gem illustrating his mastery of the present state of research. His vast erudition enlightens readers with new insights into not only the theological content but also the cultural and literary contexts to facilitate an appreciation of the contemporary relevance of two closely related but sometimes neglected Pauline letters."—**John Paul Heil**, Catholic University of America

For more information, including the series preface and an excerpt, please visit www.bakeracademic.com/paideia

Forthcoming volumes in the Paideia series include:
- **Mikeal C. Parsons** on Acts (Fall 2008)
- **Frank J. Matera** on Romans
- **Pheme Perkins** on First Corinthians
- **Raymond F. Collins** on Second Corinthians
- **James W. Thompson** on Hebrews (Fall 2008)

Editorial Board
Paul J. Achtemeier (emeritus, Union Theological Seminary)
Loveday Alexander (University of Sheffield)
C. Clifton Black (Princeton Theological Seminary)
Susan R. Garrett (Louisville Presbyterian Theological Seminary)
Francis J. Moloney, SDB (Salesian Province of Australia)

Baker Academic
a division of Baker Publishing Group

Available at your local bookstore, www.bakeracademic.com, or by calling 1-800-877-2665
Subscribe to Baker Academic's electronic newsletter (E-Notes) at www.bakeracademic.com

recent books from **EERDMANS**

IMITATING JESUS
An Inclusive Approach to New Testament Ethics
RICHARD BURRIDGE

"A welcome addition to the literature on New Testament ethics. I commend it — and recommend it — for its attention to the story of Jesus as the foundation of New Testament ethics, for its attention to genre, for its emphasis on both the rigorous moral teachings and the radically inclusive acceptance of the New Testament, and for its emphasis on the hermeneutical significance of reading the Bible in an inclusive community."
— Allen Verhey

ISBN 978-0-8028-4458-3 • 512 pages • hardcover • $35.00

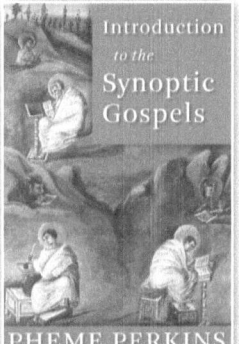

INTRODUCTION TO THE SYNOPTIC GOSPELS
PHEME PERKINS

"This book not only provides a much-needed general introduction to the Synoptic Gospels but also introduces its audience to the apocryphal Gospels, including the Gospel of Judas. Perkins's treatment is fair and balanced, and her analogies to contemporary culture are inspired and illuminating."
— Adela Yarbro Collins

ISBN 978-0-8028-1770-9 • 328 pages • hardcover • $28.00

GREED AS IDOLATRY
The Origin and Meaning of a Pauline Metaphor
BRIAN S. ROSNER

"Rosner explores the concept of greed as idolatry in rich detail from every imaginable angle — exegetical, theological, historical, sociological — and challenges contemporary Christianity to take it far more seriously. A crucial topic for anyone who wants to be faithful to biblical ethics."
— Craig L. Blomberg

ISBN 978-0-8028-3374-7 • 228 pages • paperback • $22.00

At your bookstore,
or call 800-253-7521
www.eerdmans.com

WM. B. EERDMANS
PUBLISHING CO.
2140 Oak Industrial Drive NE
Grand Rapids, MI 49505

Social Distinctives of the Christians in the First Century
Pivotal Essays by E. A. Judge
DAVID M. SCHOLER, EDITOR
This is a collection of pivotal essays by E. A. Judge, who initiated many important discussions in the establishment of social scientific criticism of the Bible.
$24.95 retail • ISBN 978-1-56563-880-8 • Paper • 248 pages • 5.5 x 8.5 inches

Paul, the Pastoral Epistles, and the Early Church
Library of Pauline Studies Series
JAMES W. AAGESON
What did the early church do with Paul's memory? How did it reshape his theology? And what role did his letters come to play in the life of the church?
$24.95 retail • ISBN 978-1-59856-041-1• Paper • 256 pages • 6 x 9 inches

Reading the Old Testament
An Inductive Introduction
MICHAEL B. DICK
April 2008
Designed to spark lively classroom discussion, this interactive introduction to the Old Testament writings leads the student-reader along a path of discovery, posing insightful questions and providing lucid explanations towards a better understanding of these extraordinary texts.
$29.95 retail • ISBN 978-1-56563-953-9 • Hardcover • 416 pages • 7 x 9.25 inches

An Exploration of Christian Theology
DON THORSEN
Though beginning theology students often find themselves bewildered by the maze of Christian thought and practice, Thorsen unravels the knots of tradition and dogma with straightforward language and an engaging format.
$34.95 retail • ISBN 978-1-56563-236-3 • Hardcover • 480 pages • 7 x 9.25 inches

God's Twilight Zone—Wisdom in the Hebrew Bible
T. A. PERRY
March 2008
With a creative impulse and a critical mind, Perry examines some of the most enigmatic portions of the Hebrew Bible, providing fresh insight into stories often avoided for their difficulty.
$19.95 retail • ISBN 978-1-59856-227-9 • Paper • 200 pages • 5.5 x 8.5 inches

HENDRICKSON PUBLISHERS

FOR MORE INFORMATION VISIT US ONLINE AT WWW.HENDRICKSON.COM

NEW READINGS

JESUS THROUGH MIDDLE EASTERN EYES
Cultural Studies in the Gospels
Kenneth E. Bailey

Kenneth Bailey draws from his extended studies and firsthand experience of Middle Eastern peasant culture to help us read the Gospels as they were meant to be read.

"[An] engaging set of studies that emphasize the concrete world presupposed in the New Testament." **—EDITH M. HUMPHREY,** Pittsburgh Theological Seminary

(Available February 2008)

REDISCOVERING PAUL
An Introduction to His World, Letters and Theology
David B. Capes, Rodney Reeves and E. Randolph Richards

"An introductory textbook to Paul that . . . [helps] us as readers to come to terms with the significance of his letters and theology for our times." **—STANLEY E. PORTER,** president, McMaster Divinity College

IVP Academic
Evangelically Rooted. Critically Engaged.

630.734.4000 · ivpacademic.com

WITHERINGTON'S LETTERS & HOMILIES

**LETTERS AND HOMILIES
FOR HELLENIZED CHRISTIANS,
VOLUME I**
*A Socio-Rhetorical Commentary on Titus,
1-2 Timothy and 1-3 John*
Ben Witherington III

Grounding his study in the distinct Hellenistic context of these letters, Ben Witherington applies his socio-rhetorical method to Titus, 1-2 Timothy and 1-3 John.

**LETTERS AND HOMILIES
FOR HELLENIZED CHRISTIANS,
VOLUME II**
A Socio-Rhetorical Commentary on 1-2 Peter
Ben Witherington III

In this commentary, Witherington helps us read 1-2 Peter using his innovative socio-rhetorical analysis.

**LETTERS AND HOMILIES
FOR JEWISH CHRISTIANS**
*A Socio-Rhetorical Commentary on Hebrews,
James and Jude*
Ben Witherington III

Witherington underscores the social tensions behind these ancient Jewish homilies and the rhetorical strategies employed to resolve them.

630.734.4000 · ivpacademic.com

New from Mohr Siebeck

Richard H. Bell
Deliver Us from Evil
Interpreting the Redemption from the Power of Satan in New Testament Theology
2007. XXIII, 439 pages (WUNT 216).
ISBN 978-3-16-149452-9 cloth $145.00

Thomas R. Blanton, IV
Constructing a New Covenant
Discursive Strategies in the Damascus Document and Second Corinthians
2007. X, 271 pages (WUNT II/233).
ISBN 978-3-16-149207-5 paper $79.00

Desta Heliso
***Pistis* and the Righteous One**
A Study of Romans 1:17 against the Background of Scripture and Second Temple Jewish Literature
2007. XIV, 292 pages (WUNT II/235).
ISBN 978-3-16-149511-3 paper $86.00

Karel Jongeling
Handbook of Neo-Punic Inscriptions
2008. 460 pages (est.). ISBN 978-3-16-149303-4 cloth $200.00 (est.) (February)

E. A. Judge
The First Christians in the Roman World
Augustan and New Testament Essays
Edited by James R. Harrison
2008. 820 pages (est.) (WUNT).
ISBN 978-3-16-149310-2 cloth $200.00 (est.) (February)

Ivar Vegge
2 Corinthians – a Letter about Reconciliation
A Psychagogical, Epistolographical and Rhetorical Analysis
2008. 440 pages (est.) (WUNT II).
ISBN 978-3-16-149302-7 paper $110.00 (est.) (February)

Jürgen Becker
Die Auferstehung Jesu Christi nach dem Neuen Testament
Ostererfahrung und Osterverständnis im Urchristentum
2007. VIII, 307 pages. ISBN 978-3-16-149426-0 paper $57.00; ISBN 978-3-16-149427-7 cloth $86.00

Mareike Verena Blischke
Die Eschatologie in der Sapientia Salomonis
2007. XI, 309 pages (FAT II/26).
ISBN 978-3-16-149459-8 paper $86.00

Nicole Chibici-Revneanu
Die Herrlichkeit des Verherrlichten
Das Verständnis der δοχα im Johannesevangelium
2007. XII, 747 pages (WUNT II/231).
ISBN 978-3-16-149296-9 paper $145.00

Werner Eck • **Rom und Judaea**
Fünf Vorträge zur römischen Herrschaft in Palästina
2007. XIX, 263 pages (Tria Corda 2).
ISBN 978-3-16-149460-4 paper $42.00

Otto Kaiser • **Des Menschen Glück und Gottes Gerechtigkeit**
Studien zur biblischen Überlieferung im Kontext hellenistischer Philosophie
2007. XVI, 269 pages (Tria Corda 1).
ISBN 978-3-16-149471-0 paper $42.00

Sven Petry • **Die Entgrenzung JHWHs**
Monolatrie, Bilderverbot und Monotheismus im Deuteronomium, in Deuterojesaja und im Ezechielbuch
2007. XIII, 463 pages (FAT II/27).
ISBN 978-3-16-149451-2 paper $115.00

Marius Reiser • **Bibelkritik und Auslegung der Heiligen Schrift**
Beiträge zur Geschichte der biblischen Exegese und Hermeneutik
2007. XI, 407 pages (WUNT 217).
ISBN 978-3-16-149412-3 cloth $138.00

Christian Rose • **Theologie als Erzählung im Markusevangelium**
Eine narratologisch-rezeptionsästhetische Studie zu Mk 1,1–15
2007. XII, 312 pages (WUNT II/236).
ISBN 978-3-16-149512-0 paper $100.00

Prices vary according to exchange rates.

Custom-made information:
www.mohr.de/form/
eKurier_e.htm

Mohr Siebeck
Tübingen
info@mohr.de
www.mohr.de

See What's New

Rachel Weeping
Jews, Christians, and Muslims at the Fortress Tomb
Fred Strickert

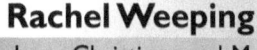

Journey into the nature and significance of Rachel's story and the story of her tomb in *Rachel Weeping*. With meticulous scholarship Fred Strickert tells the story of Rachel, the woman on the way, and gives readers a clear sense of how the monument outside Bethlehem where Christian, Jewish, and Muslim worshipers remember her fits into the current history of the Middle East.

S978-0-8146-5987-8
Paper, 176 pp., 6 x 9, $18.95

Now Available!

"*Fred Strickert* has made a unique contribution to the ongoing discussion about the relationships among members of the three monotheistic faiths. He explains the important role Rachel has in Judaism, Christianity, and Islam, and he explores how her tomb has functioned as a pilgrimage site throughout history. This creative interfacing of person and place is simultaneously a celebration of how people have cooperated in the past and a challenge to reflect on how we might get along better in the future."
   John Kaltner, Department of Religious Studies
   Rhodes College, Memphis, Tennessee

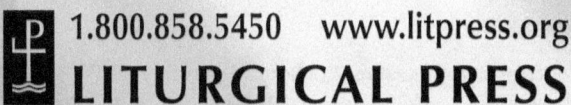

1.800.858.5450   www.litpress.org
LITURGICAL PRESS

New and Recent Titles

THE HITTITES AND THEIR WORLD
Billie Jean Collins
   This book provides a concise, current, and engaging introduction to the history, society, and religion of this Anatolian empire, from the nineteenth century B.C.E. to the eighth century B.C.E. The numerous analogues with the biblical world featured throughout the volume together represent a comprehensive and up-to-date survey of the varied and significant contributions of Hittite studies to biblical interpretation.
Paper $29.95   978-1-58983-296-1   272 pages, 2007   Code: 061707
Archaeology and Biblical Studies 7   Hardback edition www.brill.nl

APPROACHING YEHUD
New Approaches to the Study of the Persian Period
Jon L. Berquist, editor
   These essays shift the focus from the postexilic period as a staging ground for early Judaism or Christianity to Yehud on its own terms, as a Persian colony with a diverse population. Contributors include Richard Bautch, Zipporah G. Glass, Alice W. Hunt, David Janzen, John Kessler, Melody D. Knowles, Jennifer L. Koosed, Herbert R. Marbury, Christine Mitchell, Julia M. O'Brien, Donald C. Polaski, Jean-Pierre Ruiz, Brent A. Strawn, and Christine Roy Yoder.
Paper $29.95   978-1-58983-145-2   280 pages, 2007   Code: 060650
Semeia Studies 50   Hardback edition www.brill.nl

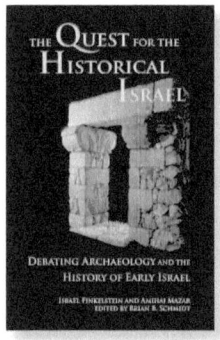

THE QUEST FOR THE HISTORICAL ISRAEL
Debating Archaeology and the History of Early Israel
Israel Finkelstein and Amihai Mazar
Brian B. Schmidt, editor
   This book brings together a currently emerging "centrist" paradigm as articulated by two leading figures in the field.
Paper $24.95   978-1-58983-277-0   220 pages, 2007   Code: 061717
Archaeology and Biblical Studies 17   Hardback edition www.brill.nl

Society of Biblical Literature • P.O. Box 2243 • Williston, VT 05495-2243
Phone: 877-725-3334 (toll-free) or 802-864-6185 • Fax: 802-864-7626
Order online at www.sbl-site.org

 New and Recent Titles

JOHN, JESUS, AND HISTORY, VOLUME 1
Critical Appraisals of Critical Views
Paul N. Anderson, Felix Just, S.J., and
Tom Thatcher, editors
   These essays critically assess the dehistoricization of John and the de-Johannification of Jesus. Diverse approaches include cognitive-critical developments of Johannine memory, distinctive characteristics of the Johannine witness, new historicism, Johannine-Synoptic relations, and fresh analyses of Johannine traditional development.
Paper $37.95   978-1-58983-293-0   356 pages, 2007   Code: 060744
Symposium 44   Hardback edition www.brill.nl

PHILOSTORGIUS: *CHURCH HISTORY*
Translated with an Introduction and Notes by
Philip R. Amidon, S.J.
   Philostorgius was a member of the Eunomian sect of Christianity, a nonconformist faction deeply opposed to the form of Christianity adopted by the Roman government as the official religion of its empire. His *Church History* offers a rare dissenting picture of the Christian world of the time.
Paper $34.95   978-1-58983-215-2   312 pages, 2007   Code: 061623
Writings from the Greco-Roman World 23   Hardback www.brill.nl

THE "WE" PASSAGES IN THE ACTS OF THE APOSTLES
The Narrator as Narrative Character
William Sanger Campbell
   This book explores the narrative significance of the "we" passages in Acts within the boundaries of acceptable ancient grammatical practice and presents narrative literary strategy as a fruitful approach to these enigmatic texts whose narrative possibilities have in the past been subordinated to their historical potential.
Paper $19.95   978-1-58983-205-3   164 pages, 2007   Code: 062514
Studies in Biblical Literature 14   Hardback edition www.brill.nl

Society of Biblical Literature • P.O. Box 2243 • Williston, VT 05495-2243
Phone: 877-725-3334 (toll-free) or 802-864-6185 • Fax: 802-864-7626
Order online at www.sbl-site.org

New! Stellar Textbooks for Biblical Studies Courses

In this ideal book for undergraduate courses in Bible, William Brown brilliantly introduces the central questions and issues of biblical authority before Marc Zvi Brettler, Michael Joseph Brown, Katie G. Cannon, Carlos F. Cardoza-Orlandi, Ellen F. Davis, Terence E. Fretheim, Robert W. Jenson, Luke Timothy Johnson, Serene Jones, Sarah Heaner Lancaster, Jacqueline E. Lapsley, Frank J. Matera, S. Dean McBride Jr., Peter Ochs, Allen Verhey, and Seung Ai Yang, each present their own view of the Bible.

Paper • $19.95 • ISBN: 978-0-664-23057-9

Paper • $24.95
ISBN: 978-0-664-22587-2

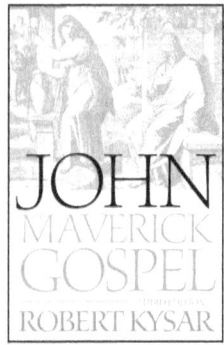

Paper • $24.95
ISBN: 978-0-664-23056-2

Paper • $24.95
ISBN: 978-0-664-23028-9

WESTMINSTER JOHN KNOX PRESS
www.wjkbooks.com

Phone: 1-800-672-1789   Fax: 1-800-445-8189   www.cokesbury.com

New Essentials for Old Testament Study

Paper • $24.95 • ISBN: 978-0-664-22991-7

Paper • $24.95 • ISBN: 978-0-664-23130-9

Perhaps the most significant and enduring series in the field, the Old Testament Library presents a critically informed, theological reading of the Old Testament. This new volume by Marvin Sweeney, Professor of Hebrew Bible at Claremont School of Theology, offers a major contribution to the series and provides a close reading of the historical books of 1 Kings and 2 Kings, concentrating on not only issues in the history of Israel but also the literary techniques of storytelling used in these books

Hardback • $49.95 • ISBN: 978-0-664-22084-6

WESTMINSTER JOHN KNOX PRESS
www.wjkbooks.com

Phone: 1-800-672-1789 Fax: 1-800-445-8189 www.cokesbury.com

BREAKING THE LOGJAM

Proto-Luke. The Oldest Gospel Account. A Christ-Centered Synthesis of Old Testament Narrative, Modelled Especially on the Elijah-Elisha Narrative. *Thomas L. Brodie O.P.*

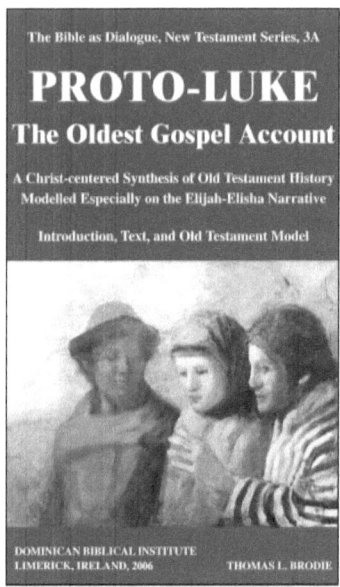

Building on R E Brown's 1971 proposal that the Elisha narrative provides the closest model for the gospels, Thomas Brodie applies awareness of ancient methods of mimesis and rewriting to clarifying Luke's use of the Septuagint, especially to identifying Proto-Luke, the document that, modelled on the entire Elijah-Elisha narrative, underlies the formation of the four gospels and Acts — far more verifiably and comprehensively than Q.

Having outlined the argument for Proto-Luke in *The Crucial Bridge. The Elijah-Elisha Narrative as ... a Model for the Gospels* (Liturgical, 2000), and especially in *The Birthing of the New Testament* (Sheffield Phoenix, 2004), Brodie now presents the text of Proto-Luke in a format that facilitates discussion.

"Students of sources and patterns in Luke-Acts will be grateful to Tom Brodie for this attractively presented reconstruction of his proposed proto-Lucan document (in both Greek and English) arranged in tabular form to bring out the diptych structures which he has detected in it." — *I Howard Marshall, University of Aberdeen.*

"Brodie's hypothetical reconstruction of a *Proto-Luke* and the development of his argument in this regard certainly deserves attention and discussion." — *Gert J Steyn, University of Pretoria.*

"An original work that will make a lasting impact on the study of Christian origins." — *David Noel Freedman, University of San Diego,* on *The Birthing of the New Testament.*

Paper, 60 pp., 14³/₈" x 9⁵/₈", $14 or €10 (postage included). ISBN 0 – 933462 – 09 -3
To order, email: administrator@dbclimerick.ie

"ABSOLUTELY THE BEST VOLUME OF ITS KIND available today. It incorporates a wealth of valuable information for classroom use or for self-study . . . [and] has been carefully prepared and organized, tested and refined in the classroom over a number of years, and handsomely produced by the publisher. I recommend it enthusiastically!"

—**Buist M. Fanning III**, Dallas Theological Seminary
Author, *Verbal Aspect in New Testament Greek*

Koine Greek Reader goes where other readers do not by providing graded readings from the New Testament, Septuagint, Apostolic Fathers, and early creeds. Its many features include four helpful vocabulary lists, numerous references to other resources, assorted translation helps, a review of basic grammar and syntax, and an introduction to BDAG. Professors will find that it integrates the full range of materials needed by intermediate students.

Retail: $25.99 • 312 pages
ISBN 978-0-8254-2442-7

Professors: Are you considering a new text in biblical languages or another discipline?

Call (1-800-733-2607) or e-mail (academic@kregel.com) us to request an examination copy.

www.ingramcontent.com/pod-product-compliance
Lightning Source LLC
Chambersburg PA
CBHW021828300426
44114CB00009BA/365